EUROPEAN CUPS
REVIEW 1993

CW01018827

Editor Mike Hammond
Published by Sports Projects Limited

A SEASON IN EUROPE

Welcome to the first edition of the European Cups Review and another addition to the Match-By-Match series of books launched by Sports Projects in 1993.

The European Cups Review is designed to be an annual publication recording the drama and excitement of a whole season of European Cup football.

As well as extensive and some exclusive statistics, the Review contains summaries and match reports for all games played in Europe's three major cup competitions for the 1992/93 season.

Facts files are also included and there are many interesting profiles and photographs of some of Europe's top players.

The European Cups Review is a pioneering publication which we are sure will become a firm favourite in the years to come with followers of the European game.

Bernard Gallagher
Publisher
July 1993

ACKNOWLEDGEMENTS

European Cups Review 1993
First published in Great Britain in July 1993
by Sports Projects Limited

© 1993 Sports Projects Limited
188 Lightwoods Hill, Smethwick, Warley,
West Midlands B67 5EH.

ISBN 0-946866-12-0

Printed and bound in Great Britain

All rights reserved.
No part of this publication may be reproduced,
stored in any retrieval system or transmitted, in
any form or by any means, without the written
consent of the publisher.

Editor: Mike Hammond

Statistical research: Dave Clayton, Jan Buitenga

Special thanks to: Marco von Ah, Rudolph
Rothenbühler (UEFA)

Photographs: Empics

Design, layout and graphics: Bernard Gallagher,
Trevor Hartley, Phil Lees, Nadine Goldingay.

CONTENTS

KEY

❏   Player booked

■   Player sent off

†   First player substituted

†56 First substitute and time
of substitution

‡   Second player substituted

‡78 Second substitute and time
of substitution

61   Figure in goals column
indicates time of goal

CHAMPIONS' CUP

PRELIMINARY ROUND DRAW

FIRST ROUND DRAW

CHAMPIONS' CUP
Preliminary Round First Leg

Wednesday 19th August 1992
Tolka Park, Dublin

SHELBOURNE 0 TAVRIA SIMFEROPOL 0

Half-time 0-0 *Attendance* 4,000

		Goals				Goals
1	Jody BYRNE			1	Oleg KOLESOV	
2	Peter COYLE			2	Sergei SHEVCHENKO ‡	
3	Kevin BRADY			3	Nikolai TURCHINENKO	
4	Mick NEVILLE			4	Aleksandr GOLOVKO	
5	Ken O'DOHERTY			5	Igor VOLKOV ❑	
6	Gary HOWLETT ❑			6	Sergei VORONEZHKY ❑	
7	Dessie GORMAN			7	Andrey OPARIN	
8	Paul DOOLIN			8	Yury GUDIMENKO	
9	Padraig DULLY			9	Sergei ANDREEV ❑	
10	Garry HAYLOCK			10	Vidmantas VISHNIAUSKAS †	
11	Mark RUTHERFORD			11	Sergei POLSTIANOV	

Substitutes

Substitutes

Sefer ALIBAEV †34

Vladislav NOVIKOV ‡78

Referee Anders FRISK (Sweden)

SUMMARY

● *Shelbourne, the League of Ireland champions, were far from overjoyed at having to begin their first European campaign for 21 years in the preliminary round. But the 1992/93 Champions' Cup entry figure of 40 teams meant that a couple of sides from established nations would have to contest the right for first round participation with the newcomers from Israel, Estonia, Latvia, Slovenia, the Faeroe Isles and the Ukraine. Shelbourne, along with Malta's Valletta, unfortunately drew the short straw. Tavria Simferopol, Shelbourne's opponents, had never appeared in Europe before, but no team which had just beaten Dinamo Kiev to capture the Ukrainian national title could be taken lightly. The Irish knew they had a task on their hands, especially with their domestic season not yet underway, and they struggled to impose themselves against a Ukrainian side which was happy to defend. Shelbourne's only previous victory in Europe had been in a Fairs' Cup preliminary round play-off back in 1964, but 28 years on there was to be no repeat and the 4,000 Dubliners in the stands had to be content with a 0-0 draw.*

TAVRIA SIMFEROPOL 2 SHELBOURNE 1

Half-time 2-1 *Aggregate* 2-1 *Attendance* 10,500

		Goals			Goals
1	Oleg KOLESOV		1	Jody BYRNE	
2	Sergei SHEVCHENKO	10	2	Peter COYLE	
3	Nikolai TURCHINENKO ❏		3	Kevin BRADY	
4	Aleksandr GOLOVKO		4	Mick NEVILLE ❏	
5	Igor VOLKOV ❏		5	Ken O'DOHERTY	
6	Sergei VORONEZHSKY		6	Gary HOWLETT	
7	Andrey OPARIN		7	Dessie GORMAN	
8	Yury GUDIMENKO ❏		8	Paul DOOLIN ❏	
9	Sergei POLSTIANOV		9	Padraig DULLY ❏	42
10	Vidmantas VISHNIAUSKAS †		10	Garry HAYLOCK †	
11	Toliat SHEYHAMETOV ‡	15	11	Mark RUTHERFORD	

Substitutes

Vladislav NOVIKOV †60

Sefer ALIBAEV ‡73

Substitute

Bobby BROWNE †84

Referee Gerd GRABHER (Austria)

SUMMARY

● Tavria Simferopol looked to have both the match and the tie sewn up within the first quarter of an hour. That was as long as it took them to establish a 2-0 lead through goals from Sergei Shevchenko and Toliat Sheyhametov. But Shelbourne showed tremendous resolve. They came back into the game with a headed goal from centre-forward Padraig Dully just before half-time and threatened on several occasions after the interval to score a second goal that would have put them into the first round proper. Tavria, though, clung to their lead and even managed to strike the crossbar late on. The 2-1 win booked their date with Swiss champions Sion in the next round and ensured that Ukrainian teams would be present in all three competitions when the European season began in earnest a fortnight later. As for Shelbourne, their defeat meant that a full decade had now passed since a League of Ireland club had won a European tie. Shamrock Rovers' 7-0 aggregate success over Fram of Iceland in the 1982/83 UEFA Cup was fast becoming a dim and distant memory.

CHAMPIONS' CUP
Preliminary Round First Leg

Wednesday 19th August 1992
National Stadium, Ta' Qali

VALLETTA 1 MACCABI TEL-AVIV 2

Half-time 0-0 *Attendance* 1,500

		Goals				Goals
1	Charles CORTIS		1	Aleksandr UVAROV		
2	Raymond BRIFFA ❏ †		2	Avi COHEN		81
3	Charles MAGRI		3	Gadi BROMER		
4	Kristian LAFERLA		4	Amir SHELACH		
5	Osnir POPULIN ❏		5	Aleksandr POLUKAROV ❏		
6	Joe CAMILLERI		6	Amit LEVY ❏		
7	Edmond LUFI ‡		7	Noam SHOAM ‡		
8	Nicky SALIBA		8	Avi NIMNY ❏		88
9	Leo REFALO		9	Nir KLINGER		
10	Joe ZARB		10	Itzak ZOHAR		
11	Jesmond ZERAFA	75	11	Aharon Meir MELIKA †		

Substitutes

William MACKAY †31
Jeremy AGIUS ‡82

Substitutes

Eli DRIEKES †70
Yaron DRORI ‡80

Referee AHMET Cakar (Turkey)

SUMMARY

● *Valletta, the champions of Malta, had been drawn against arguably the toughest of the preliminary round opponents in Maccabi Tel-Aviv. They might have fancied their chances against the champions of Estonia, Latvia and the Faeroe Isles, but against the Israelis, invited for the first time by UEFA to compete in their club competitions, they knew that they would have their work cut out to try and banish for ever their wretched record of never having won any of their 16 European ties. It looked for a long time that the match would end up goalless, but the final 15 minutes brought a flurry of activity that was to raise then crush Valletta's hopes of recording only their second ever victory in European competition. Jesmond Zerafa put the home side ahead after 75 minutes with the club's first European goal for four years and their first in open play since 1978. But the Israelis came back strongly, equalising first through captain Avi Cohen and then winning the game two minutes from time with a second goal from promising 20-year-old Israeli international midfielder Avi Nimny.*

CHAMPIONS' CUP
Preliminary Round Second Leg

Wednesday 2nd September 1992
Ramat-Gan Stadium, Tel-Aviv

MACCABI TEL-AVIV 1 VALLETTA 0

Half-time 0-0 *Aggregate* 3-1 *Attendance* 5,000

		Goals				Goals
1	Aleksandr UVAROV		1	Charles CORTIS		
2	Avi COHEN		2	Raymond BRIFFA		
3	Gadi BROMER		3	Charles MAGRI ‡		
4	Amir SHELACH		4	Kristian LAFERLA ❏		
5	Aleksandr POLUKAROV		5	Osnir POPULIN		
6	Amit LEVY		6	Joe CAMILLERI		
7	Aharon Meir MELIKA	24	7	Edmond LUFI		
8	Avi NIMNY		8	Nicky SALIBA		
9	Nir KLINGER †		9	Leo REFALO †		
10	Itzak ZOHAR		10	Joe ZARB		
11	Nezah MASOBI ‡		11	Jesmond ZERAFA		

Substitutes

Arik SHRIKI †59

Eli DRIEKES ‡59

Substitutes

Jeremy AGIUS †88

William MACKAY ‡89

Referee Vassilis NIKAKIS (Greece)

● This was the second match of a double European bill at the Ramat-Gan stadium. Just over an hour after Hapoel Petach-Tikva had booked their passage into the first round of the Cup-winners' Cup at the expense of Norway's Strømsgodset, Maccabi Tel-Aviv came out to try and ensure that Israel was also represented in the first round of the Champions' Cup. Buoyed by their late comeback in the away leg, Maccabi began strongly and with 24 minutes on the clock they extended their aggregate lead with an excellent goal from Aharon Meir Melika. Receiving a cross from the right, he controlled the ball instantly with his left foot before crashing a sweet right-footer across the 'keeper into the top corner of the net. That single goal was enough to secure the Israeli champions a first-round confrontation with Belgian side Club Bruges, a team that would surely attract more than 4,000 to the national stadium as well as providing stiffer opposition than a Valletta side which appeared more motivated by their excursion to the holy city of Jerusalem than they were by the football match.

CHAMPIONS' CUP
Preliminary Round First Leg

Wednesday 19th August 1992
Klaksvik Stadium, Klaksvik

KÍ 1 SKONTO RIGA 3

Half-time 0-1 *Attendance* 1,500

		Goals			Goals
1	Jakup MIKKELSEN		1	Oleg GRISHIN	
2	John HANSEN		2	Oleg BLAGONADEZDIN	
3	Petur Ove ELLINGSGAARD		3	Vitaly ASTAFJEV	28, 47
4	Heini HANSEN		4	Einars GNEDOI	
5	Kurt MØRKØRE		5	Mihails ZEMLINSKIS	
6	Todi JÖNSSON ❑		6	Valentin LOBANOV ‡	
7	Olgar DANIELSEN	46	7	Artur SKETOV †	
8	Jan JOENSEN		8	Aleksandr STRADIN	
9	Alan MØRKØRE		9	Aleksandr DIBRIVNY	
10	Jan ANDREASEN ‡		10	Igor TROITSKI	
11	Harley BERTHOLDSEN †		11	Aleksandr JELISEJEV	
	Substitutes			*Substitutes*	
	Sorin PETERSEN †46			Aleksei SEMJONOV †34	90
	Beinur POULSEN ‡83			Yury DERMENTIEV ‡76	

Referee Rune PEDERSEN (Norway)

SUMMARY

● *Thanks to the fact that they had been drawn to play at home in the first leg whilst B 36 were opening their Cup-winners' Cup campaign in Luxembourg, KÍ of Klaksvik became the first club to stage a European match in the Faeroe Isles. Alas, that was just about all the Faeroe Isles champions had to celebrate on an afternoon when they discovered that the champions of Latvia, themselves competing in Europe for the very first time, were a class above them in international terms. KÍ had been going well in domestic competition, beaten only once as the championship entered its decisive final phase. But Skonto Riga, the only Latvian team permitted by UEFA to represent their country in this 'trial' season, put that run into perspective with a convincing 3-1 win. Vitaly Astafjev, a Latvian international, was the man most responsible for KÍ's downfall, scoring once in the first half then restoring Skonto's lead almost instantly after Olgar Danielsen, KÍ's in-form striker (seven goals in his last six league games), had equalised. The third goal, in injury time, came from substitute Aleksei Semjonov.*

Wednesday 2nd September 1992
Daugava Stadium, Riga

SKONTO RIGA 3 KÍ 0

Half-time 2-0 Aggregate 6-1 Attendance 3,000

		Goals			Goals
1	Oleg GRISHIN		1	Jakup MIKKELSEN	
2	Oleg BLAGONADEZDIN ❏		2	John HANSEN ❏	
3	Vitaly ASTAFJEV	51	3	Petur Ove ELLINGSGAARD	
4	Einars GNEDOI		4	Heini HANSEN	
5	Mihails ZEMLINSKIS		5	Kurt MØRKØRE ❏	
6	Aleksei SEMJONOV †	37	6	Todi JÖNSSON	
7	Artur SKETOV ❏		7	Olgar DANIELSEN	
8	Aleksandr STRADIN		8	Jan JOENSEN ❏ †	
9	Aleksandr DIBRIVNY ‡		9	Alan MØRKØRE	
10	Igor TROITSKI		10	Fridrin LISKASSON	
11	Aleksandr JELISEJEV	3	11	Sorin PETERSEN ‡	

Substitutes			*Substitutes*	
Igor STEPANOV †61			Beinur POULSEN †61	
Valentin LOBANOV ‡65			Harley BERTHOLDSEN ‡64	

Referee Ilkka KOHO (Finland)

SUMMARY

● *Skonto Riga had little trouble seeing off KÍ and progressing through to a first-round confrontation with Poland's Lech Poznan. They had scored three goals in the away leg and now they repeated the feat to claim the biggest aggregate winning scoreline of the preliminary round. It took only three minutes for the Latvians to score their first of the evening, and it was netted from close range by Aleksandr Jelisejev, a man who had been on World Cup duty the previous week for the Latvian national team as they achieved a surprise goalless draw at home to European Champions Denmark. Aleksei Semjonov, a goalscoring substitute in the first leg but on from the start this time, made it 2-0 to Skonto on 37 minutes when he shot in after the KÍ offside trap had been penetrated on the left. And the scoring was completed early in the second half when Vitaly Astafjev, the two-goal hero of the first meeting, burst through the middle and fired past 'keeper Mikkelsen to claim his place as the early leading goalscorer of the Champions' Cup with three goals.*

CHAMPIONS' CUP
Preliminary Round First Leg

Wednesday 19th August 1992
Bezigrad Stadium, Ljubljana

SCT OLIMPIJA LJUBLJANA 3 NORMA TALLINN 0

Half-time 0-0 *Attendance* 3,500

		Goals			Goals
1	Marko SIMEUNOVIC		1	Tonu VANAKESA	
2	Nenad PODGAJSKI		2	Leonid KURILOV ❏	
3	Robert ENGLARO		3	Sergei BRAGIN ❏	
4	Samir ZULIC ❏		4	Vladimir URYUPIN	
5	Edin HADZIALAGIC		5	Eduard VINOGRADOV	
6	Damir VRABAC	60	6	Valery CHMIL †	
7	Andrej ZELKO		7	Valentin KOMAROV ❏	
8	Dejan DJURANOVIC ❏		8	Yury GARIFULIN	
9	Sandi VALENTINCIC †		9	Andrey BORISOV	
10	Zoran UBAVIC	48 (pen)	10	Andrey BELOKHVOSTOV	
11	Nedeljko TOPIC ‡	50	11	Aleksandr ZHURKIN	
	Substitutes			*Substitute*	
	Nenad PROTEGA †30			Dmitry TAM †57	
	Igor BENEDEJCIC ‡82				

Referee Daniel RODUIT (Switzerland)

SUMMARY

● *Three goals in the space of 12 second-half minutes gave Slovenian champions Olimpija Ljubljana a decisive first-leg lead in their confrontation with European newcomers Norma Tallinn from Estonia. Olimpija, absent from European competition for 22 years and now appearing for the first time under the Slovenian, rather than Yugoslav, flag, began the tie as clear favourites to secure a prestigious money-spinning tie with Milan in the next round. But the Estonians massed everybody into defence in the first half and succeeded in keeping their goal intact right through to the interval. Concern was growing at this stage that Olimpija might have to miss out on their big pay day in the next round, but those fears were quickly dispelled when Zoran Ubavic, scorer of 29 league goals for Olimpija the previous season, opened the scoring from the penalty spot and his strike partner, Nedeljko Topic, netted a second just two minutes later. Bosnian defender Damir Vrabac headed a third goal and by now the Estonian defensive wall had collapsed completely.*

Wednesday 2nd September 1992
Kadriorg Stadium, Tallinn

NORMA TALLINN 0 SCT OLIMPIJA LJUBLJANA 2

Half-time 0-1 *Aggregate* 0-5 *Attendance* 1,000

		Goals				Goals
1	Tonu VANAKESA		1	Marko SIMEUNOVIC		
2	Leonid KURILOV		2	Nenad PODGAJSKI		
3	Sergei BRAGIN ❑		3	Robert ENGLARO		
4	Vladimir URYUPIN		4	Samir ZULIC	27	
5	Eduard VINOGRADOV		5	Edin HADZIALAGIC		
6	Valery CHMIL		6	Damir VRABAC		
7	Valentin KOMAROV ❑		7	Igor BENEDEJCIC ❑ ‡		
8	Igor REVA †		8	Dejan DJURANOVIC	80	
9	Andrey BORISOV		9	Zoran UBAVIC		
10	Andrey BELOKHVOSTOV		10	Andrej ZELKO †		
11	Aleksandr ZHURKIN		11	Nedeljko TOPIC		

Substitute

Yury VOLKOV †53

Substitutes

Nenad PROTEGA †75

Branko ZIBERT ‡85

Referee Finn LAMBEK (Denmark)

SUMMARY

● *The first leg in Ljubljana had been played in burning heat and bright sunshine, but in the Estonian capital of Tallinn there was only cold, driving rain to welcome the two sides onto the field. Only a thousand hardy souls were prepared to brave the conditions and come to support their team, but the Estonian champions did not give them a great deal to cheer about. In effect, Olimpija Ljubljana picked up where they had left off a fortnight earlier, dominating the game and taking the lead midway through the first half with a goal from Slovenian national team defender Samir Zulic. Olimpija had won all of their first three fixtures in the new 92/93 Slovenian League scoring 14 goals in the process, and they would have totted up a similar ratio in Tallinn but for the heroics of Tenu Vanakesa, much-criticised after the first leg, in the Norma goal. They were to add just one further goal, from Dejan Djuranovic, ten minutes from time. But 5-0 was an impressive enough aggregate victory margin and the message from Olimpija Ljubljana fans now was "Milan, here we come!"*

CHAMPIONS' CUP
First Round First Leg

Wednesday 16th September 1992
Giuseppe Meazza Stadium, Milan

MILAN 4 SCT OLIMPIJA LJUBLJANA 0

Half-time 2-0 *Attendance* 14,324

		Goals				Goals
1	Francesco ANTONIOLI			1	Marko SIMEUNOVIC	
2	Mauro TASSOTTI			2	Nenad PODGAJSKI	
3	Paolo MALDINI			3	Robert ENGLARO	
4	Demetrio ALBERTINI	7		4	Samir ZULIC ❑ ■	
5	Stefano NAVA ❑			5	Edin HADZIALAGIC	
6	Alessandro COSTACURTA			6	Damir VRABAC	
7	Gianluigi LENTINI †			7	Igor BENEDEJCIC †	
8	Alberigo EVANI			8	Dejan DJURANOVIC	
9	Marco VAN BASTEN ‡	5, 50		9	Zoran UBAVIC	
10	Ruud GULLIT			10	Andrej ZELKO ‡	
11	Jean-Pierre PAPIN	64		11	Nedeljko TOPIC	

Substitutes

Roberto DONADONI †61

Daniele MASSARO ‡75

Substitutes

Branko ZIBERT †66

Nenad PROTEGA ‡85

Referee Roman STEINDL (Austria)

SUMMARY

● Milan's return to European action after their one-year suspension got off to a predictably easy start against the Slovenian champions. Within five minutes Dutch superstar Marco van Basten had opened the scoring with his 25th goal in Europe, steering in a Lentini cross from close range after turning his marker in the penalty box. The score was doubled barely two minutes later when Demetrio Albertini, on his European debut, volleyed home spectacularly from 30 yards. The match was virtually over by this stage, and there were to be only two further goals in the second half of this one-sided contest, both of them created by Ruud Gullit, playing his first competitive game of the season. The first was put away with typical power and accuracy by Van Basten. The second was despatched with a brave diving header by his striking partner Jean-Pierre Papin. It was the Frenchman's 20th Champions' Cup goal in four seasons, but, perhaps more importantly for the player himself, his first in an official game for Milan since his summer transfer from Marseille.

CHAMPIONS' CUP
First Round Second Leg

Wednesday 30th September 1992
Bezigrad Stadium, Ljubljana

SCT OLIMPIJA LJUBLJANA 0 MILAN 3

Half-time 0-1 *Aggregate* 0-7 *Attendance* 13,000

		Goals			Goals
1	Marko SIMEUNOVIC		1	Sebastiano ROSSI	
2	Nenad PODGAJSKI		2	Mauro TASSOTTI	85
3	Robert ENGLARO		3	Paolo MALDINI	
4	Dejan DJURANOVIC		4	Roberto DONADONI	
5	Edin HADZIALAGIC		5	Stefano NAVA	
6	Damir VRABAC		6	Franco BARESI	
7	Nenad PROTEGA		7	Alberigo EVANI †	
8	Zeljko MILINOVIC		8	Frank RIJKAARD	48
9	Zoran UBAVIC †		9	Zvonimir BOBAN	
10	Sandi VALENTINCIC		10	Ruud GULLIT ‡	
11	Nedeljko TOPIC ‡		11	Daniele MASSARO	31

Substitutes	*Substitutes*
Andrej ZELKO †72	Stefano ERANIO †46 ❑
Igor BENEDEJCIC ‡85	Marco SIMONE ‡61

Referee Jirí ULRICH (Czechoslovakia)

● *Six of the Milan players who had started the first leg were missing as the Italian champions took the field on a wet and unpleasant evening in Ljubljana. But the club's famed strength in depth was clear for all to see as they thoroughly outclassed the Slovenians for the second time in a fortnight. With Van Basten and Papin amongst the absentees, there was room for Croatian Zvonimir Boban to claim one of the three foreigner berths and make his debut for the club on what until recently would have been regarded as home soil for the former Yugoslav international. The other recalled foreigner was Frank Rijkaard and he celebrated his 30th birthday with a man-of-the-match performance, the highlight of which was his superb header early in the second half which put the Italians 2-0 up on the night and gave the player his first European goal since the one he scored to give Milan victory against Benfica in the 1990 Champions' Cup Final in Vienna.*

CHAMPIONS' CUP
First Round First Leg

Wednesday 16th September 1992
Lech Stadium, Poznan

LECH POZNAN 2 SKONTO RIGA 0

Half-time 2-0 *Attendance* 18,000

		Goals				Goals
1	Kazimierz SIDORCZUK		1	Oleg GRISHIN		
2	Marek RZEPKA		2	Oleg BLAGONADEZDIN		
3	Pawel WOJTALA		3	Vitaly ASTAFJEV		
4	Waldemar KRYGER		4	Einars GNEDOI		
5	Przemyslaw BERESZYNSKI		5	Mihails ZEMLINSKIS		
6	Ryszard REMIEN ‡		6	Valentin LOBANOV		
7	Kazimierz MOSKAL		7	Artur SKETOV ‡		
8	Dariusz SKRZYPCZAK		8	Aleksandr STRADIN		
9	Jerzy PODBROZNY	39	9	Aleksandr DIBRIVNY †		
10	Jaroslaw ARASZKIEWICZ		10	Igor STEPANOV		
11	Miroslaw TRCEZIAK †	27	11	Aleksandr JELISEJEV		

Substitutes

Dariusz KOFNYT †67 ❏

Igor KORNIETS ‡77

Substitutes

Sergei TARASOV †46

Aleksei SEMJONOV ‡59

Referee Mitko MITREV (Bulgaria)

S U M M A R Y

● UEFA's decision to ban all Yugoslav clubs from the 1992/93 competitions was particularly good news for Polish champions Lech Poznan. With Red Star Belgrade absent from the Champions' Cup, Lech were promoted to number eight seed for the competition, a position entitling them to the advantage of avoiding all of the top clubs in each of the first two rounds. Their first assignment looked straightforward enough. Skonto Riga, from Latvia, had come through the preliminary round with considerable ease against the champions of the Faeroe Isles, but that was no great reference. They were there for the taking, and after two first-half goals from strikers Trceziak and Podbrozny, Lech appeared set for an avalanche of goals after the interval. But with star striker Andrzej Juskowiak having been sold to Portugal, the Polish champions lacked bite up front and, to the profound disappointment of the big Poznan crowd, 2-0 was to be the final scoreline. Enough to set Lech up for a relatively trouble-free return, but insufficient to give credence to their privileged status.

CHAMPIONS' CUP
First Round Second Leg

Wednesday 30th September 1992
Daugavas Stadium, Riga

SKONTO RIGA 0 LECH POZNAN 0

Half-time 0-0 *Aggregate* 0-2 *Attendance* 3,500

		Goals				Goals
1	Oleg GRISHIN			1	Kazimierz SIDORCZUK	
2	Oleg BLAGONADDEZDIN			2	Marek RZEPKA	
3	Vitaly ASTAFJEV			3	Pawel WOJTALA	
4	Einars GNEDOI ❑			4	Waldemar KRYGER	
5	Mihails ZEMLINSKIS			5	Przemyslaw BERESZYNSKI	
6	Valentin LOBANOV			6	Ryszard REMIEN †	
7	Artur SKETOV †			7	Kazimierz MOSKAL	
8	Aleksandr STRADIN			8	Dariusz SKRZYPCZAK	
9	Igor STEPANOV ‡			9	Jerzy PODBROZNY	
10	Igor TROITSKI			10	Jaroslaw ARASZKIEWICZ	
11	Aleksandr JELISEJEV			11	Miroslaw TRZECIAK	

Substitutes		*Substitute*	
Sergei TARASOV †59		Igor KORNIETS †61	
Aleksei SEMJONOV ‡70			

Referee Frederick McKNIGHT (Northern Ireland)

SUMMARY

● *Lech Poznan became the only one of four Polish representatives to reach the second round of European competition after this uneventful encounter in Riga. 0-0 was hardly a surprising scoreline. The national teams of Denmark and Spain had also left the Latvian capital with goalless draws from recent World Cup qualifying ties. So, in that respect, there was nothing for the Polish champions to be ashamed about. They were into the second round draw and set to continue enjoying the protection afforded to those in the seeded elite. As for Skonto, they could be proud of their achievement in restricting Lech to just two goals, one a penalty, over the three hours of the tie. Like all the Champions' Cup entrants from the three ex-Soviet Baltic states, they were acting as a 'guinea pig' for the future increased participation of their country's clubs. And on the evidence of their on-field performance, if nothing else, they cannot have done the Latvian cause any harm.*

CHAMPIONS' CUP
First Round First Leg

Wednesday 16th September 1992
Philips Stadium, Eindhoven

PSV 6 ZHALGIRIS VILNIUS 0

Half-time 2-0 *Attendance* 15,650

		Goals				Goals
1	Hans VAN BREUKELEN		1	Darius SPETYLA		
2	Ernest FABER		2	Tomas ZIUKAS		
3	Adri VAN TIGGELEN		3	Tomas ZVIRGZDAUSKAS		
4	Erwin KOEMAN †	24	4	Virginius BALTUSHNIKAS		
5	Jan HEINTZE		5	Ramunas STONKUS ❑ †		
6	Gheorghe POPESCU		6	Eimantas PODERIS		
7	Juul ELLERMAN	36, 60, 64	7	Viaceslavas SUKRISTOVAS ‡		
8	Gerald VANENBURG ‡		8	Andrius TERESKINAS ❑		
9	Edward LINSKENS ❑		9	Aidas PREIKSAITIS		
10	Wim KIEFT	66	10	Aurelijus SKARBALIUS		
11	Arthur NUMAN	80	11	Ricardas ZDANCIUS		
	Substitutes			*Substitutes*		
	KALUSHA Bwalya †72			Darius MACIULEVICIUS †46		
	Raymond BEERENS ‡75			Dainius SULIAUSKAS ‡69		

Referee James McCLUSKEY (Scotland)

SUMMARY

● *PSV's credibility as a major force in the European game had dwindled somewhat during the past two years under English coach Bobby Robson. Now, with Robson having been replaced by FC Groningen boss Hans Westerhof, it was time for the Eindhoven club to re-assert themselves on the European stage. Reaching the semi-final group phase of the Champions' Cup was the club's avowed number one priority for the season, and they could scarcely have been handed an easier first round opponent than Zhalgiris Vilnius. The club from the Lithuanian capital had competed twice in Europe before, but never in the Champions' Cup and never under their own country's flag. Unlike the champions of the other new ex-Soviet Baltic states, Estonia and Latvia, Zhalgiris were excused preliminary round action. Instead, they were thrown straight into the deep end against the 1988 winners, and they did not stay afloat long. A hat-trick from Dutch international Juul Ellerman not only made him the early top scorer in the competition, but also helped PSV to their biggest win in Europe for 11 years.*

CHAMPIONS' CUP
First Round Second Leg

Wednesday 30th September 1992
Zhalgiris Stadium, Vilnius

ZHALGIRIS VILNIUS 0 PSV 2

Half-time 0-2 *Aggregate* 0-8 *Attendance* 2,800

		Goals				Goals
1	Darius SPETYLA		1	Hans VAN BREUKELEN		
2	Tomas ZIUKAS		2	Berry VAN AERLE †		
3	Tomas ZVIRGZDAUSKAS		3	Adri VAN TIGGELEN		
4	Virginius BALTUSHNIKAS		4	Erwin KOEMAN		
5	Dainius SULIAUSKAS		5	Jan HEINTZE		
6	Eimantas PODERIS		6	Gheorghe POPESCU		
7	Grazvydas MIKULENAS †		7	Juul ELLERMAN		
8	Andrius TERESKINAS		8	Edward LINSKENS		
9	Aidas PREIKSAITIS ‡		9	ROMÁRIO de Souza Faria ‡	39	
10	Aurelijus SKARBALIUS		10	Wim KIEFT		
11	Ricardas ZDANCIUS		11	Arthur NUMAN	26	
	Substitutes			*Substitutes*		
	Vytautas KARVELIS †46			Jerry DE JONG †46		
	Ramunas STONKUS ‡67			Raymond BEERENS ‡86		

Referee Markus MERK (Germany)

SUMMARY

● *With a big league game at home to Feyenoord coming up the following weekend, the long trip to Vilnius was something of an unwanted distraction for the Dutch champions. With a 6-0 advantage from the home leg, there was nothing left for PSV to play for, except perhaps to take the aggregate score into double figures, a feat they had achieved in Europe four times before. First-half goals from new signing Arthur Numan (his second of the tie) and Brazilian superstar Romário gave PSV every opportunity of stretching that record to five, but, with their minds evidently elsewhere, the team eased off noticeably after the break and they were ultimately happy to coast home to a 2-0 win. The highpoint of the match for coach Hans Westerhof was the splendid form shown by Romário. He had signalled his return from injury the previous weekend with a hat-trick in a Dutch league game against MVV and now he was on target again to maintain his impressive scoring record in the Champions' Cup - this was his ninth goal in as many games in the competition.*

Wednesday 16th September 1992
Nou Camp, Barcelona

FC BARCELONA 1 VIKING FK 0

Half-time 0-0 *Attendance* 35,000

		Goals			Goals
1	Andoni ZUBIZARRETA		1	Lars Gaute BØ	
2	Albert FERRER		2	Øyvind MELLEMSTRAND	
3	Miguel Angel NADAL		3	Ingve BØE	
4	José GUARDIOLA		4	Ulf KARLSEN	
5	EUSEBIO Sacristán		5	Roger NILSEN	
6	Goran VUCEVIC·		6	Erik PEDERSEN	
7	Jon Andoni GOIKOETXEA		7	Sander SOLBERG	
8	Guillermo AMOR	86	8	Kenneth STORVIK	
9	Michael LAUDRUP ‡		9	Egil FJETLAND †	
10	Richard WITSCHGE †		10	Egil Johan ØSTENSTAD ‡	
11	Aitor BEGUIRISTAIN		11	Børre MEINSETH	

Substitutes

Julio SALINAS †46

Miguel SOLER ‡78

Substitutes

Alf Kåre TVEIT †72

Leif Rune SALTE ‡88

Referee Lajos HARTMANN (Hungary)

SUMMARY

● *Johan Cruijff found himself the target of vehement criticism from all quarters after this inauspicious opening display by the reigning Champions' Cup holders. Barcelona's Dutch coach, a hero a few months earlier after his team's historic win at Wembley, was found guilty of complacency by supporters and media alike when he chose to 'rest' his two big foreign stars Ronald Koeman and Christo Stoichkov for what he evidently perceived as an easy first defence of the trophy. In the event, it turned out to be anything but against a Norwegian side who defended intelligently and refused to be intimidated by the occasion. Psychologically, the team from Stavanger probably felt that Cruijff had let them off the hook by deliberately fielding a weakened side. Cruijff's gamble had failed to pay off, but he was characteristically unrepentant, especially when club president Nuñez added his voice to the chorus of disapproval. "I have never been eliminated in the first round of a European competition, either as player or coach. I don't think our president can say as much!"*

CHAMPIONS' CUP
First Round Second Leg

Wednesday 30th September 1992
Stavanger Stadium, Stavanger

VIKING FK 0   FC BARCELONA 0

Half-time 0-0   *Aggregate* 0-1   *Attendance* 12,041

		Goals			Goals
1	Lars Gaute BØ		1	Andoni ZUBIZARRETA	
2	Øyvind MELLEMSTRAND		2	Albert FERRER ❑	
3	Ingve BØE		3	José GUARDIOLA ❑	
4	Ulf KARLSEN		4	Ronald KOEMAN	
5	Roger NILSEN		5	JUAN CARLOS Rodríguez	
6	Erik PEDERSEN ❑		6	José María BAKERO	
7	Sander SOLBERG		7	Miguel Angel NADAL	
8	Kenneth STORVIK †		8	Christo STOICHKOV ‡	
9	Egil FJETLAND ‡		9	Michael LAUDRUP	
10	Egil Johan ØSTENSTAD		10	Guillermo AMOR	
11	Børre MEINSETH		11	Aitor BEGUIRISTAIN †	

Substitutes

Rune GJERDE †65
Børge RANNESTAD ‡76

Substitutes

Julio SALINAS †57
Jon Andoni GOIKOETXEA ‡80

Referee Simo RUOKONEN (Finland)

● There was no messing about by Johan Cruijff for this match. Back came both Koeman and Stoichkov, together with another mainstay of the side, José María Bakero, returning from a one-match suspension. But where a patchwork Barcelona side had failed to assert their authority over their unfancied opponents in Spain, a full-strength team was to suffer similar frustration in Norway. Viking knew that eliminating the holders would constitute one of the biggest shocks in European Cup history. This was their seventh Champions' Cup campaign and they had not once passed the first round. Furthermore, no Norwegian club had managed to win a single European tie for six years. But the timing for a possible upset was perfect. Just a week earlier the Norwegian national team had made the continent sit up and take notice with a sensational 2-1 victory over Holland in a World Cup qualifier. Try as they might, though, Viking could not put the ball in the net. That said, neither could Barça, and Cruijff's team hobbled unimpressively into the next round.

CHAMPIONS' CUP
First Round First Leg

Wednesday 16th September 1992
Kisapuisto Stadium, Lahti

FC KUUSYSI 1 DINAMO BUCURESTI 0

Half-time 1-0 *Attendance* 1,330

		Goals				Goals
1	Jyrki ROVIO			1	Florin Alexandru TENE	
2	Ilkka REMES			2	Zoltan KADAR	
3	Jarmo SAASTAMOINEN			3	Tibor SELYMES	
4	Kalle LEHTINEN			4	Gheorghe MIHALI	
5	Valery GLUSAKOV			5	Adrian MATEI ❑	
6	Kimmo TARKKIO			6	Leo Florian GROZAVU ❑	
7	Petri JÄRVINEN			7	Dorinel MUNTEANU	
8	Jari RINNE ❑	16		8	Gabor GERSTENMAJER	
9	Jari KINNUNEN			9	Ioan Sebastian MOGA †	
10	Mike BELFIELD †			10	Daniel TIMOFTE ‡	
11	Juha ANNUNEN ‡			11	Sulejman DEMOLLARI	

Substitutes

Harri MUNUKKA †84

Sami VEHKAKOSKI ‡89

Substitutes

Ovidiu Cornel HANGANU †46

Nelson MENSAH ‡69

Referee Wilfred WALLACE (Republic of Ireland)

● *Kuusysi Lahti and Dinamo Bucharest were familiar foes in European competition. This was the third time in nine years that they had been paired together, with the Romanians having come out on top on both previous occasions, winning all four matches without conceding a goal. Kuusysi's overall European record was a reflection of those two results. Despite qualifying for European competition nine times in the past decade, they had only ever won two ties, both of them in the 1985/86 Champions' Cup when they reached the quarter-finals, only to be knocked out by the eventual winners - Dinamo's city rivals, Steaua! More recently, Kuusysi had gained a morale-boosting 1-0 victory over Liverpool the previous season, and against a Dinamo side featuring nine full internationals, the part-timers repeated the feat. Surprisingly, the winning goal did not come from either new signing Kimmo Tarkkio or Englishman Mike Belfield, the two top scorers in the 1991 Finnish Premier Division, but from captain Jari Rinne. His strike was enough to produce the biggest shock of the night in the Champions' Cup.*

CHAMPIONS' CUP
First Round Second Leg

Wednesday 30th September 1992
Dinamo Stadium, Bucharest

DINAMO BUCURESTI 2 FC KUUSYSI 0 (aet)

Half-time 0-0 *Aggregate* 2-1 *Attendance* 9,000

		Goals			Goals
1	Florin Alexandru TENE		1	Jyrki ROVIO	
2	Marian PANA ‡		2	Ilkka REMES	
3	Tibor SELYMES		3	Jarmo SAASTAMOINEN	
4	Gheorghe MIHALI ❑		4	Kalle LEHTINEN	
5	Adrian MATEI †		5	Valery GLUSAKOV	
6	Marius CHEREGI		6	Kimmo TARKKIO	
7	Dorinel MUNTEANU		7	Petri JÄRVINEN	
8	Gabor GERSTENMAJER	63	8	Jari RINNE ‡	
9	Ioan Sebastian MOGA		9	Jari KINNUNEN ❑	
10	Zoltan KADAR		10	Mike BELFIELD	
11	Sulejman DEMOLLARI	114	11	Juha ANNUNEN †	

Substitutes

Nelson MENSAH †46 ❑

Daniel TIMOFTE ‡78

Substitutes

Jari SULANDER †78 ❑

Harri MUNUKKA ‡103

Referee Stavros ZAKESTIDIS (Greece)

SUMMARY

● Under normal circumstances, Dinamo would have been permitted to stage their 100th European match in the Romanian National Stadium. But with priority for the use of that venue having been given to a Michael Jackson pop concert, it was in their smaller home stadium that they set about retrieving their first-leg deficit against FC Kuusysi and qualifying for the second round. The Finns clung on to their lead for over an hour, but the tie was eventually levelled with a goal from Gabor Gerstenmajer. Their resistance finally broken, Kuusysi might have been expected to collapse at this point, but they continued to defend well, succeeded in taking the tie into extra-time and were within six minutes of securing themselves a fifty-fifty chance of qualification with a penalty shoot-out when Albanian international Sulejman Demollari sent the home fans into raptures with the winning goal. Dinamo's club president Vasile Ianul was, literally, overcome with excitement at Demollari's timely strike and had to be transported to hospital suffering from a mild heart attack!

CHAMPIONS' CUP
First Round First Leg

Wednesday 16th September 1992
Ibrox Stadium, Glasgow

READY

RANGERS 2 LYNGBY BK 0

Half-time 1-0 *Attendance* 40,036

		Goals				Goals
1	Andy GORAM		1	Kim BRODERSEN		
2	Ian DURRANT		2	Svend Erik LARSEN ❏		
3	David ROBERTSON		3	Morten WIEGHORST		
4	Richard GOUGH		4	Michael GOTHENBORG		
5	Dave McPHERSON		5	Claus CHRISTIANSEN		
6	John BROWN		6	Johnny VILSTRUP ‡		
7	Aleksei MIKHAILICHENKO ❏		7	Henrik RISOM		
8	Ian FERGUSON		8	Emeka EZEUGO ❏		
9	Ally McCOIST		9	Lars HAMMER		
10	Mark HATELEY	39	10	Morten NIELSEN		
11	Pieter HUISTRA	67	11	Henrik JØRGENSEN †		

Substitutes

Substitutes

Jan Chico OLSEN †73

Anders NIELSEN ‡88

Referee Jaap UILENBERG (Holland)

SUMMARY

● *Scottish champions Rangers, appearing in Europe's premier competition for the fourth year in a row, were determined to make their mark at last in the Champions' Cup after their disappointing campaigns of the past. Lyngby represented a relatively easy first hurdle for them. The newly-crowned Danish title-holders had lost three key figures from their championship-winning side - Danish internationals Peter Nielsen, Torben Frank and Henrik Nielsen - and were not expected to improve too much on their previous performance against British opposition, a 0-1 aggregate defeat by Wrexham in the Cup-winners' Cup two years earlier. A big crowd gathered to cheer Rangers on to victory and by the final whistle the Scottish fans were able to leave Ibrox content with the 2-0 scoreline. The goals came either side of the interval. Englishman Mark Hateley scored the first, diving in where many would fear to tread to head home John Brown's left-wing cross, and it was another non-national, Pieter Huistra, who gave Rangers some breathing space for the return leg with a cool second.*

CHAMPIONS' CUP
First Round Second Leg

Wednesday 30th September 1992
Lyngby Stadium, Lyngby

LYNGBY BK 0   RANGERS 1

Half-time 0-0 *Aggregate* 0-3 *Attendance* 5,000

		Goals				Goals
1	Kim BRODERSEN		1	Andy GORAM		
2	Svend Erik LARSEN		2	Stuart McCALL		
3	Thomas RYTTER ❏ †		3	David ROBERTSON		
4	Michael GOTHENBORG		4	Ian DURRANT ❏		85
5	Claus CHRISTIANSEN		5	Dave McPHERSON		
6	Johnny VILSTRUP		6	John BROWN		
7	Henrik RISOM		7	Trevor STEVEN		
8	Morten WIEGHORST ❏		8	Ian FERGUSON ❏		
9	Henrik JØRGENSEN		9	Ally McCOIST		
10	Morten NIELSEN ‡		10	Mark HATELEY		
11	Allan KUHN		11	Pieter HUISTRA		

Substitutes

Jan Chico OLSEN †46

Henrik LYKKE ‡70

Substitutes

Referee Karl-Josef ASSENMACHER (Germany)

SUMMARY

● *The chances of Lyngby staging a dramatic comeback and turning the tie in their favour were minimal. They came into the game one place from the bottom of the Danish Super League with just one win in nine matches. Clearly they were no B 1903, the Danish side which had destroyed Aberdeen in the first round of the previous season's UEFA Cup, and Rangers, although wary of conceding a goal that might give their opponents hope, were able to settle down and dictate the pace of the game. The nearest Lyngby came to that goal was just after half-time when Johnny Vilstrup lashed a left-footed volley against the Rangers crossbar. Otherwise it was the visitors who had the best chances. One of these saw Ian Durrant hit the woodwork after a near-miss from Hateley, and it was this combination that crafted the only goal of the game five minutes from time, with Durrant breaking the offside trap and racing towards goal before pushing the ball past Brodersen to seal Rangers' passage into the second round.*

CHAMPIONS' CUP
First Round First Leg

Wednesday 16th September 1992
Tehelné pole, Bratislava

SLOVAN BRATISLAVA 4 FERENCVÁROS 1

Half-time 1-0 *Attendance* 20,000

		Goals				Goals
1	Alexander VENCEL		1	Tamás BALOGH		
2	Tomás STÚPALA		2	Tibor SIMON ❏		
3	Jozef JURIGA		3	András TELEK		
4	Ondrej KRISTOFÍK		4	József KELLER		
5	Vladimír KINDER		5	Tamás SZEKERES		
6	Milos GLONEK ❏		6	Péter LIPCSEI ❏	75	
7	Frantisek KLINOVSKY		7	Zsolt PÁLING		
8	Stefan MAIXNER ‡		8	Flórián ALBERT		
9	Pavol GOSTIC †	19	9	Gábor SCHNEIDER ‡		
10	Peter DUBOVSKY	51, 55	10	Mihaly SZÜCS		
11	Jaroslav TIMKO		11	László WUKOVICS †		
	Substitutes			*Substitutes*		
	Youssef HARAOUI †49			Sándor SZENES †52 ■		
	Stanislav MORAVEC ‡67	82		Gábor BALOGH ‡65		

Referee Serge MUHMENTHALER (Switzerland)

● This Central European 'derby' appeared on paper to be one of the most evenly-contested ties of the round. With the cities of Bratislava and Budapest just 200km apart and many Hungarians living in Slovakia, there was certainly plenty at stake. But sadly the thin line which separates local rivalry from ethnic prejudice was crossed on this occasion, leading to all sorts of brutal exchanges between the visiting supporters and the local police. A fine game of football was overshadowed completely by the unpleasant scenes on the terraces. There was no doubt that the Ferencváros fans were out to cause trouble. But the action of the Slovak police, kitted out for the occasion with helmets, batons and riot shields, was reprehensible, to say the least. The outcome of the clashes was that 15 Ferencváros fans were taken to hospital and one of them eventually died from his injuries. Ferencváros, feeling that the disturbances had affected their performance, demanded a re-match, but their protest fell on deaf ears. All they got was a fine of 15,000 Swiss Francs, the same punishment meted out to host club Slovan.

CHAMPIONS' CUP
First Round Second Leg

Wednesday 30th September 1992
Üllöi út Stadium, Budapest

FERENCVÁROS 0 SLOVAN BRATISLAVA 0

Half-time 0-0 *Aggregate* 1-4 *Attendance* 14,000

		Goals			Goals
1	Tamás BALOGH		1	Alexander VENCEL	
2	Tibor SIMON		2	Tomás STÚPALA	
3	András TELEK		3	Jozef JURIGA	
4	József KELLER		4	Ondrej KRISTOFÍK	
5	Mihaly SZÜCS		5	Vladimír KINDER	
6	Péter LIPCSEI		6	Milos GLONEK	
7	Zsolt PÁLING		7	Frantisek KLINOVSKY	
8	Flórián ALBERT		8	Stefan MAIXNER ‡	
9	Sorin CIGAN ‡		9	Pavol GOSTIC ❏ †	
10	Imre FODOR †		10	Peter DUBOVSKY	
11	László WUKOVICS		11	Jaroslav TIMKO	

Substitutes

Gábor BALOGH †46

Péter DESZATNIK ‡80

Substitutes

Stanislav MORAVEC †60

Youssef HARAOUI ‡73

Referee Sergei KHUSAINOV (Russia)

SUMMARY

● *Not surprisingly, after the tragic events of the first leg, this match was declared 'high risk' by UEFA. Ferencváros's more volatile supporters were certainly in an agitated mood. They had staged a demonstration outside the offices of the Hungarian daily sports paper 'Nemzeti Sport' in response to an editorial severely criticising their behaviour in Bratislava. Revenge was in the air, but with just a solitary courageous Slovan supporter travelling to the game to follow his team, there was thankfully no opportunity for another bout of violence. The Ferencváros diehards could only hope that their team would avenge them on the pitch. But pulling back a three-goal deficit was always going to be too much to ask. Thanks to the exploits of Alexander Vencel in the Slovan goal, the Hungarian champions did not get on the scoresheet once. Even Péter Lipcsei, the young midfielder who was the Cup-winners' Cup top scorer the previous season, was unable to break the deadlock. The 0-0 draw meant Ferencváros's first Champions' Cup campaign for 11 years ended exactly as their last, with first-round elimination by the champions of Czechoslovakia.*

Wednesday 16th September 1992
Horr Stadium, Vienna

FK AUSTRIA 3 CSKA SOFIA 1

Half-time 1-0 *Attendance* 7,000

		Goals			Goals
1	Franz WOHLFAHRT		1	Georgi VELINOV	
2	Ernst AIGNER ❏		2	Zarko MACHEV	
3	Manfred SCHMID		3	Stefan KOLEV	
4	Walter KOGLER	90	4	Krasimir BEZINSKI ❏	
5	Manfred ZSAK		5	Marius URUKOV	
6	Michael BINDER		6	Ivailo KIROV ❏	
7	Robertas FRIDRIKAS	83	7	Anatoli NANKOV †	
8	Thomas FLÖGEL †		8	Kiril METKOV	
9	Christian PROSENIK		9	Vanio SHISHKOV ‡	58
10	Peter STÖGER		10	Ivailo ANDONOV	
11	Ralph HASENHÜTTL ❏	16	11	Christo KOILOV	

Substitutes	*Substitutes*
Peter POSPISIL †72	Victorio PAVLOV †87
	Boris KHVOINEV ‡89

Referee Ion CRACIUNESCU (Romania)

SUMMARY

● There was little to choose between these two evenly-matched clubs at the outset, and at the end of the 90 minutes few could honestly predict what the eventual outcome of the tie would be. The Bulgarians, competing in the competition for the 21st time, certainly had their chances to take control of the tie after Shishkov made it 1-1 early in the second half. But at the final whistle they were left cursing both their ill-luck and their own defensive carelessness in the closing stages. Robertas Fridrikas, the only one of FK Austria's three contracted Lithuanian internationals on duty for this game, restored his side's advantage in the 82nd minute before defender Walter Kogler, a new signing from Sturm Graz, popped up seconds from time to make the final scoreline 3-1. The only goal in the first half had been scored by FK Austria striker Ralph Hasenhüttl. It was his club's 150th goal in European competition.

CHAMPIONS' CUP
First Round Second Leg

Wednesday 30th September 1992
Narodna Armia Stadium, Sofia

CSKA SOFIA 3 FK AUSTRIA 2

Half-time 1-1 *Aggregate* 4-5 *Attendance* 10,000

		Goals				Goals
1	Georgi VELINOV		1	Franz WOHLFAHRT	
2	Zarko MACHEV ❑		2	Ernst AIGNER ❑	
3	Stefan KOLEV ❑		3	Manfred SCHMID ❑	
4	Krasimir BEZINSKI †		4	Walter KOGLER	
5	Rosen KIRILOV		5	Manfred ZSAK	
6	Ivailo KIROV ❑		6	Michael BINDER	
7	Anatoli NANKOV ‡		7	Robertas FRIDRIKAS ❑ ‡	
8	Kiril METKOV ❑	2	8	Thomas FLÖGEL	28
9	Boris KHVOINEV		9	Christian PROSENIK	
10	Ivailo ANDONOV ❑	60	10	Peter STÖGER	
11	Stefan DRAGANOV ❑	73 (pen)	11	Valdas IVANAUSKAS ❑ †	67

	Substitutes			*Substitutes*	
	Christo KOILOV †46			Ralph HASENHÜTTL †75	
	Anton DIMITROV ‡69			Attila SEKERLIOGLU ‡89	

Referee David ELLERAY (England)

● Honours were even at one victory each in previous European ties between the champions of Austria and Bulgaria. And oddly enough, the two victorious teams were FK Austria (v Spartak Sofia in 1970/71) and CSKA Sofia (v Wacker Innsbruck in 1973/74). The competitive nature of the first leg was even more evident in this match, with no fewer than ten players having their names taken by the English referee. The pattern of the play was plain from the start, with the Bulgarians dominating possession and striving to peg back their first-leg deficit whilst the Austrians did their best to maintain the status quo. Kiril Metkov's early goal was the spark CSKA needed, but there was nothing they could have done about Thomas Flögel's spectacularly-struck equaliser from fully 35 yards. The swerve of the shot deceived Velinov and it crashed in off the underside of the bar. That proved a mortal blow to CSKA 's hopes of turning the tie around. Twice more they came back to take the lead on the night, the second time from a controversial penalty, but Ivanauskas's volley put the issue beyond doubt.

CHAMPIONS' CUP
First Round First Leg

Wednesday 16th September 1992
Tourbillon Stadium, Sion

FC SION 4 TAVRIA SIMFEROPOL 1

Half-time 2-0 Attendance 6,000

Goals

Goals

1	Stéphane LEHMANN	
2	Yvan QUENTIN	
3	Olivier BIAGGI ❏	
4	Dominique HERR	
5	Alain GEIGER	
6	Marc HOTTIGER	18
7	LUIS CARLOS	
8	Reto GERTSCHEN	
9	TÚLIO Humberto	35, 74
10	Roberto ASSIS ❏	78
11	David ORLANDO	

Substitutes

1	Oleg KOLESOV ■	
2	Sergei SHEVCHENKO	85
3	Nikolai TURCHINENKO	
4	Aleksandr GOLOVKO	
5	Vidmantas VISHNIAUSKAS	
6	Sergei VORONEZHSKY	
7	Andrey OPARIN	
8	Yury GUDIMENKO	
9	Sergei POLSTIANOV	
10	Sefer ALIBAEV †	
11	Toliat SHEYHAMETOV ‡	

Substitutes

Dmitry GULENKOV †21

Yury GETIKOV ‡79

Referee Léon SCHELINGS (Belgium)

● This was Sion's 11th season in Europe, but their first in the Champions' Cup. During the summer the club had undergone a radical change in personnel. Gone was not only their Swiss championship-winning coach, Enzo Trossero, but also their three top goalscorers, Baljic, Calderón and Manfreda. In to replace them were a quartet of virtually unknown Brazilians plus two Swiss international defenders from Lausanne, Marc Hottiger and Dominique Herr. And it was these new signings who were to have a profound influence on the outcome of this encounter against the Ukrainian champions, Tavria Simferopol. The visitors certainly helped Sion's cause when their goalkeeper, Kolesov, was sent off after just 20 minutes for a 'professional' foul. By that time the Swiss champions had already taken the lead through Hottiger, and they took advantage of their numerical superiority with three further goals - all of them 'made in Brazil'. Striker Túlio got two of them, one in each half, and his compatriot Assis made it 4-0 near the end. There was still time for Tavria to give themselves a glimmer of hope for the return with a late penalty.

CHAMPIONS' CUP
First Round Second Leg

Wednesday 30th September 1992
Lokomotiv Stadium, Simferopol

TAVRIA SIMFEROPOL 1 FC SION 3

Half-time 0-0 *Aggregate* 2-7 *Attendance* 10,000

		Goals			Goals
1	Dmitry GULENKOV		1	Stéphane LEHMANN	
2	Sergei SHEVCHENKO	71	2	Yvan QUENTIN	
3	Nikolai TURCHINENKO		3	Michel SAUTHIER	
4	Aleksandr GOLOVKO		4	Dominique HERR	89
5	Igor VOLKOV		5	Alain GEIGER	
6	Sergei VORONEZHSKY ❑ ‡		6	Marc HOTTIGER	
7	Andrey OPARIN		7	Blaise PIFFARETTI	
8	Yury GUDIMENKO ❑		8	LUIS CARLOS	
9	Sergei POLSTIANOV †		9	TÚLIO Humberto	68, 78
10	Vladislav NOVIKOV		10	Roberto ASSIS †	
11	Toliat SHEYHAMETOV		11	David ORLANDO ‡	

Substitutes	*Substitutes*
Yury GETIKOV †63	Johann LONFAT †80
Vidmantas VISHNIAUSKAS ‡86	Sébastien FOURNIER ‡84

Referee Christer FÄLLSTRÖM (Sweden)

● *After dominating the first leg, Sion were annoyed with themselves for conceding a late penalty and allowing Tavria Simferopol back into the tie. But they need not have feared. The club from the Crimea were no better at home than they had been in Switzerland. They made few inroads into the Sion defence and, as in the first leg, managed to score just one goal from the penalty spot. That goal came, like the three from Sion, in the final quarter of a disappointing match. Individual honours went yet again to Brazilian striker Túlio who netted his second brace of the tie to become the early top scorer of the competition. Dominique Herr's last-minute goal meant that all seven of Sion's goals in the tie had been scored by players who had not been part of the championship-winning side the previous season. It also gave Sion their best ever result away from home in Europe - they had never previously won away by more than one goal - and completed their highest aggregate scoreline. This was all in complete contrast to the previous season when, in four Cup-winners' Cup matches, Sion had scored just twice.*

CHAMPIONS' CUP
First Round First Leg

Wednesday 16th September 1992
Achille-Hammerel Stadium, Luxembourg

UNION LUXEMBOURG 1 FC PORTO 4

Half-time 0-1 *Attendance* 3,552

		Goals				Goals
1	John VAN RIJSWIJCK		1	VÍTOR BAÍA		
2	Serge THILL		2	JOÃO PINTO		
3	Thomas WOLF		3	BANDEIRINHA		
4	Patrick FEYDER		4	ALOÍSIO		
5	Yves PICARD		5	FERNANDO COUTO †	47	
6	David BORBICONI		6	RUI FILIPE		
7	Christian JOACHIM †		7	JAIME MAGALHÃES		
8	Luc FEIEREISEN		8	TONI	51	
9	Patrick MOROCUTTI		9	DOMINGOS	90	
10	Denis MOGENOT		10	SEMEDO	40	
11	Frank DEVILLE	63	11	JORGE COUTO		
	Substitute			*Substitute*		
	Fernand HEINISCH †85			JORGE COSTA †80		

Referee Pat KELLY (Republic of Ireland)

● *Being drawn against Luxembourg teams in European competition is tantamount to being given a bye into the second round. Only on two occasions have teams from the Principality progressed beyond the first round of the Champions' Cup; and the last of those was way back in the 1963/64 season when Jeunesse Esch knocked out Finnish side Haka. So 1986/87 Champions' Cup winners FC Porto knew they had it easy, especially as Union Luxembourg had never won a single European tie in 16 attempts and had been eclipsed 10-0 on aggregate by Marseille a year earlier. The Portuguese side took their time in making the breakthrough, but once Semedo had headed in a João Pinto cross just before half-time, they pressed home their advantage, adding further goals through central defender Fernando Couto and striker Toni early in the second period. Union's reply was a deflected goal from their major new summer signing Frank Deville, but the visitors had the final say, stretching their lead to 4-1 through a Domingos tap-in with virtually the last kick of the game.*

CHAMPIONS' CUP
First Round Second Leg

Wednesday 30th September 1992
Das Antas Stadium, Oporto

FC PORTO 5 UNION LUXEMBOURG 0

Half-time 3-0 *Aggregate* 9-1 *Attendance* 30,000

		Goals			Goals
1	VÍTOR BAÍA ‡		1	John VAN RIJSWIJCK	
2	JOÃO PINTO		2	Serge THILL	
3	Lubomír VLK		3	Thomas WOLF ❑	
4	JOSÉ CARLOS	66	4	Patrick FEYDER	
5	JORGE COSTA ❑		5	Marc BIRSENS	
6	BINO		6	David BORBICONI	
7	JAIME MAGALHÃES ❑		7	Christian JOACHIM	
8	Emil KOSTADINOV	16, 35	8	Luc FEIEREISEN	
9	TONI	27, 62	9	Patrick MOROCUTTI †	
10	SEMEDO		10	Denis MOGENOT	
11	ANDRÉ †		11	Frank DEVILLE ‡	
	Substitutes			*Substitutes*	
	PAULINHO †68			Yves PICARD †40	
	VALENTE ‡72			Carlos GERALDO ‡80	

Referee Eyjólfur ÓLAFSSON (Iceland)

● *A year earlier Porto had scored only a solitary last-minute goal at home to Maltese side Valletta after cruising to an easy 3-0 away win in the first leg. So victory at home to Union Luxembourg was by no means a foregone conclusion for Carlos Alberto Silva's side. But on this occasion Porto did not disappoint their supporters. Having just moved to the top of their domestic league the previous weekend, they were in a positive frame of mind and two goals apiece from strikers Kostadinov and Toni, plus a fifth from defender José Carlos, enabled them to ease into round two with the biggest aggregate score-line of the round. It was not quite up to the 13-1 victory margin they managed two years earlier against Northern Ireland's Portadown, but it was a more than satisfactory return for most of the 30,000 crowd. One intriguing aspect of this match was that Porto appeared for each half in a different strip. They replaced their traditional blue and white stripes with an all blue shirt at half-time after the Icelandic referee ruled that there was too much of a colour clash with Union's white shirts and blue shorts!*

CHAMPIONS' CUP
First Round First Leg

Wednesday 16th September 1992
Víkingsvöllur Stadium, Reykjavík

VÍKINGUR 0 CSKA MOSKVA 1

Half-time 0-0 *Attendance* 2,900

		Goals			Goals
1	Gudmundur HREIDARSSON		1	Dmitry KHARIN	
2	Atli EINARSSON		2	Aleksei GUSHIN ‡	
3	Thorsteinn THORSTEINSSON		3	Sergei KOLOTOVKIN	
4	Adalsteinn ADALSTEINSSON		4	Dmitry BYSTROV	
5	Janez ZILNIK		5	Sergei FOKIN	
6	Gudmundur Ingi MAGNÚSSON		6	Vasily IVANOV	
7	Tomislav BOSNJAK †		7	Denis MASHKARIN ▢	
8	Gudmundur STEINSSON ‡		8	Aleksandr GRISHIN	
9	Atli HELGASON		9	Oleg SERGEEV	
10	Helgi BJARNASON		10	Yevgeny BUSHMANOV †	
11	Hördur THEÓDÓRSSON		11	Ilshat FAYZULLIN	
	Substitutes			*Substitutes*	
	Helgi SIGURDSSON †29			Dmitry KORSAKOV †55	75
	Björn BJARTMARZ ‡78			Yury BAVYKIN ‡70	

Referee Gerald ASHBY (England)

SUMMARY

● *To outside observers this was probably the least appealing Champions' Cup tie of the round. But for the clubs involved it was just as important as any other. Víkingur, the champions of Iceland, were back in Europe for the first time in nine years, whilst CSKA were in the curious position of representing a country (Russia) different from the one (Soviet Union) in whose league they had qualified as champions. Both clubs were nearing the end of their domestic seasons and neither were in especially good form. So much was evident from the rather barren quality of this first leg in Reykjavík, settled in favour of the visitors with a 70th-minute winning goal from substitute Korsakov. The result left Víkingur still searching for their first home goal in Europe after five attempts. It also extended their unenviable record of losing every one of their matches in European competition. As for CSKA, the 1-0 victory seemed certain to help take them beyond the first round in Europe for the first time in 21 years.*

CHAMPIONS' CUP
First Round Second Leg

Wednesday 30th September 1992
Lenin Stadium, Moscow

CSKA MOSKVA 4 VÍKINGUR 2

Half-time 3-1 *Aggregate* 5-2 *Attendance* 10,000

		Goals			Goals
1	Dmitry KHARIN		1	Gudmundur HREIDARSSON	
2	Aleksei GUSHIN ‡		2	Atli EINARSSON	30
3	Oleg MALYUKOV		3	Thorsteinn THORSTEINSSON	
4	Dmitry BYSTROV		4	Adalsteinn ADALSTEINSSON	
5	Sergei FOKIN ❑		5	Janez ZILNIK	
6	Vasily IVANOV ❑		6	Gudmundur Ingi MAGNÚSSON ❑	
7	Vasily MINKO		7	Tomislav BOSNJAK †	
8	Aleksandr GRISHIN	44	8	Helgi SIGURDSSON	
9	Oleg SERGEEV	21	9	Atli HELGASON	
10	Dmitry KORSAKOV	34	10	Helgi BJARNASON	
11	Ilshat FAYZULLIN †		11	Hördur THEÓDÓRSSON ‡	
	Substitutes			*Substitutes*	
	Mikhail KOLESNIKOV †60	87		Gudmundur STEINSSON †72	73
	Denis MASHKARIN ‡66			Björn BJARTMARZ ‡76	

Referee ERMAN Toroglu (Turkey)

SUMMARY

● *In common with most of the clubs from the former USSR competing in the 1992/93 European Cups, CSKA were a much weakened side from the one which had competed in the last ever Soviet Supreme League in 1991. Many of their best players had since left the country, including the international triumvirate of Korneev, Kuznetsov and Galyamin, all of whom had joined Spanish First Division club Español. The only full internationals remaining in a very young team were goalkeeper Dmitry Kharin, a star at the 1992 European Championships in Sweden, and striker Oleg Sergeev. It was Sergeev who opened the scoring in this game midway through the first half, but, to their credit, the vistors from Iceland hit back straight away and forced the Russians to up the tempo. Goals from Korsakov and Grishin made it 3-1 to CSKA at half-time (4-1 on aggregate) and from then on they were always in command of the tie. Two late goals, one for either side, simply decorated the scoreline and provided CSKA with their biggest aggregate win in European competition.*

CHAMPIONS' CUP
First Round First Leg

Wednesday 16th September 1992
Ramat-Gan Stadium, Tel-Aviv

MACCABI TEL-AVIV 0 CLUB BRUGGE KV 1

Half-time 0-1 *Attendance* 12,000

		Goals				Goals
1	Aleksandr UVAROV			1	Danny VERLINDEN	
2	Avi COHEN			2	László DISZTL	
3	Gadi BROMER			3	Rudy COSSEY	
4	Amit LEVY ❑			4	Gert VERHEYEN	
5	Aleksandr POLUKAROV			5	Dominique VANMAELE	
6	Noam SHOAM			6	Stéphane VAN DER HEYDEN	
7	Aharon Meir MELIKA			7	Claude VERSPAILLE	
8	Avi NIMNY			8	Alex QUERTER ❑	
9	Nir KLINGER			9	Lorenzo STAELENS	35
10	Itzak ZOHAR			10	Marc SCHAESSENS †	
11	Yaron DRORI †			11	Tomasz DZIUBINSKI ❑	

	Substitute				*Substitute*	
	Eli DRIEKES †70				Pascal PLOVIE †75	

Referee László VAGNER (Hungary)

● *Maccabi Tel-Aviv had come through their preliminary round tie against Valletta of Malta with little difficulty, but now they were in with the big boys. 1992/93 Cup-winners' Cup semi-finalists Club Bruges represented a formidable obstacle to the Israeli side's pre-tournament objective of making it into the second round, but with three of the Belgian club's best players - captain Van der Elst and strikers Booy and Amokachi - all suspended, Maccabi had a real opportunity to make a name for themselves in their first major European encounter. Bruges's experiece, however, was to win the day. Lining up five men at the back, they gave a perfect example of the type of absorb-and-counter tactics for which Belgian teams have become famous. The match-winner was Belgian international midfielder Lorenzo Staelens, a player who had developed a reputation for scoring important away goals for his team in Europe. His 35th-minute strike gave Bruges what they had come for and for the remainder of the game they simply held their shape in defence and withstood everything the Israelis could throw at them.*

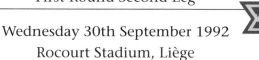

Wednesday 30th September 1992
Rocourt Stadium, Liège

CLUB BRUGGE KV 3 MACCABI TEL-AVIV 0

Half-time 0-0 Aggregate 4-0 Attendance 7,000

		Goals				Goals
1	Danny VERLINDEN		1	Aleksandr UVAROV	
2	László DISZTL		2	Avi COHEN	
3	Franky VAN DER ELST †		3	Gadi BROMER	
4	Gert VERHEYEN	77, 83	4	Alon BROMER ❏	
5	Dominique VANMAELE		5	Aleksandr POLUKAROV	
6	Stéphane VAN DER HEYDEN		6	Noam SHOAM	
7	Claude VERSPAILLE		7	Aharon Meir MELIKA ‡	
8	Rudy COSSEY		8	Avi NIMNY ❏	
9	Lorenzo STAELENS	57	9	Nir KLINGER	
10	Foeke BOOY		10	Itzak ZOHAR	
11	Marc SCHAESSENS		11	Yaron DRORI †	
	Substitute			*Substitutes*	
	Pascal PLOVIE †78			Eli DRIEKES †63	
				Nezah MASOBI ‡78	

Referee Rémy HARREL (France)

● As a result of crowd misbehaviour during their Cup-winners' Cup semi-final against Werder Bremen the previous season, Bruges were banned from their home stadium and forced to entertain their Israeli visitors on the other side of the country, in French-speaking Liège. It took Hugo Broos's side a long while to get accustomed to their new, unfamiliar surroundings, but once Lorenzo Staelens had netted his second goal of the tie early in the second half, there was no doubt which of the two sides would be entered into the hat for the second round draw. The Belgians had Van der Elst and Booy back from suspension, but it was a genuine newcomer to the side, ex-Anderlecht striker Gert Verheyen, who ensured a comfortable 3-0 victory for the home side with two late goals. Interestingly, Verheyen was the only Bruges player on the pitch who had not been a member of their Belgian championship-winning squad the previous season.

CHAMPIONS' CUP
First Round First Leg

Wednesday 16th September 1992
Neas Filadelfias Stadium, Athens

AEK 1 APOEL NICOSIA 1

Half-time 1-0 *Attendance* 28,000

		Goals			Goals
1	Antonis MINOU		1	Andreas PETRIDES	
2	Hristos VASSILOPOULOS		2	Costas COSTA	
3	Vaios KARAYANNIS ❏		3	Costas MIAMILIOTIS	
4	Stelios MANOLAS ❏		4	Demetris KLEANTHOUS	
5	Refik SABANADZOVIC		5	Lefteris KOUIS	
6	Pavlos PAPAIOANNOU		6	Toza SAPURIC ❏	
7	Alexandros ALEXANDRIS	42	7	Nicos CHARALAMBOUS	
8	Toni SAVEVSKI		8	Andros SOTIRIOU ❏	
9	Vassilis DIMITRIADIS		9	Sinisa GOGIC	
10	Zoran SLISKOVIC †		10	Yiannos IOANNOU ❏ †	
11	Stavros STAMATIS		11	Lucas HADJILUCAS ‡	75

Substitute

Yorgos AGOROYANNIS †75

Substitutes

Costas PHASOULIOTIS †61

Christodoulos CHRISTODOULOU ‡78

Referee Arie FROST (Israel)

SUMMARY

● There had been four previous meetings between Greek and Cypriot clubs in European competition. Not surprisingly, the Greeks held the upper hand with three victories. But on the one occasion that the Cypriots had come out on top, it was Apoel who had proudly carried the flag, defeating Salonika club Iraklis 2-0 on aggregate in the 1976/77 Cup-winners' Cup. The other three ties had all been lost by their Nicosia rivals Omonia, most recently in 1988 when they were beaten in both matches by Panathinaikos, the first time, surprisingly enough, that the Cypriot club had lost the away leg! Now, once again, Apoel were to avoid defeat on the 'mainland'. In a typically hyper-charged encounter, which produced five bookings, the Cypriot side put up a splendid performance to frustrate their more illustrious opponents and limit them to a single goal from Greek international Alexandros Alexandris. Apoel's equaliser, from Lucas Hadjilucas, was a considerable bonus. With an away goal in the bag, the Cypriots had given themselves a marvellous opportunity to complete the job in Nicosia and claim the most prized scalp in their European history.

CHAMPIONS' CUP
First Round Second Leg

Wednesday 30th September 1992
Makarion Stadium, Nicosia

APOEL NICOSIA 2 AEK 2

Half-time 0-1 *Aggregate* 3-3 (AEK win on away goals) *Attendance* 20,000

		Goals				Goals
1	Andreas PETRIDES		1	Antonis MINOU		
2	Costas COSTA		2	Hristos VASSILOPOULOS		
3	Costas MIAMILIOTIS		3	Vaios KARAYANNIS		
4	Demetris KLEANTHOUS †		4	Stelios MANOLAS ❑		
5	Lefteris KOUIS		5	Refik SABANADZOVIC ❑	31	
6	Toza SAPURIC		6	Pavlos PAPAIOANNOU		
7	Nicos CHARALAMBOUS		7	Alexandros ALEXANDRIS		
8	Andros SOTIRIOU ‡		8	Toni SAVEVSKI		
9	Sinisa GOGIC	77	9	Vassilis DIMITRIADIS ❑ †	71	
10	Yiannos IOANNOU		10	Zoran SLISKOVIC		
11	Lucas HADJILUCAS ❑		11	Stavros STAMATIS		

Substitutes

Willy NWAKANMA †12

Costas PHASOULIOTIS ‡69   85

Substitute

Yorgos AGOROYANNIS †82

Referee Charles AGIUS (Malta)

SUMMARY

● With Liverpool and Juventus having paid a visit to the south of the island the previous day, this might have been seen as the least attractive of the three first-round ties involving Cypriot teams. But after the results of the first leg encounters, there was no doubt where the interest of most of the country's football followers lay. A full house gathered for what most locals anticipated would be an historic occasion. A victory over big Athens club AEK was the primary objective, although a goalless draw would have been equally acceptable. That particular route to qualification disappeared, however, when Yugoslav defender Refik Sabanadzovic, a Champions' Cup winner with Red Star Belgrade in 1991, put the Greeks ahead after half an hour. In the second half the home side tried desperately to respond, but it was not until Alexandris, with his second goal of the tie, had put AEK 2-0 up that Apoel at last found the net. Two goals in seven minutes sent up a frantic finale, but in the end the visitors held on somewhat fortunately to their 'away goals' advantage.

CHAMPIONS' CUP
First Round First Leg

Wednesday 16th September 1992
Old Ullevi Stadium, Gothenburg

IFK GÖTEBORG 2 BESIKTAS 0

Half-time 0-0 *Attendance* 5,923

		Goals			Goals
1	Dick LAST		1	Jaroslaw BAKO ❏	
2	Magnus JOHANSSON		2	RECEP Cetin	
3	Tore PEDERSEN		3	KADIR Akbulut †	
4	Ola SVENSSON ❏ †		4	GÖKHAN Keskin	
5	Pontus KÅMARK		5	ULVI Güveneroglu	
6	Peter ERIKSSON		6	YÜKSEL Hamit ❏	
7	Stefan REHN		7	FEYYAZ Uçar	
8	Håkan MILD		8	RIZA Çalimbay	
9	Thomas ANDERSSON		9	MEHMET Özdilek	
10	Fredrik LEKSELL ‡		10	ZEKI Önatli	
11	Johnny EKSTRÖM	82	11	Mitar MRKELA ‡	
	Substitutes			*Substitutes*	
	Jonas OLSSON †52			MUTLU Topcu †46	
	Kaj ESKELINEN ‡70	71		TURAN Uzun ‡83	

Referee Leslie IRVINE (Northern Ireland)

SUMMARY

● Less than three months earlier the Nya (New) Ullevi Stadium in Gothenburg had been packed to the rafters for the European Championship final between Denmark and Germany. Now a paltry crowd of less than 6,000 turned up next door in the smaller Old Ullevi to witness the opening match of local side IFK Gothenburg's tenth Champions' Cup campaign. Sweden's most successful club in Europe had qualified for this competition by virtue of their Swedish championship victory in 1991, but as they took the field for this match they were toiling away in the nether reaches of the 1992 championship play-off group. Besiktas, however, held no fears for Roger Gustafsson's team. Although this was their third successive participation in the Champions' Cup, they had not passed the first round in any European competition for the past five seasons. The expected victory did go to Gothenburg, but the goals were a long time coming. Substitute Kaj Eslekinen put his side 1-0 up in the 72nd minute, two minutes after coming onto the field, and Swedish international Johnny Ekström made it 2-0 ten minutes later to give IFK a useful cushion for the difficult return in Istanbul.

CHAMPIONS' CUP
First Round Second Leg

Wednesday 30th September 1992
Inönü Stadium, Istanbul

BESIKTAS 2 IFK GÖTEBORG 1

Half-time 1-1 *Aggregate* 2-3 *Attendance* 31,462

		Goals			Goals
1	Jaroslaw BAKO		1	Dick LAST	
2	RECEP Çetin ❏		2	Jonas OLSSON ❏	
3	KADIR Akbulut		3	Tore PEDERSEN	
4	GÖKHAN Keskin		4	Ola SVENSSON	
5	ULVI Güveneroglu †		5	Pontus KÅMARK	
6	YÜKSEL Hamit		6	Peter ERIKSSON	
7	FEYYAZ Uçar	73	7	Stefan REHN	
8	RIZA Çalimbay		8	Håkan MILD	
9	MEHMET Özdilek		9	Thomas ANDERSSON	
10	Mitar MRKELA		10	Kaj ESLEKINEN ‡	10
11	METIN Tekin ❏ ‡	26	11	Johnny EKSTRÖM †	
	Substitutes			*Substitutes*	
	TURAN Uzun †60			Fredrik LEKSELL †65	
	SERGEN Yalcin ‡80			Magnus JOHANSSON ‡85 ❏	

Referee Angelo AMENDOLIA (Italy)

SUMMARY

● *First-leg scorer Kaj Eskelinen was chosen from the start in this match, and the 23-year-old striker justified his selection by extending Gothenburg's aggregate lead to a virtually insurmountable 3-0 margin with a goal after just ten minutes. This all but silenced the 30,000-strong Turkish crowd, who now knew that their side would have to score four goals without reply in the ensuing 79 minutes to remain in the competition. In their entire European Cup history stretching back 25 years Besiktas had not once managed to score more than two goals in a single game! The first half yielded one goal, from Metin Tekin, who had earlier been denied by both the crossbar and a goal-line clearance. But with Gothenburg's reserve goalkeeper Dick Last, in for broken-rib victim Thomas Ravelli, performing splendidly behind a disciplined defence, the Turks rarely looked like reaching their objective. International striker Feyyaz Uçar did score a second with a diving header (his fourth goal in the Champions' Cup - all of them against Swedish opposition!) to give his team victory on the night.*

CHAMPIONS' CUP
First Round First Leg

Wednesday 16th September 1992
The Oval, Belfast

GLENTORAN 0 OLYMPIQUE MARSEILLE 5

Half-time 0-4 *Attendance* 9,500

		Goals				Goals
1	Alan PATERSON		1	Pascal OLMETA		
2	George NEILL		2	Jocelyn ANGLOMA †		
3	Duncan LOWRY		3	Manuel AMOROS		
4	Raymond MORRISON †		4	Basile BOLI		
5	John DEVINE		5	Franck SAUZEE		41
6	Robert BOWERS		6	Jean-Philippe DURAND ‡		
7	Raymond CAMPBELL		7	Bernard CASONI		
8	Andy MATHIESON		8	Rafael MARTIN VAZQUEZ		19, 29
9	Gary McCARTNEY		9	Rudi VÖLLER		3
10	Gary HILLIS ‡		10	Abedi PELE		
11	Eamonn KAVANAGH		11	Didier DESCHAMPS		

Substitutes		*Substitutes*	
John JAMESON †72		Jean-Jacques EYDELIE †46	
James McCLOSKEY ‡72		Jean-Marc FERRERI ‡46	84

Referee Johannes REYGWART (Holland)

SUMMARY

● *Seeded number one in the Champions' Cup for the third year in a row, Marseille were rewarded with the simple task of putting out Irish League champions Glentoran. And yet it could so easily have been to Leeds instead of Belfast that the French champions travelled to begin their fourth successive Champions' Cup campaign. Just four names were left in the hat when this tie was drawn out. Leeds and Stuttgart were the other two! Quality football is none too frequent in troubled Ulster, but Marseille, featuring ten full internationals, certainly provided the Belfast spectators with plenty to savour, especially in a first half during which they scored four times. Rudi Völler opened the scoring in what, surprisingly enough, was his debut appearance in Europe's premier club competition. Rafael Martín Vázquez scored twice more and a stupendous Sauzée free-kick made it 4-0, with substitute Ferreri adding just one further goal in the second half. Glens' 38-year-old goalkeeper Alan Paterson was clearly impressed. A veteran of many European campaigns, he called Marseille "the best team I have ever seen!"*

CHAMPIONS' CUP
First Round Second Leg

Wednesday 30th September 1992
Vélodrome Stadium, Marseilles

OLYMPIQUE MARSEILLE 3 GLENTORAN 0

Half-time 2-0 *Aggregate* 8-0 *Attendance* 10,000

		Goals				Goals
1	Fabien BARTHEZ		1	Alan PATERSON		
2	Manuel AMOROS		2	George NEILL ❑		
3	Eric DI MECO		3	Duncan LOWRY		
4	Basile BOLI	71	4	Raymond MORRISON		
5	Marcel DESAILLY		5	John DEVINE ❑		
6	Jean-Jacques EYDELIE		6	Robert BOWERS		
7	Jean-Christophe THOMAS		7	Eamonn KAVANAGH †		
8	Rafael MARTIN VAZQUEZ		8	Andy MATHIESON		
9	François OMAM-BIYIK	6	9	Gary McCARTNEY		
10	Abedi PELE †	13	10	Gary HILLIS		
11	Didier DESCHAMPS ‡		11	John JAMESON ‡		

Substitutes

Jean-Philippe DURAND †46

Jean-Christophe MARQUET ‡46

Substitutes

James McCLOSKEY †59 ❑

Justin McBRIDE ‡78

Referee Fortunato AZEVEDO (Portugal)

● A spectacular overhead kick from African Footballer of the Year Abedi Pelé was the highlight of this second-leg encounter in the South of France. The Ghanaian finished off a splendid move by acrobatically converting Jean-Christophe Thomas's left-wing cross with all the style of his illustrious namesake. It was Marseille's 100th goal in European competition and a worthy strike to mark the occasion. It was also the French side's second goal of the game with just 12 minutes on the clock, another African striker, Cameroon's François Omam-Biyik, having already put Marseille in front six minutes earlier. A goal avalanche looked certain to follow at this stage, but surprisingly the visitors from Belfast managed to restrict the home side to just one further goal, headed in 18 minutes from time by another player of African descent, Ivory Coast-born Basile Boli. Glentoran's attacks on goal were scarce, which meant a relaxed and untroubled evening for young former Toulouse goalkeeper Fabien Barthez, making his club debut as a replacement for the injured Pascal Olmeta.

CHAMPIONS' CUP
First Round First Leg

Wednesday 16th September
Neckar Stadium, Stuttgart

VFB STUTTGART 3 LEEDS UNITED 0

Half-time 0-0 Attendance 36,000

		Goals				Goals
1	Eike IMMEL		1	John LUKIC		
2	Uwe SCHNEIDER		2	David ROCASTLE †		
3	Michael FRONTZECK		3	Tony DORIGO		
4	Slobodan DUBAJIC ❑		4	David BATTY		
5	Thomas STRUNZ ‡		5	Chris FAIRCLOUGH		
6	Guido BUCHWALD		6	Chris WHYTE		
7	Andreas BUCK	79	7	Eric CANTONA ‡		
8	Eyjólfur SVERRISSON		8	Gordon STRACHAN		
9	Fritz WALTER †	62, 66	9	Lee CHAPMAN		
10	Maurizio GAUDINO		10	Gary McALLISTER		
11	Ludwig KÖGL		11	Gary SPEED		

Substitutes

Adrian KNUP †80

Günther SCHÄFER ‡86

Substitutes

Steve HODGE †46 ❑

Carl SHUTT ‡62

Referee Rune LARSSON (Sweden)

FACTFILE

● *This was Leeds' first overseas visit for a European match since 1979 and their first appearance in the Champions' Cup since the 1975 final in Paris, which they lost to another German side, Bayern Munich.*
● *The reduced attendance figure was primarily due to the extensive renovation work being carried out in the stadium to prepare it for the 1993 World Athletics Championships.*
● *David Rocastle, one of the few Leeds players with previous European experience after appearing for Arsenal in the Champions' Cup a year earlier, was making his debut for his new club.*
● *Stuttgart went into the match still smarting from a German Cup defeat the previous weekend at the hands of Second Division Hansa Rostock.*

● *David Rocastle*

Defensive frailties cost Leeds dear

Leeds United boss Howard Wilkinson described this as a "meaty tie". But after 90 minutes in the Neckar Stadium he and his team were left feeding on scraps as Stuttgart dealt their European ambitions a seemingly mortal blow with three smartly-taken second-half goals.

The final 3-0 scoreline was undeniably tough on the English champions. French international Eric Cantona called it "a crazy result" and he was not far wrong. Leeds had looked to be in no great danger for an hour of the contest, with their unaccustomed man-for-man marking strategy working surprisingly well. Furthermore, they had come the closer of the two sides to opening the scoring in the first half when Cantona himself headed against a post in the 28th minute.

But once Fritz Walter, the Bundesliga's leading marksman the previous season, put Stuttgart ahead with typically ruthless efficiency after 63 minutes, the Leeds players lost all their discipline. Teams with greater European experience would probably have accepted the surrender of that goal as par for the course in an away leg and continued to play the same way as before. But Leeds panicked, tried to recover the deficit immediately, left themselves further exposed at the back and conceded a second goal, again gratefully received by the prolific Walter, just five minutes later.

All of a sudden, from being in control of the tie Leeds now knew they had a mountain to climb to stay in it. Stuttgart, on the other hand, were vibrant. 2-0 up, they pressed for a third goal which would surely have sewn the tie up for good. And with just seven minutes to play they got it. Andreas Buck, who was considered doubtful before the game with a thigh strain, robbed Fairclough of the ball in his own half and carried on to beat Lukic with a carefully placed cross-shot.

There was still time for Leeds to go forward and try to save their skins with an important away goal. But when a close-range effort in the last minute was adjudged by the Swedish official not to have crossed the line - German television coverage failed to provide sufficiently damning evidence to the contrary - all hope for Howard Wilkinson's men appeared to have gone out of the window. To English dismay and German joy, the tie of the round seemed to be over already with half of it still to play. At least, so it seemed at the time...

FRITZ WALTER
VfB Stuttgart

Fritz Walter's double strike against Leeds took his total of European goals for VfB Stuttgart into double figures. His ninth and tenth in European competition had come in his 21st match and none of his previous eight had ever been struck at a more important time for his club, not even the four he scored in helping to take Stuttgart to the UEFA Cup final in 1988/89. After all, this was the Champions' Cup and Fritz Walter, like most of his team-mates, had never played in Europe's premier club competition before. At 32 this was the furthest the little striker had gone in a career which, by the end of the 91/92 season, had produced 131 goals in 290 German League matches, 77 of them during his five seasons at Stuttgart. An impressive enough ratio, but one which has surprisingly failed to gain him any recognition at international level.

CHAMPIONS' CUP
First Round Second Leg

Wednesday 30th September 1992
Elland Road, Leeds

LEEDS UNITED 4 VFB STUTTGART 1

(later awarded LEEDS UNITED 3 VFB STUTTGART 0)

Half-time 2-1 *Aggregate* 4-4 *Attendance* 20,457

		Goals			Goals
1	John LUKIC		1	Eike IMMEL	
2	Scott SELLARS		2	Günther SCHÄFER	
3	Tony DORIGO		3	Michael FRONTZECK ❑	
4	David BATTY		4	Slobodan DUBAJIC	
5	Chris FAIRCLOUGH		5	Thomas STRUNZ	
6	Chris WHYTE		6	Guido BUCHWALD	
7	Gordon STRACHAN		7	Andreas BUCK ❑	33
8	Eric CANTONA	66	8	Eyjólfur SVERRISSON	
9	Lee CHAPMAN	78	9	Fritz WALTER †	
10	Gary McALLISTER	38 (pen)	10	Maurizio GAUDINO ‡	
11	Gary SPEED ❑	17	11	Ludwig KÖGL ❑	
	Substitutes			*Substitutes*	
				Adrian KNUP †80	
				Jovica SIMANIC ‡83	

Referee Kim NIELSEN (Denmark)

FACTFILE

● *At the final whistle Leeds United became the first reigning English champions to be eliminated in the first round of Europe since Manchester City were knocked out by Fenerbahçe of Turkey in 1968.*

● *Leeds went into the game aware that no English club had ever successfully overhauled a 0-3 deficit in the Champions' Cup.*

● *As in the Neckar Stadium for the first leg, Elland Road's capacity was severely reduced due to the building of a new stand on one side of the ground.*

● *Two of the Leeds goalscorers - Speed and McAllister - had never previously scored in European competition. Lee Chapman's only two previous goals in Europe had been scored a decade earlier when he struck once in each leg for Arsenal as they lost 8-4 on aggregate to Spartak Moscow in the first round of the UEFA Cup.*

Administrative blunder keeps Leeds alive

Leeds United gave one of the most brilliant performances in their long European history to beat Stuttgart 4-1. With a 3-0 deficit to make up from the first leg and the away goal counting against them, it was not, however, good enough to see them through into the next round. At the end of the match the Leeds fans gave their team a standing ovation for the effort which they had put in. It had been a memorable night, a captivating performance and, when all was said and done, a glorious way to go out...

But, incredibly, that was not the end of the story. Not by a long chalk. The day after the game it materialised that Stuttgart had fielded four foreign players during the course of the game. Icelandic international Eyjólfur Sverrisson and Yugoslav sweeper Slobodan Dubajic had been on from the start. Swiss striker Adrian Knup and another Yugoslav, Jovica Simanic, a player who had never appeared for the VfB first team before, were brought on as substitutes in the last frantic stages of the game.

Four non-nationals, none of them 'assimilated foreigners'. That was against UEFA rules. Amazingly, nobody had noticed it at the time. Not the referee, nor the official UEFA observer. Not the Stuttgart coaching staff. Certainly no one from Leeds. Everybody had simply been embroiled in a fascinating finale to a thrilling game of football. But the fact was that Stuttgart had broken the rules. Not deliberately, of course - that much was obvious - but through sheer administrative incompetence. In fact, the crime had been committed not when Simanic was introduced onto the field of play, but when Stuttgart coach Christoph Daum handed in the official team sheet.

So as members of the UEFA Disciplinary Committe convened to study the problem and come to a decision as to what would happen next - Stuttgart's disqualification seemed the logical outcome - the match itself was consigned to the memory banks. It had all been for nothing. Speed's brilliant opening goal, Buck's shock equaliser, Leeds' fantastic second-half fightback and the excitement and drama of the last ten minutes as the English champions sought the decisive fifth goal. All of it academic.

Three days after the match UEFA, after much deliberation, came up with a verdict. As Stuttgart had transgressed the rules, the match was to be awarded to Leeds by the statutory 3-0 scoreline. How convenient! As Stuttgart had won the first leg by precisely that score, it was declared that a third match would be played - not at Leeds, which would have seemed the fairest solution, but at a neutral venue. Leeds had come back from the dead two days earlier. Now, thanks to UEFA's generosity, it was Stuttgart's turn.

ERIC CANTONA
Leeds United

Cries of "Ooh! Aah! Cantona!" were much in evidence as the French striker produced possibly his best-ever performance for Leeds against Stuttgart. It was his neat header which set up Gary Speed for a spectacular opening goal and throughout the remainder of the game he continually tormented his marker Günther Schäfer with a succession of tricks and turns. Reward for Cantona's outstanding contribution came with Leeds' third goal.

Less than two months after this game, however, Cantona caused a real stir when he left Leeds to join Manchester United. Shockwaves though the transfer caused, especially amongst Leeds fans who, by and large, worshipped and adored him, the decision to suddenly up and leave was not wholly uncharacteristic of the turbulent Frenchman. In fact, it was the eighth time in four and a half years that he had changed club!

CHAMPIONS' CUP
First Round Play-off

Friday 9th October 1992
Nou Camp, Barcelona

LEEDS UNITED 2 VFB STUTTGART 1

Half-time 1-1 *Attendance* 10,000

		Goals				Goals
1	John LUKIC		1	Eike IMMEL		
2	Jon NEWSOME		2	Günther SCHÄFER		
3	Tony DORIGO ❏		3	Michael FRONTZECK ❏		
4	David BATTY ❏		4	Slobodan DUBAJIC		
5	Chris FAIRCLOUGH		5	Thomas STRUNZ †		
6	Chris WHYTE		6	Guido BUCHWALD		
7	Gordon STRACHAN	32	7	Andreas BUCK		
8	Eric CANTONA †		8	Eyjólfur SVERRISSON ‡		
9	Lee CHAPMAN		9	Fritz WALTER		
10	Gary McALLISTER		10	André GOLKE		38
11	Gary SPEED		11	Ludwig KÖGL		

Substitute

Carl SHUTT †76 ❏   77

Substitutes

Alexander STREHMEL †25
Adrian KNUP ‡79

Referee Fabio BALDAS (Italy)

FACTFILE

● *This was the first time in European Cup history that a tie which had apparently been settled on the field of play had been taken to a third match as a result of player ineligibility.*

● *André Golke and Carl Shutt both scored on their European debuts.*

● *Leeds' triumph gave England its tenth qualification at the expense of (West) German opposition in the Champions' Cup, as opposed to only three ties going the other way.*

● *VfB Stuttgart's second Champions' Cup appearance ultimately ended exactly as their first in 1984/85. Then they had also been knocked out in the first round, by Bulgarian side Levski Spartak.*

● *Carl Shutt scores*

Sub Shutt provides justice for Leeds

And so to Barcelona, where, after severel more days of umming and aahing, UEFA declared that this unprecedented third 'play-off' match should be staged to decide which of the two teams would progress to meet Scottish champions Rangers in the next round.

The decision to replay the match at a neutral venue had not been well received in England, where the general feeling was that Stuttgart had been lucky to get a second bite of the cherry at all. In Germany public opinion as to the rights and wrongs of UEFA's decision was overshadowed by the feeling of disbelief that the Stuttgart management team, and coach Daum in particular, could have possibly made such a startling administrative error in the first place - one which, in view of the riches on offer in the latter stages of this competition, could cost Stuttgart several million pounds.

Daum and cohorts had been reprieved by UEFA but in an eerily empty Nou Camp - filled to less than a tenth of its capacity - Leeds were in no mood to let the Germans off the hook once again. Howard Wilkinson's team, eager to see that justice would be done in the end, dominated the early passage of the game and deservedly took the lead on 33 minutes with a spectacular long-range strike from veteran midfielder Gordon Strachan. Stuttgart goalkeeper Eike Immel got his fingertips to the little Scotsman's ferocious drive, but he could not keep it out of the net and for the first time in the tie the English champions had their noses in front.

Not for long, though. Just six minutes later Stuttgart substitute Alexander Strehmel, who had replaced the injured Strunz, found André Golke with a precise cross and the Germans were level.

Boosted by this, Stuttgart began to take control after the interval but they could not find a second goal. Instead, in another dramatic turnaround, it went to Leeds. The scorer was Carl Shutt, set to celebrate his 31st birthday the following day but now, just seconds after coming onto the field to replace the extremely disappointing Cantona, becoming the centre of attention 24 hours early. It was a marvellous individual goal, fit to win a contest as closely fought as this one, and Shutt's first in any competition for more than a year!

With Leeds managing to hang on to their lead despite a typical late flourish from the Germans, this epic chapter in the story of the Champions' Cup at last reached its conclusion. For Howard Wilkinson and his team a long Friday night of celebration, let alone a money-spinning all-British clash with Rangers in the next round, lay ahead. But for Christoph Daum and Stuttgart the inquest back home in Germany was only just beginning.

GORDON STRACHAN
Leeds United

The Indian summer of Gordon Strachan's long career provided another day of sunshine in the Nou Camp. The 35-year-old Scot fired Leeds in front in the first half and he was the driving force, along with Batty and Speed, of the team's committed display in the second period, especially after Leeds had taken the lead for the second time.

Strachan is now a footballing legend in two countries. The first half of his career earned him fame in his native Scotland where, amongst other notable achievements, he helped Aberdeen to European Cup-winners' Cup success in 1983 and starred for the Scottish national team in the World Cup finals of 1982 and 1986. He had to wait a bit longer for celebrity status in England, but that was assured when he captained Leeds to the Football League title in 1991/92 three years after joining them from Manchester United when the Yorkshire outfit were a mere mid-table side in the English Second Division.

CHAMPIONS' CUP
Preliminary Round & First Round Review

PRELIMINARY ROUND RESULTS		1st leg	2nd leg	Agg.
Shelbourne	Tavria Simferopol	0-0	1-2	1-2
Valletta	Maccabi Tel-Aviv	1-2	0-1	1-3
KÍ	Skonto Riga	1-3	0-3	1-6
SCT Olimpija Ljubljana	Norma Tallinn	3-0	2-0	5-0

FIRST ROUND RESULTS		1st leg	2nd leg	Agg.
Milan	SCT Olimpija Ljubljana	4-0	3-0	7-0
Lech Poznan	Skonto Riga	2-0	0-0	2-0
PSV	Zhalgiris Vilnius	6-0	2-0	8-0
FC Barcelona	Viking FK	1-0	0-0	1-0
FC Kuusysi	Dinamo Bucuresti	1-0	0-2 aet	1-2
Rangers	Lyngby BK	2-0	1-0	3-0
Slovan Bratislava	Ferencváros	4-1	0-0	4-1
FK Austria	CSKA Sofia	3-1	2-3	5-4
FC Sion	Tavria Simferopol	4-1	3-1	7-2
Union Luxembourg	FC Porto	1-4	0-5	1-9
Víkingur	CSKA Moskva	0-1	2-4	2-5
Maccabi Tel-Aviv	Club Brugge KV	0-1	0-3	0-4
AEK	Apoel Nicosia	1-1	2-2	3-3
(AEK win on away goals)				
IFK Göteborg	Besiktas	2-0	1-2	3-2
Glentoran	Olympique Marseille	0-5	0-3	0-8
VfB Stuttgart	Leeds United	3-0	0-3*	3-3
(Leeds United win 2-1 in replay)				

* UEFA decision. Match originally won 4-1 by Leeds United.

LEADING GOALSCORERS AFTER FIRST ROUND

4 TÚLIO (FC Sion)
3 Sergei SHEVCHENKO (Tavria Simferopol)
   Vitaly ASTAFJEV (Skonto Riga)
   Juul ELLERMAN (PSV)
   TONI (FC Porto)

CHAMPIONS' CUP

CHAMPIONS' CUP
Second Round First Leg

Wednesday 21st October 1992
Old Ullevi Stadium, Gothenburg

IFK GÖTEBORG 1 LECH POZNAN 0

Half-time 0-0 *Attendance* 8,800

		Goals				Goals
1	Thomas RAVELLI			1	Kazimierz SIDORCZUK	
2	Magnus JOHANSSON			2	Marek RZEPKA	
3	Jonas OLSSON			3	Jacek BAK ❑	
4	Ola SVENSSON			4	Waldemar KRYGER	
5	Pontus KÅMARK			5	Przemyslaw BERESZYNSKI	
6	Peter ERIKSSON			6	Igor KORNIETS	
7	Stefan REHN			7	Kazimierz MOSKAL ❑	
8	Håkan MILD			8	Dariusz SKRZYPCZAK ‡	
9	Patrik BENGTSSON	86		9	Jerzy PODBROZNY	
10	Thomas ANDERSSON †			10	Jaroslaw ARASZKIEWICZ	
11	Johnny EKSTRÖM			11	Miroslaw TRZECIAK ❑ †	

Substitute

Kaj ESKELINEN †72

Substitutes

Ryszard REMIEN †74

Damian LUKASIK ‡90

Referee Roger PHILIPPI (Luxembourg)

SUMMARY

● *An extraordinary goal from Gothenburg midfielder Patrik Bengtsson just three minutes from time gave the 1991 Swedish champions a crucial first-leg lead in this potentially evenly-balanced tie. The local crowd were becoming increasingly restless when, as a result of the new backpass rule, the Lech goalkeeper, Kazimierz Sidorczuk, found himself forced to boot the ball upfield. The outcome was a miscued clearance which went straight to Bengtsoon, 40 yards from goal, close to the left touchline. The youngster, playing only as a stand-in for Swedish international Mikael Nilsson, decided, somewhat optimistically, to have a shot at goal. But he, and everybody else in the stadium, watched in amazement as the ball swerved all over the place and flew in past the hapless Sidorczuk at the near post. It was cruel luck for the Poles, who had done enough to merit their second successive 0-0 away draw of the competition., but a timely strike indeed for the Swedes, seeking to reach the latter stages of the Champions' Cup for the fourth time in nine years.*

CHAMPIONS' CUP
Second Round Second Leg

Wednesday 4th November 1992
Lech Stadium, Poznan

LECH POZNAN 0 IFK GÖTEBORG 3

Half-time 0-1 *Aggregate* 0-4 *Attendance* 28,000

		Goals				Goals
1	Kazimierz SIDORCZUK		1	Thomas RAVELLI		
2	Marek RZEPKA		2	Magnus JOHANSSON		
3	Jacek BAK		3	Jonas OLSSON		
4	Waldemar KRYGER †		4	Ola SVENSSON		
5	Przemyslaw BERESZYNSKI ‡		5	Pontus KÅMARK †		
6	Ryszard REMIEN		6	Peter ERIKSSON		
7	Kazimierz MOSKAL		7	Stefan REHN		
8	Dariusz SKRZYPCZAK		8	Håkan MILD	82	
9	Jerzy PODBROZNY		9	Mikael NILSSON	47	
10	Jaroslaw ARASZKIEWICZ		10	Thomas ANDERSSON		
11	Miroslaw TRZECIAK		11	Johnny EKSTRÖM	28	

Substitutes

Czieslaw JAKOLCEWICZ †46
Dariusz KOFNYT ‡53

Substitute

Patrik BENGTSSON †89

Referee Patrick KELLY (Republic of Ireland)

● *Lech Poznan had never previously progressed beyond the second round of any European competition, and a big crowd gathered in anticipation of a history-making performance from their team. But it was to be a night of disappointment and despair for the Poles. Gothenburg, who had been edged out by Panathinaikos at the same stage a year earlier, were determined not to let a second opportunity pass them by. The decisive blow for the home side came when a spectacular scissors-kick from Stefan Rehn was parried by goalkeeper Sidorczuk but only into the path of Johnny Ekström, who made no mistake from close range. 0-1 down at half-time, Lech knew they had precious little chance of scoring three goals without reply in the final 45 minutes, and Michael Nilsson closed all avenues by scoring Gothenburg's second just two minutes into the half. The best goal was saved till last, though, with Olympics star Håkan Mild flashing in a long-range drive off the underside of the bar to make it 3-0 eight minutes from time.*

CHAMPIONS' CUP
Second Round First Leg

Wednesday 21st October 1992
Ibrox Stadium, Glasgow

RANGERS 2 LEEDS UNITED 1

Half-time 2-1 Attendance 43,251

		Goals				Goals
1	Andy GORAM		1	John LUKIC	21 (o.g.)	
2	Stuart McCALL		2	Jon NEWSOME		
3	David ROBERTSON		3	Tony DORIGO		
4	Richard GOUGH		4	David BATTY		
5	Dave McPHERSON		5	Chris FAIRCLOUGH		
6	John BROWN		6	Chris WHYTE		
7	Trevor STEVEN †		7	Gordon STRACHAN ‡		
8	Ian FERGUSON		8	Eric CANTONA †		
9	Ally McCOIST	36	9	Lee CHAPMAN		
10	Mark HATELEY		10	Gary McALLISTER	2	
11	Ian DURRANT		11	Gary SPEED		

Substitute

Pieter HUISTRA †80

Substitutes

Rod WALLACE †83

David ROCASTLE ‡88

Referee Alphonse COSTANTIN (Belgium)

FACTFILE

● The last European tie between the champions of England and Scotland had taken place in 1980/81 when Liverpool eliminated Aberdeen 5-0 on aggregate in the second round before going on to win the trophy for the third time.

● The only other England-Scotland clash in the Champions' Cup involved Leeds United. They lost home and away to Rangers' bitter rivals Celtic in the semi-finals of the 1969/70 competition.

● There was a minute's silence before the game in memory of the recently-departed Willie Waddell, the man who had managed Rangers to their only European trophy, the Cup-winners' Cup, in 1972.

● Rangers, demonstrating their financial clout, offered a £20,000 a man win bonus for the first leg alone, while Leeds players were on just half that for actually winning the whole tie!

Lukic error puts Rangers in driving seat

Popularly dubbed the 'Battle of Britain' on both sides of the border, this tie captured the imagination of both English and Scottish fans alike. Adding further spice to the occasion was the fact that Rangers had four English players in their first-team squad - Steven, Hateley, Stevens and Gordon - while two of Leeds' most influential players - Strachan and McAllister - were Scots.

In a sensible arrangement between the two clubs, designed to avoid any potential spectator clashes, it was agreed that there should be a ban on away fans for both matches. Thus Ibrox became an even more hostile venue than usual for the visitors. Packed to capacity with 43,000 high-spirited Scots, it nonetheless echoed to the sound of almost complete silence after just 69 seconds when Gary McAllister, a self-confessed Rangers fan, fired the English champions ahead with the sweetest of volleys from the edge of the penalty area. Beforehand McAllister had referred to this as "the biggest game of my life". No wonder he was grinning from ear to ear after giving his team such a sensational start.

But it did not take long for the Rangers fans to find their voices again and they roared their team forward in search of a goal that would bring them back into the game. After 21 minutes Leeds, quite literally, handed them that sought-after equaliser. The normally dependable John Lukic was the guilty party. Seeking to punch clear a Durrant corner from the left, the Leeds goalkeeper completely misjudged the cross - he later blamed the floodlights! - and succeeded only in pushing it back towards his own goal. Despite the efforts of Dorigo to hook it clear, the ball had already crossed the line and Rangers were back in the match.

Before half-time the home fans were singing in celebration once again as arch goal poacher Ally McCoist found himself perfectly positioned to stab the ball home after Lukic had saved McPherson's header following yet another corner. As half-time arrived Leeds' dream start had suddenly turned into a nightmare. Apart from the two goals they had scarcely been under threat from the Scottish champions. For all the noise that the home fans generated, it was clear to neutrals that the better, more composed football was coming from the team from England.

And that was to be the pattern for most of the second half as well. Leeds could, and probably should, have won the match, let alone come away with a draw. But they had evidently heeded the lessons of Stuttgart and were happy to contain the opposition this time and prevent any further goals. There was one lucky escape when Hateley went clear, but that was all Rangers could muster and at the final whistle most experts were confidently predicting that Howard Wilkinson's team would turn the tie around back at Elland Road a fortnight later.

DAVID BATTY
Leeds United

The conditions at Ibrox for the first leg of the unofficial 'Championship of Great Britain' were right up David Batty's street. A fast, competitive match, played in a steady drizzle, with plenty of noisy, hostile fans and nowhere to hide. And the gritty Yorkshireman, who had played so well for Leeds in Barcelona the round before, put up another sterling performance in the heart of the Leeds midfield. Chosen for England in their opening World Cup encounter against Norway a week earlier, when he had also played well, Batty was steadily beginning to come of age as an international performer. Leeds born and bred, Batty was the only homegrown player in United's championship-winning side of 1991/92, so the triumph obviously meant more to him than most. Often regarded simply as the 'hard man' of the Leeds midfield, he is in fact much more than that. Tackling and ball-winning certainly constitute the basis of his game, but he is also a very shrewd distributor of the ball and often features in creative, attacking moves.

CHAMPIONS' CUP
Second Round Second Leg

READY

Wednesday 4th November 1992
Elland Road, Leeds

LEEDS UNITED 1 RANGERS 2

Half-time 0-1 *Aggregate* 2-4 *Attendance* 25,118

		Goals				Goals
1	John LUKIC		1	Andy GORAM		
2	Jon NEWSOME ❑		2	Stuart McCALL		
3	Tony DORIGO		3	David ROBERTSON		
4	David ROCASTLE †		4	Richard GOUGH		
5	Chris FAIRCLOUGH ‡		5	Dave McPHERSON		
6	Chris WHYTE		6	John BROWN		
7	Gordon STRACHAN		7	Dale GORDON †		
8	Eric CANTONA	85	8	Ian FERGUSON ❑		
9	Lee CHAPMAN		9	Ally McCOIST		59
10	Gary McALLISTER		10	Mark HATELEY		2
11	Gary SPEED		11	Ian DURRANT		
	Substitutes			*Substitute*		
	Steve HODGE †63			Aleksei MIKHAILICHENKO †72		
	Rod WALLACE ‡63					

Referee Aleksei SPIRIN (Russia)

FACTFILE

● *Leeds' defeat ended a disastrous night for English football, with Sheffield Wednesday and Liverpool both being eliminated, respectively, from the UEFA and Cup-winners' Cups earlier the same evening. The entire English representation had been wiped out after just two rounds.*

● *Rangers' win maintained their 100% record in the competition after the first two rounds.*

● *David Rocastle, replacing the injured David Batty, was starting a match at Elland Road for the first time since his £2 million move from Arsenal in the summer.*

● *Mark Hateley's goal was Rangers' 100th in the Champions' Cup.*

● *Mark Hateley*

Goram brilliance gives Rangers the glory

Just as a Scotsman - Gary McAllister - had scored an early goal for Leeds in the first leg at Ibrox, so an Englishman - Mark Hateley - struck at Elland Road to give Rangers the boost they needed and send the home fans into subdued silence.

Like McAllister's effort in Glasgow, Hateley's goal was spectacular and out of the blue. It came just moments after Eric Cantona had missed a glorious early opportunity to put Leeds level on aggregate. Rangers goalkeeper Andy Goram punted the ball upfield, Ian Durrant headed on, and with the ball sitting up nicely for him, Hateley let fly with his favoured left foot from the edge of the area and watched with glee as the ball soared past Lukic into the back of the net.

The onus now was on Leeds to respond as Rangers had done to McAllister's goal in the first leg. But with the influential Batty missing after sustaining an injury in a Premier League encounter against Coventry the previous weekend, the Leeds midfield took a while to get going. It was not until late in the first half that the home side, playing exclusively before their own fans, turned up the heat on the Rangers defence. First Eric Cantona had a shot saved by Goram, then Stuart McCall scrambled another effort off the line before once again Goram was on hand to deny Cantona a second time.

Rangers, meanwhile, had looked threatening on the break. Ally McCoist had one effort saved by Lukic just before the interval, but in the 58th minute, with the score still standing at 1-0 in Rangers' favour, he made no mistake. A wonderful move down the left involving Durrant and Hateley was finished off in superb style by the Rangers number nine as he met Hateley's pinpoint cross with an accurate falling header.

There was no way back for Leeds now. Even the team that had come storming back at Stuttgart a round earlier could not manage four goals in the last half hour, and with Goram continuing to thwart them at every opportunity they were ultimately glad to get just one. That came in the 85th minute from Eric Cantona, but it was no more than a consolation.

Leeds had long since abandoned all hope of retrieving the situation. A touch more luck earlier on in front of goal and they might easily have been celebrating a place in the Champions' League. But that honour belonged to Rangers. They, not Leeds, had taken the chances that had fallen their way and although the extent of their victory flattered them ,they were certainly entitled to go into the second phase of the competition as the worthy standard bearers of British football.

ANDY GORAM
Rangers

In many ways the so-called 'Battle of Britain' was a tale of two goalkeepers. John Lukic's error of judgment in the first leg had gone a long way towards giving Rangers a first-leg advantage, and Andy Goram's heroics at Elland Road ensured that the Scottish champions held on to it. Time and again he defied the Leeds attackers and despite the match-winning contributions of Hateley and McCoist at the other end, there was little doubt which player was most responsible for taking Rangers into the Champions' League. Although he is now a fixture in the Scottish national team, Goram was in fact born in England and he clocked up more than 200 appearances for Oldham Athletic before moving up north to join Hibernian in 1987. Four years later he left Hibs for Rangers, replacing England goalkeeper Chris Woods in the process. At the time the move was controversial, but there is no doubt that Rangers fans appreciate the wisdom of the deal now.

CHAMPIONS' CUP
Second Round First Leg

Wednesday 21st October 1992
Tehelné pole Stadium, Bratislava

SLOVAN BRATISLAVA 0 MILAN 1

Half-time 0-0 *Attendance* 34,467

		Goals			Goals
1	Alexander VENCEL		1	Francesco ANTONIOLI	
2	Tomás STÚPALA		2	Mauro TASSOTTI ❑	
3	Miroslav CHVÍLA		3	Paolo MALDINI	62
4	Ondrej KRISTOFÍK		4	Demetrio ALBERTINI ❑ ■	
5	Vladimír KINDER		5	Alessandro COSTACURTA	
6	Milos GLONEK ❑		6	Franco BARESI	
7	Ladislav PECKO		7	Gianluigi LENTINI ‡	
8	Frantisek KLINOVSKY ‡		8	Roberto DONADONI	
9	Pavol GOSTIC †		9	Marco VAN BASTEN	
10	Peter DUBOVSKY		10	Zvonimir BOBAN ❑	
11	Jaroslav TIMKO		11	Jean-Pierre PAPIN †	
	Substitutes			*Substitutes*	
	Stefan MAIXNER †60			Enzo GAMBARO †46	
	Youssef HARAOUI ‡69			Marco SIMONE ‡81	

Referee Kim NIELSEN (Denmark)

SUMMARY

● *Everybody wanted to see all-conquering Milan! There were no fewer than 150,000 ticket demands for this game, with all the local football followers eager to see how their team would shape up against the acknowledged best club side in the world. There was even optimism in some quarters that Slovan might actually win the game, and it was not wholly misguided. Slovan had won both of their previous home games against Italian opposition in Europe - against Inter in 1982/83 and Torino on their way to winning the Cup-winners' Cup in 1968/69. And then there was the Milan injury list, which contained the names of Rijkaard, Gullit, Savicevic, Eranio, Massaro and Evani. Not to mention the hostile atmosphere and boggy pitch! With half-time approaching the Slovak team got an even greater lift when Milan's Albertini was sent off for two bookable offences. But even against this mounting adversity Fabio Capello's men prevailed, winning the match with a single goal from left-back Paolo Maldini - his first in Europe - set up with a cunning header from man of the match, Marco van Basten.*

European Cups Review 1993

CHAMPIONS' CUP
Second Round Second Leg

Wednesday 4th November 1992
Giuseppe Meazza Stadium, Milan

MILAN 4 SLOVAN BRATISLAVA 0

Half-time 2-0 Aggregate 5-0 Attendance 30,000

		Goals				Goals
1	Francesco ANTONIOLI		1	Alexander VENCEL		
2	Mauro TASSOTTI ‡		2	Tomás STÚPALA		
3	Paolo MALDINI		3	Miroslav CHVÍLA		
4	Roberto DONADONI		4	Ondrej KRISTOFÍK		
5	Alessandro COSTACURTA		5	Vladimír KINDER		
6	Franco BARESI		6	Marián ZEMAN ❏		
7	Gianluigi LENTINI		7	Ladislav PECKO		
8	Frank RIJKAARD	30	8	Youssef HARAOUI ‡		
9	Jean-Pierre PAPIN	72	9	Pavol GOSTIC		
10	Zvonimir BOBAN	29	10	Peter DUBOVSKY		
11	Daniele MASSARO †		11	Jaroslav TIMKO †		
	Substitutes			*Substitutes*		
	Marco SIMONE †46	50		Stefan MAIXNER †46		
	Enzo GAMBARO ‡68			Stanislav MORAVEC ‡62		

Referee Antonio MARTIN NAVARRETE (Spain)

● *Milan's easy passage into the Champions' Cup last eight, the so-called 'Champions League', was secured by their second successive 4-0 home win of the competition. The individual performance of the evening belonged to Croatian midfielder Zvonimir Boban. Appearing in his third Champions' Cup match (as opposed to only one appearance in Serie A), Boban opened the scoring with a magnificent free-kick after 29 minutes and then created a second goal for Frank Rijkaard a few seconds later. The Slovakian visitors had little to offer in return and were second best in all areas of the field. Their defence, missing the suspended Glonek (soon to move to Italian side Ancona in any case) looked decidedly fragile and it was simply a question of how many more goals Milan could run up in the second period. They managed just two, the first going to Marco Simone shortly after he had come on as a substitute and the second, headed in by Papin from a brilliant Lentini cross, extending the Frenchman's remarkable scoring sequence in the Champions' Cup to 21 in 24 matches.*

CHAMPIONS' CUP
Second Round First Leg

Wednesday 21st October 1992
National Stadium, Bucharest

DINAMO BUCURESTI 0 OLYMPIQUE MARSEILLE 0

Half-time 0-0 *Attendance* 45,000

Goals | | | Goals

1	Florin Alexandru TENE		1	Fabien BARTHEZ
2	Vasile JERCALAU		2	Jocelyn ANGLOMA
3	Tibor SELYMES ❏		3	Eric DI MECO
4	Gheorghe MIHALI		4	Basile BOLI
5	Daniel TIMOFTE ❏		5	Franck SAUZEE
6	Marius CHEREGI		6	Marcel DESAILLY
7	Dorinel MUNTEANU		7	Bernard CASONI
8	Gabor GERSTENMAJER		8	Jean-Christophe THOMAS †
9	Ovidiu Cornel HANGANU		9	Rudi VÖLLER
10	Zoltan KADAR †		10	Abedi PELE ❏
11	Sulejman DEMOLLARI ‡		11	Didier DESCHAMPS ❏

Substitutes | | | *Substitute*

Costel PANA †63   Jean-Jacques EYDELIE †46

NELSON Mensuah ‡78

Referee Peter MIKKELSEN (Denmark)

SUMMARY

● *Like the Rangers-Leeds tie, this Franco-Romanian encounter should not have taken place. The Leeds-Stuttgart fiasco, and the subsequent qualification of the English champions, had deprived Dinamo Bucharest of their seeded status, pitting them against top seeds Marseille when their eighth-placed ranking warranted an easier tie. Still, there was no time for wallowing in self-pity. Dinamo had a job to do, and they responded to the fervent support of the 45,000 crowd with a fine performance of skill and industry that taxed Marseille to the full. Crucially, however, the Romanians could not turn their superiority into goals, and for that Marseille had to thank their young goalkeeper Fabien Barthez, who had now taken over the post on a permanent basis from Pascal Olmeta. He made a series of fine stops to deny the impressive forward bursts of, amongst others, Munteanu and Selymes and put Marseille in the driving seat for the return leg. It was the ideal result for the French champions, but, as coach Fernandez stressed after the match: "The important thing is that we did not concede a goal".*

CHAMPIONS' CUP
Second Round Second Leg

Wednesday 4th November 1992
Vélodrome Stadium, Marseille

OLYMPIQUE MARSEILLE 2 DINAMO BUCURESTI 0

Half-time 1-0 *Aggregate* 2-0 *Attendance* 20,000

		Goals				Goals
1	Fabien BARTHEZ			1	Florin Alexandru TENE	
2	Manuel AMOROS †			2	Vasile JERCALAU	
3	Jean-Philippe DURAND ❑			3	Tibor SELYMES	
4	Basile BOLI ❑			4	Gheorghe MIHALI	
5	Franck SAUZEE			5	Daniel TIMOFTE	
6	Marcel DESAILLY			6	Marius CHEREGI ❑	
7	Bernard CASONI			7	Dorinel MUNTEANU ❑	
8	Alen BOKSIC	32, 68		8	Gabor GERSTENMAJER	
9	Rudi VÖLLER ‡			9	Ovidiu Cornel HANGANU ‡	
10	Abedi PELE			10	Zoltan KADAR	
11	Didier DESCHAMPS			11	Sulejman DEMOLLARI †	

	Substitutes			*Substitutes*
	Jean-Jacques EYDELIE †65			Costel PANA †13
	Eric DI MECO ‡73			Nelson MENSAH ‡73

Referee Arcangelo PEZZELLA (Italy)

SUMMARY

● *Marseille recorded their 12th successive home victory in the Champions' Cup to qualify for the last eight of the competition for the third time in four seasons. They achieved it thanks to two fine goals, one in each half, from their young Croatian striker Alen Boksic. He had never previously scored in European competition, but he was a hero to the Marseille fans now as his double strike disguised a rather lacklustre and disjointed overall performance from the French champions. For such an important match the atmosphere in the Vélodrome was surprisingly muted and Marseille rarely touched the heights attained on previous big European nights in the recent past. Fortunately for them, however, Dinamo Bucharest took the field in a similarly uninspired frame of mind. The team was unchanged from the first leg, but the Mediterranean air evidently had an adverse effect on the players, who, in complete contrast from the exuberant outfit of the first leg, appeared resigned to their fate almost from the first whistle - and this with Romanian national team boss Cornel Dinu watching from the stands!*

CHAMPIONS' CUP
Second Round First Leg

Wednesday 21st October 1992
Olympia Stadium, Bruges

CLUB BRUGGE KV 2 FK AUSTRIA 0

Half-time 2-0 *Attendance* 16,000

		Goals				Goals
1	Danny VERLINDEN			1	Franz WOHLFAHRT	
2	László DISZTL			2	Manfred SCHMID ❏	
3	Franky VAN DER ELST			3	Anton PFEFFER ❏	
4	Gert VERHEYEN	22		4	Walter KOGLER ❏	
5	Rudy COSSEY			5	Manfred ZSAK	
6	Stéphane VAN DER HEYDEN ❏			6	Michael BINDER	
7	Claude VERSPAILLE			7	Robertas FRIDRIKAS †	
8	Tomasz DZIUBINSKI			8	Thomas FLÖGEL	
9	Lorenzo STAELENS			9	Christian PROSENIK	
10	Foeke BOOY ‡	42		10	Peter STÖGER	
11	Marc SCHAESSENS †			11	Valdas IVANAUSKAS	

Substitutes

Peter CREVE †68

Pascal PLOVIE ‡79

Substitute

Ralph HASENHÜTTL †65

Referee Serge MUHMENTHALER (Switzerland)

SUMMARY

● *Club Bruges embarked on their 100th match in European competition sound in the knowledge that they were favourites to knock out FK Austria and reach the next round but equally aware that they had failed to win only three of their last 16 home games in Europe, once against Milan and twice against their opponent's city rivals Rapid Vienna, who had on both occasions subsequently eliminated them! Both teams were going well in their domestic leagues, but if there was one overriding factor which favoured Bruges it was the two teams' respective recent records in Europe. While Bruges had been regular quarter-finalists in one or other of the three Cups, FK Austria had not managed to extend their European campaigns beyond Christmas for the last nine years! 2-0 is often accepted to be an ideal first-leg result for the home side, and that is what Bruges got after two first-half goals from strikers Verheyen and Booy. It was a fair reflection of play and gave Bruges every chance of emulating Anderlecht and supplying a Belgian team to the group phase for the second year in a row.*

CHAMPIONS' CUP
Second Round Second Leg

Wednesday 4th November 1992
Horr Stadium, Vienna

FK AUSTRIA 3 CLUB BRUGGE 1

Half-time 0-0 *Aggregate* 3-3 (Club Brugge win on away goals) *Attendance* 14,000

		Goals				Goals
1	Franz WOHLFAHRT		1	Danny VERLINDEN		
2	Ernst AIGNER ❑		2	László DISZTL		
3	Anton PFEFFER ❑		3	Franky VAN DER ELST		
4	Walter KOGLER †		4	Gert VERHEYEN ❑ †		
5	Manfred ZSAK	49	5	Vital BORKELMANS		
6	Michael BINDER		6	Stéphane VAN DER HEYDEN ❑	66	
7	Ralph HASENHÜTTL	90	7	Rudy COSSEY		
8	Thomas FLÖGEL		8	Pascal PLOVIE		
9	Christian PROSENIK		9	Lorenzo STAELENS ❑		
10	Peter STÖGER ❑		10	Foeke BOOY ‡		
11	Valdas IVANAUSKAS ❑		11	Claude VERSPAILLE		

Substitute

Robertas FRIDRIKAS †60   73

Substitutes

Tomasz DZIUBINSKI †71

Peter CREVE ‡86

Referee Vassilios NIKAKIS (Greece)

● Since winning the first leg Bruges had not been in the best of form in the Belgian league, whereas FK Austria had gone top of the Austrian Bundesliga the previous weekend after a 3-1 victory over local rivals Wiener Sport-Club. The tie was nicely poised, but by half-time the 0-0 scoreline clearly favoured the Belgians, whose two previous visits to the Austrian capital, by way of comparison, had both ended in 4-3 defeats! It was not long, however, before the scoring started, Austria's captain and sweeper Manfred Zsak deceiving Verlinden at the near post with a well struck free-kick after 49 minutes. The home side now had qualification firmly in their sights, but just 17 minutes later their task was rendered virtually impossible when Stéphane Van der Heyden volleyed home an all-important away goal for the visitors. Still they pressed forward, though, and their ambition was rewarded with two further goals. Alas, the second of them came on the stroke of full-time and so Austria, like Rapid in the first round of the UEFA Cup, were consigned to elimination on the away goals rule.

CHAMPIONS' CUP
Second Round First Leg

Wednesday 21st October 1992
Tourbillon Stadium, Sion

FC SION 2 FC PORTO 2

Half-time 0-0 *Attendance* 14,800

		Goals			Goals
1	Stéphane LEHMANN		1	VÍTOR BAÍA	
2	Yvan QUENTIN		2	JOÃO PINTO	
3	Michel SAUTHIER		3	BANDEIRINHA ❏	
4	Dominique HERR		4	ALOÍSIO	
5	Alain GEIGER		5	FERNANDO COUTO	82
6	Marc HOTTIGER		6	RUI FILIPE	
7	Blaise PIFFARETTI		7	JAIME MAGALHÃES	
8	MÁRCIO †		8	Emil KOSTADINOV	
9	TÚLIO Humberto		9	OLIVEIRA ‡	
10	Roberto ASSIS	59	10	SEMEDO	80
11	David ORLANDO	54	11	ANDRÉ †	

Substitute

Alexandre CLOT †79

Substitutes

JORGE COUTO †59
ANTÓNIO CARLOS ‡68

Referee John BLANKENSTEIN (Holland)

SUMMARY

● After the superb 2-2 draw the Swiss national team had gained in their World Cup qualifier against Italy a week earlier, there was considerable optimism amongst the locals that Sion, featuring four players from that team, could emulate that success at club level by becoming the first Swiss side to reach the latter stages of the Champions' Cup since Grasshoppers in 1979. For a period of 20 minutes in the second half there was every indication that it might happen. Goals from Orlando and Assis - the second a marvellous curling free-kick - had given Sion a well-deserved 2-0 lead, and Porto looked to be out for the count. But experience is so important in European competition, and where Sion, competing in the Champions' Cup for the first time, lacked it, the Portuguese champions had it in abundance. They stormed their way back into the tie with two goals in the last ten minutes, both of them coming from headers, the first from Semedo after a defensive mix-up and the second from Fernando Couto after Sion had committed the cardinal sin of substituting a player at a corner kick.

CHAMPIONS' CUP
Second Round Second Leg

Wednesday 4th November 1992
Das Antas Stadium, Oporto

FC PORTO 4   FC SION 0

Half-time 0-0   *Aggregate* 6-2   *Attendance* 35,000

		Goals				Goals
1	VÍTOR BAÍA			1	Stéphane LEHMANN	
2	JOÃO PINTO			2	Yvan QUENTIN ‡	
3	BANDEIRINHA			3	Michel SAUTHIER	
4	ALOÍSIO			4	Dominique HERR	
5	JORGE COSTA	50		5	Alain GEIGER	
6	RUI FILIPE			6	Marc HOTTIGER ❑	
7	JAIME MAGALHÃES	86		7	Blaise PIFFARETTI	
8	Emil KOSTADINOV †	64		8	Reto GERTSCHEN †	
9	DOMINGOS	85		9	David ORLANDO	
10	SEMEDO ‡			10	Roberto ASSIS	
11	ANTÓNIO CARLOS			11	LUIS CARLOS	
	Substitutes				*Substitutes*	
	ANDRÉ †74				TÚLIO Humberto †63	
	JORGE COUTO ‡77				Olivier BIAGGI ‡74	

Referee Brian HILL (England)

● Sion's spirited display in the first leg faded into oblivion after this four-goal destruction in Portugal. FC Porto warmed up for their big Portuguese league clash with Benfica the following weekend by taking the Swiss side's defence apart in the second half. Defender Jorge Costa, one of only three changes from the first leg, emulated the man he had replaced, Fernando Couto, by heading in Porto's first goal from a corner. Emil Kostadinov was next onto the scoresheet 13 minutes later, breaking the Sion offside trap and racing half the length of the field before shooting past Lehmann. Amazingly, that goal meant that the Bulgarian had scored two goals or more in European competition for the fifth season in succession. As in the first leg, Porto scored twice more in the final ten minutes. Jaime Magalhães, who netted the fourth goal, thereby became the ninth different goalscorer for Porto in their four European matches so far. Moreover, the team, which, with nine goals, had been the top scorers in the first round, now, with six goals over the two legs, repeated the feat in the second round as well!

CHAMPIONS' CUP
Second Round First Leg

Wednesday 21st October 1992
Neas Filadelfias Stadium, Athens

AEK 1 PSV 0

Half-time 0-0 *Attendance* 31,000

Goals   Goals

1	Antonis MINOU	1	Hans VAN BREUKELEN
2	Hristos VASSILOPOULOS ❑	2	Berry VAN AERLE ❑
3	Vaios KARAYANNIS	3	Adri VAN TIGGELEN
4	Stavros STAMATIS	4	Erwin KOEMAN
5	Refik SABANADZOVIC ❑	5	Jan HEINTZE
6	Pavlos PAPAIOANNOU	6	Ernest FABER ❑
7	Alexandros ALEXANDRIS †	7	Juul ELLERMAN
8	Toni SAVEVSKI ❑	8	Gerald VANENBURG †
9	Vassilis DIMITRIADIS ‡ 53	9	Edward LINSKENS
10	Zoran SLISKOVIC	10	Wim KIEFT
11	Yorgos KOUTOULAS	11	Arthur NUMAN

Substitutes   *Substitute*

Yorgos AGOROYANNIS †75 ❑   ROMÁRIO de Souza Faria †16

Anastassios MITROPOULOS ‡85 ❑

Referee Hubert FORSTINGER (Austria)

● PSV's principal objective for the season was to reach the last eight of the Champions' Cup. Winning another Dutch title was, from a financial point of view at least, of only secondary importance. Anderlecht had eliminated the Eindhoven club at the same stage a year earlier. They could not allow it to happen again. Greek champions AEK, meanwhile, had ambitions of their own, not least to match Athens rivals Panathinaikos's achievement of reaching the last eight in 1991/92. And after 90 minutes of a passionate and fiery encounter they looked to have given themselves at least an evens chance of making progress. PSV had created the better scoring opportunities, but AEK had scored the only goal - a courageous and well-directed diving header from Greek football's most prolific marksman, Vassilis Dimitriadis. There was much for the beaten Dutchmen to contemplate. Apart from losing the match and failing to score an away goal, three of their key players - Koeman, Kieft and Vanenburg - had all picked up injuries during the game. The return looked a daunting obstacle indeed.

SUMMARY

CHAMPIONS' CUP
Second Round Second Leg

Wednesday 4th November 1992
Philips Stadium, Eindhoven

PSV 3 AEK 0

Half-time 1-0 *Aggregate* 3-1 *Attendance* 26,500

		Goals				Goals
1	Hans VAN BREUKELEN		1	Antonis MINOU		
2	Berry VAN AERLE ❑		2	Hristos VASSILOPOULOS ❑		
3	Adri VAN TIGGELEN		3	Vaios KARAYANNIS		
4	Ernest FABER		4	Stelios MANOLAS ❑		
5	Jan HEINTZE		5	Manolis PAPADOPOULOS		
6	Ernest FABER		6	Pavlos PAPAIOANNOU ❑		
7	Arthur NUMAN		7	Alexandros ALEXANDRIS		
8	Gerald VANENBURG †		8	Toni SAVEVSKI		
9	ROMÁRIO de Souza Faria 5, 51, 84		9	Vassilis DIMITRIADIS		
10	Wim KIEFT		10	Zoran SLISKOVIC †		
11	Peter HOEKSTRA ❑		11	Yorgos AGOROYANNIS ‡		

Substitute

Juul ELLERMAN †70

Substitutes

Dimitris PATIKAS †36

Anastassios MITROPOULOS ‡61

Referee Fabio BALDAS (Italy)

● *"Make or break". "All or nothing". "Sink or swim". These were the sort of clichés being bandied about Eindhoven as PSV approached their most important match of the season. But cometh the hour, cometh the man. Brazilian striker Romário, whose controversial career at the club had taken another downturn when he was dropped for the first leg in Athens, emerged as PSV's hero, saviour and gold-plated superstar all rolled into one. Three times he found the net, with each goal just as important as the others. The first, coolly slotted in after just five minutes, put PSV level on aggregate. The second, a virtual replica, put them 2-1 ahead. The third, a glorious individual effort showing wonderful technique and cunning, put the Dutch champions out of reach. Until then the threat of an away goal by AEK hung perilously over any premature celebrations. But for the last five minutes the PSV fans were free to pay a vocal tribute to their goalscoring genius. Coach Westerhof called it "the team's best performance of the season", but in truth it was all about the Brazilian in the number nine shirt.*

CHAMPIONS' CUP
Second Round First Leg

Wednesday 21st October 1992
Lenin Stadium, Moscow

CSKA MOSKVA 1 FC BARCELONA 1

Half-time 1-0 *Attendance* 30,000

		Goals				Goals
1	Dmitry KHARIN		1	Andoni ZUBIZARRETA		
2	Aleksei GUSHIN		2	Albert FERRER		
3	Sergei KOLOTOVKIN		3	José GUARDIOLA †		
4	Dmitry BYSTROV		4	Ronald KOEMAN		
5	Sergei FOKIN		5	Miguel Angel NADAL		
6	Vasily IVANOV		6	José María BAKERO		
7	Denis MASHKARIN ‡		7	Jon Andoni GOIKOETXEA		
8	Aleksandr GRISHIN	17	8	Christo STOICHKOV		
9	Oleg SERGEEV ❑		9	Michael LAUDRUP		
10	Dmitry KORSAKOV †		10	EUSEBIO Sacristán		
11	Valery MINKO ❑		11	Aitor BEGUIRISTAIN ❑ ‡	58	

Substitutes

Ilshat FAYZULLIN †62

Yevgeny BUSHMANOV ‡67

Substitutes

Guillermo AMOR †46

JUAN CARLOS Rodríguez ‡80

Referee Kurt RÖTHLISBERGER (Switzerland)

SUMMARY

● *Champions' Cup holders Barcelona arrived in rainy Moscow with their spirits already dampened by a Spanish league defeat against leaders Deportivo La Coruña the previous weekend. And after just 17 minutes of the first half the alarm bells were ringing once again for Johan Cruijff's side. Midfielder José Guardiola was caught in possession in his own half and before he could rectify the damage CSKA's Grishin had shot into the far corner beyond Zubizarreta to give the home side the lead. It was just the start the 30,000 crowd had been praying for. CSKA were heading a four-strong task force of Moscow clubs in Europe and they were eager to lead by example. There were further chances for them to stretch their advantage, but Barcelona's experience brought them back into the game and they earned themselves a face-saving draw with an equaliser from Aitor Beguistáin early in the second half. That goal enabled the Basque forward to prolong his sequence of scoring at least one goal in Europe to a remarkable sixth successive season - a feat unmatched, at this stage, by any other current player.*

CHAMPIONS' CUP
Second Round Second Leg

Wednesday 4th November 1992
Nou Camp, Barcelona

FC BARCELONA 2 CSKA MOSKVA 3

Half-time 2-1 Aggregate 3-4 Attendance 70,000

		Goals				Goals
1	Andoni ZUBIZARRETA		1	Dmitry KHARIN		
2	Albert FERRER		2	Aleksei GUSHIN		
3	José GUARDIOLA †		3	Sergei KOLOTOVKIN		
4	Ronald KOEMAN		4	Oleg MALYUKOV		
5	Miguel Angel NADAL ‡	13	5	Sergei FOKIN ❑		
6	José María BAKERO		6	Mikhail KOLESNIKOV ‡		
7	Jon Andoni GOIKOETXEA		7	Denis MASHKARIN		57
8	Christo STOICHKOV		8	Aleksandr GRISHIN †		
9	Michael LAUDRUP		9	Oleg SERGEEV		
10	Guillermo AMOR		10	Yevgeny BUSHMANOV		44
11	Aitor BEGUIRISTAIN	31	11	Ilshat FAYZULLIN		
	Substitutes			*Substitutes*		
	EUSEBIO Sacristán †46			Dmitry KORSAKOV †41		60
	Julio SALINAS ‡57			Vasily IVANOV ‡78		

Referee Bernd HEYNEMANN (Germany)

● *Without doubt this was European football's shock of the season. Holders Barcelona beaten at home for the first time in 17 European matches after relinquishing a 2-0 lead. And by whom? By a club which since winning the 1991 Soviet championship, had sold their three best players to Barcelona's poor relations Español! Once Nadal and Beguiristáin had put Barcelona 2-0 up after half an hour, there appeared to be no danger whatsoever of an upset. Critically, though, the Catalans gave their opponents hope by conceding a goal just before half-time. And in the second period the unbelievable actually happened. Two goals in three minutes silenced the Nou Camp and left Barcelona needing to score twice more to stay in the competition. They had a full half an hour to do it, but by now their resolve had evaporated. Time ticked on, boos and whistles rained down from the multi-tiered stands, and the score remained the same. Incredibly the holders were out, CSKA were through, and not one of the last eight from the previous year had survived into the Champions League of 1992/93.*

CHAMPIONS' CUP
Second Round Review

SECOND ROUND RESULTS		1st leg	2nd leg	Agg.
IFK Göteborg	Lech Poznan	1-0	3-0	4-0
Rangers	Leeds United	2-1	2-1	4-2
Slovan Bratislava	Milan	0-1	0-4	0-5
Dinamo Bucuresti	Olympique Marseille	0-0	0-2	0-2
Club Brugge KV	FK Austria	2-0	1-3	3-3
(Club Brugge KV win on away goals)				
FC Sion	FC Porto	2-2	0-4	2-6
AEK	PSV	1-0	0-3	1-3
CSKA Moskva	FC Barcelona	1-1	3-2	4-3

LEADING GOALSCORERS AFTER SECOND ROUND

4 ROMÁRIO (PSV)
   TÚLIO (FC Sion)
3 Emil KOSTADINOV (FC Porto)
   Dmitry KORSAKOV (CSKA Moskva)
   Gert VERHEYEN (Club Brugge KV)
2 Jean-Pierre PAPIN (Milan)
   Frank RIJKAARD (Milan)
   Aitor BEGUIRISTAIN (FC Barcelona)
   Mark HATELEY (Rangers)
   Ally McCOIST (Rangers)
   Ralph HASENHÜTTL (FK Austria)
   Robertas FRIDRIKAS (FK Austria)
   Roberto ASSIS (FC Sion)
   SEMEDO (FC Porto)
   FERNANDO COUTO (FC Porto)
   DOMINGOS (FC Porto)
   Aleksandr GRISHIN (CSKA Moskva)
   Johnny EKSTRÖM (IFK Göteborg)
   Alen BOKSIC (Olympique Marseille)
   Gary McALLISTER (Leeds United)
   Eric CANTONA (Leeds United)
   Aleksei SEMJONOV (Skonto Riga)
   Marco VAN BASTEN (Milan)
   Arthur NUMAN (PSV)
   Peter DUBOVSKY (Slovan Bratislava)
   Lorenzo STAELENS (Club Brugge KV)
   Alexandros ALEXANDRIS (AEK)
   Kaj ESKELINEN (IFK Göteborg)
   Rafael MARTIN VAZQUEZ (Olympique Marseille)
   Fritz WALTER (VfB Stuttgart)
   Andreas BUCK (VfB Stuttgart)

CHAMPIONS' CUP

CHAMPIONS' LEAGUE DRAW   *Page*

GROUP A: Olympique Marseille (France), Club Brugge KV (Belgium), CSKA Moskva (Russia), Rangers (Scotland)

Club Brugge KV	v	CSKA Moskva	74
Rangers	v	Olympique Marseille	76
Olympique Marseille	v	Club Brugge KV	78
CSKA Moskva	v	Rangers	80
CSKA Moskva	v	Olympique Marseille	82
Club Brugge KV	v	Rangers	84
Olympique Marseille	v	CSKA Moskva	86
Rangers	v	Club Brugge KV	88
CSKA Moskva	v	Club Brugge KV	90
Olympique Marseille	v	Rangers	92
Club Brugge KV	v	Olympique Marseille	94
Rangers	v	CSKA Moskva	96

GROUP B: IFK Göteborg (Sweden), FC Porto (Portugal), Philips SV (Holland), Milan (Italy)

FC Porto	v	Philips SV	100
Milan	v	IFK Göteborg	102
IFK Göteborg	v	FC Porto	104
Philips SV	v	Milan	106
Philips SV	v	IFK Göteborg	108
FC Porto	v	Milan	110
IFK Göteborg	v	Philips SV	112
Milan	v	FC Porto	114
Philips SV	v	FC Porto	116
IFK Göteborg	v	Milan	118
FC Porto	v	IFK Göteborg	120
Milan	v	Philips SV	122

CHAMPIONS' LEAGUE
Group A

Wednesday 25th November 1992
Olympia Stadium, Bruges

CLUB BRUGGE KV 1 CSKA MOSKVA 0

Half-time 1-0 *Attendance* 17,000

		Goals			Goals
1	Danny VERLINDEN		1	Dmitry KHARIN ‡	
2	László DISZTL		2	Aleksei GUSHIN	
3	Franky VAN DER ELST		3	Sergei KOLOTOVKIN	
4	Gert VERHEYEN		4	Dmitry BYSTROV ❏	
5	Vital BORKELMANS		5	Oleg MALYUKOV ❏	
6	Rudy COSSEY		6	Mikhail KOLESNIKOV	
7	Pascal PLOVIE		7	Denis MASHKARIN	
8	Claude VERSPAILLE †		8	Aleksandr GRISHIN †	
9	Lorenzo STAELENS		9	Oleg SERGEEV	
10	Tomasz DZIUBINSKI		10	Yevgeny BUSHMANOV	
11	Daniel AMOKACHI ❏ ‡	17	11	Ilshat FAYZULLIN	

Substitutes

Peter CREVE †78

Alex QUERTER ‡89

Substitutes

Dmitry KORSAKOV †32

Aleksandr GUTEEV ‡46

Referee Bo KARLSSON (Sweden)

FACTFILE

● *Hard-up CSKA could not afford a charter flight to Belgium. They flew to Berlin then made the journey to Bruges by train with a connection at Frankfurt!*

● *This was CSKA goalkeeper Dmitry Kharin's last game for the club before his transfer to English Premier League club Chelsea.*

● *Club Bruges went into the game in relatively low spirits after losing the Bruges derby 3-1 to Cercle the previous weekend. Man of the match for their city rivals was Croatian striker Josip Weber, the Belgian League's top scorer, who hit a hat-trick.*

● *Each team had one player missing through suspension - Stéphane Van der Heyden of Bruges, Sergei Fokin of CSKA.*

● Dmitry Kharin

Belgians dominate but score just once

After CSKA Moscow's stunning victory over Barcelona none of their opponents in Champions' League Group A were likely to fall into the trap of taking the Russians lightly. Nonetheless, they appeared to be the weakest team in the section, and for Bruges an opening victory was imperative if they wished to harbour realistic ambitions of reaching the final.

Hugo Broos sent his players onto the field in a customary 5-3-2 formation, with Hungarian international László Disztl sweeping up behind the markers Cossey and Plovie, and Verspaille and Borkelmans, recently recovered from injury, raiding down the flanks. With Plovie, in particular, having a fine game against CSKA danger man Sergeev, the Bruges defence rarely came under threat throughout the 90 minutes. The counter-attacking which had undone the holders in the Nou Camp earlier in the month was virtually non-existent here.

All the goalmouth action took place at the other end of the field. Nigerian striker Daniel Amokachi got the home side off to the perfect start when he broke through the Russian offside trap and held his balance long enough to round the goalkeeper and slide the ball into the unguarded net. That early goal gave Bruges the encouragement they needed to take the game to CSKA and it was only the goalkeeping of former USSR/CIS international Dmitry Kharin which prevented the Belgians from going in at half-time with a greater advantage.

To CSKA's misfortune, Kharin was injured by a challenge from Staelens just before the interval and he had to be replaced for the second 45 minutes by substitute goalkeeper Aleksandr Guteev. This may have seemed like good news for Bruges at the time, but if anything Guteev's exploits were to surpass those of his predecessor. Still the Belgians pressed forward seeking the second goal that would confirm their superiority, but Guteev kept them out with a series of spectacular stops, the best of them being a wonderful reaction save from Amokachi's point-blank header and, in the last minute, a one-handed effort at full stretch to deny Polish striker Dziubinski.

At the final whistle, however, Bruges were delighted simply to have pocketed the two points. This was no longer a two-legged Cup tie. This was a league, and one in which goal difference, in terms of qualification for the final, was relatively unimportant.

DANIEL AMOKACHI
Club Brugge KV

Injured whilst playing for Nigeria in an African Nations' Cup qualifier in August and subsequently out of action for three months, Daniel Amokachi returned to the Bruges side for his first European appearance of the season in triumphant form. As in the first leg of the Cup-winners' Cup semi-final against Werder Bremen the previous season, it was his single, early goal which ensured a crucial European victory for his team in the Olympia Stadium.
Amokachi came to Belgium from Nigerian club Ranchers Bees as a raw 17 year old in 1990. He had impressed onlookers with his power, speed and goalscoring whilst playing for a Nigerian selection on tour to the Low Countries, and Bruges snapped him up before anybody else had the opportunity to size up his potential. That foresight paid off handsomely in Amokachi's first full season in the first team. His 12 goals in 26 games went a long way towards taking Bruges to the Belgian title and into the Champions' Cup.

CHAMPIONS' LEAGUE
Group A

Wednesday 25th November 1992
Ibrox Stadium, Glasgow

RANGERS 2 OLYMPIQUE MARSEILLE 2

Half-time 0-1 *Attendance* 41,624

		Goals				Goals
1	Andy GORAM		1	Fabien BARTHEZ		
2	Neil MURRAY		2	Jocelyn ANGLOMA		
3	David ROBERTSON		3	Eric DI MECO ❑		
4	Richard GOUGH †		4	Basile BOLI ❑		
5	Dave McPHERSON		5	Franck SAUZEE		
6	John BROWN		6	Marcel DESAILLY		
7	Trevor STEVEN ‡		7	Bernard CASONI		
8	Stuart McCALL		8	Alen BOKSIC †		31
9	Ian DURRANT		9	Rudi VÖLLER ‡		56
10	Mark HATELEY	81	10	Abedi PELE		
11	Aleksei MIKHAILICHENKO		11	Didier DESCHAMPS		

Substitutes

Steven PRESSLEY †46

Gary McSWEGAN ‡77   78

Substitutes

Jean-Philippe DURAND †84

Jean-Jacques EYDELIE ‡90

Referee Sándor PUHL (Hungary)

FACTFILE

● *Both Rangers and Marseille were knocked out of the Champions' Cup the previous season by Czechoslovakian champions Sparta Prague.*

● *Alen Boksic's goal enabled Marseille to become the top-scoring French club in European competition. This was their 104th European goal, surpassing the previous record of 103 held by Saint-Etienne.*

● *Rangers were the only team drawn in Group A to have previously won a European trophy (1971/72 Cup-winners' Cup). Conversely, all four teams in Group B were former European winners.*

● *The Scottish champions were also the only Group A side to go into the Champions' League with a 100% record from their previous four games.*

● *Gary McSwegan*

Late fightback denies impressive Marseille

Five days before this game Olympique Marseille had taken a 2-0 lead in a French League fixture away to Strasbourg before eventually being pegged back to a 2-2 draw. Now, on a filthy evening in Glasgow, history was to repeat itself and deny Marseille victory once again.

For 78 minutes the French champions belied their shaky league form and put on a display which oozed class in every quarter. Rangers were made to look the European novices which, strictly speaking, they were, as Marseille dominated possession with tremendous skill and vivacity, taking the game to their hosts in almost contemptible 'British' style.

Rangers, so used to being masters on their own turf in domestic competition, had little answer to the French side's guile and application. Granted, they took the field without the injured Ally McCoist, scorer of 32 goals already in the 92/93 season, and the suspended midfielder Ian Ferguson, but there was still enough talent and experience in the team for them to offer more attacking options than the one they chose - simply ballooning long balls on to the head of lone striker Mark Hateley and hoping that their midfielders would feed off his knockdowns.

Marseille took a deserved lead on the half-hour mark when Alen Boksic, hero of the previous round against Dinamo Bucharest, scored his third goal in successive European games, pouncing in the area after some excellent work on the left from his strike partner Rudi Völler. Early in the second half it was Völler himself who put the visitors further ahead after a dreadful mix-up in the Rangers defence between goalkeeper Goram and young defender Pressley, who had replaced injured captain Richard Gough at half-time.

That second goal looked certain to have finished Rangers off. But if Rangers' first substitution had proved disastrous, their second, made after 77 minutes, was to provide instant dividends. Gary McSwegan, a young striker who had never played in Europe before, rose to send a glorious header past Barthez after a superb move involving Durrant and Mikhailichenko. Then, barely three minutes later, McSwegan was involved again as Mark Hateley stooped to head in a deflected cross from close range that sent the Ibrox crowd into raptures and earned the Scottish champions a crucial point.

Rangers boss Walter Smith accurately summed up the night's proceedings when he said: "We were physically inferior to the French. But my team showed tremendous character after being outplayed for so long."

RUDI VÖLLER
Olympique Marseille

When 32-year-old Rudi Völler left Roma for Marseille in the summer of 1992, many regarded the move as a first step in the winding-down process of an illustrious career. But Marseille president Bernard Tapie has never been interested in has-beens, and he evidently felt that the German striker still had plenty to offer at the highest level. Replacing Jean-Pierre Papin was never going to be easy, but the prolific French striker would have been hard pressed to put on a more convincing and effective all-round display than Völler produced in the mudbath of Ibrox.

Although this was Völler's first season in the Champions' Cup, he had previously starred for Roma in the UEFA Cup, scoring 10 goals to take them to the final in 1990/91. It is for his feats at international level, though, that the former Werder Bremen striker is best known. A World Cup winner in 1990, he also shone in the German team which finished runners-up in Mexico four years earlier. His final game for Germany came in October 1992 when he scored in a friendly against Mexico. It was his 44th goal in 85 internationals.

CHAMPIONS' LEAGUE
Group A

Wednesday 9th December 1992
Vélodrome Stadium, Marseilles

OLYMPIQUE MARSEILLE 3 CLUB BRUGGE KV 0

Half-time 3-0 Attendance 29,000

		Goals			Goals
1	Fabien BARTHEZ		1	Danny VERLINDEN	
2	Jean-Christophe THOMAS		2	László DISZTL	
3	Eric DI MECO		3	Franky VAN DER ELST	
4	Jocelyn ANGLOMA		4	Gert VERHEYEN	
5	Franck SAUZEE	4 (pen)	5	Vital BORKELMANS	
6	Marcel DESAILLY		6	Stéphane VAN DER HEYDEN ❏	
7	Bernard CASONI		7	Pascal PLOVIE	
8	Alen BOKSIC ‡	10, 26	8	Claude VERSPAILLE	
9	Jean-Jacques EYDELIE †		9	Lorenzo STAELENS	
10	Abedi PELE		10	Tomasz DZIUBINSKI	
11	Didier DESCHAMPS		11	Daniel AMOKACHI †	

Substitutes

Jean-Philippe DURAND †82

Jean-Marc FERRERI ‡86

Substitute

Rudy COSSEY †46

Referee Aron SCHMIDHUBER (Germany)

FACTFILE

● *This was Marseille's first competitive match for 11 days. Their extra preparation time had been assisted by the cancellation of their French League match at Lille the previous Friday.*

● *Bruges' last European game in France had ended in similar disappointment - a 6-1 beating by Monaco in the 1988/89 Champions' Cup. Only two survivors from that game made the team in Marseille - Pascal Plovie and Franky Van der Elst.*

● *Marseille's victory completed a hat-trick of triumphs for French clubs against Belgian opposition. In the same week Paris-Saint-Germain knocked Anderlecht out of the UEFA Cup and Auxerre did the same to Standard Liège.*

● *Marseille's victory was achieved without two key men - Basile Boli was suspended, Rudi Völler was out through injury.*

Boksic batters Bruges into early submission

"Our best performance of the season!" exclaimed Marseille boss Raymond Goethals. "My best match for Marseille!" declared star striker Alen Boksic. Both men had good reason to be proud after a display which not only enabled Marseille to leapfrog Bruges into top position in Group A but which also confirmed them as the most likely qualifiers for the Champions' Cup final.

Marseille tore at the Belgians from the word go. Hugo Broos, the Bruges coach, had sent his players onto the field with the expressed intention of gaining a draw. But what appeared to be a well-armoured defence was pierced with less than five minutes on the clock. When Bruges' Belgian international left-back Vital Borkelmans lunged at Alen Boksic from behind in the penalty area, the German referee had little option but to point to the penalty spot. Franck Sauzée converted the kick powerfully and accurately to send Verlinden the wrong way and give Marseille the early lead.

Not long afterwards the Belgian defence was unhinged again. Thomas swung in a corner from the right. Angloma tried to stab it in at the near post but failed to connect. The ball then curved through the crowd to hit the other upright before Boksic, ever alert in the danger zone, blasted the ball into the net with a posse of Bruges defenders looking on helplessly.

2-0 became 3-0 after 26 minutes when the in-form Croatian striker brushed aside Disztl on the right before weaving his way into the box and, with apparently all the time in the world to pick his spot, placing a left-foot shot inside Verlinden's near post.

That third goal put the seal on the match. It was now just a question of how many more times the home team could breach the Belgian defence. Bruges coach Hugo Broos appeared to recognise this when he brought on an extra defender, Rudy Cossey, for striker Amokachi at half-time. Normally, when a team is 0-3 down with half the match still left to play, reinforcing the defence would seem to be the least likely course of action to take. But the Belgians had evidently thrown in the towel. Now it was simply a case of salvaging as much pride as possible, and in that respect, with Marseille failing to add to their tally in the second period, it was mission accomplished for the Bruges coach.

But in the final analysis goalkeeper Verlinden was the only Bruges player to emerge from the match with any real credit. He made some telling saves, especially from Deschamps and Pelé in the second half, and it was his efforts alone that saved the Belgian champions from complete annihilation.

ALEN BOKSIC
Olympique Marseille

Croatian-born Alen Boksic was the man responsible for taking Marseille through to the Champions' League with his two-goal blast against Dinamo Bucharest in round two. Against Bruges he produced an even more convincing display to take Marseille to the top of the Group A table. Without his injured striking partner Rudi Völler, Boksic took it upon himself to destroy the Bruges defence single-handed, and that was precisely what he did. He not only scored two goals, but also obtained the penalty from which Sauzée opened the scoring and then sent a header crashing against the post in the second half. Boksic began his career at Hajduk Split, where he scored 27 goals in 96 Yugoslav League games. After scoring the winning goal to beat Red Star Belgrade in the 1991 Yugoslav Cup final he signed up with Marseille, only to discover that there was no room for an extra foreigner at the club. The 1991/92 season was therefore a sabbatical one for him, but, judging by his brilliant form since, it did not appear to do him any harm.

CHAMPIONS' LEAGUE
Group A

Wednesday 9th December 1992
Ruhr Stadium, Bochum

CSKA MOSKVA 0 RANGERS 1

Half-time 0-1 *Attendance* 9,000

		Goals				Goals
1	Aleksandr GUTEEV		1	Andy GORAM		
2	Aleksei GUSHIN ❏ ‡		2	Stuart McCALL		
3	Sergei KOLOTOVKIN		3	David ROBERTSON		
4	Dmitry BYSTROV		4	Ian DURRANT		
5	Sergei FOKIN ❏		5	Dave McPHERSON		
6	Oleg MALYUKOV		6	John BROWN		
7	Valery MINKO †		7	Trevor STEVEN		
8	Dmitry KORSAKOV		8	Ian FERGUSON		13
9	Oleg SERGEEV		9	Ally McCOIST		
10	Yevgeny BUSHMANOV		10	Mark HATELEY		
11	Ilshat FAYZULLIN		11	Aleksei MIKHAILICHENKO		

Substitutes | | | *Substitutes*

Aleksandr GRISHIN †59
Vasily IVANOV ‡66

Referee Kim NIELSEN (Denmark)

FACTFILE

● *The victory was Rangers' third in succession away from home.*
● *Like Marseille in the other Group A match, Rangers had the advantage of their league fixture the previous weekend (against Dundee United) being called off due to bad weather.*
● *CSKA, whose league had long since finished, were obliged to play this home fixture outside Russia because of the unplayable conditions in their homeland in December. In order not to disadvantage the other two teams in the group, that meant that all three of their 'home' games would have to be held on foreign territory*
● *This was Rangers' 18th European match on German soil but their first victory there for 31 years!*

● *Ian Ferguson*

Rangers cruise home after early scare

A thousand miles from Moscow and with only a few hundred of their fans to support them, CSKA could draw little or no benefit from the fact that this was, on paper at least, their first 'home' game in the Champions' League. With the Russian winter having already set in back home, they chose the German city of Bochum and the splendid setting of the Ruhr Stadium, to host this encounter with Rangers.

The Scottish champions, relieved to have got away with a point from their first match at home to Marseille, knew that they needed to beat CSKA to remain in touch with the French side. With barely 15 seconds on the clock, however, they very nearly found themselves having to chase the game when a rapid CSKA attack resulted in two shots from Sergeev and an extraordinary goalmouth scramble before Rangers cleared the ball to safety.

Thereafter the Russians continued to look threatening and it was against the run of play that Rangers took the lead after 13 minutes. Aleksandr Guteev, keeping goal from the start in this game now that Kharin had quit the club, failed to catch a high ball lofted into the penalty area from deep. The ball fell into play, Mark Hateley latched on to it, played it back to Ian Ferguson and his shot deflected up off Fokin before looping over Guteev's head into the net.

At that stage of the game Rangers' lead was undeserved, but as time went on, especially after CSKA had had a goal ruled out - correctly - for offside, the game began to swing their way. Just before half-time Ally McCoist went desperately close to increasing Rangers' lead when Guteev could only parry Trevor Steven's shot into his path. And after the interval there was really only one team in it.

Rangers had ample opportunity to clinch the two points as CSKA visibly ran out of steam. First McCoist was denied by Guteev. Then Hateley and Durrant both wasted chances created for them by Mikhailichenko before Robertson sent a soaring left-foot drive just past the upright. In the very last minute Rangers were almost made to pay for their profligacy when Sergeev escaped on a counter-attack. But Brown's crucial tackle saved the day and ensured that the victory, and the £400,000 prize money which went with it, belonged to Rangers.

ALEKSEI MIKHAILICHENKO
Rangers

Rangers looked to midfielder Aleksei Mikhailichenko for a little 'local knowledge' against the 1991 Soviet Union champions. But given that when he last appeared in the same league as the opposition - in 1990 - less than half of the players on show in Bochum were in the CSKA first team, it was perhaps asking too much of the former Dinamo Kiev player. But on the field of play 'Mikha' evidently enjoyed taking on his former countrymen, producing one of his most convincing displays for Rangers since joining them from Sampdoria in 1991. On the whole, Mikhailichenko has not enjoyed the best of times since leaving Kiev. Although he has won championship medals with both Sampdoria and Rangers, he has never been an integral member of the team nor has he been able to reproduce consistently the sort of form he showed in his great year of 1988 when he shone at both the European Championships and the Olympic Games and was voted fourth in the European Footballer of the Year poll.

CHAMPIONS' LEAGUE
Group A

Wednesday 3rd March 1993
Olympia Stadium, Berlin

CSKA MOSKVA 1 OLYMPIQUE MARSEILLE 1

Half-time 0-1 *Attendance* 13,000

		Goals				Goals
1	Yevgeny PLOTNIKOV		1	Fabien BARTHEZ		
2	Sergei MAMCHUR ❑		2	Jean-Jacques EYDELIE		
3	Sergei KOLOTOVKIN		3	Eric DI MECO		
4	Dmitry BYSTROV		4	Jocelyn ANGLOMA		
5	Oleg MALYUKOV		5	Franck SAUZEE		
6	Yury ANTONOVICH		6	Marcel DESAILLY		
7	Valery MINKO ‡		7	Bernard CASONI		
8	Vasily IVANOV ❑ †		8	Alen BOKSIC		
9	Oleg SERGEEV		9	Igor DOBROVOLSKY †		
10	Yevgeny BUSHMANOV		10	Abedi PELE		28
11	Ilshat FAYZULLIN	56	11	Didier DESCHAMPS		

Substitutes

Yury DUDNIK †46

Dmitry KORSAKOV ‡54

Substitute

Jean-Philippe DURAND †57

Referee Fabio BALDAS (ITA)

FACTFILE

● *This was CSKA's first competitive game of any sort since their previous Champions' League encounter, three months earlier, against Rangers.*

● *The match was originally due to be staged in the Rhineland town of Leverkusen, but was later switched to Berlin where it was felt that CSKA would obtain better support, notably from the Russian military presence in the city.*

● *This was the fourth European Cup tie that Marseille had played on neutral territory. The previous three were in Lyons against Juventus in 1972/73, in Lecce against Finnish side RoPS in 1987/88 and, of course, the 1990/91 Champions' Cup final against Red Star Belgrade in Bari.*

● *New signing Yevgeny Plotnikov was the third different goalkeeper used by CSKA in their three Champions' League matches.*

Marseille drop a point in Berlin

CSKA had forfeited the right to play their home games in Moscow because of the notoriously bad Russian winter, but the conditions in Berlin - their chosen venue - were equally as harsh for both sets of players. Although there was no snow on the pitch, the temperature at the start of the game was -6 degrees and most of the players came onto the field wearing gloves.

But irrespective of the conditions, Marseille were aware that they needed to take both points from the Russians. CSKA had lost both of their first two matches and were only just emerging from their winter hibernation. Marseille, on the other hand, were going well in the French League, although they had just relinquished top place the previous weekend after going down unluckily to a 0-1 defeat in Monaco.

There was little to choose between the sides in the opening skirmishes. Igor Dobrovolsky, a Russian international signed from Italian club Genoa during the winter, had a good chance to score on his European debut for Marseille, but his shot hit the post and rebounded to safety. At the other end one of CSKA's new signings, Antonovich, could only find the side-netting with an equally good opportunity. With almost half an hour gone, though, Marseille took the lead. It was a goal fashioned by the pace and strength of Boksic, who shrugged off Kolotovkin's challenge on the right before pulling the ball back from the byline and setting up Abedi Pelé for a glorious left-foot finish.

Boksic himself had an excellent opportunity to make it 2-0 early in the second half when he burst through the Russian defence again, but the hard pitch got the better of him and he sliced the ball horribly wide of the target. It was an important miss, because shortly afterwards CSKA equalised. Their first goal scored in the Champions' League was a wonderful individual effort by teenage striker Fayzullin, who cut in past Casoni and steered a precise shot beyond Barthez into the far corner. The same player wasted a much easier chance later on when the Marseille goalkeeper miskicked the ball straight to him, but Fayzullin's shot, though on target, was not struck hard enough and Desailly had no problem in scrambling back to clear it off the line.

Marseille also went close to a winner when Sauzée's shot took a wicked deflection off Bystrov, but Plotnikov, who had looked impressive all evening, showed splendid athleticism to save. So the score stayed at 1-1 and despite having 29 shots during the course of the 90 minutes the Group A favourites had to make do with just one goal and, more importantly, just one point.

ABEDI PELE
Olympique Marseille

With his country, Ghana, having surprisingly been knocked out of the World Cup by Algeria the previous Friday, Abedi Pelé could focus all his attention on his other main objective for the season - winning the Champions' Cup with Marseille. He certainly played his part in Berlin with the superb sliding hook shot which gave the French champions the lead, but with Rudi Völler missing from the attack with injury, Marseille lacked the necessary firepower to finish off the Russians for good.

Pelé has been regarded as one of the most skilful players in the French League for several seasons now. He began with Second Division sides Niort and Mulhouse before joining Marseille in 1988. But foreign player restrictions meant that he had to spend two seasons at Lille before he became a permanent fixture in the 'OM' first team. He helped the club to the Champions' Cup final in his first full season and has since been voted African Footballer of the Year two years in a row (1991, 1992) - the first player ever to have achieved that distinction.

CHAMPIONS' LEAGUE
Group A

Wednesday 3rd March 1993
Olympia Stadium, Bruges

CLUB BRUGGE KV 1 RANGERS 1

Half-time 1-0 *Attendance* 19,000

		Goals			Goals
1	Danny VERLINDEN		1	Andy GORAM	
2	Rudy COSSEY		2	Scott NISBET ❑ †	
3	Franky VAN DER ELST		3	David ROBERTSON	
4	Gert VERHEYEN		4	Neil MURRAY	
5	Vital BORKELMANS ❑		5	Dave McPHERSON	
6	Tomasz DZIUBINSKI	44	6	John BROWN	
7	Peter CREVE †		7	Aleksei MIKHAILICHENKO	
8	Alex QUERTER ❑		8	Stuart McCALL	
9	Lorenzo STAELENS		9	Ally McCOIST	
10	Foeke BOOY		10	Mark HATELEY	
11	Daniel AMOKACHI		11	Pieter HUISTRA	73

Substitute
Claude VERSPAILLE †79

Substitute
Steven PRESSLEY †84

Referee Antonio MARTIN NAVARRETE (Spain)

FACTFILE

● *This was the third time in the competition that Rangers had come from behind to deny their opponents victory. It had also happened in the home matches against both Leeds and Marseille.*

● *The game was originally scheduled by UEFA to be played behind closed doors as a punishment for the behaviour of the Bruges fans in Marseilles. But the Belgian club won their appeal.*

● *This was the third Belgium-Scotland confrontation in the 92/93 European campaign. Hibernian and Anderlecht had met in the first round of the UEFA Cup, with Hearts and Standard Liège playing each other in the same competition a round later.*

● *Pieter Huistra's goal was the first conceded at home by Bruges in five European ties.*

Gallant Rangers storm back to draw

Both Club Bruges and Rangers went into this third match of the Champions' League with injury problems, but that did not prevent them from providing an enthralling game of football. The Belgians were missing two key defenders in Plovie and Disztl and a useful midfielder in the suspended Van der Heyden, whilst the Scots were forced to leave out internationals Gough, Durrant and Steven, not to mention the former England right-back Gary Stevens, whose foot injury had kept him out of every one of their European matches during the season.

The pace of the game was established early on as both sides set about gaining the victory that would keep them firmly on course for a place in the Champions' Cup final. There was no let up in the action as first Bruges went close when both their captain Franky Van der Elst and their star striker Amokachi made contact with the Rangers woodwork and then Ally McCoist sent a delicate chip onto the top of the Bruges crossbar only for Aleksei Mikhailichenko to head the rebound into the crowd from only a couple of yards out.

The Ukrainian almost redeemed himself shortly afterwards when Bruges goalkeeper Verlinden went walkabout and his beautifully flighted lob was cleared off the line, but instead Mikhailichenko blotted his copybook further still when, just a minute before the interval, he made a miserable attempt to head a clearance out of his own box. The ball fell to Bruges' Polish striker Dziubinski and, with the Rangers defence wrongfooted, he crashed the ball into the net via the right-hand post to give his team the lead.

But the Belgians were not allowed to build on that lead in the second half. Rangers simply came at them with renewed vigour and dominated completely. Hateley and Huistra were both denied in quick succession by Verlinden and the Bruges 'keeper gained even louder applause from the home fans when he pulled off a tremendous save to deny a McPherson header a few minutes later. A goal had to come for Rangers, and it duly arrived after 72 minutes. Bruges failed to clear Mikhailichenko's corner adequately, Stuart McCall sent the ball back into the danger area and Pieter Huistra, running in on the right, found himself perfectly placed to fire it unerringly into the roof of the net past several Bruges defenders on the line.

Rangers were level, they had a point, and it was no more than they deserved.

STUART McCALL
Rangers

No player was more committed to getting Rangers a result in Bruges than flame-haired midfielder Stuart McCall. He was the heart and lungs of the side's second-half fightback, and although his through-ball to Huistra for the equalising goal was unintentional - it was a mishit shot with his unfavoured left foot! - it certainly had the desired effect. McCall has enjoyed a meteoric rise to stardom over the past five years. In 1988 he was still playing Second Division football in England with Bradford City - he had been on the pitch the day of the appalling fire three years earlier - when Everton came in with an offer for him. He remained at Goodison for three years during which time he scored twice on the losing side against Liverpool in the FA Cup final at Wembley and starred for Scotland at the 1990 World Cup. Rangers brought him to Ibrox in 1991 and he is now not only a firm favourite at the club but also one of their most consistent players.

CHAMPIONS' LEAGUE
Group A

Wednesday 17th March 1993
Vélodrome Stadium, Marseilles

OLYMPIQUE MARSEILLE 6 CSKA MOSKVA 0

Half-time 3-0 *Attendance* 30,000

		Goals				Goals
1	Fabien BARTHEZ			1	Aleksandr GUTEEV	
2	Jocelyn ANGLOMA			2	Sergei MAMCHUR	
3	Eric DI MECO			3	Sergei KOLOTOVKIN	
4	Basile BOLI			4	Dmitry BYSTROV	
5	Franck SAUZEE ‡	5 (pen), 34, 49		5	Oleg MALYUKOV	
6	Marcel DESAILLY	79		6	Yury ANTONOVICH	
7	Jean-Philippe DURAND			7	Valery MINKO	
8	Alen BOKSIC			8	Denis MASHKARIN †	
9	Rudi VÖLLER †			9	Oleg SERGEEV	
10	Abedi PELE	43		10	Yevgeny BUSHMANOV ‡	
11	Didier DESCHAMPS			11	Ilshat FAYZULLIN	

Substitutes

Jean-Marc FERRERI †65   71
Jean-Jacques EYDELIE ‡67

Substitutes

Dmitry KORSAKOV †40
Aleksandr GRISHIN ‡46

Referee Serge MUHMENTHALER (Switzerland)

FACTFILE

● *Marseille's victory was their 14th in succession on home soil in European competition.*

● *CSKA went back to Barcelona, scene of their glorious second-round triumph, to prepare for this match. And history repeated itself in a warm-up game when they beat Barcelona's 'other club', Español, by the same 3-2 margin that they had knocked out the Champions' Cup holders!*

● *The 6-0 scoreline was the biggest victory margin at this stage of the competition since UEFA revamped the quarter and semi-finals in 1991/92.*

● *Rudi Völler, back from injury, was also in the Roma side which knocked CSKA out of the Cup-winners' Cup the previous season.*

● *Jocelyn Angloma*

Russians taken apart by mighty Marseille

In the aftermath of Marseille's disappointing draw in Berlin a fortnight earlier, coach Raymond Goethals had made no bones about the fact that he felt CSKA were " by far the weakest of our opponents in Group A.". The result on that occasion had not borne him out, but in the Vélodrome, on a warm early spring evening that offered a complete contrast in climate to that of the first game, he hardly needed to add another word to his assessment.

Marseille destroyed their opponents with an ease that was barely credible at this stage of the competition. Anybody watching from Barcelona could scarcely have imagined that this was the same CSKA team which had humbled their heroes at the Nou Camp a few months earlier. The Russians had been forced to endure a seven-hour coach trip up from Catalonia before the game, and it showed in the weary way in which they began the game, conceding a penalty after just four minutes to give Marseille the early impetus they wanted.

Midfielder Franck Sauzée blasted home that spot-kick, and he had more to celebrate half an hour later when he fired in a fierce left-footer after an astute back-heel from Rudi Völler. Abedi Pelé made it 3-0 to the home side with the goal of the night soon afterwards and at half-time the match was all but over.

Still, Marseille were in no mood for mercy. Seeking to establish a healthy goal-difference should it prove useful later on in the competition, they subjected the Russians to more pressure in the second half. Sauzée completed his hat-trick with a perfectly-placed 25-yard drive in the 49th minute after the CSKA defence had allowed him all the time in the world to choose his target. Substitute Jean-Marc Ferreri made it 5-0 midway through the half when he headed in Durand's cross from what was probably an offside position. And defender Marcel Desailly, who had

not scored a goal at any level for more than five years, completed the rout with Marseille's sixth goal when he deflected in a Deschamps shot on the edge of the six-yard box.

● *Raymond Goethals*

The extent of Marseille's destruction was wonderful for their supporters, who now saw the gates to the final opening up before them. But as an advert for the new Champions' League, it certainly didn't win any new converts.

FRANCK SAUZEE
Olympique Marseille

Franck Sauzée's hat-trick against CSKA brought his total of European goals for Marseille to nine - the second-highest total of any Marseille player, although still some distance behind front-runner Jean-Pierre Papin, who scored 23 European goals in 29 matches during his time at the club. Sauzée's treble strike also crowned a marvellous season for the player, his best so far in a career which began in the French Second Division with Sochaux where he first gained recognition as a star of the French Under-21 team that won the European Championships in 1988. Sauzée spent two seasons at Marseille before he surprisingly moved to Monaco for the 1990/91 season. But the lure of success brought him back to 'OM' after just a year away. A dead-ball specialist with a fierce shot in either foot, he has now won over 30 caps for France and will be a key member of Gérard Houllier's squad if, as expected, they qualify for the World Cup Finals in the United States.

CHAMPIONS' LEAGUE
Group A

Wednesday 17th March 1993
Ibrox Stadium, Glasgow

RANGERS 2 CLUB BRUGGE KV 1

Half-time 1-0 *Attendance* 42,731

		Goals				Goals
1	Andy GORAM		1	Danny VERLINDEN		
2	Scott NISBET	75	2	László DISZTL		
3	Neil MURRAY		3	Franky VAN DER ELST		
4	Richard GOUGH		4	Gert VERHEYEN		
5	Dave McPHERSON		5	Vital BORKELMANS		
6	John BROWN ❑		6	Stéphane VAN DER HEYDEN		
7	Trevor STEVEN		7	Peter CREVE ❑		
8	Stuart McCALL		8	Rudy COSSEY		
9	Ally McCOIST		9	Lorenzo STAELENS		55
10	Mark HATELEY ■		10	Marc SCHAESSENS †		
11	Ian DURRANT †	39	11	Daniel AMOKACHI		

Substitute

Davy HAGEN †87

Substitute

Tomasz DZIUBINSKI †76

Referee Ryszard WÓJCIK (Poland)

FACTFILE

● In order to try and avoid any crowd disturbances of the type which had occurred in the previous away match in Marseille, Club Bruges refused to sell any tickets to their supporters for this match.

● Mark Hateley became the first player to be sent off in Group A and the second, after PSV's Adri van Tiggelen, in the Champions' League.

● As in the first match between these two sides, it was the away team which took the field in their traditional colours. Rangers, like Bruges a fortnight earlier, appeared before their own supporters in unfamiliar white shirts.

● Lorenzo Staelens' equaliser was his seventh goal in Europe and his fourth away from home.

Fluke goal wins it for 10-man Rangers

It was becoming something of a tradition for Rangers that all their big European matches at Ibrox should be accompanied by torrential rain. It had poured throughout against both Leeds and Marseille and now, for the visit of Bruges, the skies opened again, leaving the pitch wet and uneven and hardly in the best condition for a game of such importance.

Both teams needed a win to maintain their hopes of staying the distance with Marseille, although Bruges boss Hugo Broos admitted beforehand that he would not be displeased with a draw. Ally McCoist, still searching for his first Champions' League goal, might have put Rangers in front early on but for some fine goalkeeping by Verlinden, whilst Bruges striker Gert Verheyen wasted a glorious opportunity at the other end.

Just before half-time Rangers sent the crowd into raptures with a superb goal by Ian Durrant. A brilliant first-time pass by Trevor Steven, who, like Durrant, had missed the game in Bruges, put the Rangers number 11 through and his shot was both powerful and accurate enough to beat Verlinden at the near post. But the joy of the crowd did not last long. Four minutes later an off-the-ball scuffle between Bruges defender Rudy Cossey and Rangers striker Mark Hateley resulted in a red card for the former England international. If the dismissal of Hateley seemed fair enough given that he had raised an arm at his opponent, it was illogical and unjust that Cossey should get off scot free. After all, it was because he had had his arm around Hateley's neck that the Rangers player swung out at him.

So Rangers had to play the entire second half with a man short. And their plight was worsened when, just ten minutes into the half, Bruges got an equaliser. Van der Heyden's pass found a way through the Rangers defence and Staelens slid the ball under Goram. It seemed now that there was no way back for Rangers, but with 15 minutes of the game left, they scored a quite amazing goal to go ahead once again. Right-back Scott Nisbet took a swing at the ball out on the right, it cannoned up into the air off Van der Heyden's foot and as it landed in the penalty area, goalkeeper Verlinden seemed likely to deal with it comfortably. But because of the spin imparted by Van der Heyden's boot, the ball shot up off the turf almost at a right-angle, deceiving Verlinden as it bounced over his head into the goal.

Ian Ferguson had scored with a similar efort against CSKA Moscow two games earlier, and now Rangers had gained their second Champions' League victory with an even odder goal. The feeling was beginning to grow in Glasgow that this might just be Rangers' year after all!...

IAN DURRANT
Rangers

When Ian Durrant returned to football in 1991 after almost three years out of the game with a knee injury, Rangers fans breathed a collective sigh of relief. For it meant that one of the finest young talents in Scotland had not been lost forever, as had frequently been feared during his extended absence. Durrant made a slow, gentle recovery during the 1991/92 season, but by the beginning of the 92/93 campaign he was fit and raring to go. His season began well with goals against Celtic and Aberdeen at Ibrox and a winning strike in Europe against Lyngby. Also, there was his return to the Scottish national team for the first time in exactly four years when he took the field as a substitute in Switzerland. Against Bruges, the 26-year-old midfielder was the star of the show. He showed admirable composure in giving Rangers an early lead and, with Mark Hateley off the field for the second half, continued to make life difficult for the Belgian defence with his intelligent support play up front for Ally McCoist.

CHAMPIONS' LEAGUE
Group A

Wednesday 7th April 1993
Olympia Stadium, Berlin

CSKA MOSKVA 1 CLUB BRUGGE KV 2

Half-time 1-1 *Attendance* 2,000

		Goals			Goals
1	Yevgeny PLOTNIKOV		1	Danny VERLINDEN	
2	Aleksei GUSHIN		2	Rudy COSSEY	
3	Sergei KOLOTOVKIN		3	Franky VAN DER ELST	
4	Denis MASHKARIN		4	Gert VERHEYEN	86
5	Oleg MALYUKOV		5	Vital BORKELMANS	
6	Yevgeny BUSHMANOV		6	Stéphane VAN DER HEYDEN ❑	
7	Valery MINKO		7	Peter CREVE	
8	Dmitry KORSAKOV ‡		8	Tomasz DZIUBINSKI †	
9	Vasily IVANOV †		9	Lorenzo STAELENS	
10	Oleg SERGEEV	19	10	Marc SCHAESSENS	43
11	Ilshat FAYZULLIN		11	Daniel AMOKACHI ‡	

Substitutes

Yury ANTONOVICH †32

Sergei MAMCHUR ‡74

Substitutes

Foeke BOOY †46

Dominique VAN MAELE ‡89

Referee Angelo AMENDOLIA (Italy)

FACTFILE

● *Oleg Sergeev's 19th-minute strike was only the second goal scored by CSKA Moscow in the Champions' League. Both of them had come in Berlin.*

● *Bruges made only one change from their previous starting line-up against Rangers in Glasgow, bringing in Polish striker Tomasz Dziubinski for Hungarian defender László Disztl.*

● *Bruges midfielder Stéphane Van der Heyden's yellow card (harshly awarded for a supposed foul on Korsakov) was his fourth of the competition. It meant that he had to miss the next game against Marseille - his third suspension of the campaign!*

● *Oleg Sergeev*

Late header wins it for Bruges

A virtually empty, rain-soaked Olympic Stadium in Berlin was the scene for Group A's 'other match' as Marseille and Rangers fought it out for a place in the Champions' Cup final down in the south of France.

Apart from the fact that a sizeable amount of money was still on offer, the confrontation between the group's third and fourth-placed teams was a non-event. Neither side maintained a competitive interest in the tournament. It was simply a matter of turning up to fulfil fixture obligations and collect the cash.

For much of the game it looked as if the £200,000 prize money would be shared equally. CSKA Moscow, once again forfeiting home advantage, put on their best performance of the Champions' League so far and thrilled their modest contingent of supporters in the barely visible crowd by taking a surprise lead in the 19th minute. But Bruges equalised just before half-time and it was only four minutes from the end of full-time that the Belgians stole a winner to complete a Champions' League double over the former Soviet Army side.

The opener came from Oleg Sergeev, the only international in the CSKA line-up. He turned brilliantly to shake off his marker Cossey in the penalty area before slotting the ball past Verlinden with his left foot to give CSKA the lead. There were a number of opportunities for Bruges to get back into the game before the interval. Most of them fell the way of muscular striker Gert Verheyen, but his finishing left a lot to be desired. First he sent a header sailing over the bar, then he hit the post from close in after a defensive error from Kolotovkin. It was another blunder by the CSKA left-back, however, which led to Bruges's equaliser two minutes before the break. In attempting to head clear a Borkelmans cross, Kolotovkin could only nudge the ball to the edge of the penalty area where Marc Schaessens was waiting to drive it back across Plotnikov into the far corner.

There were few moments of drama in the second half. Verheyen had one great chance to put his team in front when sent clean through the middle. But his composure was lacking and Plotnikov managed to save with his legs. Verheyen's evening of frustration was to come to an end, though, late in the game. After a free-kick had been hammered into the wall, the ball was worked back into the danger area by Van der Elst and Schaessens, and Verheyen, with visible relief, headed in from five yards out. The Russians might have had a case for offside, but the goal stood and Bruges were the victors.

GERT VERHEYEN
Club Brugge KV

The match against CSKA Moscow was so close to being a nightmare for Bruges striker Gert Verheyen. Three clear chances were spurned by him before he redeemed himself with the winning header shortly before the end. The 22-year-old was a late addition to the Bruges squad at the start of their Champions' Cup campaign. Surplus to requirements at Anderlecht, where he had scored just three league goals in four seasons as a second-choice midfielder, Verheyen moved to the reigning Belgian champions just before the start of the 92/93 season and quickly settled in as a striker, becoming the club's most reliable goalscorer both in domestic competition and in Europe, where he netted three goals in the first two rounds against Maccabi Tel-Aviv and FK Austria.

Wednesday 7th April 1993
Vélodrome Stadium, Marseilles

OLYMPIQUE MARSEILLE 1 RANGERS 1

Half-time 1-0 *Attendance* 46,000

		Goals				Goals
1	Fabien BARTHEZ		1	Andy GORAM		
2	Jocelyn ANGLOMA		2	Stuart McCALL		
3	Eric DI MECO ❑		3	David ROBERTSON †		
4	Basile BOLI		4	Richard GOUGH		
5	Franck SAUZEE	16	5	Dave McPHERSON		
6	Marcel DESAILLY ❑		6	John BROWN		
7	Jean-Jacques EYDELIE		7	Trevor STEVEN		
8	Alen BOKSIC ❑		8	Ian FERGUSON		
9	Rudi VÖLLER		9	Ally McCOIST ❑		
10	Abedi PELE		10	Ian DURRANT		52
11	Didier DESCHAMPS		11	Pieter HUISTRA ‡		

Substitutes

Substitutes

Neil MURRAY †53 ❑

Gary McSWEGAN ‡79

Referee Mario VAN DER ENDE (Holland)

FACTFILE

● *Trevor Steven, the Rangers midfielder, was playing against his old club. He scored three goals in 28 French League appearances for Marseille during the 1991/92 season.*

● *Both teams went into the match having registered important domestic victories the previous weekend. Marseille had won 2-0 away to Saint-Etienne in the French League while Rangers had beaten Hearts in the semi-finals of the Scottish Cup.*

● *Franck Sauzee's goal made him top scorer in the Champions' League, taking his total to five, one ahead of Milan's Marco van Basten.*

● *Rangers became the first visitors in 15 matches to deny Marseille victory on their own ground in European competition.*

● *Trevor Steven*

Draw leaves qualification wide open

"Winner takes all" was how this match was billed. Should either team gain a victory, they would be mathematically certain of reaching the Champions' Cup final in Munich. The Champions' League rules stipulated that if two sides finished with the same number of points in the final table, the deciding factor would be the results of the matches played between the two clubs concerned. As the first meeting had ended 2-2 in Glasgow, the winner of this encounter in Marseille would not only have a two-point lead going into the final game, but would also have three points out of four against their only challengers - a decisive advantage.

Marseille were most people's pre-match favourites. Not just because their home record in Europe was so impressive. But also because they were able to field a full-strength side - no injuries or suspensions - while Rangers were forced to do without one of their most important players, striker Mark Hateley, sent off in the previous encounter with Bruges.

With so much at stake, there was bound to be a lot of tension on the field, and that showed in the early exchanges. Four players were booked in the first half as the Dutch referee struggled to maintain his authority. The home side had more of the play, and they deserved their half-time lead, given to them by Franck Sauzée in the 16th minute when he lashed in a right-footer after Robertson's needless concession of possession had allowed Rudi Völler a run at the Rangers defence.

Early in the second half Sauzée went close to extending Marseille's lead when his deftly struck free-kick hit the crossbar. But within a minute the Scottish champions were level. Steven's corner was not properly cleared and Ian Durrant rifled home a glorious right-footer for what he later described as "the most important goal of my career." For the remainder of the match Marseille continued to press forward in search of the winner, but the well-organised Rangers defence held firm. The Scots clearly felt that a 1-1 draw was a good result, even though another goal for them would have booked their passage into the final.

In reality, though, the result meant that qualification was still in Marseille's hands. If they won their final game in Bruges, then Rangers were helpless to do anything about it. The extra away goal that the French had scored in Glasgow was almost as good as an additional point, and although their task of winning in Bruges looked more difficult than Rangers' at home to CSKA Moscow, they still held the key to their own destiny.

RICHARD GOUGH
Rangers

Together with his defensive colleagues McPherson and Brown, Rangers captain Richard Gough ensured that his club's interest in the competition remained very much alive with a resounding display in the Vélodrome. The much-feared Marseille strike-force of Völler and Boksic, both of whom had been on target at Ibrox, barely got a look-in on this occasion, and that was due mainly to the know-how and big-match experience of the 60-times capped Scottish international. There is little doubt that Gough now ranks amongst the finest Scottish defenders of all time. He enjoyed considerable success during his formative years at Dundee United, including a Scottish championship victory, and since joining Rangers in 1987 after a brief flirtation with the English League at Tottenham Hotspur he has been a cornerstone of the club's recent triumphs under Graeme Souness and Walter Smith.

CHAMPIONS' LEAGUE
Group A

Wednesday 21st April 1993
Olympia Stadium, Bruges

CLUB BRUGGE KV 0 OLYMPIQUE MARSEILLE 1

Half-time 0-1 *Attendance* 23,000

		Goals				Goals
1	Danny VERLINDEN			1	Fabien BARTHEZ	
2	László DISZTL			2	Jocelyn ANGLOMA	
3	Rudy COSSEY ❑			3	Jean-Christophe THOMAS	
4	Gert VERHEYEN			4	Basile BOLI	
5	Vital BORKELMANS			5	Jean-Jacques EYDELIE	
6	Dominique VAN MAELE ‡			6	Marcel DESAILLY	
7	Peter CREVE			7	Jean-Marc FERRERI †	
8	Marc SCHAESSENS ❑			8	Alen BOKSIC	3
9	Lorenzo STAELENS †			9	Rudi VÖLLER ‡	
10	Tomasz DZIUBINSKI			10	Abedi PELE	
11	Daniel AMOKACHI			11	Didier DESCHAMPS	

Substitutes		*Substitutes*
Alex QUERTER †78		Franck SAUZEE †46
Pascal RENIER ‡83		Jean-Philippe DURAND ‡89

Referee Ion CRACIUNESCU (Romania)

FACTFILE

● *Marseille not only reached the final in Bruges. They also did it without incurring any red or yellow cards, meaning that the five players who started the match under threat of suspension - Boksic, Deschamps, Desailly, Pelé and Boli - were all available for the final.*
● *Marseille's victory enabled them to become the seventh French club to reach a European final.*
● *Alen Boksic's goal was his sixth of the competition, with exactly half of them coming against Bruges!*
● *Bruges had to make do without their influential captain Franky Van der Elst, injured and absent for the first time from the team's Champions' League campaign.*

● Franky Van der Elst

Lone Boksic goal sees Marseille through

In the end Alen Boksic's third-minute goal was sufficient to win the game and, irrespective of the simultaneous goings-on at Ibrox, send Marseille through to their second Champions' Cup final in three years. But how the French champions were made to sweat before referee Craciunescu blew the final whistle. For this was a match which Marseille should have sewn up long before the end. They created a whole host of chances, but the security they sought from a second goal would just not come their way and as the match gradually drew to its close the fear still remained that Bruges might just nick a late goal to deprive Raymond Goethals and his men of their place in Munich.

Marseille, needing to win to ensure qualification for the final, made no secret of their game plan right from the opening whistle. They tore upfield and with 100 seconds on the clock came very close to taking the lead when Boksic headed inches wide from a corner. A minute later, however, the Croatian found himself with another opportunity in front of goal, and this time he found the net. Bruges left-back Vital Borkelmans was twice at fault in the build-up to the goal. In fact, his attempts to clear the danger appeared so half-hearted as to suspect some sort of collusion. First he completely missed a header as the ball was lofted forward towards Rudi Völler. Then, as the German trod on the ball in his attempt to race clear, Borkelmans simply passed it back to the opposition in the shape of Jean-Marc Ferreri. He knocked it forward and Boksic, in his stride, hammered the ball unerringly against the stanchion in the far corner to put Marseille ahead.

The noise coming from the stands indicated that the Bruges fans expected their team to recover from this early setback and put up a fight, but the Bruges players' minds were evidently elsewhere. They showed little inclination to come forward and even when, for once, they did break clear of the disciplined Marseille defence at the end of the first half, Lorenzo Staelens, normally a cool finisher, could only blast high and wide into the stands.

Marseille, on the other hand, continued to create numerous opportunities to extend their advantage. Boksic twice rattled the woodwork in the second half. Then, later in the game, he spooned a glorious opportunity over the bar after a pass inside from Völler.

Raymond Goethals was angry at his team's failure to kill off the opposition, but he was ultimately as pleased as anybody else at the club that his team had made it again to the final. "We were without doubt the best team in the group" he said. Outside of Glasgow, there were few ready to disagree with him.

MARCEL DESAILLY
Olympique Marseille

Marcel Desailly was in a difficult predicament for this game. He was faced with the task of marking Bruges's most dangerous forward Daniel Amokachi out of the game while at the same time making sure that he did not go too far and get booked, which would have meant suspension from the final. In the event, he achieved both of his objectives and was roundly acknowledged as one of Marseille's real heroes of the night.

Desailly moved to Marseille at the beginning of the season from Nantes, where he had been a defensive stalwart for a number of years since making his French First Division debut as a 17-year-old in 1986. He originally joined as a sweeper to replace Benfica-bound Carlos Mozer, but with Bernard Casoni gradually falling out of favour, he began increasingly to take on man-marking responsibilities. A native of Ghana, he has nevertheless earned French Under-21 recognition and is a possible candidate for full international selection at the 1994 World Cup.

CHAMPIONS' LEAGUE
Group A

Wednesday 21st April 1993
Ibrox Stadium, Glasgow

RANGERS 0 CSKA MOSKVA 0

Half-time 0-0 *Attendance* 43,142

		Goals				Goals
1	Andy GORAM		1	Yevgeny PLOTNIKOV		
2	Stuart McCALL		2	Aleksei GUSCHIN		
3	David ROBERTSON		3	Sergei MAMCHUR		
4	Richard GOUGH		4	Denis MASHKARIN		
5	Dave McPHERSON		5	Oleg MALYUKOV		
6	John BROWN		6	Yevgeny BUSHMANOV		
7	Trevor STEVEN †		7	Valery MINKO ❏		
8	Ian FERGUSON		8	Dmitry KORSAKOV		
9	Ally McCOIST		9	Yury ANTONOVICH ❏		
10	Ian DURRANT		10	Oleg SERGEEV		
11	Pieter HUISTRA		11	Ilshat FAYZULLIN †		

Substitute

Gary McSWEGAN †81

Substitute

Yury DUDNIK †62

Referee Peter MIKKELSEN (Denmark)

FACTFILE

● *The goalless draw left Rangers eliminated from the competition but unbeaten in all ten of their Champions' Cup/League matches.*

● *This was the only one of 24 Champions' League matches to finish without a goal.*

● *This was the first time CSKA had kept a clean sheet in the competition since their opening first-round match in Iceland. Likewise, it was the first time that Rangers had failed to score in 10 European games.*

● *Yevgeny Plotnikov's selection meant that for the first time in the Champions' League CSKA Moscow had fielded the same goalkeeper for two matches in a row!*

● *Yevgeny Plotnikov*

Night of frustration for goalless Rangers

Rangers' highly impressive European campaign finished on a frustrating note as they failed to beat Group A whipping-boys CSKA Moscow before another full house at Ibrox.

Had Marseille lost in Bruges, the goalless draw would have taken Rangers through to meet Milan in the final. But with news of the French side's early goal filtering through to the players, the evening was always going to be an uphill struggle for Walter Smith's team. Not that they imagined for a moment that they would not defeat the Russians. Had Marseille themselves not put six goals past them in their home fixture?

Breaking down a packed defence, collective in its endeavour, is never the easiest of tasks at any level of football. But with more good fortune Rangers would surely have scored the one goal they needed to secure victory. They created a whole host of chances, but it was not to be their night. CSKA goalkeeper Yevgeny Plotnikov gave an outstanding performance, every bit as good as those of his predecessors Kharin and Guteev in previous games, and he was to deny Rangers time and again as the Scottish side lay siege to his goal for the bulk of the 90 minutes.

Ally McCoist, the prolific Rangers striker, still seeking his first Champions' League goal, had a particularly fraught evening. His adventures started in the first half with two off-target headers within the space of a minute, both from Pieter Huistra crosses, and continued after the interval when he failed to finish off at least another three gilt-edged opportunities.The closest Rangers otherwise came to breaking the deadlock came just after halftime when Trevor Steven hit the crossbar and in the very last minute when Plotnikov saved brilliantly from John Brown, Gough had a shot blocked and Durrant's chip was cleared off the line.

CSKA might even have scored themselves near the end as Rangers poured everything into attack. But Andy Goram, recently acclaimed as the Scottish Player of the Year, lived up to his reputation by making two important saves to deny the Russians' best outfield player, Oleg Sergeev.

And so it ended goalless. CSKA were delighted with the point - their first away from home in the Champions' League - while Rangers could gain some consolation from the fact that even if they had put 10 goals past Plotnikov, Marseille's victory in Belgium would still have consigned them to the runners-up spot.

ALLY McCOIST
Rangers

Rarely, if ever, could Ally McCoist have experienced such a soul-destroying evening as he did against CSKA. Seeking to score his 50th goal of the season for Rangers, as well as attempting to equal the club record of goals in Europe held by '60s star Ralph Brand, the 30-year-old Scottish international striker could only draw his fifth successive blank in the Champions' League. McCoist's failure to score against CSKA also meant that his only European goals of the season had been scored against British opponents, namely Leeds United, adding further fuel to the fire concerning his ability to cut it against top-class foreign opposition. At domestic level, though, McCoist has no equal. Scottish football has rarely seen a striker with such lethal opportunism in front of goal, and his goalscoring exploits in the last two seasons have made an enormous contribution to Rangers' amazing trophy haul.

Group A Review

CHAMPIONS' LEAGUE GROUP A RESULTS

Club Brugge KV	CSKA Moskva	1-0
Rangers	Olympique Marseille	2-2
Olympique Marseille	Club Brugge KV	3-0
CSKA Moskva	Rangers	0-1
CSKA Moskva	Olympique Marseille	1-1
Club Brugge KV	Rangers	1-1
Olympique Marseille	CSKA Moskva	6-0
Rangers	Club Brugge KV	2-1
CSKA Moskva	Club Brugge KV	1-2
Olympique Marseille	Rangers	1-1
Club Brugge KV	Olympique Marseille	0-1
Rangers	CSKA Moskva	0-0

CHAMPIONS' LEAGUE GROUP A FINAL TABLE

		Pd	W	D	L	F	A	Pts
1	OLYMPIQUE MARSEILLE	6	3	3	0	14	4	9
2	RANGERS	6	2	4	0	7	5	8
3	CLUB BRUGGE KV	6	2	1	3	5	8	5
4	CSKA MOSKVA	6	0	2	4	2	11	2

CHAMPIONS' LEAGUE GROUP A GOALSCORERS

5 Franck SAUZEE (Olympique Marseille)
4 Alen BOKSIC (Olympique Marseille)
2 Abedi PELE (Olympique Marseille)
  Ian DURRANT (Rangers)
1 VÖLLER, FERRERI, DESAILLY (Olympique Marseille)
  McSWEGAN, HATELEY, FERGUSON, HUISTRA, NISBET (Rangers)
  AMOKACHI, DZIUBINSKI, STAELENS, SCHAESSENS,
  VERHEYEN (Club Brugge KV)
  FAYZULLIN, SERGEEV (CSKA Moskva)

CHAMPIONS' LEAGUE GROUP A PLAYER APPEARANCES

OLYMPIQUE MARSEILLE

	Pos	Apps(subs)	Gls
Jocelyn ANGLOMA	D	6	
Fabien BARTHEZ	G	6	
Alen BOKSIC	A	6	4
Basile BOLI	D	4	
Bernard CASONI	D	3	
Marcel DESAILLY	D	6	1
Didier DESCHAMPS	M	6	
Eric DI MECO	D	5	
Igor DOBROVOLSKY	A	1	
Jean-Philippe DURAND	M	1 (4)	
Jean-Jacques EYDELIE	D	4 (2)	
Jean-Marc FERRERI	M	1 (2)	1
Franck SAUZEE	M	5 (1)	5
Abedi PELE	M	6	2
Jean-Christophe THOMAS	D	2	
Rudi VÖLLER	A	4	1

RANGERS

	Pos	Apps(subs)	Gls
John BROWN	D	6	
Ian DURRANT	M	5	2
Ian FERGUSON	M	3	1
Andy GORAM	G	6	
Richard GOUGH	D	4	
David HAGEN	M	(1)	
Mark HATELEY	A	4	1
Pieter HUISTRA	M	3	1
Stuart McCALL	M	6	
Ally McCOIST	A	5	
Dave McPHERSON	D	6	
Gary McSWEFGAN	A	(3)	1
Aleksei MIKHAILICHENKO	M	3	
Neil MURRAY	D	3 (1)	
Scott NISBET	D	2	1
Steven PRESSLEY	D	(2)	
David ROBERTSON	D	5	
Trevor STEVEN	M	5	

CLUB BRUGGE KV

	Pos	Apps(subs)	Gls
Daniel AMOKACHI	A	6	1
Vital BORKELMANS	D	6	
Foeke BOOY	A	1 (1)	
Rudy COSSEY	D	5 (1)	
Peter CREVE	M	4 (1)	
László DISZTL	D	4	
Tomasz DZIUBINSKI	A	5 (1)	1
Pascal PLOVIE	D	2	
Alex QUERTER	D	1 (2)	
Pascal RENIER	D	(1)	
Marc SCHAESSENS	M	3	1
Lorenzo STAELENS	M	6	1
Franky VAN DER ELST	M	5	
Stéphane VAN DER HEYDEN	M	3	
Dominique VAN MAELE	M	1 (1)	
Gert VERHEYEN	A	6	1
Danny VERLINDEN	G	6	
Claude VERSPAILLE	M	2 (1)	

CSKA MOSKVA

	Pos	Apps(subs)	Gls
Yury ANTONOVICH	M	3 (1)	
Yevgeny BUSHMANOV	M	6	
Dmitry BYSTROV	D	4	
Yury DUDNIK	M	(2)	
Ilshat FAYZULLIN	A	6	1
Sergei FOKIN	D	1	
Aleksandr GRISHIN	M	2 (2)	
Aleksei GUSHIN	D	3	
Aleksandr GUTEEV	G	2 (1)	
Vasily IVANOV	D	2 (1)	
Dmitry KHARIN	G	1	
Mikhail KOLESNIKOV	M	1	
Sergei KOLOTOVKIN	D	5	
Dmitry KORSAKOV	A	3 (3)	
Oleg MALYUKOV	D	6	
Sergei MAMCHUR	D	3 (1)	
Denis MASHKARIN	D	4	
Valery MINKO	M	5	
Yevgeny PLOTNIKOV	G	3	
Oleg SERGEEV	A	6	1

CHAMPIONS' LEAGUE
Group B

Wednesday 25th November 1992
Das Antas Stadium, Oporto

FC PORTO 2 PHILIPS SV 2

Half-time 1-1 *Attendance* 34,000

		Goals				Goals
1	VÍTOR BAÍA		1	Hans VAN BREUKELEN		
2	JOÃO PINTO		2	Edward LINSKENS		
3	ANDRÉ		3	Adri VAN TIGGELEN ▫ ■		
4	ALOÍSIO		4	Erwin KOEMAN ‡		
5	JOSÉ CARLOS ▫	75	5	Jan HEINTZE †		
6	RUI FILIPE		6	Gheorghe POPESCU		
7	JAIME MAGALHÃES ▫	34	7	Juul ELLERMAN		
8	Emil KOSTADINOV		8	Gerald VANENBURG		
9	DOMINGOS		9	ROMÁRIO de Souza Faria	43, 59	
10	SEMEDO †		10	Wim KIEFT		
11	JORGE COUTO		11	Arthur NUMAN		

Substitute		*Substitutes*
TOZÉ †62		Ernest FABER †33
		Jerry DE JONG ‡78

Referee Antonio MARTIN NAVARRETE (Spain)

FACTFILE

● FC Porto number three André was a late replacement for original choice Bandeirinha, who injured himself during the pre-match warm-up.

● Both teams went into the match as leaders of their own domestic leagues.

● Romário's two goals were his fifth and sixth of the competition, enabling him to join Marco van Basten - four-goal hero for Milan the same evening - as the competition's top goalscorer.

● The only previous meeting of these two teams was in the 1988/89 Champions' Cup. Porto won their home game 2-0 but were eliminated by the then holders PSV after losing the first match 5-0 in Eindhoven.

● *Hans van Breukelen*

All-square between Milan's main rivals

Milan were clear favourites to win Group B and qualify for the Champions' Cup final, but FC Porto and PSV, both recent winners of the competition, were the two teams expected to give the Italian side a run for their money.

PSV had lost their previous away match - a Dutch League game in Utrecht - and there were early signs of discomfort in this encounter too. Veteran goalkeeper Hans van Breukelen, one of five survivors from the 1988 Champions' Cup-winning side in the PSV starting line-up, looked decidedly shaky in the opening minutes as Porto began to dominate. But he did make one fine save from Bulgarian striker Emil Kostadinov before the home side went ahead with a speculative 25-yard drive from long-serving midfielder Jaime Magalhães.

This setback stirred PSV, and especially chief goalgetter Romário, into action at the other end and before half-time they were level. The Brazilian had just clipped one opportunity over the bar before he stretched out a leg in the penalty area to meet a left-wing cross and prod the ball past 'keeper Vítor Baía.

Prior to this match Porto had established a remarkable record by going more than a year with a 100% record, all competitions included, in the Das Antas stadium - Tottenham Hotspur had been the last team to deny them victory there in the previous season's Cup-winners' Cup - but that record looked to be seriously threatened when Romário scored a second goal for PSV. It was a classic dead-ball strike from the Brazilian. One step and a nonchalant chip into the near corner of the net. But there was considerable debate as to whether the free-kick should have been awarded in the first place.

Stung into action by what they perceived as an injustice, the Portuguese champions went on to dominate completely the last third of the game. A couple of ambitious penalty claims were denied them before the Spanish referee eventually decided to take pity. A challenge outside the box by Adri van Tiggelen earned the PSV defender a red card for his second bookable offence - his first yellow card had been for a perfectly fair tackle! - and from the resulting free-kick central defender José Carlos saw his shot cannon off the heel of PSV's Gheorghe Popescu and into the net past the helpless Van Breukelen.

Porto's tails were up now and there was plenty of late drama as first Tozé, the substitute, hit a post and then Popescu spectacularly cleared the ball off the line. But 2-2 remained the score, and it was a result which, judging by the reaction to the final whistle, evidently suited the Dutch more than the Portuguese.

ROMÁRIO
Philips SV

Romário's two goals in Oporto made him PSV's hero for the second European match in a row. His hat-trick against AEK had ensured the Dutch champions' presence in the Champions' League, and now his double strike against FC Porto enabled them to take a very valuable point from one of their most difficult fixtures in the group.

Although his five-year spell at PSV has been a never-ending saga of dispute and controversy, Romário has always been allowed to get away with his off-field indiscretions because of his phenomenal goal-scoring record. His average of a goal a game since he joined PSV from Brazilian club Vasco da Gama in 1988 speaks for itself. The Brazilian was bought for his goals after he had finished as the top scorer in the 1988 Olympic Games, and he has always delivered. Top scorer in the Dutch League for each of his first three seasons, he is sure to go down in history as one of the most successful foreign players ever to have appeared in the Eredivisie.

CHAMPIONS' LEAGUE
Group B

Wednesday 25th November 1992
Giuseppe Meazza Stadium, Milan

MILAN 4 IFK GÖTEBORG 0

Half-time 1-0 *Attendance* 60,000

Goals

Goals

1	Francesco ANTONIOLI		1	Thomas RAVELLI ❑
2	Mauro TASSOTTI		2	Magnus JOHANSSON
3	Daniele MASSARO		3	Tore PEDERSEN
4	Demetrio ALBERTINI		4	Ola SVENSSON
5	Alessandro COSTACURTA †		5	Pontus KÅMARK
6	Franco BARESI		6	Peter ERIKSSON
7	Gianluigi LENTINI ‡		7	Stefan REHN †
8	Frank RIJKAARD		8	Håkan MILD
9	Marco VAN BASTEN 34,53 (pen),61,62		9	Mikael NILSSON
10	Jean-Pierre PAPIN		10	Thomas ANDERSSON
11	Stefano ERANIO		11	Johnny EKSTRÖM

Substitutes

Substitute

Stefano NAVA †67

Fredrik LEKSELL †68

Marco SIMONE ‡73

Referee Frans VAN DEN WIJNGAERT (Belgium)

FACTFILE

● *Marco van Basten had scored four goals once before for Milan in a European match - against Bulgarian club Vitosha Sofia in the first round of the 1988/89 Champions' Cup, which Milan went on to win.*

● *The last of Van Basten's four goals was his 18th for Milan in Europe - two short of José Altafini's club record - and his 29th in total.*

● *IFK Gothenburg's last visit to Milan had been in the quarter-finals of the 1986/87 UEFA Cup when they drew 1-1 against Inter to win the tie on away goals. They eventually went on to win the competition for the second time in six years.*

● *Milan's victory maintained their 100% record in the competition after five matches.*

Van Basten brilliance buries the Swedes

Marco van Basten went a step closer towards being proclaimed as the undisputed best player in the world after this magnificent individual display in Milan's opening Champions' League encounter. The Dutchman was in masterful form, scoring all four of his team's goals as the tournament favourites demolished Group B outsiders FK Gothenburg to take an early grip on their group.

The Swedish side came to the San Siro with nothing to lose. They had already surpassed their expectations by reaching this stage of the competition. Nobody believed they had a prayer of upsetting the Italian champions on their own turf, especially as they had just finished the Swedish domestic season in very disappointing form, failing even to claim a berth for the 1993/94 European competitions.

But it was Gothenburg who actually had the best of the early chances. European Cup veteran Johnny Ekström danced his way down the left and offered an inviting opportunity for Peter Eriksson to stun the great stadium into silence. But the midfielder hurried his shot and the ball sailed harmlessly over the bar. That was the closest they would get to scoring, for the remainder of the game belonged almost exclusively to Milan.

Jean-Pierre Papin was the first of the home side's world-class strike-force to figure prominently. First he smashed a brilliant effort against the inside of the post and then he saw another effort saved by Thomas Ravelli. But the night belonged not to Papin, but to Marco van Basten.

The Dutchman's first goal was a gem. He superbly finished off a glorious one-touch move involving Papin and Eranio, scooping the ball high into the net as he fell under a challenge from a Swedish defender. His second was not so spectacular. A penalty kick, almost saved by Ravelli, which had been awarded after a foul on Van Basten himself by Pedersen. But the hat-trick goal was a classic. Eranio pulled the ball back from the right and Van Basten, back to goal, connected perfectly with his acrobatic scissors-kick to send it soaring, via Ravelli's fingertips again, into the Gothenburg net. A minute later Van Basten had another when he sneaked in and rounded Ravelli to make the most of an unfortunate ricochet in the Swedish defence.

Gothenburg simply had no answer to all this. They barely broke out of their own half for the entire second half and were ultimately happy just to restrict the Italians to four goals. Milan, on the other hand, had served notice to everybody watching that it would take something special to stop them going on to lift the trophy.

MARCO VAN BASTEN
Milan

This stunning four-goal display was the deciding factor in taking Marco van Basten to his record-equalling third European Footballer of the Year crown. Barcelona's Christo Stoichkov and Ajax's Dennis Bergkamp had looked equally strong contenders up until this game, but Van Basten's magnificent performance, highlighted by the truly spectacular third goal, swung the floating voters in his favour.

Van Basten joined Milan from Ajax in 1987 just after he had captained the Dutch side to the European Cup-winners' Cup, scoring the winning goal in the final against Lokomotive Leipzig. He scored 127 goals in 133 league games for Ajax and although that ratio has inevitably gone down during his time in Italy, Van Basten can still claim a marvellously consistent goalscoring record. He has twice been Serie A's top scorer (1989/90 and 1991/92) and has now scored over 100 goals for Milan.

CHAMPIONS' LEAGUE
Group B

Wednesday 9th December 1992
Nye Ullevi Stadium, Gothenburg

IFK GÖTEBORG 1 FC PORTO 0

Half-time 0-0 *Attendance* 18,000

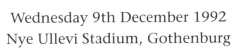

		Goals				Goals
1	Thomas RAVELLI		1	VÍTOR BAÍA		
2	Magnus JOHANSSON		2	JOÃO PINTO		
3	Pontus KÅMARK		3	BANDEIRINHA		
4	Ola SVENSSON		4	ALOÍSIO		
5	Mikael NILSSON		5	FERNANDO COUTO		
6	Peter ERIKSSON	87	6	ANTÓNIO CARLOS ❏ †		
7	Stefan REHN		7	JORGE COUTO		
8	Håkan MILD		8	Emil KOSTADINOV		
9	Patrik BENGTSSON †		9	DOMINGOS		
10	Thomas ANDERSSON		10	SEMEDO		
11	Johnny EKSTRÖM		11	ANDRÉ		
	Substitute			*Substitute*		
	Stefan LINDQVIST †72			TOZÉ †65		

Referee Jozef MARKO (Czechoslovakia)

FACTFILE

● *This was the first ever meeting of two clubs which, between them, had played over 200 European matches.*

● *Both Gothenburg and FC Porto were winners of European trophies in 1986/87. But while the Swedes retained not one single survivor from their UEFA Cup-winning side, Porto still had João Pinto and André from the side that beat Bayern Munich 2-1 in the Champions' Cup final in Vienna.*

● *While Porto, six points clear in the Portuguese league, looked odds on to qualify for the Champions' Cup again in 1993/94, Gothenburg, with the Swedish domestic season completed, had already failed to qualify for any of the three European competitions.*

● *João Pinto*

Late goal clinches victory for Gothenburg

UEFA's new Champions' League formula has many advocates. But this match was one for its critics. A conventional Cup tie would surely have brought more fire and ambition from two teams who seemed content with a share of the points and another £200,000 in their club kitty.

In the end, though, the match did have a winner. And, to considerable surprise, it was Gothenburg, humbled by Milan in their first encounter, who got the victory to put themselves in second place in the Group B table.

Just three minutes were left on the clock, with a goalless draw looking increasingly inevitable, when Peter Eriksson, the Gothenburg midfielder, galloped down the right-wing and into the Porto penalty area close to the goal line. From his position a cross seemed the only possible option. But instead he fired in a shot and watched with glee as the ball struck the goalkeeper's right foot and deflected into the net at the near post.

It was the decisive moment of a very disappointing match and enough to induce delirious acclaim from the 18,000 crowd, who were witnessing their first European match of the season in the new Ullevi Stadium, venue of the 1992 European Championship Final.

If either of the teams deserved victory, it was probably Gothenburg. Porto, for reasons best known to themselves, came simply to defend. The first half saw the Swedes get lots of bodies forward, but against one of the tightest defences in Europe they made very little impact. In fact the only clear-cut chance of the first 45 minutes fell to Eriksson, but his shot was blocked

after he had found himself free on the right side of the area. In the second half it was substitute Stefan Lindqvist who came closest to breaking the deadlock when he headed across the goal after good work by Rehn and Ekström.

Gothenburg took delight in their victory, but with Milan winning the same night in Eindhoven, this result virtually cleared the way for the Italian champions to reach the final with four games still left to play!

• *Stefan Lindqvist*

PETER ERIKSSON
IFK Göteborg

Peter Eriksson's late winner against FC Porto enabled IFK Gothenburg to end what had been a disappointing year for the club on a happy note. The Swedish champions of 1991 had finished only fifth in 1992 despite having arguably the best squad of players in the country.

For Eriksson, though, it had been a very good year, probably the best of his career. In addition to appearing in every one of IFK's matches from the start and scoring a career-best six goals in the process, he also earned a call-up to the Swedish national team and his first cap in a friendly against Tunisia. Unfortunately Eriksson did not make it into the European Championship squad - though his namesakes Lars and Jan did! - but his performances in Europe for Gothenburg have certainly brought him to the attention of Swedish coach Tommy Svensson and he is now seen as a reliable option on the right side of midfield if and when the likes of Ingesson and Limpar are unavailable.

CHAMPIONS' LEAGUE
Group B

Wednesday 9th December 1992
Philips Stadium, Eindhoven

PHILIPS SV 1 MILAN 2

Half-time 0-1 *Attendance* 27,500

		Goals			Goals
1	Hans VAN BREUKELEN		1	Sebastiano ROSSI	
2	Raymond BEERENS		2	Mauro TASSOTTI	
3	Ernest FABER		3	Paolo MALDINI	
4	Edward LINSKENS		4	Demetrio ALBERTINI	
5	Jan HEINTZE ❑		5	Alessandro COSTACURTA	
6	Gheorghe POPESCU		6	Franco BARESI	
7	Juul ELLERMAN †		7	Gianluigi LENTINI	
8	Gerald VANENBURG		8	Frank RIJKAARD	20
9	ROMÁRIO de Souza Faria ❑	66	9	Marco VAN BASTEN	
10	Wim KIEFT		10	Ruud GULLIT †	
11	Arthur NUMAN		11	Marco SIMONE ‡	63

Substitute			*Substitutes*	
Peter HOEKSTRA †38			Stefano ERANIO †60 ❑	
			Daniele MASSARO ‡89	

Referee Aleksei SPIRIN (Russia)

FACTFILE

● *Both teams played in change strips. PSV appeared in all blue, while Milan donned black shorts and socks to go with their usual red and black striped shirts.*

● *Match-winner Marco Simone was the only player in the Milan starting line-up who had not yet received full international recognition.*

● *Romário's goal was the first conceded by Milan in the competition. It was also the Brazilian's 15th goal in 15 European games for PSV.*

● *PSV's only previous encounter with Italian opposition in Europe was in the 1969/70 Cup-winners' Cup when, after two 1-0 home wins in their tie against Roma, they were eliminated by the drawing of lots!*

● *Gerald Vanenburg*

Milan pass first big test with flying colours

When the Champions' League draw was made, this looked to be the most difficult match for Milan. But in the event they won it at a canter. 2-1 was the final score, but the margin of victory could easily have been much greater.

Admittedly, PSV went into the match with problems at the back. Berry van Aerle and Jerry de Jong were injured and veteran man-marker Adri van Tiggelen was suspended after his controversial sending-off in the previous match against FC Porto. That left Romanian sweeper Gheorghe Popescu and Danish left-back Jan Heintze as the only players of any great experience in defence. Still, at least they did not have to face up to the brilliant Jean-Pierre Papin. He had been left out to allow Ruud Gullit to face his old club alongside fellow Dutchmen Frank Rijkaard and Marco van Basten.

On a pitch where an Italian national team featuring no fewer than seven Milan players had beaten Holland 3-2 in a friendly international earlier in the season, the visitors seemed very much at home. Long-range efforts from Simone and Albertini kept Hans van Breukelen on his toes, but the PSV 'keeper was beaten after just 19 minutes when Frank Rijkaard headed the ball back across him from Van Basten's centre to give Milan the lead. At the other end Romário was the only PSV forward to make an impression. He showed one glorious piece of skill to turn Baresi on the edge of the area and create a chance in the centre, but the other side of his character was in evidence shortly afterwards when he got himself booked for a deliberate hand-ball.

17 minutes into the second half Milan were 2-0 up. Rijkaard's measured through-ball was knocked into the danger area by Eranio for Marco Simone to drive in ferociously at the near post. That two-goal lead did not last long, though, as Romário pulled one back for PSV with a glorious individual effort three minutes later. Juggling the ball with his back to goal, he turned and whipped a brilliant right-foot shot into the roof of the net.

The remainder of the match was dominated by two controversial refereeing decisions. First Milan were denied a penalty when Van Basten's legs appeared to be caught by Beerens. But if that one was debatable, there was no question that Rijkaard handled the ball just inside the area when attempting to head the ball away from Romário moments later.

2-1 it remained, though, and Milan had a hugely significant victory under their belts. They were now the only team in either group to have won both of their Champions' League matches and were looking increasingly invincible with every game.

FRANK RIJKAARD
Milan

Frank Rijkaard certainly enjoyed his first club match in his native Holland for over five years. As well as scoring the opening goal for Milan he started the move that led to the second goal and was involved in just about all of his team's best moves. And all this despite playing with a badly bruised knee!
Rijkaard is widely considered to be one of the best players in Europe. Although he began his career, for both Ajax and Holland, in defence, he has matured into one of the most complete all-round midfielders in the game. Competitive and creative in equal measure, he has been one of the mainstays in the Milan success story of the past few years. Although he disgraced himself with a red card for spitting at the 1990 World Cup, and subsequently 'retired' from international football, he returned to the Dutch colours a year later and starred for the Oranje at the European Championships in 1992, just as he had done in the same competition four years earlier when Holland won the trophy.

CHAMPIONS' LEAGUE
Group B

Wednesday 3rd March 1993
Philips Stadium, Eindhoven

PHILIPS SV 1 IFK GÖTEBORG 3

Half-time 1-3 *Attendance* 27,500

		Goals			Goals
1	Hans VAN BREUKELEN		1	Thomas RAVELLI	
2	Berry VAN AERLE		2	Magnus JOHANSSON	
3	Adri VAN TIGGELEN		3	Joachim BJÖRKLUND	
4	Ernest FABER		4	Ola SVENSSON	
5	Jan HEINTZE		5	Pontus KÅMARK	
6	Gheorghe POPESCU		6	Peter ERIKSSON	
7	Arthur NUMAN	8	7	Stefan REHN	
8	Edward LINSKENS †		8	Håkan MILD	
9	ROMÁRIO de Souza Faria		9	Mikael NILSSON	20
10	Wim KIEFT		10	Mikael MARTINSSON †	
11	Peter HOEKSTRA		11	Johnny EKSTRÖM ‡	35, 45

Substitute

Gerald VANENBURG †46

Substitutes

Thomas ANDERSSON †67
Stefan LINDQVIST ‡89

Referee Keith BURGE (Wales)

FACTFILE

● *Two of the Gothenburg players were new signings during the winter break - Joachim Björklund, signed from Norwegian club Brann, and Mikael Martinsson, from Djurgården. A third newcomer, Magnus Erlingmark, was ineligible as he had already appeared in the UEFA Cup for Örebro.*

● *PSV's defeat came in a week when the Big Three in Holland all lost in Europe. Ajax went down 4-2 at Auxerre in the UEFA Cup, whilst Feyenoord lost 0-1 at home to Spartak Moscow in the Cup-winners' Cup.*

● *This was IFK Gothenburg's first competitive match of 1993. The Swedish League did not start for another five and a half weeks.*

● *Arthur Numan*

Dutch champions fall to shock defeat

There had been few surprises in the first eight Champions' League matches played before Christmas. But this result was to send shockwaves right across Europe. IFK Gothenburg had been expected merely to 'make up the numbers' in Group B while Porto and PSV slugged it out for second place behind the mighty Milan. But in Eindhoven, against all odds, Roger Gustafsson's side suddenly emerged as the only team that could possibly stop the Italian champions from reaching the final.

The result was as much about PSV's failings as Gothenburg's success. Nevertheless, the early moments of the game went distinctly to plan for Hans Westerhof's men. Arthur Numan shot them into an early lead with a scorching left-foot shot after some brilliant approach work from Romário, and they should have made it 2-0 moments later when poor defending by the Swedes left the Brazilian striker unmarked in the penalty area. But now Romário reverted to type, shooting himself when Kieft was free with an open goal a few yards to his right, and Ravelli deflected the ball wide of the post.

That was a crucial miss for PSV. Shortly afterwards the Swedes, who had not looked at all threatening, got themselves back into the game with a stunning individual goal from midfielder Mikael Nilsson. Receiving the ball on the edge of his own penalty area, he strode forward, played a one-two with a colleague, turned inside Van Aerle and unleashed a ferocious dipping right-foot shot that completely foxed Hans van Breukelen. The goal completely took the wind out of PSV's sails. They could not get it out of their system. And as they pondered on it for the remainder of the half, Gothenburg dealt them two further telling blows.

Mikael Martinsson, making his debut for Gothenburg, had just sent one opportunity wide of the target when he received the ball once again in a dangerous position. This time he laid it forward into the path of team-mate Håkan Mild, whose shot at goal hit the near post and rolled across the goalline before Johnny Ekström tapped it into the net. Ten minutes later the lanky number 11 scored again. This time he did all the work himself. Stefan Rehn sent him away down athe right-wing with a shrewd pass and Ekström used all his pace to stride past Van Tiggelen and clip the ball over Van Breukelen.

The home side were predictably, and justifiably, whistled off the field at the interval. They put up a better performance in the second half, but despite an abundance of openings could not score the goal that would have raised morale and got them back into the game.

JOHNNY EKSTRÖM
IFK Göteborg

With his wonderful pace and goalscoring instinct, Johnny Ekström is often regarded as one of the best counter-attacking players in Europe. Against PSV in Eindhoven he did much to enhance that reputation with two decisive goals, the second of which bore all of his trademarks.

When he first hit the headlines in IFK Gothenburg's 1985/86 Champions' Cup campaign - the club reached the semi-final before losing on penalties to Barcelona - it was expected that Ekström would develop into a major international star. But unconvincing spells in Italy (at Empoli), Germany (Bayern Munich) and France (Cannes) sent him back to Gothenburg in 1991, where he immediately made an impact again, helping the club to win the Swedish title with six goals in the championship play-offs. Ekström has over 40 caps for Sweden, but he was only ever used as a substitute at Euro '92 - very effectively, as it proved, in the final group game against England in Stockholm.

CHAMPIONS' LEAGUE
Group B

Wednesday 3rd March 1993
Das Antas Stadium, Oporto

FC PORTO 0 MILAN 1

Half-time 0-0 *Attendance* 55,000

		Goals				Goals
1	VÍTOR BAÍA		1	Sebastiano ROSSI ‡		
2	JOÃO PINTO		2	Mauro TASSOTTI		
3	RUI JORGE		3	Paolo MALDINI		
4	ALOÍSIO		4	Demetrio ALBERTINI		
5	FERNANDO COUTO		5	Alessandro COSTACURTA		
6	Ion TIMOFTE		6	Franco BARESI ❏		
7	JORGE COSTA ❏		7	Gianluigi LENTINI		
8	Emil KOSTADINOV ‡		8	Zvonimir BOBAN		
9	JORGE COUTO †		9	Jean-Pierre PAPIN ❏		72
10	SEMEDO		10	Ruud GULLIT		
11	PAULINHO SANTOS		11	Marco SIMONE †		

Substitutes

DOMINGOS †68

TONI ‡77

Substitutes

Alberigo EVANI †79

Carlo CUDICINI ‡88

Referee Aron SCHMIDHUBER (Germany)

FACTFILE

● *Milan's victory was their seventh in succession in the Champions' Cup - a record for an Italian club.*

● *Carlo Cudicini made his first-team debut for Milan when he came on late in the game to replace injured goalkeeper Sebastiano Rossi. But in two minutes of play, he did not touch the ball once.*

● *A week earlier Italy had defeated Portugal 3-1 in a World Cup qualifier in the same stadium. Five players from each club appeared in both games. Vítor Baía, João Pinto, Fernando Couto, Semedo and Domingos from Porto; Costacurta, Maldini, Tassotti, Albertini and Lentini from Milan.*

● *This was Milan's 57th consecutive game, all competitions included, without defeat.*

Papin wonder goal sets Milan up for final

If there had been any doubts beforehand, there were none now. Victory in Oporto, where the home side had not lost a match for almost two years, confirmed Milan's domination of Champions' League Group B and set the Italian champions up for an easy route to the final.

A large crowd packed the Das Antas stadium hoping to see their team take revenge for the Portuguese national team's World Cup defeat at the hands of Italy a week earlier. But if victory was what the fans sought, it appeared not to be the priority for the Porto management. Oddly enough, considering the team's position in the group, they sent out a team containing five defenders and just one man up front - Bulgarian striker, Emil Kostadinov. That meant no place for Domingos, the man who had led the Portuguese attack the previous week!

Milan, without injury victims Van Basten and Rijkaard, the heroes of their first two Champions' League games, still looked powerful in every department. And it was a measure of their strength in depth that they could still field nine full internationals.

A disappointing first-half should have ended with a goal for the Portuguese champions, but Semedo failed to connect properly with his header from a Timofte free-kick and the ball hit the ground before bouncing up over the bar. Porto's well-organised defence had restricted Milan's forwards to long-range shots in the first period, but by the second half they were beginning to find their range. First Tassotti sent a blockbuster just over the bar. Then Simone forced Vítor Baía into a spectacular save. But in the 72nd minute the Portuguese international goalkeeper was given no chance when Jean-Pierre Papin, latching onto Simone's head-

● Ion Timofte

er on the edge of the penalty area, sent a sensational right-foot volley soaring past him into the roof of the net.

It was a glorious strike, and one the little Frenchman almost repeated a few minutes later. This time Vítor Baía did get in the way, but by now Milan were on top and, despite the gallant work put in at the other end by Kostadinov, who gave Franco Baresi one of his most uncomfortable evenings for many a while, there was no way back into the match for the home side.

JEAN-PIERRE PAPIN
Milan

When Milan went to Eindhoven for their previous Champions' League match against PSV, Jean-Pierre Papin was not even included in the travelling party. At the time it seemed certain that his stay at Milan would not last long. Disaffected and angry at being left out of the team, the Frenchman was threatening to quit after less than half a season in Italy. But after Marco van Basten's operation at Christmas and his subsequent inactivity, the opportunity knocked for Papin, and the prolific French international striker grabbed it with both hands.
Papin's spectacular strike against Porto was his tenth goal in as many games for Milan. Suddenly there was no talk of quitting. The man who had scored goals for fun at Marseille - 134 in the French league, and 23 in Europe, to be precise - was back in business, and both player and management had never been happier!

CHAMPIONS' LEAGUE
Group B

Wednesday 17th March 1993
Nya Ullevi Stadium, Gothenburg

IFK GÖTEBORG 3 PHILIPS SV 0

Half-time 2-0 *Attendance* 35,225

		Goals			Goals
1	Thomas RAVELLI		1	Hans VAN BREUKELEN	
2	Magnus JOHANSSON		2	Berry VAN AERLE	
3	Joachim BJÖRKLUND		3	Adri VAN TIGGELEN ❑	
4	Ola SVENSSON		4	Erwin KOEMAN ❑	
5	Pontus KÅMARK		5	Jan HEINTZE	
6	Peter ERIKSSON †		6	Ernest FABER	
7	Stefan REHN		7	Edward LINSKENS	
8	Håkan MILD		8	Gerald VANENBURG	
9	Mikael NILSSON	1	9	ROMÁRIO de Souza Faria	
10	Mikael MARTINSSON	47	10	Arthur NUMAN †	
11	Johnny EKSTRÖM	45	11	Peter HOEKSTRA	
	Substitute			*Substitute*	
	Thomas ANDERSSON †57			KALUSHA Bwalya †12 ❑	

Referee Ion CRACIUNESCU (Romania)

FACTFILE

● *Johnny Ekström's goal was his fifth of the 92/93 competition and the 11th of his European career.*

● *Three players from each side participated in the 1992 European Championships. Ravelli, Björklund and Ekström from IFK; Van Breukelen, Van Aerle and Van Tiggelen from PSV. Gothenburg's Rehn and Nilsson were also members of the Swedish squad but did not play.*

● *PSV's defeat was their heaviest in European competition since French side Saint-Etienne thrashed them 6-0 in the second round of the 1979/80 UEFA Cup. It was their worst defeat in the Champions' Cup since Rapid Vienna beat them 6-1 in the first round of the inaugural competition back in 1955/56.*

● *Thomas Ravelli*

Gothenburg complete remarkable 'double'

On a night when the Swedish President of UEFA, Lennart Johansson, announced plans to merge the Champions' Cup and UEFA Cup into a single competition, recent double UEFA Cup winners IFK Gothenburg destroyed the 87/88 Champions' Cup victors PSV for the second time in a fortnight.

There was no escape for the Dutch champions after their humiliating reverse in Eindhoven two weeks earlier. Their chances of qualification had already disappeared with that 1-3 defeat, but in Gothenburg they showed a pitiful lack of determination to exact revenge. Granted, two of their most experienced players, Gheorghe Popescu and Wim Kieft, were out with injury and their goalscorer in the first encounter, Arthur Numan, joined them on the sidelines when he sustained a nasty ankle injury after just 12 minutes. But Hans Westerhof's men played without spirit. In the first 45 minutes they did not even manage a single shot on goal, and by the time they woke up in the second half, they were already 0-3 down.

The Swedes revival in Eindhoven had been initiated by a wonderful long-range goal from Mikael Nilsson, and here again it was the 24-year-old midfielder who opened the scoring with a picture-book strike after just 58 seconds. His immaculately taken free-kick bent like a banana around the PSV wall. Hans van Breukelen was totally deceived by the flight and Gothenburg were 1-0 up within a minute.

The home side dominated the remainder of the half. Johnny Ekström might have made it 2-0 when Håkan Mild intercepted Van Aerle's wayward pass and sent him through with a clear run on goal, but he fired just wide. Not long afterwards, however, the galloping forward made amends with almost a carbon copy of his second goal in the first match.

The match was sewn up early in the second half with a third goal for Gothenburg, new signing Mikael Martinsson getting his first goal for the club with a straightforward header from a deflected Peter Eriksson cross. And there should have been more. Van Breukelen was fortunate both to stay on the field and avoid conceding a penalty when he brought Martinsson down with a rash challenge. Although the foul was clearly inside the area, the Romanian referee awarded only a free-kick and the PSV 'keeper was not even cautioned. Still, with PSV failing to score, it mattered not to the Swedes. They now had six points from four games and were the only team still in a position to challenge group leaders Milan - the next visitors to the Ullevi!

MIKAEL NILSSON
IFK Göteborg

Mikael Nilsson's goal in Eindhoven had been spectacular enough. But the 30-yard free-kick with which he opened the scoring in this game was even more sensational. Most dead-ball experts have mastered the art of chipping the ball over a wall and into one of the top corners, but few have the ability to curve the ball around the wall, as Nilsson did in this instance, and still beat one of the world's most respected goal-keepers.
Nilsson has spent much of his career flitting backwards and forwards between defence and midfield. In his early days, when he joined Gothenburg as a teenager in 1987, he received strong recognition for his versatility. Then he was tried out at sweeper and it worked so well - back-to-back Swedish championships in 1990 and 1991 - that he began to fill the position in the Swedish national team as well. But when coach Tommy Svensson reverted to 4-4-2 for the European Championships, Nilsson suddenly found himself out of favour and, for most of 1992, out of form.

CHAMPIONS' LEAGUE
Group B

Wednesday 17th March 1993
Giuseppe Meazza Stadium, Milan

MILAN 1 FC PORTO 0

Half-time 1-0 *Attendance* 67,389

Goals

Goals

1	Sebastiano ROSSI			1	VÍTOR BAÍA	
2	Enzo GAMBARO			2	JOÃO PINTO ❑	
3	Paolo MALDINI			3	RUI JORGE	
4	Demetrio ALBERTINI ❑			4	ALOÍSIO	
5	Alessandro COSTACURTA			5	FERNANDO COUTO ❑	
6	Franco BARESI ❑			6	Ion TIMOFTE †	
7	Gianluigi LENTINI †			7	PAULINHO SANTOS	
8	Stefano ERANIO ❑	32		8	Emil KOSTADINOV	
9	Jean-Pierre PAPIN			9	JORGE COUTO ❑	
10	Alberigo EVANI			10	SEMEDO	
11	Marco SIMONE ‡			11	ANDRÉ ‡	

Substitutes

Daniele MASSARO †65

Substitutes

DOMINGOS †64

Dejan SAVICEVIC ‡77

BINO ‡78

Referee Philip DON (England)

FACTFILE

● *The absence of right-back Mauro Tassotti meant that not one Milan player had appeared in each of their eight Champions' Cup/League matches. On the contrary, three FC Porto players - Vítor Baía, João Pinto and Semedo - were ever-presents so far in their team's European campaign.*

● *Frenchman Jean-Pierre Papin was the only one of the six foreign players on Milan's books to start the game. Yugoslav international Dejan Savicevic came on as a late substitute to make his debut appearance in the competition for Milan.*

● *FC Porto's three permitted foreign players were Brazilian Aloísio, Romanian Timofte and Bulgarian Kostadinov.*

● *Aloísio*

Maximum points with minimum fuss

Milan consolidated their position at the head of the Group B table with this laboured 1-0 victory over FC Porto. It was without question their least convincing performance of the competition so far, although with virtually half of their first-choice team missing, they had to take some credit for extending their winning sequence to eight games.

FC Porto travelled to Milan knowing that if they were to have any chance of progressing through to the Champions' Cup final they would have to win all three of their remaining games. And first of all that meant taking both points from Milan in the San Siro. A week or so earlier that might have seemed an impossible task, but that was before Milan's long unbeaten run had finally come to an end in an Italian Cup semi-final against Roma. Fabio Capello's men had only just managed to preserve their unbeaten Serie A record a few days later in the same Olympic stadium when they were held 2-2 by Lazio, so if ever there was a chance for Porto to make a name for themselves, this was it.

The opening half-hour produced little quality football from either side. As in the first game, Milan were restricted to trying long-range shots, while Porto rarely threatened at all. But then, out of the blue, a moment of magic from Italian international midfielder Stefano Eranio suddenly raised the 67,000 spectators from their slumber. Served on the edge of the area by a cunning back-heel from Marco Simone, Eranio lashed the ball first time with his right foot past Vítor Baía in the Porto goal.

The visitors had an excellent opportunity to equalise just before half-time. Ion Timofte appeared to have done the hard bit when he skilfully beat Franco Baresi in the penalty area, but his shot lacked conviction and Rossi made a fine save to preserve Milan's lead. Rossi made another good stop in the second half, from Fernando Couto's blockbuster free-kick, but otherwise he was untroubled. Milan, for their part, made no great attempt to add to their one goal. The closest they came was when Evani grazed Vítor Baía's right-hand upright with a powerful right-foot drive midway through the half.

● *Fernando Couto*

Milan were in no mood for heroics. They could come later. For the moment they were happy enough just to collect the points and take another step closer towards the final.

STEFANO ERANIO
Milan

Match-winner Stefano Eranio was making only his second start for Milan in the Champions' Cup. His only previous selection had been in the opening Champions' League victory at home to IFK Gothenburg when, amongst other things, he laid on Marco van Basten's spectacular hat-trick goal. Now, his 32nd-minute strike ensured that Milan remained at the top of the Group B table with maximum points from their four matches.

Eranio, a UEFA Cup semi-finalist with Genoa in 1991/92, was one of several players to join Milan for a huge fee in the close season. Like most of the newcomers, he discovered that his chances of first-team action would be severely restricted by the club's 'turnover' policy. But that proved no hindrance to Italian national coach Arrigo Sacchi, who retained his faith in the player and, like most of his countrymen, jumped for joy as Eranio crashed home a vital last-minute equaliser in Italy's World Cup opener against Switzerland.

CHAMPIONS' LEAGUE
Group B

Wednesday 7th April 1993
Philips Stadium, Eindhoven

PHILIPS SV 0 FC PORTO 1

Half-time 0-0 *Attendance* 27,750

Goals

			Goals
1	Hans VAN BREUKELEN ❏	1 VÍTOR BAÍA	
2	Raymond BEERENS	2 BANDEIRINHA	
3	Ernest FABER	3 Lubomír VLK ‡	
4	Erwin KOEMAN	4 JOSÉ CARLOS	71 (pen)
5	Jan HEINTZE	5 FERNANDO COUTO	
6	René KLOMP	6 PAULINHO SANTOS	
7	Edward LINSKENS	7 JORGE COUTO	
8	Gerald VANENBURG ❏	8 JORGE COSTA	
9	ROMÁRIO de Souza Faria	9 PAULINHO CÉSAR	
10	Wim KIEFT †	10 BINO ❏	
11	Peter HOEKSTRA ‡	11 TOZÉ †	

Substitutes

Juul ELLERMAN †62

KALUSHA Bwalya ‡81

Substitutes

DOMINGOS †38

RUI JORGE ‡65

Referee Leslie MOTTRAM (Scotland)

FACTFILE

● *PSV's defeat meant that they had lost all three of their home games in the Champions' League.*

● *Only three Porto players remained from the team which had started the first game against PSV in Oporto - goalkeeper Vítor Baía, defender José Carlos and midfielder Jorge Couto.*

● *José Carlos was only asked to take the winning penalty because regular spot-kick takers Ion Timofte and João Pinto were not in the team.*

● *This result ensured that, regardless of what happened in the final round of matches, PSV would finish bottom of the Group B table and Porto would end up third.*

● *Peter Hoekstra*

Penalty condemns PSV to another home defeat

Whilst the leadership of the group was being decided in Gothenburg, Philips SV and FC Porto contested the wooden spoon in Eindhoven. Both teams took the field with severely depleted line-ups. Van Aerle, Numan and Popescu were all injured for the Dutch champions, with Van Tiggelen again joining them on the sidelines through suspension. Many of the changes in the Porto line-up were not enforced, but done through choice. After all, they still had the Portuguese title to defend, and that was of far more importance to the club than this relatively meaningless Champions' League fixture.

The last time Porto had visited Eindhoven for a European Cup tie they had been turned over 5-0 by a PSV side that was at the time defending the Champions' Cup. But although the size of the crowd was comparable to that occasion, the sense of purpose amongst the players was very different.

The home side had the majority of the play in the first half, but the Porto defence, renowned for its discipline and solidity, restricted them to long-range efforts, none of which caused any great concern to Portuguese international goalkeeper Vítor Baía. Jan Heintze had the first effort, from fully 35 yards, then Peter Hoekstra rapped the Porto 'keeper's knuckles from just inside the area. Before the interval Romário also had an opportunity to add to the two goals he scored in the first meeting, but his snap-volley sailed harmlessly over the bar.

The visitors came into it more in the second half. PSV's resolve was on the wane and Porto began to take advantage by launching a series of counter-attacking raids. One of them produced the best chance of the game. An error of judgment by Raymond Beerens allowed Porto substitute striker Domingos a clear run on goal, but as Van Breukelen came out to meet him, he chipped it wide of the target. Soon afterwards, though, the same player went some way towards making up for his miss when his nimble footwork in the area forced Van Breukelen into pulling him down and conceding a penalty. The veteran Dutch 'keeper received a yellow card for his misdemeanour and then watched agonisingly as José Carlos, a scorer from a free-kick in the first meeting, steered home the winning goal from the spot.

Not surprisingly, PSV left the field to boos and whistles from all around the ground. Their Champions' League campaign had been nothing short of a disaster. Just one point from five games, none at all at home, and with their final fixture to play away to all-conquering Milan!

VÍTOR BAÍA
FC Porto

Another clean sheet in Eindhoven added to the growing reputation of Vítor Baía as one of the most reliable young goalkeepers in Europe. Well into his fourth full season with FC Porto he still maintained a record of conceding less than a goal every other game - a splendid record for a man of such little experience.
Vítor Baía has taken to big-time international competition like a duck to water. His consistency of performance at all levels has meant that since making his debut for Portugal as a second-half substitute against the United States in December 1990 he has missed only one international in the past two and a half years - ironically against the USA again, in June 1992. At club level he made the headlines during the 1991/92 season when he went 12 matches without conceding a goal, establishing a new Portuguese League record of 1,192 minutes undefeated. Over the whole season he let in just 11 goals in 34 matches to help Porto to the title.

CHAMPIONS' LEAGUE
Group B

Wednesday 7th April 1993
Nya Ullevi Stadium, Gothenburg

IFK GÖTEBORG 0 MILAN 1

Half-time 0-0 *Attendance* 40,323

		Goals				Goals
1	Thomas RAVELLI			1	Sebastiano ROSSI	
2	Magnus JOHANSSON			2	Mauro TASSOTTI	
3	Joachim BJÖRKLUND			3	Stefano NAVA	
4	Ola SVENSSON			4	Alberigo EVANI	
5	Pontus KÅMARK			5	Alessandro COSTACURTA	
6	Peter ERIKSSON			6	Paolo MALDINI	
7	Stefan REHN			7	Gianluigi LENTINI ❑	
8	Håkan MILD			8	Frank RIJKAARD	
9	Mikael NILSSON			9	Zvonimir BOBAN	
10	Mikael MARTINSSON			10	Dejan SAVICEVIC	
11	Johnny EKSTRÖM			11	Daniele MASSARO †	70

Substitutes

Substitute

Enzo GAMBARO †87

Referee Karl-Josef ASSENMACHER (Germany)

F A C T F I L E

● *Milan's ninth European victory on the trot equalled the record set by Borussia Mönchengladbach on their way to winning the UEFA Cup in 1974/75.*

● *Gothenburg's defeat was their first at home in European competition for 36 games - a sequence stretching back eight years to when Panathinaikos beat them 1-0 in the quarter-finals of the 1984/85 Champions' Cup.*

● *This was Milan's first victory on Swedish soil in three attempts. They had previously drawn against IFK Norrköping and lost to Malmö FF.*

● *Victory took Milan into the sixth Champions' Cup final in their history and their third in five seasons.*

● *Mauro Tassotti*

Underststrength Milan too good for Swedes

In Sweden it was billed as the "Match of the Century". Three straight victories had put Gothenburg within touching distance of Milan at the top of the Group B table. The rules of the competition meant that they would have to beat the Italian champions by a five-goal margin if they wanted to leapfrog them to the top of the table with one match left to play, but first and foremost in the Swedes' minds was winning the game and thereby putting unexpected pressure on Fabio Capello's men for their final match at home to PSV.

Swedish optimism was fuelled by the fact that Milan came to Gothenburg without most of their best-known players. Foreign stars Van Basten, Gullit and Papin were all injured and Italian internationals Baresi, Albertini and Eranio were all missing through suspension. Furthermore, Milan were undergoing a period of crisis in domestic competition. They had not won a Serie A match for precisely one month and rivals Inter, their next opponents four days later, were rapidly closing in on them.

The Swedish season had not yet begun, but Gothenburg were buoyant after their two comprehensive victories over PSV the previous month and a sell-out crwod of over 40,000 was in the Ullevi to see if they could record an historic victory.

Gothenburg indeed looked to be the more confident of the two teams in the first half, but they made few inroads into the Italian defence and when they did, Sebastiano Rossi was in commanding form between the posts. He made one excellent stop from a long-range Stefan Rehn shot and was also well positioned to deny Mikael Nilsson when the Gothenburg number nine attempted a repeat of his stunning free-kick goal against PSV.

Gianluigi Lentini was Milan's most effective player going forward. The second-choice foreign triumvirate of Rijkaard, Boban and Savicevic were in very disappointing form and it was left to the ex-Torino man to provide virtually all of Milan's better attacking moments. It was no surprise, therefore, when a piece of Lentini magic produced a goal with just 20 minutes left on the clock. Not for the first time in the match he broke down the left, shrugging off the challenge of Johansson. Approaching the byline, he cut the ball back for Daniele Massaro, who, with a perfectly timed left-voot volley, despatched the ball past Ravelli at the near post before he had time to move.

Fabio Capello, delighted to have reached his first Champions' Cup final as Milan coach, acknowledged "We played well, but a draw would have been a fairer result", while his Gothenburg counterpart Roger Gustafsson confessed "The Italians denied us space and we were never able to get round the back of them like we did against PSV."

GIANLUIGI LENTINI
Milan

Being known first and foremost as the world's most expensive footballer is a burden most players could do without. And it is fair to say that Gianluigi Lentini's first season at Milan since his £13 million move from Torino has hardly justified such an excessive outlay. But in this vital confrontation in Gothenburg the young Italian international winger produced one of the finest performances of his career. He was a constant scourge to the Swedish defence and it was his run on the left that led to Massaro's winning goal. By helping to secure victory over the Swedes, Lentini ensured himself a second European final appearance in successive seasons. The previous season he had played a major role in taking Torino to the UEFA Cup final. Lentini has not yet fully convinced Italian national coach Arrigo Sacchi of his effectiveness for the Azzurri, but it seems certain that he will be a squad member should Italy make it to World Cup '94.

CHAMPIONS' LEAGUE
Group B

Wednesday 21st April 1993
Das Antas Stadium, Oporto

FC PORTO 2 IFK GÖTEBORG 0

Half-time 1-0 *Attendance* 6,000

		Goals			Goals
1	VÍTOR BAÍA		1	Thomas RAVELLI	
2	BANDEIRINHA		2	Magnus JOHANSSON ❑	
3	RUI JORGE †		3	Joachim BJÖRKLUND ‡	
4	JOSÉ CARLOS	42	4	Pontus KÅMARK	
5	FERNANDO COUTO		5	Mikael NILSSON ❑	
6	Ion TIMOFTE	56	6	Stefan LINDQVIST ❑	
7	JAIME MAGALHÃES		7	Stefan REHN	
8	Emil KOSTADINOV ‡		8	Håkan MILD ❑	
9	DOMINGOS		9	Patrik BENGTSSON	
10	SEMEDO		10	Mikael MARTINSSON †	
11	ANDRÉ		11	Johnny EKSTRÖM	

Substitutes

JORGE COSTA †46

BINO ‡82

Substitutes

Peter ERIKSSON †55

Jonas OHLSSON ‡66

Referee David ELLERAY (England)

FACTFILE

● *This was IFK Gothenburg's 50th match in the European Champions' Cup.*
● *Four Gothenburg players were booked in the second half by the pedantic English referee, David Elleray. That was as many yellow cards as the team had received throughout their previous nine and a half matches in the competition!*
● *Although Porto's victory was not enough to take them above Gothenburg in the final Group B table, they could, under traditional European Cup rules, consider themselves to have been the second best team in the group having 'beaten' both PSV (3-2) and Gothenburg (2-1) on aggregate.*
● *As in the first meeting between the sides in Gothenburg, the Swedes were the team to relinquish their normal blue and white striped shirts and take the field in all red.*

● *Patrik Bengtsson*

Timofte inspires Porto to insignificant win

A tiny crowd of just 6,000 braved chilly temperatures - unusual for a late April evening in Portugal - to witness FC Porto record their first home victory in the Champions' League at the expense of Group B runners-up IFK Gothenburg.

Earlier in the day the UEFA Club Competitions Executive Committee had been meeting in Berne to discuss ways of improving the Champions' League for the following season. The one major amendment they had agreed upon was to introduce single-match semi-finals for the 1993/94 event, with the games being played on the home ground of the group winners. Had that been introduced for this inaugural Champions' League, however, it would not have made a bit of difference to the situation in Group B. All four positions in the group had already been determined by the penultimate matches and this game in Oporto would still have been of only academic and, of course, financial, interest.

Porto's big match of the week had come a few days earlier when they managed to snatch a vital 0-0 draw away to Benfica in the Portuguese League. So it was in a relatively relaxed mood that they approached this encounter. Once again, coach Carlos Alberto had decided to shuffle his team around, and there were only four survivors from the team that had started the previous Champions' League game away at PSV.

One of the absentees in Eindhoven, Romanian midfielder Ion Timofte, was to have a major influence on this game. He was instrumental in most of the many good moves which Porto produced in the first half and was twice close to opening the scoring, firstly when he lobbed just wide after Thomas Ravelli had come off his line, then when he blasted a long-range left-footer which the Gothenburg 'keeper spectacularly pushed away for a corner. With half-time approaching, however, the Swedish defences were finally broken. A corner was only half-cleared, Timofte retrieved the ball over by the right touchline and then swung in a curling cross which José Carlos nodded into the corner of the net for his third goal of the competition.

Gothenburg came back into the game in the second period, but by that stage they were fighting a lost cause, Porto having scored a second goal when Johansson's attempted clearance struck Jaime Magalhães and dropped perfectly for Timofte to sweep the ball into the net. The Swedes protested that the ball had come off Jaime Magalhães' hand, but referee Elleray showed no sympathy and Porto were well on their way to collecting the two points and securing their second Champions' League victory on the trot.

ION TIMOFTE
FC Porto

Ion Timofte stood head and shoulders above everybody else on the pitch as Porto finished off their Champions' League campaign with victory over IFK Gothenburg. The Romanian provided virtually all of the touches of individual class on view, and the goal he scored to kill the tie in the 56th minute - his first of the competition - could not have been more richly deserved. Timofte is one of many foreign stars on the FC Porto books, but few have been quite so influential as him over the two seasons he has spent at the club since arriving as a relative unknown from Romainan provincial side Politehnica Timisoara. His knack of scoring important goals, especially against Benfica, has helped to tilt the domestic balance in Porto's favour over their great Lisbon rivals. So too has his invention in midfield, where his magical left foot often works wonders, especially from dead-ball situations.

CHAMPIONS' LEAGUE
Group B

Wednesday 21st April 1993
Giuseppe Meazza Stadium, Milan

MILAN 2 PHILIPS SV 0

Half-time 2-0 *Attendance* 56,862

		Goals			Goals
1	Carlo CUDICINI		1	Wim DE RON	
2	Stefano NAVA		2	Berry VAN AERLE †	
3	Enzo GAMBARO		3	Adri VAN TIGGELEN	
4	Fernando DE NAPOLI		4	Erwin KOEMAN	
5	Alessandro COSTACURTA		5	Mitchel VAN DER GAAG	
6	Paolo MALDINI		6	Gheorghe POPESCU	
7	Roberto DONADONI		7	Edward LINSKENS ‡	
8	Zvonimir BOBAN		8	Gerald VANENBURG	
9	Marco SIMONE †	5, 19	9	ROMÁRIO de Souza Faria	
10	Dejan SAVICEVIC		10	Juul ELLERMAN	
11	Alberigo EVANI		11	Peter HOEKSTRA ▫	

Substitute

Daniele MASSARO †33

Substitutes

Raymond BEERENS †37

René KLOMP ‡77

Referee Sándor PUHL (Hungary)

FACTFILE

● Both goalkeepers, Milan's Carlo Cudicini and PSV's Wim de Ron, were making their first full appearances in European competition.

● Milan's tenth straight victory established a new record for all three European competitions. It was also the first time that a club had ever reached a European final by winning all of its matches en route.

● Although he did not get on the scoresheet this time, PSV striker Romário still had the personal satisfaction of being the only player to score against Milan in the Champions' League after his earlier effort in Eindhoven.

● This was PSV's fifth straight defeat in the Champions' League and their third in a row without a goal.

● Romário

Simone double maintains perfect record

With Milan's place in the Munich final already assured after their victory in Gothenburg a fortnight earlier, coach Capello was in the enviable position of being able to leave out all those players who were on a yellow card and risked suspension for the final. That meant no place for such stalwarts as Tassotti, Albertini, Baresi, Lentini, Eranio and Papin. Of all those under threat, Capello opted to play only Nava and Boban, neither of whom evidently figured in his plans for the game in Munich. The only players selected who could conceivably be regarded as indispensables in Capello's first-choice XI were defenders Costacurta and Maldini.

With the Italians so badly understrength - their three Dutchmen were all injured as well - PSV might have fancied their chances of regaining some sort of respect and credibility from what had been a calamitous Champions' League campaign. But any hopes they had of pulling off a shock win were killed off within the first 20 minutes. That was all the time it took for Milan striker Marco Simone to make his mark on the game with two excellent goals, the first with a well-directed header from an Enzo Gambaro cross, the second with a chip from a tight angle after a shrewd through-ball from Zvonimir Boban.

That was that as far as the contest was concerned. PSV showed little inclination to haul themselves back into the game and the Italians, eager to please a sizeable crowd in the San Siro, continued to push forward in search of a third goal. Goal hero Simone had to leave the field after 33 minutes after a bad foul, and the man who replaced him, Daniele Massaro, should have scored soon afterwards when, after an error in the PSV defence, he raced through on goal, only to balloon the ball into the stands. Shortly before the interval Paolo Maldini also went close, but his flying header from a right-wing corner was cleared off the line.

The second half was something of a non-event. PSV had by now admitted defeat and their priorities had already switched back to their Dutch League campaign where, after good wins over Fortuna Sittard and Utrecht, they were well placed to defend their title. Milan, after their home defeat by Juventus the previous weekend, still had some work to do to hold onto their domestic crown, but as far as Europe was concerned, their job of qualifying for the final had already been completed and now it was simply a matter of showing off to the world just how strong and well-endowed their playing squad actually was.

MARCO SIMONE
Milan

Milan's final Champions' League fixture was quite an eventful one for Marco Simone. Making the most of the famous number nine shirt, habitually worn by either Van Basten or Papin, he scored both of the early goals which ensured the continuation of Milan's 100% record in the competition. But with thoughts of a first ever hat-trick looming in his mind, he was cruelly tackled from behind in the 33rd minute and forced to leave the field.

Simone began his career just up the road from Milan in Como. He had one season in Serie C1 on loan to Virescit, before returning to the lakeside club and playing in every one of their games as they finished bottom of Serie A the following season. That was when Arrigo Sacchi brought him to Milan. In four seasons with the 'Rossoneri' Simone has never quite managed to secure himself a permanent berth in the side, but he has often provided important goals and was awarded his first Italian national cap in December 1992 in a World Cup qualifier away to Malta.

CHAMPIONS' CUP
Group B Review

CHAMPIONS' LEAGUE GROUP B RESULTS

FC Porto	Philips SV	2-2
Milan	IFK Göteborg	4-0
IFK Göteborg	FC Porto	1-0
Philips SV	Milan	1-2
Philips SV	IFK Göteborg	1-3
FC Porto	Milan	0-1
IFK Göteborg	Philips SV	3-0
Milan	FC Porto	1-0
Philips SV	FC Porto	0-1
IFK Göteborg	Milan	0-1
FC Porto	IFK Göteborg	2-0
Milan	Philips SV	2-0

CHAMPIONS' LEAGUE GROUP B FINAL TABLE

		Pd	W	D	L	F	A	Pts
1	MILAN	6	6	0	0	11	1	12
2	IFK GÖTEBORG	6	3	0	3	7	8	6
3	FC PORTO	6	2	1	3	5	5	5
4	PHILIPS SV	6	0	1	5	4	13	1

CHAMPIONS' LEAGUE GROUP B GOALSCORERS

4 Marco VAN BASTEN (Milan)
3 Marco SIMONE (Milan)
   Johnny EKSTRÖM (IFK Göteborg)
   JOSÉ CARLOS (FC Porto)
   ROMÁRIO (Philips SV)
2 Mikael NILSSON (IFK Göteborg)
1 RIJKAARD, PAPIN, ERANIO, MASSARO (Milan)
   ERIKSSON, MARTINSSON (IFK Göteborg)
   JAIME MAGALHÃES, TIMOFTE (FC Porto)
   NUMAN (Philips SV)

CHAMPIONS' LEAGUE GROUP B PLAYER APPEARANCES

MILAN

	Pos	Apps(subs)	Gls
Demetrio ALBERTINI	M	4	
Francesco ANTONIOLI	G	1	
Franco BARESI	D	4	
Zvonimir BOBAN	M	3	
Alessandro COSTACURTA	D	6	
Carlo CUDICINI	G	1 (1)	
Fernando DE NAPOLI	M	1	
Roberto DONADONI	M	1	
Stefano ERANIO	M	2 (1)	1
Alberigo EVANI	M	3 (1)	
Enzo GAMBARO	D	2 (1)	
Ruud GULLIT	M	2	
Gianluigi LENTINI	M	5	
Paolo MALDINI	D	5	
Daniele MASSARO	A	2 (3)	1
Stefano NAVA	D	2 (1)	
Jean-Pierre PAPIN	A	3	1
Frank RIJKAARD	M	3	1
Sebastiano ROSSI	G	4	
Dejan SAVICEVIC	M	2 (1)	
Marco SIMONE	A	4 (1)	3
Mauro TASSOTTI	D	4	
Marco VAN BASTEN	A	2	4

IFK GÖTEBORG

	Pos	Apps(subs)	Gls
Thomas ANDERSSON	M	2 (2)	
Patrik BENGTSSON	M	2	
Joachim BJÖRKLUND	D	4	
Johnny EKSTRÖM	A	6	3
Peter ERIKSSON	M	5 (1)	1
Magnus JOHANSSON	D	6	
Pontus KÅMARK	D	6	
Fredrik LEKSELL	A	(1)	
Stefan LINDQVIST	A	1 (2)	
Mikael MARTINSSON	A	4	1
Håkan MILD	M	6	
Mikael NILSSON	M	6	2
Jonas OHLSSON	D	(1)	
Tore PEDERSEN	D	1	
Thomas RAVELLI	G	6	
Stefan REHN	M	6	
Ola SVENSSON	D	5	

FC PORTO

	Pos	Apps(subs)	Gls
ALOÍSIO	D	4	
ANDRÉ	M	4	
ANTÓNIO CARLOS	M	1	
BANDEIRINHA	D	3	
BINO	A	1 (2)	
DOMINGOS	A	3 (3)	
FERNANDO COUTO	D	5	
JAIME MAGALHÃES	M	2	1
JOÃO PINTO	D	4	
JORGE COSTA	D	2 (2)	
JORGE COUTO	A	5	
JOSÉ CARLOS	D	3	3
Emil KOSTADINOV	A	5	
PAULINHO CÉSAR	M	1	
PAULINHO SANTOS	A	3	
RUI FILIPE	M	1	
RUI JORGE	D	3 (1)	
SEMEDO	M	5	
Ion TIMOFTE	M	3	1
TONI	A	(1)	
TOZÉ	A	1 (2)	
VÍTOR BAÍA	G	6	
Lubomír VLK	D	1	

PHILIPS SV

	Pos	Apps(subs)	Gls
Raymond BEERENS	D	2 (2)	
Wim DE RON	G	1	
Juul ELLERMAN	M	3 (1)	
Ernest FABER	D	4 (1)	
Jan HEINTZE	D	5	
Peter HOEKSTRA	A	4 (1)	
KALUSHA Bwalya	A	(2)	
Wim KIEFT	A	4	
René KLOMP	M	1 (1)	
Erwin KOEMAN	M	4	
Edward LINSKENS	M	6	
Arthur NUMAN	M	4	1
Gheorghe POPESCU	D	4	
ROMÁRIO de Souza Faria	A	6	3
Berry VAN AERLE	D	3	
Hans VAN BREUKELEN	G	5	
Mitchel VAN DER GAAG	D	1	
Gerald VANENBURG	M	5 (1)	
Adri VAN TIGGELEN	D	4	

CHAMPIONS' CUP
Final

Wednesday 26th May 1993
Olympia Stadium, Munich

OLYMPIQUE MARSEILLE 1   MILAN 0

Half-time 1-0   *Attendance* 72,300

		Goals			Goals
1	Fabien BARTHEZ ❑		1	Sebastiano ROSSI	
2	Jocelyn ANGLOMA †		2	Mauro TASSOTTI	
3	Eric DI MECO ❑		3	Paolo MALDINI	
4	Basile BOLI	44	4	Demetrio ALBERTINI	
5	Franck SAUZEE		5	Alessandro COSTACURTA	
6	Marcel DESAILLY		6	Franco BARESI	
7	Jean-Jacques EYDELIE		7	Gianluigi LENTINI ❑	
8	Alen BOKSIC		8	Frank RIJKAARD	
9	Rudi VÖLLER ‡		9	Marco VAN BASTEN ‡	
10	Abedi PELE		10	Roberto DONADONI †	
11	Didier DESCHAMPS		11	Daniele MASSARO	

Substitutes

Jean-Philippe DURAND †62

Jean-Christophe THOMAS ‡79

Substitutes

Jean-Pierre PAPIN †55

Stefano ERANIO ‡86

Referee Kurt RÖTHLISBERGER (Switzerland)

FACTFILE

● *Basile Boli became the first non-Dutchman to score in a Champions' Cup final since 1987.*

● *Both finalists wrapped up their domestic titles the following weekend, Milan getting the point they needed in a 1-1 draw at home to Brescia and Marseille beating closest rivals Paris-Saint-Germain 3-1 at home in the Vélodrome.*

● *Only three Marseille players survived from their previous Champions' Cup final two years earlier against Red Star Belgrade - Boli, Di Meco and Pelé.*

● *Milan's defeat deprived Italy of their second European 'Grand Slam' in four seasons. 1989/90 therefore remains the only season in which one country has landed all three European trophies.*

● *Didier Deschamps*

Marseille bring Euro glory at last to France

It had taken 37 years and 106 attempts, but at last France had a European triumph to celebrate. No French club had ever won any of the three European trophies, but in the glorious setting of the Munich Olympic Stadium, and against the supposed best team in the world, Olympique Marseille brought all those years of agony and frustration for French football to an end.

Marseille went into the final as underdogs, but form was certainly in their favour. Whilst they had produced a tremendous burst of form to see off their rivals in the French title race, Milan had won only one of their last ten Serie A matches. Both Fabio Capello and Raymond Goethals were able to field full-strength sides. Extraordinarily, there were no suspensions or injuries affecting either team. But while the Marseille side virtually selected itself, Capello, faced with all sorts of alternatives, made the controversial decision to field only two foreigners, meaning no place at all for Ruud Gullit and only a seat on the bench for ex-Marseille sharpshooter Jean-Pierre Papin.

It was a decision Capello would later be forced to regret as Papin's replacement, Daniele Massaro, squandered a whole host of opportunities in a first half that was full of open play and littered with defensive inadequacies on both sides. Within the first ten minutes four clear opportunities had been created - two for each team. Massaro missed both of Milan's, heading just wide with his first effort, then shooting straight at Barthez with his second. At the other end Rudi Völler had a shot saved by Rossi and then Alen Boksic fired over with an even better opportunity.

With the score still goalless after those opening salvoes, both defences at last began to function normally and it was Milan who started to dictate the pattern of the game. Maldini headed over from a corner, then Van Basten, back in action again after his lengthy lay-off, forced a good save from Barthez after Massaro, again, had dallied too long over an easier shooting chance. Marseille were not figuring at all when, just a couple of minutes before the interval, Pelé broke down the right and earned his side their first corner. The Ghanaian took the kick himself, Völler went up to head it but it was the man standing just behind him, defender Basile Boli, who made contact, and he succeeded in angling his header into the unguarded far corner of the net.

The second half was as disappointing for the neutral as the first 45 minutes had been exciting and entertaining. Marseille, intent on preserving their advantage, did so with relative ease as the Milan superstars, including Papin, belatedly introduced for Donadoni, failed to live up to their reputations. At the final whistle the delight on the faces of Marseille players, officials and supporters was plain for all to see. The joy was perhaps most intense for Marseille president Bernard Tapie and retiring 72-year-old coach Raymond Goethals, the unlikely double-act that had at last succeeded where so many French teams had failed in the past. History indeed belonged to them.

BASILE BOLI
Olympique Marseille

Basile Boli had wept openly after Marseille's penalty shoot-out defeat against Red Star Belgrade in Bari. But two years on the big Marseille centre-back was radiant with joy, the hero of Marseille's historic triumph thanks both to his match-winning goal just before half-time and his masterful handling of European Footballer of the Year Marco van Basten.
Boli is still only 26 years of age, but he is regarded as something of a veteran in French football circles. Born in the Ivory Coast, he moved to France as a youngster and actually made his First Division debut for Auxerre at the age of just 16 in April 1983 against Monaco. The following season he was a regular in the Auxerre defence and continued to be so until he left the club for Marseille in 1990. Boli made his debut for the French national team against Switzerland in their first match after the 1986 World Cup and he has largely remained a key figure in the side, under three different coaches, ever since.

CHAMPIONS' CUP
Review

TOP GOALSCORERS

7 ROMÁRIO (PSV)
6 Alen BOKSIC (Olympique Marseille)
 Franck SAUZEE (Olympique Marseille)
 Marco VAN BASTEN (Milan)
5 Johnny EKSTRÖM (IFK Göteborg)
4 Gert VERHEYEN (Club Brugge KV)
 Marco SIMONE (Milan)
 JOSÉ CARLOS (FC Porto)
 TÚLIO (FC Sion)
3 Lorenzo STAELENS (Club Brugge KV)
 Mark HATELEY (Rangers)
 Ian DURRANT (Rangers)
 Abedi PELE (Olympique Marseille)
 Frank RIJKAARD (Milan)
 Jean-Pierre PAPIN (Milan)
 Mikael NILSSON (IFK Göteborg)
 Arthur NUMAN (PSV)
 Emil KOSTADINOV (FC Porto)
 Dmitry KORSAKOV (CSKA Moskva)
 Sergei SHEVCHENKO (Tavria Simferopol)
 Vitaly ASTAFJEV (Skonto Riga)
 Juul ELLERMAN (PSV)
 TONI (FC Porto)

RED CARDS

1 Samir ZULIC (SCT Olimpija Ljubljana)
 Sándor SZENES (Ferencváros)
 Oleg KOLESOV (Tavria Simferopol)
 Demetrio ALBERTINI (Milan)
 Adri VAN TIGGELEN (PSV)
 Mark HATELEY (Rangers)

YELLOW CARDS

4 Stéphane VAN DER HEYDEN
 (Club Brugge KV)
3 Stefano ERANIO (Milan)
 Sergei FOKIN (CSKA Moskva)
 Basile BOLI (Olympique Marseille)
 Eric DI MECO (Olympique Marseille)
 Stelios MANOLAS (AEK)
 Demetrio ALBERTINI (Milan) (inc. red card)
 Adri VAN TIGGELEN (PSV) (inc. red card)
 Samir ZULIC (SCT Olimpija Ljubljana)
2 VOLKOV, VORONEZHSKY,
 GUDIMENKO (Tavria Simferopol)
 NIMNI, LEVY (Maccabi Tel-Aviv)
 KOMAROV, BRAGIN (Norma Tallinn)
 KIROV (CSKA Sofia)
 FRONTZECK (VfB Stuttgart)
 VAN AERLE, HOEKSTRA (PSV)
 FERGUSON (Rangers)
 GLONEK (Slovan Bratislava)
 AIGNER, IVANAUSKAS, SCHMID,
 PFEFFER (FK Austria)
 SABANDZOVIC, VASSILOPOULOS (AEK)
 BARESI, LENTINI (Milan)
 JORGE COSTA, JAIME MAGALHÃES
 (FC Porto)
 MINKO, MAMCHUR (CSKA Moskva)
 QUERTER (Club Brugge KV)
 JOHANSSON (IFK Göteborg)

CUP-WINNERS' CUP

CUP-WINNERS' CUP
Preliminary Round First Leg

Wednesday 19th August 1992
Ljudski Vrt Stadium, Maribor

MARIBOR BRANIK 4 HAMRUN SPARTANS 0

Half-time 2-0 *Attendance* 7,000

		Goals			Goals
1	Mladen DABANOVIC		1	Alan ZAMMIT	
2	Emil STERBAL		2	Emanuel BRINCAT ‡	
3	Bostjan RATKOVIC		3	Mario GORLA ❏	
4	Zarko TARANA	49	4	Marco GRECH	
5	Saso LUKIC		5	Joe BRINCAT	
6	Ales KRIZAN		6	Raymond VELLA	
7	Ante SIMUNDZA	16, 30	7	Ivan ZAMMIT ❏	
8	Peter BINKOVSKI	77	8	Miguel CORBALAN	
9	Mirsad BICAKCIC †		9	Cesar PAIBER ❏	
10	Marko KRIZANIC ‡		10	Michael DEGIORGIO †	
11	Marijan BAKULA		11	Stefan SULTANA	

Substitutes		*Substitutes*
Saso GAJSER †76 ❏		David CAMILLERI †22
Simon DVORSAK ‡80		Noel FENECH ‡56

Referee Bernd HEYNEMANN (Germany)

SUMMARY

● *Maribor Branik preceded Olimpija Ljubljana by an hour and 15 minutes to become the first club to represent the newly-formed independent state of Slovenia in European competition. And by the time the country's champion club kicked off in the capital, Maribor were already three goals to the good against Hamrun Spartans of Malta, provisionally booking themselves a place in the first round against Spanish giants Atlético Madrid. A fourth goal 13 minutes from time all but confirmed it. Maribor had never previously appeared in European competition, but they were far too strong for Hamrun Spartans, a club embarking on its eighth European campaign in the last ten seasons. 20-year-old forward Ante Simundza, a scorer of 17 league goals for Maribor the previous season, was the man of the first half, netting both of the goals which gave the Slovenians a 2-0 half-time lead. Bosnian defender Zarko Tarana then made it three early in the second period and young midfielder Peter Binkovski finished off the scoring late on to complete Hamrun Spartans' 13th defeat in 17 European fixtures.*

CUP-WINNERS' CUP
Preliminary Round Second Leg

Wednesday 2nd September 1992
National Stadium, Ta' Qali

HAMRUN SPARTANS 2 MARIBOR BRANIK 1

Half-time 1-1 *Aggregate* 2-5 *Attendance* 1,000

		Goals				Goals
1	Alan ZAMMIT		1	Mladen DABANOVIC	
2	John MICALLEF		2	Emil STERBAL	
3	Mario GORLA		3	Bostjan RATKOVIC ❑	
4	Marco GRECH		4	Zarko TARANA	38
5	Joe BRINCAT	34, 59	5	Saso LUKIC	
6	David CAMILLERI		6	Ales KRIZAN	
7	Ivan ZAMMIT		7	Ante SIMUNDZA ‡	
8	Noel FENECH		8	Peter BINKOVSKI	
9	Cesar PAIBER ‡		9	Mirsad BICAKCIC	
10	Michael DEGIORGIO		10	Marko KRIZANIC †	
11	Stefan SULTANA †		11	Marijan BAKULA	

Substitutes		*Substitutes*
Alex AZZOPARDI †86		Saso GAJSER †74
Miguel CORBALAN ‡90		Enver CIRIC ‡83

Referee Arcangelo PEZZELLA (Italy)

● *A double from Maltese international defender Joe Brincat gave Hamrun Spartans their first victory and first goals in Europe for four years, but, as in 1989 when they beat 17 Nëntori of Albania 2-1 in the first round of the Champions' Cup, it was not enough to take the team through to the next round. In fact, Hamrun's elimination, along with that of Valletta in the Champions' Cup, meant that the first round proper of the European competitions would start with only one team from Malta - UEFA Cup qualifiers Floriana. Brincat had never previously scored in Europe, although he had found the target twice for the Maltese national team. Four minutes after his first strike, however, Maribor Branik. also found the net, through their first-leg scorer Tarana, and that was sufficient to kill off any thoughts the home side had of recovering their 0-4 deficit from the away leg. Brincat's second goal did give Hamrun a rare European victory, though, and it also meant that Maribor became the only preliminary round qualifiers (including those in the Champions' Cup) to go through to the first round carrying a defeat.*

CUP-WINNERS' CUP
Preliminary Round First Leg

Wednesday 19th August 1992
Marienlyst Stadium, Drammen

STRØMSGODSET IF 0 HAPOEL PETACH-TIKVA 2

Half-time 0-0 *Attendance* 4,000

		Goals				Goals
1	Erik ARILDSET ❑		1	Rafi COHEN		
2	Ståle SKAU †		2	Benny KOZOSHVILY		
3	Frode JOHANNESSEN		3	Mordachy KAKON		
4	Vegard HANSEN		4	Alex BREMCHER		
5	Jan WENDELBORG ‡		5	Carlos OLERAN		
6	Geir ANDERSEN		6	Avi KEISY ❑		
7	Trond NORDEIDE		7	Yossi LEVY		
8	Glenn KNUTSEN		8	Meny BASSON	48, 59	
9	Halvor STORSKOGEN		9	Nir LEVIN		
10	Krister Åre ISAKSEN		10	Ely MACHPOD ❑		
11	Juro KUVICEK		11	Yosef SHOSHANI		

Substitutes

Arne GUSTAVSEN †46

Odd JOHNSEN ‡63

Substitutes

Referee Wojciech RUDY (Poland)

SUMMARY

● *Strømsgodset of Norway were one of the more surprising entries into the 92/93 Cup-winners' Cup, but they were certainly there on merit having produced one of the biggest upsets for years in their homeland when they beat hot favourites Rosenborg 3-2 in the 1992 Norwegian Cup final. As many as ten of the players who had taken part in that sensational victory were again on duty for this, the club's first European encounter in 18 years. Strømsgodset had been regular European participants in the early '70s, but since losing 11-0 to Liverpool in the first round of the 1974/75 Cup-winners' Cup (the English club's biggest ever European victory), they had not returned...until now, as a Norwegian Second Division club! But against Israeli debutants Hapoel Petach-Tikva there was to be no fairytale repeat of their Cup final triumph. The team now coached by former PSV Eindhoven star Hallvar Thoresen were no match for the Israelis, and two goals early in the second half from striker Meny Basson three days before his 24th birthday seemed certain to take Hapoel through to the next round.*

CUP-WINNERS' CUP
Preliminary Round Second Leg

Wednesday 2nd September 1992
Municipal Stadium, Petach-Tikva

HAPOEL PETACH-TIKVA 2 STRØMSGODSET IF 0

Half-time 1-0 *Aggregate* 4-0 *Attendance* 2,000

		Goals				Goals
1	Rafi COHEN			1	Erik ARILDSET	
2	Benny KOZOSHVILY			2	Arne GUSTAVSEN	
3	Avi KEISY			3	Frode JOHANNESSEN	
4	Uda BAHAGAT			4	Vegard HANSEN	
5	Carlos OLERAN			5	Jan WENDELBORG	
6	Noam KEISY			6	Krister Åre ISAKSEN ❑	
7	Yossi LEVY ❑			7	Ulf CAMITZ	
8	Meny BASSON	68		8	Geir ANDERSEN	
9	Nir LEVIN	17		9	Glenn KNUTSEN	
10	Ely MACHPOD ‡			10	Odd JOHNSEN †	
11	Oz ILIA †			11	Juro KUVICEK	

Substitutes

Uzi HOAION †70

Ofir KOPEL ‡72

Substitute

Ståle SKAU †46

Referee Loizos LOIZOU (Cyprus)

● *Less than a thousand spectators were present in the 55,000-capacity Ramat-Gan stadium at kick-off for the first match of Israel's European 'double header' featuring Cup winners Hapoel Petach-Tikva. Whether it was over-confidence on the part of the club's supporters after the convincing first-leg win in Norway or simply the baking 40 degree heat in the afternoon sunshine, there was an unreal atmosphere in the ground as Hapoel set about their task of confirming their first-leg superiority and clinching an attractive first-round confrontation with the previous season's semi-finalists Feyenoord. A goal from former Belgian League player Nir Levin after just 17 minutes put the tie out of the Norwegians' reach and Meny Basson was on target again in the second half to score his third goal of the tie and repeat the 2-0 scoreline of the first match. Strømsgodset never looked remotely like recovering their first-leg deficit. They suffered badly in the tropical temperatures and their bid to become the first Norwegian club to win a European tie in five years never even got off the ground.*

CUP-WINNERS' CUP
Preliminary Round First Leg

Wednesday 19th August 1992
National Stadium, Vaduz

FC VADUZ 0 CHERNOMORETS ODESSA 5

Half-time 0-1 *Attendance* 2,000

		Goals				Goals
1	Peter HARTMANN		1	Oleg SUSLOV	
2	Roland MOSER ‡		2	Yury NIKIFOROV	
3	Patrick HEFTI		3	Sergei PROTSYUK	
4	Roland MOSER		4	Yury BUKEL	
5	Heinrich NIGG ❑		5	Vladimir LEBED	47
6	Alex QUADERER		6	Dmitry PARFONOV †	
7	Franco ROTUNNO		7	Ilya TSYMBALAR	45
8	Wolfgang OSPELT		8	Viktor YABLONSKI	
9	Franz SCHÄDLER †		9	Oleg KOSHELYUK ‡	
10	Beat LOHNER		10	Yury SAK	52
11	Harry SCHÄDLER		11	Sergei GUSEV	80, 82

	Substitutes			*Substitutes*	
	Daniel HASLER †46			Ruslan ROMANCHUK †55	
	Daniel HEMMERLE ‡77			Konstantin KULIK ‡55	

Referee Erny KESSELER (Luxembourg)

S U M M A R Y

● *All of a sudden European competition was open to everybody. Even Liechtenstein, where there is no such thing as a national league, were now being permitted to enter a team in the Cup-winners' Cup. FC Vaduz had the dubious privilege of being the first team to represent their tiny country in Europe, but after this 0-5 drubbing by Ukrainian Cup winners Chernomorets Odessa, the club might have wished that it had never bothered to apply. In fairness, Vaduz held their opponents at bay for almost the entire first 45 minutes. But once Chernomorets' star midfielder Ilya Tsymbalar had opened the scoring on the stroke of half-time, the Liechtenstein Cup winners appeared to lose all their spirit, not to mention their fitness, and it became a stroll for the visitors in the second half. Two quick goals from Lebed and Sak followed shortly after the resumption and the rout was completed with two late strikes from Odessa's star forward Sergei Gusev, scorer of seven goals in 17 games in the 1992 Ukrainian League. It was men against boys, and one feared greatly for the Liechtensteiners in the return...*

134

European Cups Review 1993

Wednesday 2nd September 1992
Central Stadium, Odessa

CHERNOMORETS ODESSA 7 FC VADUZ 1

Half-time 3-0 *Aggregate* 12-1 *Attendance* 4,600

		Goals				Goals
1	Oleg SUSLOV		1	Peter HARTMANN †		
2	Yury NIKIFOROV	9, 49 (pen), 78, 90	2	Daniel HASLER ‡		
3	Sergei PROTSYUK		3	Patrick HEFTI		
4	Yury BUKEL		4	Beat LOHNER		
5	Vladimir LEBED	77	5	Heinrich NIGG		
6	Dmitry PARFONOV		6	Alex QUADERER		
7	Ilya TSYMBALAR	27	7	Franco ROTUNNO		
8	Viktor YABLONSKI †	23	8	Roland MOSER		
9	Oleg KOSHELYUK		9	Christian STÖBER		87
10	Yury SAK ‡		10	Franz SCHÄDLER		
11	Sergei GUSEV		11	Harry SCHÄDLER		

Substitutes		*Substitutes*	
Andrey LOZOVSKY †46		Oliver GASSNER †69	
Konstantin KULIK ‡46		Rigobert WOLF ‡69	

Referee Jozef MARKO (Czechoslovakia)

SUMMARY

● *True to expectation, FC Vaduz were lambs to the slaughter against Chernomorets in Odessa. Former CIS international Yury Nikiforov, in particular, had a field day. He opened the scoring with a stunning free-kick after nine minutes and closed it, with his fourth goal of the afternoon, in the 90th. In between Viktor Yablonski, Ilya Tsymbalar and Vladimir Lebed also added their names to the scoresheet to run up an unforgiving aggregate scoreline of 12. That one goal for Vaduz was probably the most celebrated of the lot, even amongst the Chernomorets fans. It arrived three minutes from time and was headed in off the post by Swiss striker Christian Stöber, one of the three permitted non-nationals in the Vaduz side, the other two being goalkeeper Peter Hartmann and defender Heinrich Nigg. Whilst Vaduz headed back to Liechtenstein to lick their wounds, Chernomorets were now faced with an appealing first-round tie against Olympiakos of Greece, a team with a strong Ukrainian connection in the shape of coach Oleg Blokhin and former USSR internationals Protasov and Litovchenko.*

CUP-WINNERS' CUP
Preliminary Round First Leg

Wednesday 19th August 1992
Beggen Stadium, Luxembourg

AVENIR BEGGEN 1 B 36 0

Half-time 1-0 *Attendance* 1,500

		Goals			Goals
1	Paul KOCH		1	Wiscek ZAKREWSKI	
2	Ralph FERRON		2	Danjal Petur JOHANSEN †	
3	Théo SCHOLTEN		3	Tummas Eli HANSEN	
4	Jean VANEK		4	Bogi JACOBSEN	
5	Alex WILHELM		5	Rogvi THORSTEINSSON	
6	Jaba MOREIRA		6	Jon HARDLEI	
7	Markus KRAHEN †		7	Jakup MØRK ❑	
8	Carlo WEIS		8	Jens Christian HANSEN	
9	Frank GOERGEN ‡		9	Jan POULSEN	
10	Armin KRINGS	1	10	Kari REYNHEIM	
11	Luc HOLTZ		11	Jakup SIMONSEN	

Substitutes			*Substitute*		
Mario NOWAK †75			Samal HANSEN †67		
Serge JENTGEN ‡81					

Referee Marnix SANDRA (Belgium)

SUMMARY

● *Avenir Beggen were evidently on a roll. The club which at one time held the worst record in European Cup football - 20 defeats in 20 games - had now, with this narrow victory over B 36 of the Faeroe Isles, been victorious in each of their last two home games! Two years earlier Beggen had at last brought their long losing run to an end with a 2-1 victory at home to Inter Bratislava in the UEFA Cup. Now the taste of victory was catching. A goal in the very first minute from German-born Luxembourg international striker Armin Krings proved sufficient to win the game and set the Luxembourg side up for a possible first-ever qualification. The side from the Faeroe Isles were equally happy with the final scoreline. They had been going through a rocky spell in domestic competition - only three wins in 13 league games - but by restricting Beggen to just a single goal, they at least kept alive their hopes of turning the tie around back home in Tórshavn.*

Wednesday 2nd September 1992
Gundadalur Stadium, Tórshavn

B 36 1 AVENIR BEGGEN 1

Half-time 1-1 *Aggregate* 1-2 *Attendance* 665

		Goals				Goals
1	Wiscek ZAKREWSKI		1	Paul KOCH		
2	Danjal Petur JOHANSEN		2	Ralph FERRON ❑		
3	Tummas Eli HANSEN		3	Rolf JENTGEN		
4	Bogi JACOBSEN ❑		4	Jean VANEK ❑		
5	Rogvi THORSTEINSSON		5	Alex WILHELM		
6	Samal HANSEN		6	Serge JENTGEN		
7	Jakup MØRK ❑ †		7	Markus KRAHEN †	27
8	Jens Christian HANSEN		8	Carlo WEIS		
9	Jan POULSEN ‡		9	Théo SCHOLTEN		
10	Kari REYNHEIM	8	10	Armin KRINGS		
11	Jakup SIMONSEN		11	Luc HOLTZ ‡		
	Substitutes			*Substitutes*		
	Jon HARDLEI †67			Mario NOWAK †84		
	Frodi MADSEN ‡84			Jaba MOREIRA ‡89		

Referee Joseph TIMMONS (Scotland)

SUMMARY

● *Avenir Beggen had managed to win their home game, but now came the best chance they had ever had of actually winning a tie and making progress in European competition. They got off to the worst possible start, though, when B 36, playing in front of a depressingly low three-figure crowd, took the lead after just eight minutes. The goalscorer was Faeroe Isles international Kari Reynheim, the man who had already made headlines for himself in international competition when he scored a sensational equaliser away to Northern Ireland in the qualifying round for the 1992 European Championship. But Beggen also had their man for the big occasion in German striker Marcus Krahen. His had been the winning goal in the 1992 Luxembourg Cup final that had brought the team into this competition and it was to be his strike again, after 27 minutes, that put Beggen in the driving seat once and for all. That precious away goal left the home side having to score twice more to save the tie. They couldn't manage one of them, which left the Luxembourg side celebrating their first ever European triumph.*

CUP-WINNERS' CUP
First Round First Leg

Wednesday September 16 1992
Zaglebie Stadium, Lubin

MIEDZ LEGNICA 0 AS MONACO 1

Half-time 0-1 *Attendance* 6,000

		Goals			Goals
1	Dariusz PLACZKIEWICZ		1	Jean-Luc ETTORI	
2	Grzegorz KOCHANEK		2	Patrick VALERY	
3	Cezary MICHALSKI		3	Patrick BLONDEAU	
4	Bogdan PISZ		4	Lilian THURAM ❑	
5	Andrzej CYMBALA		5	Franck DUMAS	
6	Mariusz URBANIAK		6	Claude PUEL	
7	Artur WÓJCIK †		7	Jürgen KLINSMANN	
8	Marcin CILINSKI		8	Jérôme GNAKO	
9	Jaroslaw GIEREJKIEWICZ		9	LUIS HENRIQUE	
10	Dariusz DZIARMAGA		10	RUI BARROS †	
11	Wojciech GÓRSKI		11	Youri DJORKAEFF	3

Substitute		*Substitute*	
Pawel PRIMA †78		Sylvain LEGWINSKI †46	

Referee Hans-Peter DELLWING (Germany)

SUMMARY

● *Monaco, the competition's top seeds and previous season's beaten finalists, looked to have been handed a simple passage into round two. The draw had paired them with Polish Second Division side Miedz Legnica, who had qualified for their first ever European campaign by defeating Górnik Zabrze in the Polish Cup final on a penalty shoot-out. For security reasons this match had to be switched from Legnica's tiny stadium to that of nearby Zaglebie Lubin. Monaco fielded only four of the team which had started the 91/92 Cup-winners' Cup final in Lisbon against Werder Bremen (Ettori, Valéry, Gnako and Rui Barros), but it was a substitute from that game, Youri Djorkaeff, who got them off to the perfect start when he collected a lay-off from new signing Jürgen Klinsmann to fire home a 25-yard shot after just two minutes. 88 minutes later the score still remained at 0-1, although both teams had squandered ideal opportunities to increase their tally. Ettori saved Kochanek's penalty in the 27th minute and Placzkiewicz pushed Klinsmann's spot-kick onto the post four minutes from time.*

CUP-WINNERS' CUP
First Round Second Leg

Wednesday 30th September 1992
Louis II Stadium, Monaco

AS MONACO 0 MIEDZ LEGNICA 0

Half-time 0-0 *Aggregate* 1-0 *Attendance* 4,000

		Goals				Goals
1	Jean-Luc ETTORI		1	Dariusz PLACZKIEWICZ	
2	Patrick BLONDEAU		2	Piotr PRZERYWACZ	
3	Luc SONOR ❏		3	Cezary MICHALSKI	
4	Lilian THURAM		4	Bogdan PISZ	
5	Franck DUMAS		5	Andrzej CYMBALA	
6	Claude PUEL		6	Mariusz URBANIAK ‡	
7	Jürgen KLINSMANN		7	Artur WÓJCIK	
8	Marcel DIB		8	Marcin CILINSKI	
9	LUIS HENRIQUE †		9	Jaroslaw GIEREJKIEWICZ	
10	Jérôme GNAKO		10	Dariusz DZIARMAGA †	
11	Youssouf FOFANA ‡		11	Wojciech GÓRSKI ❏	

Substitutes		*Substitutes*	
Youri DJORKAEFF †63		Tadeusz GAJDZIS †16	
Bruno RODRIGUEZ ‡82		Krzysztof WOJTKOWSKI ‡61 ❏	

Referee Manuel DIAZ VEGA (Spain)

● With a 1-0 advantage from the away leg, Monaco were expected to dispose of the Polish Division Two side without undue concern. But things did not quite go to plan. With Portuguese international Rui Barros out with an ankle injury, coach Arsène Wenger forced to watch from the stands (he had been expelled from the touchline in the first leg) and the three-pronged strike-force of Luis Henrique, Klinsmann and Fofana having an unproductive evening in front of goal, Monaco struggled to impose themselves against their unfancied opponents. The Poles gave a good account of themselves and were evidently happy with the result, but, like Monaco, they created few chances and the overall quality of the game was very poor. Not that Monaco themselves were particularly distressed. The 0-0 draw meant that they had passed the first round of European competition for the fifth season in a row. A complete contrast to a spell in the early '80s when they were dumped out of the first round on five successive occasions.

CUP-WINNERS' CUP
First Round First Leg

Wednesday 16th September 1992
Avni Aker Stadium, Trabzon

TRABZONSPOR 2 TPS 0

Half-time 0-0 *Attendance* 22,000

		Goals
1	Viktor GRISHKO	
2	Jacek CYZIO †	
3	OGÜN Temizkanoglu	
4	KEMAL Serdar	
5	HAMDI Aslan	
6	ABDULLAH Ercan	
7	TURGUT Uçar	
8	ÜNAL Karaman ‡	
9	Yury SHELEPNITSKY	
10	HAMI Mandirali	52, 65
11	ORHAN Çikrikçi	

Substitutes

SONER Boz †46

ISMAIL Gökçek ‡83

		Goals
1	Petri JAKONEN	
2	Ari HEIKKINEN	
3	Petteri VILJANEN ❑	
4	Petri SULONEN	
5	Jyrki HÄNNIKÄINEN	
6	Jani KEULA	
7	Mika LIPPONEN ‡	
8	Janne LEHTINEN †	
9	György KAJDY	
10	Lars DALSBORG ❑	
11	Marko RAJAMÄKI ❑	

Substitutes

Kim LEHTONEN †61

Jasse JALONEN ‡81

Referee Kaj ØSTERGAARD (Denmark)

SUMMARY

● *Two second-half goals from Turkish international forward Hami Mandirali were enough to secure a comfortable first-leg lead for Trabzonspor in front of a sizeable crowd on the banks of the Black Sea. The 24-year-old's brace took his tally of European goals to seven in as many games. He had scored five the season before as Trabzonspor registered their best-ever performance in European competition, reaching the third round of the UEFA Cup. Now the Turkish Cup winners were aiming, under new Belgian coach Georges Leekens (ex-Anderlecht, Club Bruges and Mechelen), to go one better and reach their first European quarter-final. 2-0 is often cited as the ideal result for a team playing the first leg at home, and the Trabzonspor supporters were happy enough at the final whistle after they had suffered, along with the players, in a frustrating, barren first 45 minutes. The Finnish side, making their Cup-winners' Cup debut, never looked at ease in one of Europe's most hostile venues and rarely threatened to score the away goal which would have given them hope for the return.*

Wednesday 30th September 1992
Kupittaan Stadium, Turku

TPS 2 TRABZONSPOR 2

Half-time 1-1 *Aggregate* 2-4 *Attendance* 1,376

		Goals				Goals
1	Petri JAKONEN		1	Viktor GRISHKO		
2	Ari HEIKKINEN		2	METIN Altinay †		
3	Petteri VILJANEN ❏		3	OGÜN Temizkanoglu		
4	Petri SULONEN		4	KEMAL Serdar		
5	Jyrki HÄNNIKÄINEN		5	HAMDI Aslan	13	
6	Lars DALSBORG		6	ABDULLAH Ercan		
7	Mika LIPPONEN †		7	TURGUT Uçar		
8	Janne LEHTINEN		8	Jacek CYZIO		
9	György KAJDY	1	9	Yury SHELEPNITSKY ‡		
10	Mika AALTONEN ❏		10	HAMI Mandirali		
11	Marko RAJAMÄKI		11	ORHAN Çikrikçi	60	

	Substitute		*Substitutes*	
	Kim LEHTONEN †4 ❏	83	SEYHMUZ Suna †85	
			ISMAIL Gökçek ‡89	

Referee Hugh WILLIAMSON (Scotland)

SUMMARY

● TPS went into this game aware that no Finnish side had ever before eliminated a team from Turkey in European competition. Few locals considered their team capable of ending that record. That much was evident from the small crowd which turned up to support them. But those who did attend were in good voice after less than a minute's play when TPS's Hungarian import, former Ferencváros player György Kajdy, scored the opening goal. The promise of a miracle comeback lasted only a few minutes, however, Trabzonspor destroying the Finnish side's hopes with a precious away goal on the break. TPS, going through a very lean goalscoring spell in domestic football (they were the lowest scorers in the Finnish Premier Division), were hardly going to score another three goals without reply to take the tie, and when Turkish international left winger Orhan scored a second for the visitors on the hour, that left no room for argument. Trabzonspor were through, joining Istanbul clubs Fenerbahçe and Galatasaray in an unprecedented three-club Turkish assault on the second round.

CUP-WINNERS' CUP
First Round First Leg

Wednesday 16th September 1992
Dalymount Park, Dublin

BOHEMIANS 0 STEAUA BUCURESTI 0

Half-time 0-0 *Attendance* 4,500

		Goals				Goals
1	David HENDERSON		1	Daniel GHERASIM		
2	Tommy BYRNE		2	Aurel PANAIT		
3	Declan GEOGHEGAN		3	Ionel PIRVU		
4	Robbie BEST		4	Anton DOBOS ❏		
5	Paul WHELAN		5	Bogdan BUCUR		
6	Alan BYRNE ❏		6	Stefan IOVAN		
7	Lee KING		7	Ion VLADOIU		
8	Maurice O'DRISCOLL		8	Ilie DUMITRESCU		
9	Joe LAWLESS		9	Viorel ION ‡		
10	Pat FENLON		10	Nica Basarab PANDURU		
11	David TILSON		11	Ilie STAN †		

Substitutes

Ion SBURLEA †10 ❏

Iulian FILIPESCU ‡75

Referee Gilles VEISSIERE (France)

SUMMARY

● *Steaua Bucharest, Champions' Cup winners in 1986, were given a very tough game on their first-ever visit to Dublin in European competition. Bohemians, early leaders of the League of Ireland, celebrated their return to Europe after a five-year absence with a spirited performance. It was the first time that the 'Bohs' had faced continental opposition since 1979. Their three European campaigns since then had seen them paired each time with Scottish opposition. But there were three players in their line-up who had already played against a Romanian team in Europe. Two years earlier Maurice O'Driscoll, Joe Lawless and Pat Fenlon had all played for St. Patrick's Athletic against Dinamo Bucharest in the Champions' Cup. The Dublin side had drawn their home leg on that occasion (Fenlon scoring in a 1-1 draw) and Bohemians were to repeat that feat against Steaua. Another ex-St. Patrick's player, veteran goalkeeper Dave Henderson, was their star as he denied Dumitrescu, Stan and Panduru to keep a clean sheet and give his team a chance, albeit an outside one, in the return.*

CUP-WINNERS' CUP
First Round Second Leg

Tuesday 29th September 1992
Steaua Stadium, Bucharest

STEAUA BUCURESTI 4   BOHEMIANS 0

Half-time 3-0 *Aggregate* 4-0 *Attendance* 15,000

		Goals			Goals
1	Daniel GHERASIM		1	David HENDERSON	
2	Aurel PANAIT ❏ ‡		2	Tommy BYRNE	
3	Ionel PIRVU		3	Declan GEOGHEGAN	
4	Anton DOBOS		4	Robbie BEST	
5	Bogdan BUCUR		5	Paul WHELAN	
6	Ionel FULGA †		6	Alan BYRNE ❏ †	
7	Ion VLADOIU	45	7	Tony O'CONNOR	
8	Ilie DUMITRESCU ❏		8	Maurice O'DRISCOLL ‡	
9	Alexandru ANDRASI	26, 34	9	Joe LAWLESS	
10	Nica Basarab PANDURU ❏		10	Pat FENLON	
11	Ilie STAN		11	David TILSON	
	Substitutes			*Substitutes*	
	Viorel ION †52	85		Lee KING †72	
	Adrian STATE ‡69			Mark DEVLIN ‡82	

Referee Friedrich KAUPE (Austria)

● *Similarities with the Champions' Cup tie between Dinamo Bucharest and St. Patrick's two years earlier were again in evidence as Steaua, like their city rivals before them, showed a much more ruthless streak towards their League of Ireland opponents on home soil and ran out easy 4-0 winners. The Dubliners kept the Steaua attack at bay until the 26th minute, but once former Brasov striker Alexandru Andrasi had put the Romanian Cup holders ahead, the floodgates opened and by half-time Bohemians were 0-3 down and, effectively, out of the competition. Steaua added just one further goal in the second half, a late effort by new signing from Otelul Galati, Viorel Ion, but with the efforts of a big derby win over Dinamo three days earlier still in their limbs, that was hardly surprising. The victory ensured that Steaua maintained their run of not having lost a first-round European tie since 1984. Since then, of course, they had twice reached the Champions' Cup final, winning the trophy in 1986 against Barcelona and losing to Milan three years later.*

CUP-WINNERS' CUP
First Round First Leg

Thursday 17th September 1992
Karaiskakis Stadium, Piraeus

OLYMPIAKOS 0 CHERNOMORETS ODESSA 1

Half-time 0-1 *Attendance* 30,000

		Goals				Goals
1	Yorgos MIRTSOS		1	Oleg SUSLOV		
2	Theodoros PAHATOURIDIS †		2	Yury NIKIFOROV		
3	Kiriakos KARATAIDIS		3	Sergei PROTSYUK		
4	Yorgos MITSIBONAS		4	Yury BUKEL		
5	Mihalis VLAHOS		5	Vladimir LEBED		
6	Panayiotis TSALOUHIDIS		6	Dmitry PARFONOV		
7	Gennady LITOVCHENKO		7	Ilya TSYMBALAR		
8	Nikos TSIANTAKIS		8	Konstantin KULIK		
9	Oleg PROTASOV		9	Oleg KOSHELYUK		
10	Vassilis KARAPIALIS		10	Yury SAK ❑		4
11	Yorgos VAITSIS		11	Sergei GUSEV		

Substitute

Ilias SAVVIDIS †62

Substitutes

Referee Brian HILL (England)

SUMMARY

● *To most outsiders, this result looked to be one of the shocks of the round. But to followers of Greek football, and of Olympiakos in particular, it was just the latest in a long list of European setbacks for the country's biggest football club. Olympiakos's record in Europe had long been a constant source of embarrassment to the club's officials and supporters. It was only on their 25th participation, in the 1989/90 season, that they at last managed to go beyond the second round of any of the three competitions for the first time. But just as their fortunes appeared to be changing, they lost at home to Sampdoria in the following year's Cup-winners' Cup, their notorious fans rioted, and UEFA banned them for a year. Now here they were back in Europe, failing again in front of a big crowd. Chernomorets, who had sailed through their preliminary tie against Vaduz of Liechtenstein, scored early on through midfielder Yuri Sak and managed to hold on to that lead right through to the final whistle, successfully withstanding a barrage of Greek attacks in the process.*

CUP-WINNERS' CUP
First Round Second Leg

Wednesday 30th September 1992
Central Stadium, Odessa

CHERNOMORETS ODESSA 0 OLYMPIAKOS 3

Half-time 0-2 Aggregate 1-3 Attendance 23,000

		Goals				Goals
1	Oleg SUSLOV		1	Yorgos MIRTSOS		
2	Yury NIKIFOROV ❏		2	Theodoros PAHATOURIDIS		
3	Sergei PROTSYUK		3	Kiriakos KARATAIDIS		
4	Yury BUKEL		4	Yorgos MITSIBONAS	15	
5	Vladimir LEBED ‡		5	Mihalis VLAHOS		
6	Dmitry PARFONOV		6	Panayiotis TSALOUHIDIS		
7	Ilya TSYMBALAR		7	Gennady LITOVCHENKO	27	
8	Konstantin KULIK		8	Nikos TSIANTAKIS		
9	Oleg KOSHELYUK †		9	Oleg PROTASOV ‡	80	
10	Yury SAK		10	Vassilis KARAPIALIS ❏ †		
11	Sergei GUSEV		11	Yorgos VAITSIS		

Substitutes

Ruslan ROMANCHUK †72

Andrey LOZOVSKY ‡79

Substitutes

Ilias SAVVIDIS †81

Daniel BATISTA ‡86

Referee Gianni BESCHIN (Italy)

● *The odds were stacked against Olympiakos turning this tie around. For a start, they had never before won a European tie after losing the home leg. And furthermore, Chernomorets had not been beaten in any of their previous six home games in Europe. But this was a night on which the only happy Ukrainians belonged to Olympiakos - coach Oleg Blokhin, a winner of this competition twice as a player with Dinamo Kiev, and former Soviet World Cup stars Gennady Litovchenko and Oleg Protasov. It was an inspired homecoming for the trio. After new signing from PAOK, Yorgos Mitsibonas, had scrambled in the Greeks' first goal on 15 minutes, Litovchenko and Protasov took centre stage, scoring a goal apiece to give Olympiakos an improbable 3-0 victory, and with it a place in round two. Litovchenko's goal was a splendid solo effort, a long-range shot after a run from the halfway line, but Protasov's was even better. A swift, clinical three-man move carved open the Odessa defence before the ace ex-Kiev marksman finished it off with customary aplomb to seal one of the club's best ever results in Europe.*

First Round First Leg

Thursday 17th September 1992
Laugardalsvöllur, Reykjavík

VALUR 0 BOAVISTA FC 0

Half-time 0-0 *Attendance* 400

		Goals				Goals
1	Bjarni SIGURDSSON		1	ALFREDO		
2	Ágúst GYLFASON		2	CASACA		
3	Izudin DERVIC		3	RUI BENTO ❏		
4	Salih PORCA		4	TAVARES		
5	Einar Páll TOMASSON		5	CAETANO		
6	Jón S. HELGASON		6	GARRIDO		
7	Jón Grétar JÓNSSON		7	BOBÓ		
8	Steinar ADÓLFSSON		8	MARLON †		
9	Anthony GREGORY		9	Richard OWUBOKIRI "RICKY"		
10	Gunnlaugur EINARSSON		10	Erwin SANCHEZ		
11	Baldur BRAGASON ❏		11	NELO ❏		

Substitutes

Substitute

TOZÉ †39

Referee Jef VAN VLIET (Holland)

● *A pitiful total of only 400 spectators turned up for this low-key confrontation between the Icelandic and Portuguese Cup winners. And, judging by the desperate quality of the football on display, there was plenty to back the arguments of those who had stayed away. Nobody expected much from Valur in any case. They had never previously won any of their ten Cup-winners' Cup matches, and the last, and only, time they had won a European tie of any description had been 25 years earlier - an away-goals success against Jeunesse Esch of Luxembourg. For this match they also had to do without the services of their only current international, experienced defender Saevar Jónsson, who was out through suspension. The picture was grim enough without Boavista adding to it by playing defensively for a draw. But after 90 uneventful minutes, that is what they got. They were the only one of the five Portuguese entrants in Europe who failed to win their opening match, but with a home game to come against such weak opposition, they remained justifiably confident of qualifying for the second round.*

CUP-WINNERS' CUP
First Round Second Leg

Wednesday 30th September 1992
Dr Alves Vieira Stadium, Torres Novas

BOAVISTA FC 3   VALUR 0

Half-time 2-0 Aggregate 3-0 Attendance 5,000

		Goals				Goals
1	ALFREDO			1	Bjarni SIGURDSSON	
2	JAIME ALVES			2	Ágúst GYLFASON	
3	RUI BENTO			3	Izudin DERVIC	
4	TAVARES			4	Salih PORCA ‡	
5	CAETANO			5	Einar Páll TOMASSON	
6	NOGUEIRA			6	Jón S. HELGASON	
7	CASACA			7	Jón Grétar JÓNSSON	
8	MARLON	13, 81		8	Steinar ADÓLFSSON	
9	Richard OWUBOKIRI "RICKY" ‡	25		9	Anthony GREGORY	
10	Erwin SANCHEZ †			10	Gunnlaugur EINARSSON †	
11	NELO			11	Baldur BRAGASON	
	Substitutes				*Substitutes*	
	BOBÓ †74				Arnljótur DAVÍDSSON †66	
	BAMBO ‡81				Gunnar GUNNARSSON ‡72	

Referee Eric BLAREAU (Belgium)

SUMMARY

● *In the first round of the Cup-winners' Cup a year earlier Valur had gone to Switzerland and drawn 1-1 with FC Sion. It had not been enough on that occasion to take them into the second round, but after the goalless draw in the first leg against Boavista, an identical result this time around in Portugal would have seen the Reykjavík club lay their Cup-winners' Cup bogey to rest once and for all. Alas, it was not to be for the Icelandic minnows. Boavista, despite being suspended from their home stadium, were simply too good for them. Brazilian-born striker Marlon, who had been one of the team's goal-scoring heroes when they eliminated holders Internazionale from the UEFA Cup a year earlier, scored two goals, one in each half, to put his team in the hat for the second round draw. Nigerian striker Ricky, the Portuguese league's top scorer with 30 goals in 1991/92, netted the other goal in a one-sided 3-0 victory which gave Boavista their biggest aggregate winning total in Europe for 13 years.*

CUP-WINNERS' CUP
First Round First Leg

Tuesday 15th September 1992
Broomfield Park, Airdrie

AIRDRIEONIANS 0 SPARTA PRAHA 1

Half-time 0-0 Attendance 7,000

		Goals				Goals
1	John MARTIN		1	Petr KOUBA		
2	Walter KIDD		2	Jan SOPKO		89
3	Sandy STEWART		3	Lumír MISTR		
4	Jimmy SANDISON		4	Petr VRABEC		
5	Chris HONOR		5	Michal HORNÁK		
6	Kenny BLACK		6	Michal BÍLEK ❑		
7	Jimmy BOYLE		7	Jirí NEMEC		
8	Evan BALFOUR		8	Jozef CHOVANEC		
9	Andy SMITH		9	Viktor DVIRNIK †		
10	Alan LAWRENCE		10	Roman VONASEK ❑		
11	Owen COYLE		11	Martin FRYDEK ‡		

Substitutes

Substitutes

Marek TRVAL †70

Pavel NEDVED ‡90

Referee Rune PEDERSEN (Norway)

SUMMARY

● *On paper this looked to be no contest. Airdrie were only playing in the competition because Rangers had done the double in Scotland the previous season. Furthermore, the Lanarkshire club had never featured in European competition before and only three of their players - Hearts old-boys Kidd, Sandison and Black - boasted any sort of European experience. Sparta Prague, on the other hand, were competing at this level for the 10th season on the trot and indeed were being touted by many as the Cup-winners' Cup dark horses after their superb Champions' Cup run in 1991/92. One unfortunate legacy of that campaign, however, was the suspension for this match of two of their best players, defender Jirí Novotny and striker Horst Siegl. In the event, the Scottish side gave their supporters plenty to cheer, but their honest toil and endeavour was not translated into goals, and they paid the price for that when Sparta defender Jan Sopko headed in the only goal of the game from a right-wing corner with just 90 seconds left on the clock.*

CUP-WINNERS' CUP
First Round Second Leg

Tuesday 29th September 1992
Letna Stadium, Prague

SPARTA PRAHA 2 AIRDRIEONIANS 1

Half-time 2-0 *Aggregate* 3-1 *Attendance* 8,989

		Goals				Goals
1	Petr KOUBA		1	John MARTIN		
2	Jan SOPKO		2	Walter KIDD		
3	Lumír MISTR		3	Sandy STEWART ❏		
4	Petr VRABEC	31	4	Jimmy SANDISON		
5	Michal HORNÁK		5	Gus CAESAR ❏ †		
6	Michal BÍLEK		6	Kenny BLACK ❏	56	
7	Jirí NEMEC		7	Jimmy BOYLE ‡		
8	Jozef CHOVANEC		8	Evan BALFOUR		
9	Roman VONASEK	37	9	Andy SMITH		
10	Horst SIEGL ‡		10	Owen COYLE		
11	Martin FRYDEK †		11	Chris HONOR		

Substitutes

Pavel NEDVED †87

Viktor DVIRNIK ‡89

Substitutes

Davie KIRKWOOD †54

Alan LAWRENCE ❏ ‡65

Referee Atanas UZUNOV (Bulgaria)

SUMMARY

● *Two first-half goals within the space of six minutes killed off this tie and ensured that Sparta Prague eliminated Scottish opposition in the first round of European competition for the second year running following their away goals success against Rangers in the Champions' Cup a year earlier. Left-back Petr Vrabec, an ever-present in Sparta's 1991/92 European run, and striker Roman Vonasek, a relative newcomer to the side, were the men who found a way past barely-fit Airdrie 'keeper John Martin to ease their side into round two. Airdrie's pride was salvaged with a goal from Kenny Black early in the second period, but 'Rough Diamonds' was arguably the most appropriate headline to sum up the team's overall performance after no fewer than four of their players had their names pencilled into the Bulgarian referee's notebook.*

CUP-WINNERS' CUP
First Round First Leg

Tuesday 15th September 1992
Mourneview Park, Lurgan

GLENAVON 1 ROYAL ANTWERP FC 1

Half-time 1-0 *Attendance* 2,500

		Goals				Goals
1	Robbie BECK		1	Ratko SVILAR		
2	Trevor McMULLAN		2	Geert EMMERECHTS		
3	Tony SCAPPATICI ❑		3	Nico BROECKAERT		
4	Paul BYRNE		4	Rudy SMIDTS		
5	Michael McKEOWN †		5	Didier SEGERS		
6	Colin CRAWFORD		6	Wim KIEKENS		
7	Sammy SMITH	45	7	Ronny VAN RETHY		
8	Brian KENNEDY		8	Patrick VAN VEIRDEGHEM ❑		
9	Glenn FERGUSON		9	Dragan JAKOVLJEVIC		
10	Geoff FERRIS		10	Hans-Peter LEHNHOFF	46	
11	Michael CROWE		11	Alex CZERNIATYNSKI †		
	Substitute			*Substitute*		
	Fintan McCONVILLE †89			Francis SEVEREYNS †76		

Referee Nemus DJURHUUS (Faeroe Isles)

SUMMARY

● *Antwerp might have wished for a grander setting than Glenavon's tiny Mourneview Park ground for their debut appearance in the Cup-winners' Cup, but they could take nothing for granted against their Irish League opponents. The Lurgan club had qualified for Europe for four of the past five seasons and although they had never managed to pass the first round, they had been unlucky to go down to Finnish side Ilves on away goals the previous season after winning the home leg 3-2. There was plenty of local optimism for a repeat performance, and that was heightened on the stroke of half-time when Sammy Smith latched on to a loose ball in the area to put Glenavon ahead. But the half-time interval was all the time the home supporters had to enjoy their lead. The first attacking move of the second half brought Antwerp's equaliser, with German playmaker Hans-Peter Lehnhoff beating Glenavon 'keeper Robbie Beck at the near post from a tight angle after he had been set free on the left by Jakovljevic.*

Wednesday 30th September 1992
Bosuil Stadium, Antwerp

ROYAL ANTWERP FC 1   GLENAVON 1 (aet)

Half-time 0-0 *Aggregate* 2-2 (Antwerp win 3-1 on penalties) *Attendance* 4,000

		Goals			Goals
1	Ratko SVILAR		1	Robbie BECK	
2	Wim KIEKENS	65 (pen)	2	Trevor McMULLAN	
3	Nico BROECKAERT		3	Tony SCAPPATICI †	
4	Geert EMMERECHTS ❑		4	Paul BYRNE	
5	Rudy SMIDTS		5	Michael McKEOWN	
6	Nourédine MOUKRIM		6	Brian KENNEDY	
7	Ronny VAN RETHY ‡		7	Colin CRAWFORD ❑	
8	Didier SEGERS		8	Fintan McCONVILLE ‡	
9	Francis SEVEREYNS		9	Glenn FERGUSON ❑	
10	Hans-Peter LEHNHOFF ❑		10	Geoff FERRIS	81
11	Alex CZERNIATYNSKI †		11	Michael CROWE	

Substitutes		*Substitutes*	
Willy VINCENT †78		Keith PERCY †75	
Patrick VAN VEIRDEGHEM ‡107		Sammy SMITH ‡77	

Referee Heinz HOLZMANN (Austria)

● It had been elimination on the away goals rule the previous season. Now Irish League part-timers Glenavon had to suffer the agony of defeat in a penalty shoot-out as their dreams of passing the opening round in Europe for the first time disappeared for yet another year. That they came so close to putting out the Belgian Cup holders, however, was a mark of their achievement, and this was recognised by the club's directors who agreed to pay their players a win bonus even though they did not actually win the game. Antwerp had won the Belgian Cup final a few months earlier by defeating Mechelen in a penalty shoot-out and they certainly appeared the calmer of the two teams when it came down to the dreaded spot-kick lottery, winning it easily by three goals to one after three Glenavon players failed to hold their nerve. All this unexpected drama had been made possible by a shock 80th-minute goal from 30-year-old Glenavon striker Geoff Ferris which cancelled out Antwerp's opener from right-back Wim Kiekens - scored, need it be said, from the penalty spot!

CARDIFF CITY 1 FC ADMIRA WACKER 1

Half-time 0-1 *Attendance* 9,624

		Goals			Goals
1	Mark GREW		1	Franz GRUBER	
2	Tony BIRD †		2	Alois DÖTZL	
3	Damon SEARLE		3	Thomas ZINGLER	
4	Lee BADDELEY		4	Michael GRUBER	
5	Gareth ABRAHAM		5	Gerald MESSLENDER ❑	
6	Derek BRAZIL		6	Johannes ABFALTERER	44
7	Paul RAMSEY ❑		7	Andreas GUTLEDERER †	
8	Cohen GRIFFITH		8	Peter ARTNER	
9	Chris PIKE	59	9	Kurt TEMM	
10	Carl DALE		10	Roger LJUNG	
11	Nathan BLAKE ❑		11	Olaf MARSCHALL	

Substitute		*Substitute*	
Andy GORMAN †72		Gerald BACHER †53	

Referee Jorge MONTEIRO COROADO (Portugal)

SUMMARY

● *Unbeknown to many of the watching public at Ninian Park, Cardiff City were making history in this tie. It was the 13th time that the Welsh club had set out on a Cup-winners' Cup campaign, beating the previous record of 12 entries held jointly with the three-time winners of the competition, FC Barcelona. Unfortunately, though, the Bluebirds could not celebrate their achievement with a victory. In fact, they were extremely fortunate to emerge from the contest with a 1-1 draw. Their opponents, Austrian club Admira Wacker, outplayed them for long periods and deservedly took the lead just before the interval with a 'pin-ball'-type goal from Johannes Abfalterer, the ball deflecting off the limbs of three Cardiff players before it crossed the line. The home side's equaliser arrived 14 minutes into the second half when Chris Pike soared above a static Austrian defence to head in Damon Searle's free-kick. On the evidence of the overall play, however, that single goal looked insufficient to help Cardiff's cause in the return.*

CUP-WINNERS' CUP
First Round Second Leg

Tuesday 29th September 1992
Südstadt Stadium, Vienna

FC ADMIRA WACKER 2 CARDIFF CITY 0

Half-time 0-0 *Aggregate* 3-1 *Attendance* 4,700

Goals   Goals

1	Franz GRUBER			1	Mark GREW		
2	Alois DÖTZL			2	Robbie JAMES		
3	Uwe MÜLLER †			3	Damon SEARLE		
4	Michael GRUBER			4	Lee BADDELEY		
5	Gerald MESSLENDER			5	Gareth ABRAHAM †		
6	Johannes ABFALTERER ❑ 90			6	Derek BRAZIL		
7	Gerald BACHER ❑			7	Paul RAMSEY ❑		
8	Peter ARTNER			8	Cohen GRIFFITH		
9	Kurt TEMM			9	Chris PIKE		
10	Roger LJUNG			10	Carl DALE		
11	Olaf MARSCHALL 47			11	Nathan BLAKE		

Substitute   *Substitute*

Thomas ZINGLER †53   Tony BIRD †49

Referee Lube SPASOV (Bulgaria)

SUMMARY

● *Cardiff manager Eddie May was adamant. "We will score!" he proclaimed, citing Admira Wacker's defensive vulnerability as the reason for his optimism before this second leg clash in the south of Vienna. But it was a comedy of errors in his own defence which was to decide the outcome of the tie. The Welsh Cup winners were still in contention for an improbable qualification when, just two minutes into the second half, an 'air-shot' from a Cardiff defender allowed Admira's Swedish international Roger Ljung to shoot at goal. Goalkeeper Mark Grew looked to have it covered, but the ball bounced up, went through his arms, rebounded off his forehead and fell perfectly for ex-East German international Olaf Marschall to nod Admira in front. Despite the graft and experience of veteran international Robbie James, back on the European stage he graced on several occasions in the '80s with Swansea City, Cardiff could not fulfil their manager's promise and equalise, and Abfalterer's second goal of the tie, poked in from close range in the last minute, was simply the icing on the cake for the home side.*

CUP-WINNERS' CUP
First Round First Leg

Wednesday 16th September 1992
Ennio Tardini Stadium, Parma

PARMA 1 ÚJPESTI TE 0

Half-time 0-0 *Attendance* 11,603

		Goals			Goals
1	Claudio TAFFAREL		1	Attila GRÓF ❑	
2	Antonio BENARRIVO		2	János TOMKA	
3	Alberto DI CHIARA		3	Zoltán ACZÉL	
4	Lorenzo MINOTTI		4	Zoltán SZLEZÁK	
5	Luigi APOLLONI		5	Balázs BÉRCZY ■	
6	Georges GRÜN		6	Tamás SZÖNYI	
7	Alessandro MELLI		7	Zoltán KECSKÉS	
8	Daniele ZORATTO †		8	Sándor BÁCSI †	
9	Marco OSIO		9	Zoltán MIOVECZ	
10	Gabriele PIN ❑ ‡		10	György VÉBER	
11	Faustino ASPRILLA	49	11	Zsolt FÜZESI ‡	
	Substitutes			*Substitutes*	
	Giovanni SORCE †73			Tamás TIEFENBACH †55	
	Ivo PULGA ‡90			Csaba HETESI ‡68	

Referee Michal LISTKIEWICZ (Poland)

SUMMARY

● Parma's European debut the previous season had ended in tears with a shock away-goals elimination in the first round of the UEFA Cup by CSKA Sofia. Eager to avoid a similar fate against another Eastern European team, the Italian Cup holders went all out for a clear victory in this home leg, making use of the full width of the pitch through their enterprising wing-backs Benarrivo and Di Chiara. So prominent were these two players and their ability to cross the ball into threatening positions that Parma should have set up a sizeable first-leg advantage against their modest opponents. But with Swedish striker Tomas Brolin still recovering from an injury sustained at the Olympics, the Italians lacked ingenuity up front. The one goal of the evening was scored by Brolin's replacement in the team, Colombian international Faustino Asprilla, but that solitary strike was poor reward for Parma's domination. Újpesti's best player was unquestionably their goalkeeper Attila Gróf, a close-season signing from Second Division Volán, but even he blotted his copybook with a yellow card.

CUP-WINNERS' CUP
First Round Second Leg

PARMA A.C.

Thursday 1st October 1992
Megyeri út Stadium, Budapest

ÚJPESTI TE 1   PARMA 1

Half-time 0-0   Aggregate 1-2   Attendance 10,000

		Goals				Goals
1	Attila GRÓF		1	Marco BALLOTTA		
2	János TOMKA ❑		2	Ivo PULGA		
3	Zoltán ACZÉL		3	Salvatore MATRECANO		
4	Zoltán SZLEZÁK		4	Lorenzo MINOTTI		
5	Zoltán MIOVECZ		5	Luigi APOLLONI		
6	Tamás SZÖNYI		6	Georges GRÜN ❑	53	
7	Zoltán KECSKÉS		7	Alessandro MELLI ❑		
8	János ZSINKA †		8	Daniele ZORATTO †		
9	Tamás TIEFENBACH		9	Gabriele PIN		
10	György VÉBER ❑		10	Stefano CUOGHI		
11	Ferenc LOVÁSZ ‡		11	Faustino ASPRILLA ‡		

Substitutes

Sándor BÁCSI †54	Aldo MONZA †60
Csaba HETESI ‡56 62	Sergio BERTI ‡82

Referee Frans VAN DEN WIJNGAERT (Belgium)

● *Parma, despite missing their first-leg stars Benarrivo and Di Chiara, were once again a class above Újpesti in all areas of the field. Except one. Namely, the art of putting the ball in the back of the net. As in the first leg, strikers Melli and Asprilla failed to cement Parma's superiority, wasting a number of opportunities to get their names on the scoresheet. In the end, it was left to defender Georges Grün to save his team-mates' blushes. In 45 previous European matches, the bulk of them for Anderlecht, the Belgian national team captain had scored just one goal. Now he made it two with a header early in the second half that virtually ensured Parma's passage into the next round. The Hungarians replied less than 10 minutes later with a goal from their substitute Hetesi, but it was an equaliser that was barely deserved. Under their old name of Újpesti Dózsa the club had reached the semi-finals of all three European competitions, plus the final of the Fairs' Cup against Newcastle in 1969. This team, however, was, like Hungarian football in general, a pale shadow of its once glorious past.*

CUP-WINNERS' CUP
First Round First Leg

Tuesday 15th September 1992
Råsunda Stadium, Solna (Stockholm)

AIK 3 AGF 3

Half-time 0-2 *Attendance* 3,976

		Goals				Goals
1	Bernt LJUNG		1	Troels RASMUSSEN		
2	Krister NORDIN		2	Lasse SKOV		
3	Björn KINDLUND		3	Kent NIELSEN		
4	Anders HJELM		4	Claus THOMSEN		
5	Peter LARSSON		5	Claus CHRISTIANSEN		
6	Vadim YEVTUSHENKO	85	6	Bo HARDER		
7	Michael BORGQVIST		7	Jan Halvor HALVORSEN ❏		
8	Kim BERGSTRAND		8	Torben CHRISTENSEN †	36, 54	
9	Pascal SIMPSON	51	9	Stig TØFTING ❏		15
10	Peter HALLSTRÖM †	56	10	Jan BARTRAM		
11	Gary SUNDGREN		11	Søren ANDERSEN ‡		

Substitute

Dick LIDMAN †74

Substitutes

Ole MORTENSEN †65
Palle SØRENSEN ‡74

Referee Stephen LODGE (England)

S U M M A R Y

● *Swedish and Danish clubs had met four times before in European competition, but this was the first confrontation in the Cup-winners' Cup. With Scandinavian football enjoying a boom after the success of both Denmark and Sweden at the Euro '92 finals, both AIK and AGF were eager to put on a good show. AIK were going well in their domestic league, having just moved to the top of the Swedish championship play-off table the previous weekend after a 4-2 triumph over reigning champions IFK Gothenburg. But they found themselves 0-2 down at half-time. Stig Tøfting, a member of Denmark's Olympic Games squad in Barcelona, scored AGF's 50th goal in Europe after a quarter of an hour and former Danish international Torben Christensen made it 2-0 to the visitors 21 minutes later. But the second half saw the Swedes raise their game and eventually grab an improbable 3-3 draw with a late equaliser from Ukrainian Vadim Yevtushenko. The former Soviet international had also scored a goal in his last Cup-winners' Cup appearance - for Dinamo Kiev in their 3-0 victory over Atlético Madrid in the 1986 final!*

CUP-WINNERS' CUP
First Round Second Leg

Tuesday 29th September 1992
Aarhus Stadium, Aarhus

AGF 1 AIK 1

Half-time 0-1 *Aggregate* 4-4 (AGF win on away goals) *Attendance* 9,000

		Goals				Goals
1	Troels RASMUSSEN			1	Bernt LJUNG	
2	Lasse SKOV †			2	Krister NORDIN ❏	
3	Kent NIELSEN			3	Björn KINDLUND	
4	Claus THOMSEN			4	Anders HJELM	
5	Claus CHRISTIANSEN ‡			5	Peter LARSSON	
6	Bo HARDER	67		6	Vadim YEVTUSHENKO	
7	Jan Halvor HALVORSEN			7	Michael BORGQVIST ❏	
8	Torben CHRISTENSEN			8	Kim BERGSTRAND	
9	Stig TØFTING			9	Pascal SIMPSON	20
10	Jan BARTRAM			10	Peter HALLSTRÖM †	
11	Søren ANDERSEN ❏			11	Gary SUNDGREN ❏	

Substitutes			*Substitute*	
Palle SØRENSEN †57			Dick LIDMAN †75	
Gunner Lind PEDERSEN ‡71				

Referee Arturo MARTINO (Switzerland)

● AIK's increasingly notorious hooligan following was on the warpath in the build-up to this return fixture on Denmark's Jutland peninsula. 30 members of the self-proclaimed 'Black Army' were arrested as they attacked innocent Danes and burned down a house on their way to the game. And further woe was inflicted on the locals when after just 20 minutes AIK's coloured Under-21 star, Pascal Simpson, latched on to a deflected cross to volley home his second goal of the tie and put the Swedes in front. There might have been further goals for the visitors in a first half which they dominated. But after the break AGF took command and were rewarded with an equaliser midway through the half from Bo Harder, who lashed home a first-time right-foot shot after a clever cut-back from the byline. Young striker Søren Andersen had two good opportunities after that to seal the Danes' qualification, but at 1-1 the home side were through to the next round. Remarkably, it was the first time ever in European competition that a Danish club had won a tie on the away goals rule!

CUP-WINNERS' CUP
First Round First Leg

Wednesday 16th September 1992
Olympic Stadium, Moscow

SPARTAK MOSKVA 0 AVENIR BEGGEN 0

Half-time 0-0 *Attendance* 5,000

Goals   Goals

1	Stanislav CHERCHESOV		1	Paul KOCH	
2	Dmitry KHLESTOV		2	Ralph FERRON	
3	Andrey IVANOV		3	Rolf JENTGEN	
4	Nikolai PISAREV †		4	Jean VANEK	
5	Mikhail RUSYAEV		5	Alex WILHELM ‡	
6	Andrey CHERNYSHOV		6	Jaba MOREIRA	
7	Viktor ONOPKO		7	Théo SCHOLTEN	
8	Valery KARPIN		8	Carlo WEIS	
9	Andrey PYATNITSKY		9	Frank GOERGEN	
10	Igor LEDYAKHOV ❏		10	Armin KRINGS ❏ †	
11	Dmitry RADCHENKO		11	Luc HOLTZ	

Substitute

Vladimir BESCHASTNYKH †50

Substitutes

Markus KRAHEN †58
Serge JENTGEN ‡74

Referee Luben ANGELOV (Bulgaria)

S U M M A R Y

● *This was a sensational result in so many ways. If ever there was a 'home banker', this was it. Spartak, the Champions' Cup semi-finalists in 1991 and a team on the verge of capturing the inaugural Russian championship after a brilliant 5-2 away victory over closest rivals Spartak Vladikavkaz five days earlier, against Avenir Beggen of Luxembourg, a club which had only just scraped past the Cup winners of the Faeroe Isles in the preliminary round to register their first ever success in 12 seasons of European competition. But with everybody fully expecting Spartak to record their best-ever home win in Europe, the Russians proved incapable of finding a way past Beggen's international 'keeper Paul Koch even once. The draw meant that after losing every one of their first 20 games in Europe, Beggen had now been beaten in only one of their last five! More importantly, there remained the very real possibility that they might even win the return match at home and reach the dizzy heights of the second round for the very first time...*

CUP-WINNERS' CUP
First Round Second Leg

Wednesday 30th September 1992
Beggen Stadium, Luxembourg

AVENIR BEGGEN 1 SPARTAK MOSKVA 5

Half-time 0-2 *Aggregate* 1-5 *Attendance* 2,000

		Goals				Goals
1	Paul KOCH		1	Stanislav CHERCHESOV		
2	Ralph FERRON		2	Dmitry KHLESTOV		
3	Théo SCHOLTEN †		3	Andrey IVANOV ‡		
4	Jean VANEK		4	Dmitry POPOV		59
5	Jaba MOREIRA ‡		5	Mikhail RUSYAEV †		
6	Serge JENTGEN		6	Andrey CHERNYSHOV		
7	Markus KRAHEN		7	Viktor ONOPKO		6
8	Carlos WEIS		8	Valery KARPIN		
9	Frank GOERGEN ❏		9	Andrey PYATNITSKY		9, 79
10	Armin KRINGS		10	Igor LEDYAKHOV		
11	Luc HOLTZ		11	Dmitry RADCHENKO		55

Substitutes

Substitutes

DOS SANTOS LOPES †46

Vladimir BESCHASTNYKH †26

Mario NOVAK ‡77   87

Oleg KUZHLEV ‡76

Referee Sten JOHANSSON (Sweden)

SUMMARY

● *Avenir Beggen's dreams of glory did not last long. With only ten minutes of the match elapsed, they had already conceded two goals. Spartak were clearly intent on erasing the embarrassment of the first leg as swiftly as possible, and those early strikes from ex-CIS internationals Viktor Onopko and Andrey Pyatnitsky were just what they needed. Beggen had won both of their last two home games in Europe, but there was clearly no way back for them now. They had never scored three goals in a European tie before, and with Spartak proving a far more effective outfit than they had been in the first leg, the contest was already effectively over. The Russians' superiority was reflected in the second half with three further goals, from Radchenko, Popov and Pyatnitsky again, before Novak scored a consolation goal five minutes from time. It was the fifth time that Spartak had managed to score five goals away from home in Europe (the most memorable example being their 5-2 thrashing of Arsenal at Highbury in 1982/83), a feat they had achieved only once at home (against Toulouse in 1986/87).*

Wednesday 16th September 1992
Anfield, Liverpool

LIVERPOOL 6 APOLLON LIMASSOL 1

Half-time 3-0 Attendance 12,769

		Goals				Goals
1	David JAMES			1	Michalis CHRISTOPHI	
2	Steve HARKNESS †			2	Andonis ELIA "ANDRELIS"	
3	David BURROWS ❏			3	Charalambos PITTAS ❏	
4	Steve NICOL			4	Dimitris IOANNOU	
5	Jamie REDKNAPP			5	David KENNY	
6	Mark WRIGHT			6	Yiannakis YIANGOUDAKIS	
7	Mike MARSH			7	George IOSIPHIDES	
8	Paul STEWART ‡	4, 38		8	Milenko SPOLJARIC	83 (pen)
9	Ian RUSH	39, 50, 55, 74		9	Chrysostomos JURAS	
10	Jan MØLBY			10	Pambos CHRISTOPHI †	
11	Mark WALTERS			11	Marios CHARALAMBOUS ❏ ■	

Substitutes

Philip CHARNOCK †58

Ronny ROSENTHAL ‡85

Substitute

Andreas SOFOCLEOUS †60

Referee José Alberto VEIGA TRIGO (Portugal)

SUMMARY

● *Liverpool set out on their quest for the one European title that had so far eluded them without the man who had scored nine goals for them in the UEFA Cup the previous season. Dean Saunders had just been transferred to Aston Villa a few days earlier, but against the small fry of Apollon Limassol, the Merseysiders did not need him. After all, they still had his Welsh international colleague Ian Rush. And this was to be Rush's night! The lean number nine scored four goals, all of them stamped with his trademark, that of the penalty-box poacher. The goal which completed his hat-trick was his 18th in European competition and it enabled him to overtake the previous club record held by Roger Hunt. Liverpool's other two goals in this 6-1 victory, and the ones which began the rout, were scored by new signing from Tottenham, Paul Stewart. The only disappointment for Liverpool on a night when they created an incredible 39 goal attempts was the size of the crowd - their second lowest ever for a European match.*

Tuesday 29th September 1992
Tsirion Stadium, Limassol

APOLLON LIMASSOL 1 LIVERPOOL 2

Half-time 0-0 *Aggregate* 2-8 *Attendance* 10,000

		Goals				Goals
1	Michalis CHRISTOPHI		1	Bruce GROBBELAAR		
2	Andonis ELIA "ANDRELIS"		2	Mike MARSH ❏		
3	Charalambos PITTAS		3	David BURROWS		
4	Dimitris IOANNOU ❏		4	Nicky TANNER		
5	Pambos CHRISTOPHI		5	Jamie REDKNAPP		
6	Yiannakis YIANGOUDAKIS		6	Don HUTCHISON	68	
7	George IOSIPHIDES		7	Steve McMANAMAN		
8	Milenko SPOLJARIC	60	8	Paul STEWART ■		
9	Chrysostomos JURAS †		9	Ian RUSH	62	
10	Angelos TSOLAKIS ‡		10	Jan MØLBY		
11	David KENNY		11	Mark WALTERS †		

Substitutes

Andreas SOFOCLEOUS †6
Avgoustinos GENNARIS ‡66

Substitute

Steve HARKNESS †81

Referee Loris STAFOGGIA (Italy)

SUMMARY

● *A year earlier Liverpool had opened their European season with a 6-1 win at Anfield before going to Finland and losing 1-0 to FC Kuusysi. Now, once again, they travelled to one of Europe's less celebrated footballing outposts with a 6-1 first-leg advantage. But unfortunately for their Cypriot hosts, history did not repeat itself. Not that a victory for Apollon would have been such a big surprise. The Limassol club had beaten Universitatea Craiova 3-0 the previous season in the Champions' Cup. As for Liverpool, their form in domestic competition had just reached a new low, conceding 11 goals in their previous three fixtures not having won away for almost nine months! So when Apollon's Milenko Spoljaric scored his second goal of the tie with a full-blooded drive on the hour, a home win was a distinct possibility. Ian Rush quickly levelled matters, though, and six minutes later Don Hutchison marked a fine European debut with a well-taken winner. All was not sweetness and light, however, for Graeme Souness's team as Paul Stewart subsequently got himself sent off for a gentle pat in Apollon 'keeper Christophi's face.*

CUP-WINNERS' CUP
First Round First Leg

Wednesday 16th September 1992
Levski Stadium, Sofia

LEVSKI SOFIA 2 FC LUZERN 1

Half-time 0-1 *Attendance* 8,000

		Goals			Goals
1	Plamen NIKOLOV		1	Beat MUTTER	
2	Petar KHUBCHEV		2	Peter GMÜR	
3	Valentin DARTILOV		3	Urs BIRRER †	
4	Zlatko YANKOV		4	René VAN ECK ❏	
5	Nikolai ILIEV		5	Martin RUEDA	
6	Georgi SLAVCHEV ‡		6	Christoph GILLI	
7	Daniel BORIMIROV	53	7	Hanspeter BURRI ❏	
8	Plamen GETOV	70 (pen)	8	Roberto FREGNO ❏	
9	Rumen STOIANOV		9	Urs GÜNTENSPERGER ‡	
10	Ilian ILIEV ❏		10	Oliver CAMENZIND ❏	9
11	Ivailo YOTOV †		11	Semir TUCE	

Substitutes		*Substitutes*	
Nikolai MITOV †17 ❏		Adalbert KOCH †37	
Vladko SHALAMANOV ‡46		Stefan WOLF ‡55	

Referee Václav KRONDL (Czechoslovakia)

● Levski Sofia had every reason to feel confident going into this tie. They had made an excellent start to their domestic championship and were up against opponents who had been relegated the previous season into the Swiss Second Division (NLB). Furthermore, Levski were embarking on their 23rd campaign in Europe, as opposed to Luzern's fifth. The last time Luzern had competed in the Cup-winners' Cup was the very first year it was held, in 1960/61, when they lost 9-2 on aggregate to eventual winners Fiorentina. But, against the odds, it was the Swiss Cup holders who took the lead as early as the ninth minute through Under-21 international Oliver Camenzind, and it stayed that way until half-time. The Bulgarians eventually won the game with two second-half goals from youngster Daniel Borimirov and 1986 World Cup veteran Plamen Getov, but 2-1 was far from the ideal scoreline for Ivan Voutsov's team. Whenever Levski had won their home legs by that scoreline previously in European competition - it had occurred four times - they had lost the away leg.

CUP-WINNERS' CUP
First Round Second Leg

Wednesday 30th September 1992
Allmend Stadium, Lucerne

FC LUZERN 1 LEVSKI SOFIA 0

Half-time 1-0 *Aggregate* 2-2 (FC Luzern win on away goals) *Attendance* 12,000

		Goals				Goals
1	Beat MUTTER			1	Plamen NIKOLOV	
2	Peter GMÜR			2	Petar KHUBCHEV †	
3	Urs BIRRER			3	Valentin DARTILOV ❑	
4	René VAN ECK			4	Krasimir KOEV ❑	
5	Martin RUEDA			5	Nikolai ILIEV	
6	Urs SCHÖNENBERGER			6	Zlatko YANKOV	
7	Hanspeter BURRI ‡			7	Daniel BORIMIROV	
8	Roberto FREGNO			8	Plamen GETOV	
9	Urs GÜNTENSPERGER †			9	Dimitar VASILEV	
10	Oliver CAMENZIND	23		10	Ilian ILIEV	
11	Semir TUCE			11	Georgi DONKOV ‡	

Substitutes

Brian BERTELSEN †69

Stefan WOLF ‡89

Substitutes

Nikolai MITOV †55

Valeri VALKOV ‡77

Referee Joaquín URIO VELAZQUEZ (Spain)

● Oliver Camenzind's second goal of the tie, struck home in the 24th minute, was enough to take Luzern into the second round on the away goals rule and maintain Swiss interest in all three competitions. It was only their second ever aggregate victory in European competition, the first having come two years earlier in the UEFA Cup against Hungarian side MTK-VM, ironically enough the team with whom their coach, Bertalan Bicskei, had reached the Cup-winners' Cup quarter-finals as a goalkeeper back in 1977. Levski Sofia had only themselves to blame for not going through. They spurned chances galore throughout the 90 minutes and that consigned them to the first-round scrapheap along with the three other Bulgarian representatives, CSKA Sofia and the two Plovdiv clubs, Lokomotiv and Botev. It meant that Levski had now lost six European ties in succession, their last success stretching back to 1986 when they defeated Velez Mostar whilst competing under their former name of Vitosha.

Wednesday 16th September 1992
Ljudski Vrt Stadium, Maribor

MARIBOR BRANIK 0   ATLETICO MADRID 3

Half-time 0-2   Attendance 5,000

		Goals				Goals
1	Mladen DABANOVIC		1	ABEL Resino		
2	Emil STERBAL		2	Carlos AGUILERA ❑		
3	Bostjan RATKOVIC		3	Antonio Muñoz "TONI" †		
4	Zarko TARANA ❑		4	Roberto SOLOZABAL		
5	Saso LUKIC		5	Francisco FERREIRA		
6	Ales KRIZAN		6	DONATO Gama da Silva		
7	Ante SIMUNDZA		7	ALFREDO Santaelena	26	
8	Peter BINKOVSKI †		8	Bernd SCHUSTER		
9	Ermin SUSIC		9	Juan VIZCAINO		
10	Renato KOTNIK		10	Paulo FUTRE ‡		
11	Marijan BAKULA ❑ ‡		11	LUIS GARCIA	42, 56	

Substitutes

Saso GAJSER †60

Marko KRIZANIC ‡73

Substitutes

Juan Francisco Rodríguez "JUANITO" †46

Manuel ALFARO ‡53

Referee HASAN Ceylan (Turkey)

SUMMARY

● *Two goals for Mexican international striker Luis García, signed in the summer by Atlético as the 'new Hugo Sánchez', completed a comprehensive first-leg victory for one of the pre-tournament favourites against the Slovenian novices of Maribor Branik. Maribor had thrashed Maltese Trophy holders Hamrun Spartans 4-0 at home in the preliminary round, but they found the Spanish giants a different proposition altogether. Once Alfredo had headed skilfully across the 'keeper to put Atlético ahead midway through the first half, there was only one team in it. Luis García made it 2-0 just before half-time, tapping in Alfredo's cross, and he rounded off an impressive European debut with a delightful first-time chip from the edge of the area shortly after the interval. 3-0 up and with the home leg still to come, Atlético were virtually certain to prolong their record of never having been eliminated from the Cup-winners' Cup in the first round.*

Wednesday 30th September 1992
Vicente Calderón Stadium, Madrid

ATLETICO MADRID 6 MARIBOR BRANIK 1

Half-time 2-1 *Aggregate* 9-1 *Attendance* 3,000

		Goals				Goals
1	Angel MEJIAS		1	Darko DUBRAVICA		
2	PIZO GOMEZ	70	2	Saso GAJSER †		
3	PEDRO González		3	Bostjan RATKOVIC		
4	Francisco FERREIRA		4	Zarko TARANA	84 (og)	
5	TOMAS Reñones		5	Saso LUKIC ❑		
6	Juan Francisco Rodríguez "JUANITO" 45		6	Ales KRIZAN		
7	Gabriel MOYA		7	Ante SIMUNDZA ■		
8	Antonio ACOSTA		8	Peter BINKOVSKI		
9	Juan VIZCAINO †		9	Mirsad BICAKCIC	22	
10	Manuel ALFARO ‡	17	10	Renato KOTNIK ‡		
11	Juan SABAS	48 (pen)	11	Marijan BAKULA ❑		

Substitutes			*Substitutes*		
Manuel Sánchez "MANOLO" †50 ❑			Simon DVORSAK †49		
Carlos AGUILERA ‡75	80		Marko KRIZANIC ‡65		

Referee Gerhard KAPL (Austria)

● *There were only 3,000 spectators in the Vicente Calderón stadium to watch a deliberately understrength Atlético notch up six more goals against Maribor Branik and thereby complete their biggest aggregate victory in Europe since their very first tie, against Drumcondra in the preliminary round of the 1958/59 Champions' Cup (13-1). The Slovenians provided cannon fodder for the Atlético attack in a rip-roaring second-half display. Up until a minute before the interval Maribor were actually holding their own, with Bikakcic having equalised Alfaro's early goal after a fine counter-attack on the right. But Juanito's header in the 45th minute heralded a rout in the second period. Four goals followed, each of them from a different scorer. The most memorable was saved until last, a bizarre own goal from Tarana, who must have had a rush of blood to the head as he met a left-wing cross with the instinct of a seasoned striker and sent the ball flashing past his own bewildered 'keeper into the net!*

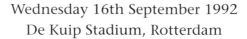

CUP-WINNERS' CUP
First Round First Leg

Wednesday 16th September 1992
De Kuip Stadium, Rotterdam

FEYENOORD 1 HAPOEL PETACH-TIKVA 0

Half-time 0-0 *Attendance* 19,000

		Goals			Goals
1	Ed DE GOEY		1	Rafi COHEN	
2	Arnold SCHOLTEN †		2	Benny KOZOSHVILY	
3	John DE WOLF ❑ ‡		3	Avi KEISY	
4	John METGOD		4	Uda BAHAGAT ❑	
5	Errol REFOS		5	Carlos OLERAN	
6	Peter BOSZ		6	Noam KEISY	
7	Henk FRÄSER		7	Yossi LEVY	
8	Gaston TAUMENT		8	Uzi HOAION	
9	József KIPRICH	89	9	Nir LEVIN	
10	Rob WITSCHGE		10	Ely MACHPOD	
11	Regi BLINKER		11	Mordachy KAKON ❑	

Substitutes

Mike OBIKU †60

Ulrich VAN GOBBEL ‡75

Substitutes

Referee Erny KESSELER (Luxembourg)

SUMMARY

● *Hapoel Petach-Tikva's 4-0 aggregate demolition of Norway's Strømsgodset in the preliminary round was an impressive enough achievement for the Israeli club on their first outing in European competition. But for 89 minutes it looked as if they would surpass that by holding the 91/92 Cup-winners' Cup semi-finalists Feyenoord to an unexpected goalless draw in Rotterdam. Time was almost up when Hungarian striker József Kiprich beat his marker to the ball in the penalty area and rifled home a right-foot shot to give Feyenoord a 1-0 victory. It was the continuation of a good goalscoring run by the former Tatabánya player. Despite being under threat for his place by the club's new Nigerian striker Mike Obiku, Kiprich was at the head of the Dutch 'Eredivisie' top scorer charts with five goals in five games, only two of which he had started. His only previous goal in Europe had come six months earlier in the 91/92 quarter-final when he scored the only goal of the tie against Tottenham Hotspur.*

Wednesday 30th September 1992
Ramat Gan Stadium, Tel-Aviv

HAPOEL PETACH-TIKVA 2 FEYENOORD 1

Half-time 1-0 *Aggregate* 2-2 (Feyenoord win on away goals) *Attendance* 7,500

		Goals				Goals
1	Rafi COHEN		1	Ed DE GOEY		
2	Benny KOZOSHVILY		2	Arnold SCHOLTEN ❏		
3	Avi KEISY		3	John DE WOLF		
4	Uda BAHAGAT		4	John METGOD		
5	Carlos OLERAN		5	Dean GORRE		
6	Noam KEISY		6	Peter BOSZ		
7	Mordachy KAKON	48	7	Henk FRÄSER	69	
8	Meny BASSON †		8	Gaston TAUMENT ‡		
9	Nir LEVIN	3	9	József KIPRICH †		
10	Uzi HOAION ❏		10	Rob WITSCHGE		
11	Oz ILIA ❏ ‡		11	Regi BLINKER		

Substitutes		*Substitutes*	
Ely MACHPOD †49		Mike OBIKU †63	
Yossi LEVY ‡86		Ulrich VAN GOBBEL ‡89	

Referee Sándor PILLER (Hungary)

SUMMARY

● *A second-half goal from former Dutch international defender Henk Fräser kept alive Feyenoord's Cup-winners' Cup hopes just when it appeared that the famous Rotterdam club were about to suffer one of the shocks of the competition at the hands of Israel's European debutants Hapoel Petach-Tikva. Until Fräser headed in Regi Blinker's cross in the 69th minute, Wim van Hanegem's side were floundering. Their first-leg lead had been wiped out as early as the third minute when Kakon broke the Feyenoord offside trap to create a goal for Levin. Buoyed by the return from injury of their star striker Meny Basson, who had scored three of their four goals in the preliminary round tie, Hapoel deservedly went ahead 2-1 on aggregate at the start of the second half with a Kakon header from Ilia's cross. Fräser' goal, however, completely changed the course of the tie. In the final half-hour Hapoel's energy was visibly sapped and they never looked likely to score again. So it was Feyenoord, thanks to the away goals rule, who breathed a sigh of relief and progressed into round two.*

CUP-WINNERS' CUP
First Round First Leg

Tuesday 15th September 1992
Weser Stadium, Bremen

SV WERDER BREMEN 3 HANNOVER 96 1

Half-time 3-1 *Attendance* 17,003

		Goals			Goals
1	Oliver RECK		1	Jörg SIEVERS	
2	Manfred BOCKENFELD ❑		2	Bernd HEEMSOTH	
3	Uwe HARTTGEN ❑		3	Jörg-Uwe KLÜTZ	
4	Rune BRATSETH	45	4	André SIROCKS	
5	Dietmar BEIERSDORFER †		5	Roman WÓJCICKI	26 (pen)
6	Marco BODE		6	Axel SUNDERMANN	
7	Dieter EILTS		7	Michael SCHÖNBERG ❑ ■	
8	Miroslav VOTAVA		8	Hakan BICICI ❑	
9	Wynton RUFER ‡	19, 28	9	Martin GROTH	
10	Andreas HERZOG ❑		10	Milos DJELMAS †	
11	Klaus ALLOFS		11	Michael KOCH ❑ ‡	

Substitutes		*Substitutes*	
Günter HERMANN †30		Reinhold MATHY †64	
Thomas WOLTER ‡69		Jörg KRETSCHMAR ‡66	

Referee David ELLERAY (England)

FACTFILE

● *Werder Bremen embarked on their defence of the Cup-winners' Cup in the knowledge that no team had ever won the trophy two years in a row.*

● *This was the first all-German encounter in the history of the European Cup-winners' Cup. There had been several ties between Bundesliga teams in the UEFA Cup, notably in the 1979/80 competition, when all four semi-finalists were from (West) Germany.*

● *Of the seven German clubs competing in Europe, Hannover were the only one to lose their opening game.*

● *Face to face in this match were two veterans of the 1982 World Cup in Spain - Roman Wójcicki of Poland and Wynton Rufer of New Zealand.*

● *Bremen goalscorer Rune Bratseth*

Rufer double gives holders opening win

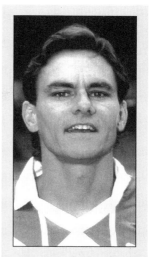

By a quirk of fate, the last two names to be picked out of the hat for the Cup-winners' Cup draw were both German. Cup-winners' Cup holders Werder Bremen against DFB Cup holders Hannover.

There was little doubt, however, which of the two teams set out as favourites. While Bremen had considerably strengthened their squad during the summer, using the cash from their successful European campaign to purchase German international defender Dietmar Beiersdorfer from Hamburg and Austrian star Andreas Herzog from Rapid Vienna, Hannover remained ensconced in the German Second Division, occupying a disappointing mid-table position after 13 games of the season.

Furthermore, the club from Lower Saxony had been absent from Europe for 24 years and had never appeared in any European competition other than the old Inter Cities Fairs' Cup.

Predictably, Hannover went to Bremen with one objective in mind - to keep the Bremen attack at bay and give themselves at least something to aim for in the return leg. To this end they tried to close Werder down with tight man-to-man marking, not only on the strikers Rufer and Allofs, but also on the two flank players, Bockenfeld and Bode, and playmaker Herzog.

But the New Zealander got away from his marker Klütz on two occasions in the first half hour and on both occasions made him pay with well-struck goals, the first after a pass from Herzog and the second with assistance from Bode. Not that the Bremen defence escaped punishment either. A rash challenge by Beiersdorfer earned Hannover a penalty just before Rufer's second strike and Wójcicki banged it in for a significant away goal.

A header from Rune Bratseth on the stroke of half-time made it 3-1 to Bremen, but they should have extended their lead after the interval, with Bode, in particular, missing a number of chances to kill off the tie for good. Hannover, in fairness, were not blessed with luck. They suffered a double blow just after the hour mark when two of their foreign players, Schönberg and Djelmas, left the field together in unfortunate circumstances. The Dane was controversially dismissed by the English referee for delaying a free-kick (his second bookable offence) while his Yugoslav colleague lay injured awaiting treatment! After that, the 1-3 final scoreline did not look too bad at all for the Second Division side...

WYNTON RUFER
SV Werder Bremen

Wynton Rufer's double strike against Hannover took his total of European goals for Werder Bremen to 10 in 19 games. The most important of all those, of course, had come in the previous season's final against Monaco in Lisbon, but the New Zealander also retains equally fond memories of the two goals he scored to help eliminate holders Napoli from the 1989/90 UEFA Cup. Bremen went on to reach the semi-finals of the UEFA Cup that season, and Rufer was also on hand to help the team to their German Cup success a year later.
Prior to joining Bremen in 1989 Rufer had spent seven seasons in Switzerland, first with FC Zürich, then with Aarau and latterly, for one season only, with Grasshoppers. A teenage member of New Zealand's World Cup squad back in 1982, he is widely considered to be one of the best footballers ever to have emerged from the Oceania region.

Wednesday 30th September 1992
Niedersachsen Stadium, Hanover

HANNOVER 96 2 SV WERDER BREMEN 1

Half-time 2-1 Aggregate 3-4 Attendance 27,436

		Goals				Goals
1	Jörg SIEVERS			1	Oliver RECK	
2	André SIROCKS			2	Manfred BOCKENFELD	
3	Jörg-Uwe KLÜTZ			3	Marco BODE	
4	Jörg KRETSCHMAR			4	Rune BRATSETH	
5	Dejan RAICKOVIC ❑			5	Dietmar BEIERSDORFER †	
6	Axel SUNDERMANN			6	Thomas WOLTER ❑	
7	Reinhold DASCHNER ‡	29, 34		7	Dieter EILTS ❑	
8	Hakan BICICI			8	Miroslav VOTAVA	
9	Martin GROTH			9	Wynton RUFER	18 (pen)
10	Milos DJELMAS ❑			10	Andreas HERZOG ‡	
11	Uwe JURSCH †			11	Klaus ALLOFS ❑	

Substitutes		*Substitutes*
Michael KOCH †62		Uwe HARTTGEN †28
André BREITENREITER ‡74		Günter HERMANN ‡58 ❑

Referee Mario VAN DER ENDE (Holland)

FACTFILE

● *All seven goals in the two legs of the tie were scored in the first half.*

● *The Hannover players were on approximately £10,000 per man to reach the second round.*

● *The Niedersachsen Stadium, although a Second Division venue since Hannover were relegated in 1989, remains one of Germany's most impressive stadiums. It was used as a venue for two matches at the 1988 European Championships (Denmark v Spain and Republic of Ireland v USSR) and also for Germany's big Euro '92 qualifying match against Belgium.*

● *The six yellow cards handed out by Dutch referee Van der Ende took the total for the tie to 12, although no one player was cautioned in both games.*

Holders struggle through after shock defeat

It all looked so comfortable for Werder Bremen when Wynton Rufer scored his third goal of the tie from the penalty spot after just 18 minutes. That extended Bremen's aggregate lead to 4-1 and the chances of a Hannover comeback appeared at this stage to be very remote. But a rash substitution by Werder boss Otto Rehhagel in the 28th minute suddenly allowed Hannover back into the game and within five minutes they had scored twice to pull themselves back into contention.

As in the first leg, Rehhagel decided to take off Dietmar Beiersdorfer with less than a third of the match gone. The former Hamburg defender, whose only international cap had been won in this same stadium against Belgium 17 months previously, was again having trouble containing Yugoslav striker Djelmas. But his premature removal only brought chaos to the Bremen defence, and Hannover wasted no time in exploiting the freedom they suddenly discovered up front to score two goals and peg back their aggregate deficit to just one goal.

The scorer of both goals was former Bayern Munich and Cologne midfielder Reinhold Daschner. He had not been selected for the first leg in Bremen and was only in the starting line-up for this game because of the thigh injury which sidelined first-leg scorer Roman Wójcicki.

Roared on by a big home crowd, Hannover sensed that a major shock might be on the cards. They pressed forward and could easily have taken the tie into extra-time with a third goal but for the acrobatics of Oliver Reck in the Bremen goal. Twice he made splendid saves from free-kicks and it was ultimately his contribution that proved to be the difference between the two sides.

Having held on for the duration of the second half against mounting pressure to keep their aggregate advantage intact, Bremen were clearly relieved to take their place in the draw for the next round and happy to have their revenge over the team that had beaten them in the German Cup semi-finals the previous season. But victory on the night was a source of great satisfaction, too, for the underdogs. As in their sensational run to the German Cup final, they had shown once again that they could live with the best the Bundesliga had to offer - even in the special environment of a European Cup tie.

OLIVER RECK
SV Werder Bremen

Werder Bremen's unlikely hero in their first defence of the Cup-winners' Cup trophy was the man who sadly missed the previous season's final triumph against Monaco through suspension. Goalkeeper Oliver Reck had been an ever-present between the posts for Bremen on their march to the final, conceding just four goals in eight games, but a second yellow card in the semi-final second leg against Club Bruges denied him a place in Lisbon.
Although never capped at international level by Germany, Reck came very close to making the 1990 World Cup squad in Italy. A string of classy performances for Werder in the UEFA Cup that season brought him to Franz Beckenbauer's attention but he was eventually overlooked in favour of Andy Köpke as the squad's third 'keeper behind Illgner and Aumann. Reck had previously made a name for himself in 1987/88 when he set a new Bundesliga record by conceding a mere 22 goals in Bremen's championship-winning season.

CUP-WINNERS' CUP
Preliminary Round & First Round Review

PRELIMINARY ROUND RESULTS

		1st leg	2nd leg	Agg.
Maribor Branik	Hamrun Spartans	4-0	1-2	5-2
Strømsgodset IF	Hapoel Petach-Tikva	0-2	0-2	0-4
FC Vaduz	Chernomorets Odessa	0-5	1-7	1-12
Avenir Beggen	B 36	1-0	1-1	2-1

FIRST ROUND RESULTS

		1st leg	2nd leg	Agg.
Miedz Legnica	AS Monaco	0-1	0-0	0-1
Trabzonspor	TPS	2-0	2-2	4-2
Bohemians	Steaua Bucuresti	0-0	0-4	0-4
Olympiakos	Chernomorets Odessa	0-1	3-0	3-1
Valur	Boavista FC	0-0	0-3	0-3
Airdrieonians	Sparta Praha	0-1	1-2	1-3
Glenavon	Royal Antwerp FC	1-1	1-1aet	2-2
(Royal Antwerp FC won 3-1 on penalties)				
Cardiff City	FC Admira Wacker	1-1	0-2	1-3
Parma	Újpesti TE	1-0	1-1	2-1
AIK	AGF	3-3	1-1	4-4
(AGF win on away goals)				
Spartak Moskva	Avenir Beggen	0-0	5-1	5-1
Liverpool	Apollon Limassol	6-1	2-1	8-2
Levski Sofia	FC Luzern	2-1	0-1	2-2
(FC Luzern win on away goals)				
Maribor Branik	Atlético Madrid	0-3	1-6	1-9
Feyenoord	Hapoel Petach-Tikva	1-0	1-2	2-2
(Feyenoord win on away goals)				
SV Werder Bremen	Hannover 96	3-1	1-2	4-3

LEADING GOALSCORERS AFTER FIRST ROUND

5	Ian RUSH (Liverpool)
4	Yury NIKIFOROV (Chernomorets Odessa)
3	Meny BASSON (Hapoel Petach-Tikva)
	Wynton RUFER (SV Werder Bremen)

CUP-WINNERS' CUP

SECOND ROUND DRAW

CUP-WINNERS' CUP
Second Round First Leg

Wednesday 21st November 1992
Allmend Stadium, Lucerne

FC LUZERN 1 FEYENOORD 0

Half-time 0-0 *Attendance* 11,700

		Goals			Goals
1	Beat MUTTER		1	Ed DE GOEY	
2	Peter GMÜR		2	Arnold SCHOLTEN ❑	
3	Urs BIRRER ❑		3	John DE WOLF ■	
4	René VAN ECK		4	John METGOD	
5	Martin RUEDA	75	5	Errol REFOS	
6	Christoph GILLI		6	Peter BOSZ	
7	Hanspeter BURRI ❑ ‡		7	Henk FRÄSER ❑	
8	Roberto FREGNO		8	Gaston TAUMENT	
9	Urs GÜNTENSPERGER		9	József KIPRICH †	
10	Oliver CAMENZIND		10	Rob WITSCHGE	
11	Adalbert KOCH †		11	Regi BLINKER	

Substitutes

Peter NADIG †66

Brian BERTELSEN ‡68

Substitute

Ulrich VAN GOBBEL †64

Referee Loizos LOIZOU (Cyprus)

● *For the second year in a row Feyenoord were drawn to meet the holders of the Swiss Cup in the second round of the Cup-winners' Cup. A year earlier they had knocked out Sion in a penalty shoot-out after two goalless draws en route to the semi-finals. On paper this should have been an easier task. Luzern were now in the Swiss Second Division and Feyenoord were a year more experienced. But as in the first round against Hapoel Petach-Tikva, Feyenoord looked uncomfortable away from home and it was no surprise when Luzern's Martin Rueda gave the Swiss side victory with a headed goal from a Bertelsen free-kick 12 minutes from time. Feyenoord had begun the match at full strength, but finished it with only ten men on the pitch. The fact that it was the wrong ten men was lost on the Cypriot referee, but not on UEFA, who later, after studying video evidence, conceded that John De Wolf had been the victim of mistaken identity and that it was in fact Henk Fräser who had thrown a punch at an opponent and merited the red card. So he, not De Wolf, would have to sit out the second leg.*

CUP-WINNERS' CUP
Second Round Second Leg

Wednesday 4th November 1992
Feyenoord Stadium, Rotterdam

FEYENOORD 4 FC LUZERN 1

Half-time 2-1 *Aggregate* 4-2 *Attendance* 26,000

		Goals			Goals
1	Ed DE GOEY		1	Beat MUTTER ❑	
2	Ulrich VAN GOBBEL		2	Peter GMÜR †	
3	John DE WOLF		3	Urs BIRRER	
4	John METGOD		4	René VAN ECK ■	
5	Errol REFOS		5	Martin RUEDA ❑	
6	Peter BOSZ		6	Urs SCHÖNENBERGER ❑	
7	Dean GORRE ‡		7	Herbert BAUMANN	
8	Gaston TAUMENT †	2	8	Brian BERTELSEN ■	
9	József KIPRICH	55, 83 (pen)	9	Peter NADIG ‡	12
10	Rob WITSCHGE		10	Roberto FREGNO	
11	Regi BLINKER	15	11	Oliver CAMENZIND	
	Substitutes			*Substitutes*	
	Mike OBIKU †78			Christoph GILLI †57	
	Orlando TRUSTFULL ‡86			Adalbert KOCH ‡69	

Referee Alan SNODDY (Northern Ireland)

SUMMARY

● *Feyenoord made it through to the Cup-winners' Cup quarter-finals for the second year on the trot, but they made hard work of it, having to rely in part on the ill-discipline and lack of composure of their modest opponents. With only 35 minutes left on the clock the Dutch side were on their way out of the competition. Their exciting Rastafarian double act of Gaston Taument and Regi Blinker had both found the target in the first half, but sandwiched between these two goals was a 12th-minute strike from Luzern's Peter Nadig, made possible by a rare aberration from Feyenoord goalkeeper Ed de Goey. Once again, though, Feyenoord were to be indebted to the goalscoring of their Hungarian striker József Kiprich, again preferred ahead of Obiku to lead the attack. He scored twice in the second half, the second from the penalty spot after a foul on the aforementioned Obiku, now on as a substitute. By this stage, however, Luzern were down to nine men after the dismissal of their two foreign players Bertelsen and Van Eck, and any chance they had of sneaking another goal had long since vanished.*

CUP-WINNERS' CUP
Second Round First Leg

Wednesday 21st October 1992
Louis II Stadium, Monaco

AS MONACO 0 OLYMPIAKOS 1

Half-time 0-0 *Attendance* 8,000

Goals	Goals

		Goals				Goals
1	Jean-Luc ETTORI		1	Yorgos MIRTSOS	
2	Patrick VALERY		2	Theodoros PAHATOURIDIS	
3	Luc SONOR		3	Kiriakos KARATAIDIS ❏	
4	Lilian THURAM		4	Yorgos MITSIBONAS	
5	Franck DUMAS		5	Mihalis VLAHOS ‡	
6	Marcel DIB †		6	Panayiotis TSALOUHIDIS	
7	Jürgen KLINSMANN		7	Gennady LITOVCHENKO	
8	Jérôme GNAKO		8	Nikos TSIANTAKIS	
9	LUIS HENRIQUE		9	Minas HANTZIDIS	
10	Youri DJORKAEFF ❏		10	Vassilis KARAPIALIS †	
11	Christian PEREZ		11	Yorgos VAITSIS	86

Substitute

Kelvin SEBWE †62

Substitutes

Daniel BATISTA †40 ❏

Ilias SAVVIDIS ‡62 ❏

Referee Michal LISTKIEWICZ (Poland)

SUMMARY

● *The Louis II stadium in Monaco is normally one of the more tranquil sporting arenas in Europe. But 3,000 travelling fans from Greece ensured that the decibel level went up considerably for this encounter. And at the final whistle it was those Olympiakos supporters who were doing all the cheering and chanting. An 86-minute goal from Yorgos Vaitsis, created by Gullit-lookalike Daniel Batista on the right wing, was sufficient to give Olympiakos a rare away win in Europe and put them in sight of a first ever European quarter-final place. Monaco were disappointing, but they did not deserve to lose. Jürgen Klinsmann was denied a clear penalty in the 75th minute when hauled to the ground by Vlahos, but this was an occasion where his reputation for 'diving' probably counted against him! And so Monaco's barren goalscoring run in the Louis II continued. Since establishing a goalscoring record for a French team in Europe with an 8-1 demolition of Swansea a year or so earlier the club had managed just three goals in five European matches at home in the Principality, and none at all in the last two.*

Wednesday 4th November 1992
Karaiskakis Stadium, Piraeus

OLYMPIAKOS 0   AS MONACO 0

Half-time 0-0   *Aggregate* 1-0   *Attendance* 40,000

Goals   Goals

1 Yorgos MIRTSOS ❏	1 Jean-Luc ETTORI
2 Theodoros PAHATOURIDIS ❏	2 Patrick VALERY †
3 Kiriakos KARATAIDIS	3 Patrick BLONDEAU
4 Yorgos MITSIBONAS ❏	4 Lilian THURAM
5 Mihalis VLAHOS ❏	5 Franck DUMAS
6 Panayiotis TSALOUHIDIS	6 Claude PUEL
7 Gennady LITOVCHENKO ❏	7 Jürgen KLINSMANN
8 Nikos TSIANTAKIS	8 Marcel DIB ‡
9 Sotiris MAVROMATIS †	9 LUIS HENRIQUE
10 Ilias SAVVIDIS ‡	10 Jérôme GNAKO
11 Yorgos VAITSIS	11 Christian PEREZ ❏
Substitutes	*Substitutes*
Daniel BATISTA †53	Youri DJORKAEFF †59
Oleg PROTASOV ‡85	Youssouf FOFANA ‡68

Referee Alphonse COSTANTIN (Belgium)

● *After all the trouble which had occurred at the PAOK v Paris-Saint-Germain encounter in the UEFA Cup, this second Greece-France confrontation of the season clearly fell into UEFA's 'high risk' category. Olympiakos had done their bit to try and prevent further problems by limiting tickets to one per customer on presentation of an I.D. card, and given the explosive nature of the contest, it was probably a good job that they did. No fewer than five Olympiakos players received yellow cards as the Greeks tried all they knew, both fair and foul, to cling on to their first-leg lead and achieve an historic qualification. Even the ball boys were taking their time to retrieve the ball as the final minutes ticked on with the score still goalless. Monaco, playing in an unfamiliar all sky blue kit, were desperately unlucky not to score. Both Klinsmann and Djorkaeff struck the post, but it was not to be their night. Olympiakos coach Oleg Blokhin, who had celebrated his 40th birthday the day before, was honest in his appraisal of the match: "Monaco did everything to qualify. I was very nervous, especially in the last five minutes."*

Wednesday 21st October 1992
Aarhus Stadium, Aarhus

AGF 3 STEAUA BUCURESTI 2

Half-time 2-0 Attendance 9,000

		Goals				Goals
1	Troels RASMUSSEN		1	Daniel GHERASIM †	
2	Lasse SKOV ❑		2	Constantin GILCA	
3	Martin NIELSEN	80 (pen)	3	Ionel PIRVU ❑	
4	Claus THOMSEN		4	Anton DOBOS ❑	
5	Palle SØRENSEN		5	Bogdan BUCUR	
6	Gunner Lind PEDERSEN ‡		6	Viorel ION ‡	
7	Jan Halvor HALVORSEN		7	Ion VLADOIU	64
8	Torben CHRISTENSEN	19	8	Ilie DUMITRESCU	89
9	Stig TØFTING		9	Ion SBURLEA	
10	Jan BARTRAM ❑ †		10	Nica Basarab PANDURU ❑	
11	Søren ANDERSEN	12	11	Ilie STAN	

Substitutes

Claus CHRISTIANSEN †69

Bo HARDER ‡74

Substitutes

Dumitru STINGACIU †46

Alexandru ANDRASI ‡64

Referee Aron SCHMIDHUBER (Germany)

SUMMARY

● *Clubs from Denmark and Romania had faced each other four times before in European competition, and on every occasion the Romanians had come out on top. In fact Steaua themselves had eliminated a Danish club - Vejle - on their way to winning the Champions' Cup in 1985/86. They did not have that same Cup-winning potential now, but they were nevertheless able to field a number of exciting young players, notably Dumitrescu and Stan. It was the home side, however, who looked the stronger of the two in the first half. Lack of organisation in the Steaua defence twice allowed Danish forwards to break clear and score in the first 19 minutes and there might have been more goals for the home crowd to savour in the 45 minutes before Vladoiu's volley put Steaua back in the match. AGF's two-goal cushion was restored with a coolly taken Michael Nielsen penalty but they could not hang onto it and in the last minute goalkeeper Troels Rasmussen could only watch helplessly as his save from Dumitrescu's strong shot looped up into the air and dropped in just over the line.*

Wednesday 4th November 1992
Steaua Stadium, Bucharest

STEAUA BUCURESTI 2   AGF 1

Half-time 0-1 *Aggregate* 4-4 (Steaua win on away goals) *Attendance* 26,000

		Goals				Goals
1	Dumitru STINGACIU		1	Troels RASMUSSEN		
2	Cornel CRISTESCU	81	2	Lasse SKOV		
3	Ionel PIRVU ‡		3	Kent NIELSEN ❏		
4	Ion SBURLEA		4	Claus THOMSEN		
5	Bogdan BUCUR		5	Martin NIELSEN		
6	Constantin GILCA		6	Gunner Lind PEDERSEN ❏		
7	Ion VLADOIU	89	7	Jan Halvor HALVORSEN		
8	Ilie DUMITRESCU		8	Torben CHRISTENSEN	12	
9	Alexandru ANDRASI †		9	Stig TØFTING		
10	Viorel ION ❏		10	Jan BARTRAM †		
11	Ilie STAN ❏		11	Søren ANDERSEN ‡		

Substitutes	*Substitutes*
Ionel FULGA †55	Claus CHRISTIANSEN †72
Iulian FILIPESCU ‡62	Palle SØRENSEN ‡81

Referee AHMET Cakar (Turkey)

● *After the outcomes of the various first-leg matches, Denmark's hopes of having a club in the the quarter-finals of European competition for the third year running rested squarely on the shoulders of AGF. Similarly, Steaua also bore the bulk of their country's expectations. There was much to play for, but with only ten minutes of the tie remaining Romanian hopes appeared to be forlorn. AGF had increased their aggregate lead to 4-2 with a Torben Christensen header, and although the home side pressed forward relentlessly for the remainder of the game, the best chance to add to the scoring actually fell to AGF, Stig Tøfting missing an easy chance with just the goalkeeper to beat. It was a moment the Danes would later live to regret. A superb individual goal by right-back Cornel Cristescu in the 81st minute set up a frantic climax and, as in the first leg, with the final whistle just seconds away, Steaua scored a second. Ion Vladoiu was the hero, sending the crowd into raptures with a sweetly-struck volley after some magical dribbling on the right by Gilca, and sending Steaua through on away goals.*

CUP-WINNERS' CUP
Second Round First Leg

Wednesday 21st October 1992
Avni Aker Stadium, Trabzon

TRABZONSPOR 0 ATLETICO MADRID 2

Half-time 0-1 *Attendance* 24,000

		Goals			Goals
1	Viktor GRISHKO		1	ABEL Resino	
2	OGÜN Temizkanoglu		2	Carlos AGUILERA	
3	SEYHMUZ Suna ❑ ‡		3	TOMAS Reñones ❑	
4	KEMAL Serdar		4	Roberto SOLOZABAL	
5	HAMDI Aslan		5	Juan Manuel LOPEZ	
6	ABDULLAH Ercan ❑		6	DONATO Gama da Silva	
7	TURGUT Uçar		7	Manuel Sánchez "MANOLO" †	
8	ÜNAL Karaman		8	Bernd SCHUSTER	
9	Jacek CYZIO		9	Juan VIZCAINO	
10	HAMI Mandirali		10	Paulo FUTRE ‡	38
11	ORHAN Cikrikçi †		11	Gabriel MOYA	59
	Substitutes			*Substitutes*	
	SONER Boz †46			ALFREDO Santaelena †52	
	LEMI Çelik ‡78			LUIS GARCIA ‡60	

Referee Aleksei SPIRIN (Russia)

SUMMARY

● *Security was tight in and around the Avni Aker stadium. Three days earlier there had been major disturbances at the ground following Trabzonspor's 3-4 defeat by Fenerbahçe in a Turkish league encounter. Nearly 50 people had been arrested and several spectators and policemen injured as hundreds of hooligans invaded the pitch at the final whistle, trapping players and officials in the dressing rooms. Fortunately there was a much calmer atmosphere all round for this encounter, although once again the home fans were to be disappointed with the outcome. Atlético, whose president Jesús Gil had advised the club's fans not to travel to the match, put up a very professional display and won the game thanks to two moments of inspiration from their star forward Paulo Futre, who had been so impressive for Portugal in a World Cup tie against Scotland a week earlier. He it was who opened the scoring after 38 minutes with a splendid rising shot after a one-two with Manolo, and it was a typically penetrating diagonal run of his which set up Moya for the second goal early in the second half.*

CUP-WINNERS' CUP
Second Round Second Leg

Wednesday 4th November 1992
Vicente Calderón Stadium, Madrid

ATLETICO MADRID 0 TRABZONSPOR 0

Half-time 0-0 Aggregate 2-0 Attendance 9,000

Goals

Goals

	Atletico Madrid			Trabzonspor	
1	DIEGO Garrido		1	Viktor GRISHKO	
2	TOMAS Reñones		2	LEMI Çelik ❏	
3	PEDRO González		3	OGÜN Temizkanoglu	
4	Roberto SOLOZABAL ❏		4	KEMAL Serdar	
5	Juan Manuel LOPEZ ❏		5	HAMDI Aslan	
6	Francisco FERREIRA †		6	ABDULLAH Ercan ■	
7	Gabriel MOYA		7	TURGUT Uçar †	
8	DONATO Gama da Silva		8	ÜNAL Karaman ‡	
9	Juan VIZCAINO		9	Jacek CYZIO ❏	
10	Paulo FUTRE		10	SONER Boz	
11	LUIS GARCIA ‡		11	ORHAN Çikrikçi	

Substitutes

Substitutes

Antonio ACOSTA †8

SEYHMUZ Suna †72

Juan SABAS ‡52

SÜLEYMAN Usta ‡88

Referee Rémy HARREL (France)

● With a 2-0 lead from the first leg in Turkey, Atlético were all but certain of reaching the quarter-finals of the Cup-winners' Cup for the sixth time in nine participations. The club's fans evidently thought that way, because only 9,000 of them felt it worth their while to come along and see the team finish off Trabzonspor. In the event, those who chose to stay away probably made the right decision. With the home team lacking a number of important players - notably Schuster and Manolo - Atlético struggled to get out of first gear for most of the game, and even with their opponents down to ten men after the expulsion of Abdullah just after half-time the Spanish Cup holders could not add to their first-leg tally. The Turks, without their star striker Hami, rarely posed a threat to Atlético's stand-in goalkeeper Diego. They defended well at the other end to keep Futre and co. at bay, but it was often at the expense of fair play, as their final card count testified.

Wednesday 21st October 1992
Südstadt Stadium, Vienna

FC ADMIRA WACKER 2 ROYAL ANTWERP FC 4

Half-time 2-1 *Attendance* 3,000

		Goals				Goals
1	Franz GRUBER			1	Wim DE CONINCK	
2	Alois DÖTZL			2	Wim KIEKENS	
3	Thomas ZINGLER			3	Nico BROECKAERT	
4	Michael GRUBER			4	Geert EMMERECHTS	
5	Gerald MESSLENDER ❑			5	Rudy SMIDTS	
6	Gerald BACHER †	41		6	Didier SEGERS †	55
7	Ernst OGRIS			7	Ronny VAN RETHY	
8	Peter ARTNER			8	Patrick VAN VEIRDEGHEM	
9	Uwe MÜLLER			9	Francis SEVEREYNS	
10	Roger LJUNG			10	Hans-Peter LEHNHOFF ❑	
11	Olaf MARSCHALL	24		11	Alex CZERNIATYNSKI	34, 62, 73
	Substitute				*Substitute*	
	Johannes ABFALTERER †60				Nourédine MOUKRIM †83	

Referee Sergei KHUSAINOV (Russia)

SUMMARY

● *Alex Czerniatynski, the veteran World Cup forward recently recalled to the Belgian national team colours, continued his splendid start to the season by scoring a superb opportunist hat-trick to give Antwerp a decisive 4-2 victory away to Admira. But if Czerniatynski was the Belgians' hero, Admira goalkeeper Franz Gruber had to carry the can for his team's downfall. He was badly at fault for all three of Czerniatynski's goals, the second of which might conceivably have been credited to Francis Severeyns, who blasted the ball home on the goal-line after his in-form striking partner had headed the ball-back over the head of the despairing 'keeper. The best of Antwerp's goals was scored by midfielder Didier Segers, but the most spectacular of the lot was Gerald Bacher's precise 40th-minute volley which at that stage actually took Admira into a 2-1 lead. The second half, however, belonged entirely to Antwerp who, with Bruges beating FK Austria in the Champions' Cup the same evening, made it a Belgian double over Austria in the top two competitions.*

CUP-WINNERS' CUP
Second Round Second Leg

Wednesday 4th November 1992
Bosuil Stadium, Antwerp

ROYAL ANTWERP FC 3 FC ADMIRA WACKER 4 (aet)

Half-time 2-0 Aggregate 7-6 Attendance 6,000

		Goals				Goals
1	Ratko SVILAR		1	Wolfgang KNALLER		
2	Wim KIEKENS		2	Gerald BACHER		46
3	Nico BROECKAERT		3	Thomas ZINGLER ❑ †		
4	Geert EMMERECHTS ❑		4	Helmut GRAF ❑		
5	Rudy SMIDTS		5	Uwe MÜLLER		
6	Nourédine MOUKRIM ‡		6	Johannes ABFALTERER		57
7	Ronny VAN RETHY		7	Andreas GUTLEDERER ‡		
8	Didier SEGERS †		8	Peter ARTNER		
9	Francis SEVEREYNS	43	9	Michael GRUBER		
10	Kari UKKONEN		10	Roger LJUNG		62, 77
11	Alex CZERNIATYNSKI	21, 97	11	Olaf MARSCHALL ■		
	Substitutes			*Substitutes*		
	Patrick VAN VEIRDEGHEM †21			Kurt TEMM †106		
	Willy VINCENT ‡73			Ernst OGRIS ‡106 ❑		

Referee Zbigniew PRZESMYCKI (Poland)

● *The dust had barely settled on this extraordinary match when the news broke that Admira Wacker were launching an official complaint to UEFA over the size of the Antwerp goals! Given that the match had produced seven goals, it seemed illogical that the Austrians should protest that they were 5cm too small! But that was their claim, and UEFA initially took it seriously before rejecting it and officially eliminating Admira. In the circumstances the Austrians might have been excused their desperation. After all, they had come from being 6-2 down on aggregate with just 45 minutes left to level at 6-6 with just 10 men, only for Antwerp to snatch the winner in extra-time. Admira's comeback was quite extraordinary, but having surrendered a virtually unassailable lead, the Belgians too deserved credit for not allowing their heads to drop in extra-time. Antwerp coach Walter Meeuws did not see it that way, though. He called his team's performance "shameful" and was still fuming several days later, even after UEFA had confirmed his club's second appearance in a European quarter-final in four seasons.*

Thursday 22nd October 1992
Lenin Stadium, Moscow

SPARTAK MOSKVA 4 LIVERPOOL 2

Half-time 1-0 *Attendance* 55,000

		Goals				Goals
1	Stanislav CHERCHESOV		1	Bruce GROBBELAAR ■		
2	Dmitry KHLESTOV ❏		2	Mike MARSH		
3	Andrey IVANOV		3	David BURROWS		
4	Nikolai PISAREV	10	4	Rob JONES ‡		
5	Vladimir BESCHASTNYKH †		5	Mark WRIGHT	66	
6	Andrey CHERNYSHOV		6	Don HUTCHISON		
7	Viktor ONOPKO		7	Steve McMANAMAN	74	
8	Valery KARPIN	69, 84 (pen)	8	Mark WALTERS		
9	Andrey PYATNITSKY		9	Ian RUSH †		
10	Igor LEDYAKHOV	89	10	Jamie REDKNAPP ❏		
11	Dmitry RADCHENKO		11	Michael THOMAS		

Substitute

Mikhail RUSYAEV †53

Substitutes

Ronny ROSENTHAL †53

Nicky TANNER ‡78

Referee Rune LARSSON (Sweden)

FACTFILE

● *With Spartak playing in an exact replica of Liverpool's usual all-red kit, the English club took the field in all green.*

● *The Spartak side included five members of the squad that had represented the CIS at the previous summer's European Championship Finals - Cherchesov, Ivanov, Chernyshov, Onopko and Ledyakhov. Conversely, none of the Liverpool team were in Sweden.*

● *Liverpool had never previously played a European match in Moscow. Their only previous fixture in the former Soviet Union was in Georgia, against Dinamo Tbilisi, in 1979/80, when, as holders, they lost 3-0 and were eliminated from the Champions' Cup in the very first round.*

● *Spartak had just secured the inaugural Russian championship the previous weekend with a 4-1 victory over city rivals Lokomotiv.*

Grobbelaar madness hands it to Spartak

Five minutes of mayhem at the end of a dramatic tie in Moscow gave Spartak a crucial two-goal cushion to take to Anfield a fortnight later. It was an advantage they probably deserved on the balance of play, but the manner in which they achieved it owed more than a little to the generosity of the Liverpool defence, and in particular of goalkeeper Bruce Grobbelaar.

A year earlier the Zimbabwean had been a hero as he kept Liverpool in the UEFA Cup with a superb display in Auxerre, but on a night of driving sleet and rain in the Russian capital Grobbelaar could do nothing right. Twice he was caught out when attempting to dribble the ball outside his area. The first time he got away with it as the ball just skimmed past his right post. But in the second half, just minutes after Mark Wright had equalised Nikolai Pisarev's early strike, the Liverpool 'keeper was not so lucky. Caught in possession, he tried to clear the ball to safety but found only Spartak midfielder Valery Karpin 35 yards out on the right. As Grobbelaar chased back, he could only watch in dismay as the ball flashed past him into the unguarded net.

That incident was bad enough, but Grobbelaar's nightmare was only just beginning. A marvellous individual goal from young forward Steve McManaman had brought the scores level again and Liverpool, battling bravely in the adverse conditions, appeared to be back in control of the tie. But with just a few minutes left on the clock Grobbelaar left his line once again to confront Spartak striker Radchenko as he burst through towards the Liverpool goal. Committing himself early, Grobbelaar missed the ball. He probably missed the man too, but Radchenko went down, a penalty was given and the Liverpool number one was ordered off the field, leaving left-back David Burrows to take over in goal.

Commendably, Burrows got his fingertips to Karpin's spot-kick, but he could not keep it out and, for the third time, Spartak again had the lead. At this stage a 3-2 defeat would probably have suited Liverpool, but in the very last minute they made their task extremely difficult for the return leg when they conceded another goal, Ledyakhov pouncing after the besieged defence failed properly to clear the danger. It was all too much for Liverpool manager Graeme Souness. His verbal assault on the Swedish referee as the teams left the pitch was later to earn him a five-match dressing room and touchline ban from UEFA.

MARK WALTERS
Liverpool

If Bruce Grobbelaar was the most talked-about Liverpool player in Moscow, the man who had done most to court good publicity for his team was Mark Walters. After a torrid first half, in which Liverpool had not mustered a single shot on goal, the Birmingham-born winger took it upon himself to drive the FA Cup holders forward. It was his cross which created the first equaliser for Mark Wright and his 20-yard shot which smashed against the Spartak crossbar just before McManaman's second.

For all his natural talent, Walters has never made it into the big time of international football - just one England cap against New Zealand in 1991 - but he has frequently shone in European club football. He was just on the verge of breaking through into the Aston Villa first team when they won the Champions' Cup in 1982. During his time at Rangers in Scotland he scored important European goals against both Katowice and Bayern Munich. And for Liverpool his was the dramatic late winner which saw off Auxerre in the 91/92 UEFA Cup.

Wednesday 4th November 1992
Anfield, Liverpool

LIVERPOOL 0 SPARTAK MOSKVA 2

Half-time 0-0 Aggregate 2-6 Attendance 37,993

		Goals
1	Mike HOOPER	
2	Rob JONES †	
3	David BURROWS ❑	
4	Steve NICOL	
5	Mark WRIGHT	
6	Don HUTCHISON	
7	Steve McMANAMAN	
8	Mike MARSH ■	
9	Ian RUSH	
10	Jamie REDKNAPP	
11	Michael THOMAS	

Substitute

Ronny ROSENTHAL †55

		Goals
1	Stanislav CHERCHESOV	
2	Dmitry KHLESTOV	
3	Andrey IVANOV	
4	Nikolai PISAREV ❑ †	
5	Vladimir BESCHASTNYKH ❑	
6	Andrey CHERNYSHOV ❑	
7	Viktor ONOPKO ❑	
8	Valery KARPIN	
9	Andrey PYATNITSKY	89
10	Igor LEDYAKHOV ‡	
11	Dmitry RADCHENKO	63

Substitutes

Mikhail RUSYAEV †63

Vladimir BAKSCHEV ‡85

Referee Manuel DIAZ VEGA (Spain)

FACTFILE

● *Spartak took the field with precisely the same 11 players who had started the first leg in Moscow.*

● *Helped by reduced admission prices, the 37,993 crowd was the biggest of the season so far at Anfield, with almost three times as many spectators present as had attended the first round match against Apollon Limassol.*

● *This was only the fifth home defeat for Liverpool in 72 European matches. Victory at Anfield had previously gone to Ferencváros (67/68), Leeds United (70/71), Red Star Belgrade (73/74) and Genoa (91/92).*

● *Mike Hooper, replacing the suspended Grobbelaar in the Liverpool goal, was making his first appearance of the season.*

● *Mike Hooper*

Counter-punches floor the Reds

The conditions were perfect for Liverpool to repeat their come-back of a season earlier when, needing to reverse a two-goal deficit from the away leg, they came back to beat Auxerre 3-0 and qualify for the third round of the UEFA Cup. Now the prize was a quarter-final place in the Cup-winners' Cup and, bearing in mind the modest quality of the rest of the field, a reasonable chance of landing the only European trophy that had so far eluded them.

But against Auxerre the Merseysiders had scored early. Now, despite dominating possession, they struggled to find a way through a disciplined Spartak defence, in which Russian national team goalkeeper Stanislav Cherchesov was in particularly fine form. Liverpool's early assault produced few chances. The best of them fell to young Don Hutchison, a player enjoying an excellent scoring run in the Liverpool midfield, but he half-volleyed the opportunity over the bar.

Five minutes after the interval, with Liverpool now, as is their custom, facing towards the Kop, an even better chance was squandered when Michael Thomas saw his close-range effort cleared off the line. Had that gone in, Liverpool would surely have gone on to score another and take the tie. But it didn't and not long afterwards they were made to pay as Spartak took the lead with a splendid counter-attacking goal. Beschastnykh, a raw talent in the Spartak attack, found Radchenko with a glorious long diagonal ball and the number 11 sent Hooper the wrong way with a coolly steered right-foot shot.

Although the crowd noise merely intensified after this setback, the chances of Liverpool scoring the three goals they needed were minimal, especially with Spartak defending so well. And so it proved when, after Mike Marsh had become the third Liverpool player to be sent off in successive European matches for a violent high-tackle on Radchenko, Spartak completed a night of Merseyside misery by scoring a second goal in the dying seconds. Andrey Pyatnitsky was the scorer, sliding the ball home after a neat move involving Radchenko and substitute Rusyaev.

Liverpool's defeat was their second in Europe at Anfield in 1992. Genoa had beaten them there with a similar brand of counter-attacking football some eight months earlier. Clearly, the long Heysel-induced ban was still having its effects. As for Spartak, their comprehensive 6-2 aggregate victory gave them a European quarter-final place for the second time in three seasons. CSKA Moscow's shock win in Barcelona later the same evening was to steal some of the thunder from their performance, but the recently-crowned Russian champions nonetheless remained their country's best bet for a European trophy.

DMITRY RADCHENKO
Spartak Moskva

Dmitry Radchenko had been in the headlines in the spring of 1991 when he scored two goals in Spartak's amazing 3-1 victory away to Real Madrid in the quarter-finals of the Champions' Cup and then found himself the subject of an investigation by UEFA over whether he had indeed been eligible to play in that match after moving to the club from Zenit Leningrad the previous winter.

There was no question mark, however, about Radchenko's right to appear for Spartak at Anfield (although, ironically, doubts did later surface over the eligibility of substitute Rusyaev!) where he again displayed great counter-attacking ability, scoring the first of his team's goals and then having a hand in the second. Radchenko was certainly a man in form, having scored a hat-trick for Spartak in their penultimate Russian League fixture the previous Friday - a 5-2 victory away to Dinamo Moscow.

CUP-WINNERS' CUP
Second Round First Leg

Wednesday 21st October 1992
Weser Stadium, Bremen

SV WERDER BREMEN 2 SPARTA PRAHA 3

Half-time 0-2 *Attendance* 10,747

		Goals			Goals
1	Oliver RECK		1	Petr KOUBA	
2	Thomas WOLTER		2	Jan SOPKO	25
3	Thorsten LEGAT †		3	Lumír MISTR	
4	Rune BRATSETH		4	Petr VRABEC	
5	Dietmar BEIERSDORFER ‡		5	Michal HORNÁK	
6	Ulrich BOROWKA		6	Michal BÍLEK †	
7	Dieter EILTS		7	Jirí NEMEC	
8	Miroslav VOTAVA		8	Jozef CHOVANEC ■	
9	Wynton RUFER	80	9	Viktor DVIRNIK ‡	35
10	Andreas HERZOG ❏		10	Horst SIEGL ❏	
11	Marco BODE		11	Roman VONASEK	90

Substitutes			*Substitutes*	
Frank NEUBARTH †46 ❏	56		Martin FRYDEK †48	
Klaus ALLOFS ‡46			Marek TRVAL ‡88	

Referee Angelo AMENDOLIA (Italy)

SUMMARY

● *Cup holders Werder Bremen suffered a big blow to their chances of successfully defending the trophy with this surprise home defeat. But they could have no complaint about the result. The Czech side were good value for their win. They were already 2-0 up at half-time, defender Jan Sopko having scored his second away goal of the competition when he deflected in a Petr Vrabec shot after 25 minutes and Ukrainian striker Viktor Dvirnik having doubled the lead with a close-range header ten minutes later. But Sparta's command of the tie received a serious setback just before the interval when Jozef Chovanec received a red card for a so-called 'professional' foul on Marco Bode. Down to ten men and with Klaus Allofs and Frank Neubarth on to strengthen Bremen's attack, the momentum was all with the home side for the second 45 minutes and they cemented their dominance with two goals from Neubarth and Wynton Rufer. The final word, though, belonged to Sparta when striker Roman Vonasek broke away to score the winning goal in the very last minute.*

Wednesday 4th November 1992
Letna Stadium, Prague

SPARTA PRAHA 1 SV WERDER BREMEN 0

Half-time 1-0 *Aggregate* 4-2 *Attendance* 29,704

		Goals			Goals
1	Petr KOUBA		1	Oliver RECK	
2	Jan SOPKO		2	Manfred BOCKENFELD	
3	Lumír MISTR		3	Thorsten LEGAT ❑	
4	Petr VRABEC		4	Rune BRATSETH	
5	Michal HORNÁK		5	Thomas WOLTER ❑	
6	Michal BÍLEK ❑		6	Ulrich BOROWKA †	
7	Jirí NEMEC		7	Dieter EILTS	
8	Roman VONASEK		8	Miroslav VOTAVA	
9	Viktor DVIRNIK †		9	Wynton RUFER ❑ ■	
10	Horst SIEGL	7	10	Frank NEUBARTH	
11	Martin FRYDEK		11	Marco BODE ‡	

Substitute

Pavel NEDVED †88

Substitutes

Klaus ALLOFS †46

Stefan KOHN ‡80

Referee Egil NERVIK (Norway)

● Almost 30,000 fans turned up at the Letna stadium to see if Sparta could maintain their advantage and qualify for a European quarter-final for the second year in succession. The Czech fans had only seven minutes to wait before that aggregate advantage had been stretched to 4-2. Horst Siegl, the young striker who had scored match-winning goals against both Marseille and Barcelona the previous season, did it again. Winning the ball somewhat fortuitously from an opposing defender just inside the Bremen half, he sped forward before threading the ball through the goalkeeper's legs. Urged on passionately by the crowd, Sparta refused to allow the Germans a sniff of the three goals they now required to qualify. The nearest they came was when Rufer had a header brilliantly saved by Petr Kouba. It was to be a black night indeed for the New Zealander, sent off in the final minute for his second yellow card offence, and a disappointing one all round for Bremen, who, in defeat, simply prolonged the remarkable tradition of no Cup-winners' Cup holders ever having managed to retain the trophy.

CUP-WINNERS' CUP
Second Round First Leg

Wednesday 21st October, 1992
Ennio Tardini Stadium, Parma

PARMA 0 BOAVISTA FC 0

Half-time 0-0 Attendance 8,675

		Goals				Goals
1	Marco BALLOTTA		1	ALFREDO		
2	Gabriele PIN		2	JAIME ALVES		
3	Alberto DI CHIARA		3	RUI BENTO		
4	Lorenzo MINOTTI		4	VENÂNCIO		
5	Luigi APOLLONI		5	CAETANO †		
6	Georges GRÜN ❏ ‡		6	NOGUEIRA ❏		
7	Alessandro MELLI		7	BOBÓ ❏		
8	Daniele ZORATTO ❏		8	MARLON ‡		
9	Marco OSIO		9	Richard OWUBOKIRI "RICKY"		
10	Stefano CUOGHI		10	NELO ❏		
11	Faustino ASPRILLA †		11	TAVARES		

Substitutes   *Substitutes*

Fausto PIZZI †55 ❏   CASACA †65

Salvatore MATRECANO ‡63   GARRIDO ‡89 ❏

Referee Jan DAMGAARD (Denmark)

SUMMARY

● *Boavista had knocked holders Internazionale out of the UEFA Cup the previous season, so a trip to Italy held few fears for them.. And, as in the San Siro a year earlier, they succeeded in achieving the result they set out for - a goalless draw. With Nigerian striker Ricky, the Portuguese League's top scorer in 1991/92, ploughing a lonely furrow up front, Boavista spent virtually the entire 90 minutes camped in defence. The policy paid off, but only because the Parma strike-force of Melli and Asprilla failed to show sufficient composure in front of goal when the chances came. The Colombian, in particular, seemed more concerned with showing off his technical repertoire than giving his team a first-leg lead to take to Portugal. Parma's man of the match was Georges Grün. But even he spoiled an impressive individual performance by collecting a yellow card, one of seven shown by the no-nonsense Danish referee. And with that being Grün's second booking in successive European games, it meant that Parma would have to travel to Portugal for the second leg without their experienced Belgian international defender.*

Wednesday 4th November, 1992
Dr Alves Vieira Stadium, Torres Novas

BOAVISTA FC 0 PARMA 2

Half-time 0-1 *Aggregate* 0-2 *Attendance* 6,000

		Goals				Goals
1	ALFREDO		1	Claudio TAFFAREL		
2	JAIME ALVES †		2	Salvatore MATRECANO		
3	RUI BENTO		3	Alberto DI CHIARA ❑		
4	VENÂNCIO ❑		4	Lorenzo MINOTTI		
5	CAETANO		5	Luigi APOLLONI		
6	NOGUEIRA	11 (og)	6	Gabriele PIN		
7	BOBÓ ❑		7	Alessandro MELLI ‡		78
8	MARLON		8	Daniele ZORATTO ❑		
9	Richard OWUBOKIRI "RICKY"		9	Fausto PIZZI		
10	TAVARES		10	Stefano CUOGHI ❑		
11	Erwin SANCHEZ ‡		11	Tomas BROLIN †		

Substitutes

TOZÉ †32

LITOS ‡46

Substitutes

Gianluca FRANCHINI †52 ❑

Cornelio DONATI ‡86

Referee Hans-Jürgen WEBER (Germany)

S U M M A R Y

● With the UEFA ban on Boavista's Bessa stadium still in force, the Portuguese Cup holders headed once again to the tiny Third Division ground at Torres Novas, 60 km north-east of Lisbon, to plot their course into a first-ever European quarter-final. But it was Parma who took more kindly to the unfamiliar surroundings. Just 11 minutes had elapsed when Italian international left-back Alberto Di Chiara set off on a 50-metre diagonal run into the Boavista penalty area. His resulting shot was heading off target, but a kind deflection off the knee of retreating defender Nogueira took the ball into the net to give the Italians a crucial away goal. The pressure now off, Parma went on to produce their best performance of the season so far, and with their hosts looking bereft of ideas when it came to breaking down the Italians' five-man defence, the Serie A side clinched qualification with a late close-range second from star striker Alessandro Melli. This was Parma's sixth outing in European competition and they had still not lost a game.

CUP-WINNERS' CUP
Second Round Review

SECOND ROUND RESULTS		1st leg	2nd leg	Agg.
FC Luzern	Feyenoord	1-0	1-4	2-4
AS Monaco	Olympiakos	0-1	0-0	0-1
AGF	Steaua Bucuresti	3-2	1-2	4-4
(Steaua Bucuresti win on away goals)				
Trabzonspor	Atlético Madrid	0-2	0-0	0-2
FC Admira Wacker	Royal Antwerp FC	2-4	4-3aet	6-7
Spartak Moskva	Liverpool	4-2	2-0	6-2
SV Werder Bremen	Sparta Praha	2-3	0-1	2-4
Parma	Boavista FC	0-0	2-0	2-0

LEADING GOALSCORERS AFTER SECOND ROUND

5   Alex CZERNIATYNSKI (Royal Antwerp FC)
     Ian RUSH (Liverpool)
4   Torben CHRISTENSEN (AGF)
     Wynton RUFER (SV Werder Bremen)
     Yury NIKIFOROV (Chernomorets Odessa)
3   József KIPRICH (Feyenoord)
     Ion VLADOIU (Steaua Bucuresti)
     Andrey PYATNITSKY (Spartak Moskva)
     Meny BASSON (Hapoel Petach-Tikva)

CUP-WINNERS' CUP

CUP-WINNERS' CUP
Quarter-Final First Leg

Wednesday 3rd March 1993
Letna Stadium, Prague

SPARTA PRAHA 0 PARMA 0

Half-time 0-0 *Attendance* 30,000

		Goals				Goals
1	Petr KOUBA		1	Marco BALLOTTA		
2	Pavel NEDVED †		2	Antonio BENARIVO ❑		
3	Lumír MISTR		3	Alberto DI CHIARA		
4	Petr VRABEC		4	Lorenzo MINOTTI ❑		
5	Michal HORNÁK		5	Luigi APOLLONI ❑		
6	Roman VONASEK		6	Georges GRÜN		
7	Jirí NEMEC		7	Faustino ASPRILLA		
8	Jozef CHOVANEC		8	Gabriele PIN		
9	Viktor DVIRNIK		9	Tomas BROLIN		
10	Horst SIEGL		10	Stefano CUOGHI		
11	Martin FRYDEK		11	Fausto PIZZI		

Substitute

Tomás VOTAVA †82 ❑

Substitutes

Referee Alfred WIESER (Austria)

FACTFILE

● *Parma became the first team in two and a half years to prevent Sparta Prague from scoring at home in a European tie.*

● *This was Parma's seventh game in Europe and their fifth draw.*

● *Three important players were suspended from this game.- Czechoslovakian internationals Michal Bílek and Jirí Novotny and Parma midfielder Daniele Zoratto. This was Novotny's last match out as a result of the five-match ban imposed on him after his sending-off in Kiev the previous season.*

● *This was Parma defender Georges Grün's second visit to Prague in the 1992/93 season. Six months earlier he had been a member of the Belgian national team which defeated Czechoslovakia 2-1 in a World Cup qualifier.*

Parma hold firm in icy Prague

Early March is never the easiest of times for Mediterranean football sides to visit Eastern Europe. With the chill of winter still in the air, many surprise results have been recorded at this stage of the European competitions. But Italian Cup holders Parma, appearing in a European quarter-final for the very first time, came to frost-bound Prague well prepared for the ordeal. Kitted out in gloves and thermals, they applied themselves superbly to their task and were ultimately unlucky to come away from the Czech capital with only a draw.

Sparta, backed, as ever on big European nights, by a large crowd, sought yet another big scalp to add to those of Marseille, Barcelona and Werder Bremen. But Parma boss Nevio Scala had done his homework. His five-man defence, backed by an in-form Marco Ballotta - now undisputed first-choice goalkeeper ahead of Brazilian international Taffarel - made light work of the home side's attacks. Both Benarrivo and Minotti had their names taken in the first 15 minutes, but once they grew accustomed to the irregular bounce of the ball on the frozen surface, they had little difficulty in snuffing out the threat of Siegl and co. in the Sparta attack. The closest the home side came to scoring was when sweeper Chovanec strode forward to fire in a free-kick, which Ballotta did well to push over at the last moment.

It was Parma who created the clearest scoring opportunities of the game, but with central striker Alessandro Melli consigned to the bench after a recent spell of erratic form, there was nobody up front to finish them off. Swedish international Tomas Brolin had three clear openings during the course of the 90 minutes, but he failed to find the target every time. His most embarrassing miss came as early as the ninth minute when, again a victim of the surface, he blasted high and wide with just the goalkeeper to beat.

Unimpressed with the sterile nature of the game, the local fans began to show their disapproval by hurling snowballs onto the pitch. Serious trouble really began when the Sparta 'Ultras' switched their target to the small group of supporters that had travelled from Italy. Not only that, but the snowballs were also replaced by more threatening projectiles. The result was that police had to be drafted in and several fans were arrested.

The match itself slowly petered out into a goalless draw. Sparta were aware that the away goals rule still gave them a chance of qualification in the return leg, but Parma, though proud to maintain their unbeaten record in Europe, knew that with better finishing in front of goal they could easily have made the second game an irrelevance.

JOZEF CHOVANEC
Sparta Praha

Back from the one-match suspension imposed after his red card in Bremen, Jozef Chovanec proved a tower of strength in the Sparta defence against Parma. Leading by example, the Sparta skipper's ability to read and intercept the opposition's attacking moves had a lot to do with his side's clean sheet, and it was his ferocious left-footed free-kick which almost gave the Czechoslovakian Cup holders a shock victory.

Chovanec is regarded in his homeland as one of the best players of his generation. With over 50 Czechoslovakian caps to his name, he has been just as influential at international level as in his two spells at Sparta. By far the biggest disappointent of his career, however, was his failure to make the grade at PSV Eindhoven. Originally signed as a replacement for Barcelona-bound Ronald Koeman, he eventually made only 34 Dutch League appearances for the club in three years before returning to Sparta midway through the 1991/92 season.

CUP-WINNERS' CUP
Quarter-Final Second Leg

Wednesday 17th March 1993
Ennio Tardini Stadium, Parma

PARMA 2 SPARTA PRAHA 0

Half-time 2-0 *Aggregate* 2-0 *Attendance* 17,942

		Goals				Goals
1	Marco BALLOTTA		1	Petr KOUBA		
2	Antonio BENARRIVO		2	Jirí NOVOTNY		
3	Alberto DI CHIARA		3	Roman VONASEK		
4	Lorenzo MINOTTI		4	Petr VRABEC		
5	Luigi APOLLONI ❑		5	Michal HORNÁK ❑ ■		
6	Georges GRÜN		6	Michal BÍLEK		
7	Alessandro MELLI †	11	7	Jirí NEMEC ❑		
8	Daniele ZORATTO		8	Jozef CHOVANEC		
9	Tomas BROLIN ‡		9	Viktor DVIRNIK †		
10	Stefano CUOGHI		10	Horst SIEGL		
11	Faustino ASPRILLA	33	11	Martin FRYDEK ‡		

Substitutes

Fausto PIZZI †77

Gabriele PIN ‡84

Substitutes

Pavel NEDVED †46

Lumír MISTR ‡70

Referee John BLANKENSTEIN (Holland)

FACTFILE

● *Parma strikers Alessandro Melli and Faustino Asprilla each scored their second goal of the competition.*

● *Kick-off time in the Ennio Tardini Stadium was brought forward to 14.30 in order to avoid a clash with other matches involving Italian sides taking place later the same day.*

● *Michal Hornák became the third Sparta defender to be sent off in four successive European away games.*

● *Sparta's elimination was their fifth out of five against Italian teams in Europe. They had also gone out previously to Bologna (66/67), Inter (69/70), Milan (72/73) and Juventus (84/85), and on each occasion they had lost the away leg in Italy.*

Early strikes see Parma safely through

Parma required just 45 minutes to book their place in the Cup-winners' Cup semi-finals. A goal apiece from their twin strike force of Melli and Asprilla, plus the sending off of Sparta Prague defender Michal Hornák for violent play, put the Italians in an unassailable position at the interval. Their job done, Nevio Scala's side turned off the heat in the second half in an evident attempt to conserve energy for their big Serie A confrontation with runaway leaders Milan the following weekend.

Parma began the match in breathtaking fashion. Tomas Brolin was determined to make up for his poor display in the first leg and turned the Sparta defence inside out on several occasions in the early minutes. A goal was inevitable, and it arrived from the boot of first-leg absentee Alessandro Melli after 11 minutes. In fact, Melli's task of putting the ball over the line was simple. The goal had been manufactured for him by Brolin and Asprilla, with the Swede setting the Colombian up for a shot which Sparta goalkeeper Petr Kouba could only half-save, deflecting it towards the goal for Melli to finish off with the greatest of ease.

There was nothing straightforward, though, about Parma's second goal - a rising first-time shot from Asprilla that swerved majestically into the far corner of Kouba's net for one of the European goals of the season. The Colombian, so anonymous in the first leg, was now bang in form, and four days later he would earn himself even more widespread publicity for an equally spectacular free-kick which finally ended Milan's long unbeaten run in Serie A.

Four minutes after Asprilla had brought the house down with his glory goal, Sparta's hopes of a comeback, and a third successive away win, were ruined for good when Hornák got his marching orders from the Dutch referee. As in the first leg, the Czech forwards got no change out of Parma's disciplined defence, and there was only one occasion - a Vrabec free-kick - when Ballotta's goal came under significant threat.

Sparta coach Dusan Uhrín admitted afterwards: "We didn't play the right way. Parma deserved to go through." As for Parma boss Scala, he could look forward with quiet confidence to the semi-finals, sound in the knowledge that his still unbeaten team were improving all the time and that, with Asprilla, Melli and Brolin on form in attack, he had more to offer than just an extremely reliable and flexible five-man defence.

ALESSANDRO MELLI
Parma

Italian national team boss Arrigo Sacchi was amongst the spectators at the Ennio Tardini Stadium. Ostensibly he was there to watch his old club qualify for their first European semi-final, but his official mission was to observe Parma striker Alessandro Melli with a view to selecting him for the World Cup qualifier against Malta. Melli evidently passed the test, because he duly gained his first Italian cap in Palermo a week later.
Melli first sprang to the attention of Italian football watchers when he scored 11 goals to help Parma into Serie A for the first time in the 1989/90 season. The following year he did even better, scoring 13 times in 29 games, including two goals against Milan, who subsequently expressed an interest in buying him. Melli remained at Parma, however, helping them to win the Italian Cup the following season and establishing himself as one of the finest all-round strikers in Italy.

Thursday 4th March 1993
OAKA Stadium, Athens

OLYMPIAKOS 1 ATLETICO MADRID 1

Half-time 0-1 *Attendance* 55,000

		Goals				Goals
1	Yorgos MIRTSOS		1	ABEL Resino		
2	Theodoros PAHATOURIDIS		2	Juan Manuel LOPEZ ❑		
3	Kiriakos KARATAIDIS ❑		3	Antonio Muñoz "TONI"		
4	Yorgos MITSIBONAS		4	Roberto SOLOZABAL		
5	Mihalis VLAHOS ❑ †		5	Francisco FERREIRA ❑		
6	Panayiotis TSALOUHIDIS		6	Juan Francisco Rodríguez "JUANITO"		
7	Sotiris MAVROMATIS		7	ALFREDO Santaelena †		
8	Nikos TSIANTAKIS ‡		8	Bernd SCHUSTER		
9	Daniel BATISTA		9	Gabriel MOYA	11	
10	Vassilis KARAPIALIS		10	Manuel ALFARO ‡		
11	Yorgos VAITSIS	64	11	Luis GARCIA		
	Substitutes			*Substitutes*		
	Ilias SAVVIDIS †61			TOMAS Reñones †83 ❑		
	Panayiotis SOFIANOPOULOS ‡75			Antonio OREJUELA ‡87		

Referee Rune LARSSON (Sweden)

FACTFILE

● *Atlético Madrid had only made one previous visit to Greece. That was in the 1971/72 season when they were eliminated in the first round of the UEFA Cup by a Panionios side making their European debut. That was the only time in nine confrontations that a Greek team had ever eliminated a Spanish team from a European Cup.*

● *Since the second round both teams had changed their coaches. Ljubomir Petrovic, the Champions' Cup-winning boss of Red Star Belgrade in 1991, had replaced Oleg Blokhin at Olympiakos, while Atlético now had Omar Pastoriza on the bench instead of Luis Aragonés.*

● *This was Olympiakos's first ever meeting with a Spanish club in Europe.*

● *Vaitsis's second-half equaliser was Olympiakos's first goal at home in the competition.*

Terrace warfare overshadows football

Atlético Madrid players and officials were happy to come away from Greece with a 1-1 draw. More importantly, though, they were just grateful to emerge in one piece from what had been a genuinely frightening experience in the Athens Olympic Stadium.

The occasional excesses of Greek football fans had been well documented throughout Europe. But nothing could have prepared the Spanish side for the extent of the hostility which they faced in Athens. Even larger-than-life president Jesús Gil admitted afterwards, in the relative safety of the charter plane flying back to Madrid, that he had never seen anything quite like it! His official protest to UEFA was as outspoken as it was inevitable.

During the course of the match the Atlético players had been bombarded with missiles thrown from the stands. At half-time and, especially, full-time they had to run the gauntlet through a hailstorm of fireworks, cans and seat cushions to get to their dressing-rooms. It was even alleged by some of the Atlético players that their Olympiakos counterparts were throwing punches at them and preventing them from getting through as well. Chaotic scenes indeed, but, sad to say, nothing new in Greece.

In view of all this off-pitch activity, the football itself took something of a back seat. The crowd's ire was fuelled early on when Olympiakos, appearing in their very first European quarter-final, conceded a soft goal to hand their opponents the lead. The Olympiakos defenders allowed a harmless-looking Schuster free-kick to float over their heads and that gave Gabriel Moya the chance to chest the ball down and fire it home at his leisure.

Not long afterwards Atlético should have gone 2-0 up. Alfaro, wearing the number ten shirt vacated by Benfica-bound Paulo Futre, showed all the cunning of his predecessor to dupe the Swedish referee into awarding his team a penalty. But justice was done when Mexican striker Luis García struck the post with his spot-kick as Mirtsos came dancing off his line - illegally, of course - to distract him.

The home fans had to wait until the 64th minute before their team got back into the game. Again, defensive uncertainty was to blame for the goal. Abel came out to collect a high ball, failed to do so and Yorgos Vaitsis, the Greeks' match-winner in the previous round against Monaco, skilfully flicked the ball into the net to make it 1-1.

BERND SCHUSTER
Atlético Madrid

With Futre back in Portugal and Atlético's two new foreign signings José Luis Villareal and Vladan Lukic ineligible, Bernd Schuster had a key role to play as Atlético sought to gain a semi-final foothold in Athens. Not renowned as one for the big occasion, the German midfielder nevertheless produced one of his most polished performances in an Atlético shirt.

Schuster's career has been one long saga of controversy. A revelation as a 20-year-old at the 1980 European Championship Finals, he quit Cologne for Barcelona a few months later and looked set for a glittering career at club and international level But a mixture of unavailiability, injuries and, most of all, sheer downright stubbornness on his part, restricted his German national team appearances to just 21, with his last game being at the age of just 23. He played a prominent part at Barcelona in bringing the club its long-awaited Spanish League title in 1985, but a year later he walked out on them during the Champions' Cup final against Steaua Bucharest and did not play at all the following season. He later joined Real Madrid and in 1990 became the only man ever to play for the Big Three in Spain when he moved across town to join Atlético.

CUP-WINNERS' CUP
Quarter-Final Second Leg

Thursday 18th March 1993
Vicente Calderón Stadium, Madrid

ATLETICO MADRID 3 OLYMPIAKOS 1

Half-time 1-0 *Aggregate* 4-2 *Attendance* 50,000

	Atletico Madrid	Goals		Olympiakos	Goals
1	ABEL Resino		1	Yorgos MIRTSOS	
2	Francisco FERREIRA		2	Minas HANTZIDIS †	
3	Antonio Muñoz "TONI" ❏		3	Ilias SAVVIDIS	
4	Roberto SOLOZABAL		4	Yorgos MITSIBONAS	
5	Juan VIZCAINO		5	Sotiris MAVROMATIS	
6	Juan Francisco Rodríguez "JUANITO"		6	Panayiotis TSALOUHIDIS	60
7	ALFREDO Santaelena ❏		7	Gennadi LITOVCHENKO	
8	Bernd SCHUSTER		8	Nikos TSIANTAKIS	
9	Gabriel MOYA †		9	Daniel BATISTA ‡	
10	Manuel Sánchez "MANOLO"	10, 59	10	Vassilis KARAPIALIS	
11	Luis GARCIA ‡		11	Yorgos VAITSIS ❏	

Substitutes

	Manuel ALFARO †56	67		Panayiotis SOFIANOPOULOS †70	
	Juan SABAS ‡88			Oleg PROTASOV ‡75	

Referee James McCLUSKEY (Scotland)

FACTFILE

● *Four of the five players booked in the first leg were suspended for the return - Vlahos and Karataidis of Olympiakos and López and Tomás of Atlético Madrid. Only Atlético's Francisco Ferreira was still available for selection.*

● *Atlético's win enabled them to go one better than the previous year when they had been knocked out of the quarter-finals on away goals by Club Bruges.*

● *Manolo's two goals were his first of the season in Europe. When he scored his first in the tenth minute, he became the tenth different Atlético goalscorer in the competition.*

● *Victory left Atlético as the only Spanish side remaining in the three European Cups.*

● *Manuel Alfaro - substitute scorer*

Night of euphoria in the Calderón

MANOLO
Atlético Madrid

It was difficult to tell which were the louder cheers. Those which greeted an Atlético goal or those which indicated that hated city rivals Real Madrid had conceded another in Paris. At the end of the night's proceedings Atlético fans duly had cause for a double celebration. Real had fallen to an injury-time goal from Paris-Saint-Germain in the UEFA Cup and Atlético had knocked out the club that had given them such an unwelcome reception in Athens a fortnight earlier.

Fortunately, there was no repeat of the violent and ugly scenes of the first leg in Madrid. If there was revenge in the air, it was sensibly saved for the field of play, where Atlético got off to the perfect start and went on to dominate their opponents throughout the 90 minutes.

Spanish international striker Manolo wasted no time in giving Atlético the lead. The Madrid side had started very strongly, with Schuster and the fit-again Vizcaíno driving them forward, and it was no more than they deserved when Manolo slid in after just ten minutes to fire them in front. There might have been further goals in the first period, with Atlético continuing to control the play from midfield, but the Olympiakos defence held out manfully through to the interval.

14 minutes into the second period, however, Atlético did get the second goal they had been threatening for so long. Once again Manolo was the scorer. After substitute Alfaro had beaten Hantzidis on the wing, Manolo met his centre with considerable force to give Atlético a comfortable two-goal cushion. Barely seconds later, though, the home side were back where they were as Greek international midfielder Panayiotis Tsalouhidis, so often the scorer of crucial goals for club and country, pulled a goal back for Olympiakos completely out of the blue.

Until that stage the Greeks had looked outclassed in all areas. None of their celebrated individual stars such as Batista, Karapialis and Tsiantakis had been able to get into the game and as time went on they increasingly began to resort to hopeful long punts upfield. Tsalouhidis's strike gave them fresh hope, but only for a matter of seven minutes. In conceding a third goal - a superb individual effort by the 22-year-old Alfaro - Olympiakos's quest for glory was over once and for all.

The night instead belonged to Atlético. They successfully meted out their revenge on the Greeks and were now through to the Cup-winners' Cup semi-finals for the fifth time in their history.

Atlético Madrid's match-winner Manolo was, surprisingly enough, starting only his second European game of the season. But he certainly made up for lost time with his double strike that went a long way towards taking the Spanish Cup holders into the semi-finals. Manolo was something of an unknown quantity when he joined Atlético from Murcia in 1988. But he made an immediate impact in his first season at the club, most notably in the Spanish national team, for whom he scored on his debut in a World Cup qualifier against the Republic of Ireland and subsequently found the target on four more occasions as Luis Suárez's team qualified for Italia '90. Manolo's best season for Atlético was in 1991/92 where he scored 27 league goals to take the 'Pichichi' top goalscorers' crown and another five in the European Cup-winners' Cup.

CUP-WINNERS' CUP
Quarter-Final First Leg

Thursday 4th March 1993
Bosuil Stadium, Antwerp

ROYAL ANTWERP FC 0 STEAUA BUCURESTI 0

Half-time 0-0 *Attendance* 9,500

		Goals				Goals
1	Stevan STOJANOVIC		1	Dumitru STINGACIU		
2	Wim KIEKENS ❑		2	Bogdan BUCUR ❑ ■		
3	Nico BROECKAERT		3	Aurel PANAIT		
4	Rudy TAEYMANS		4	Anton DOBOS ❑		
5	Rudy SMIDTS		5	Constantin GILCA ❑		
6	Dragan JAKOVLJEVIC		6	Daniel PRODAN ❑		
7	Didier SEGERS		7	Ion VLADOIU †		
8	Patrick VAN VEIRDEGHEM		8	Ilie DUMITRESCU ‡		
9	Francis SEVEREYNS		9	Iulian FILIPESCU		
10	Hans-Peter LEHNHOFF		10	Nica Basarab PANDURU		
11	Alex CZERNIATYNSKI		11	Ilie STAN ❑		

Substitutes

Substitutes

Ion SBURLEA †63

Daniel IFTODE ‡85

Referee Vadim ZHUK (Bielorussia)

FACTFILE

● *Steaua had received five yellow cards in each of the previous two rounds of the competition. Now they surpassed that total in just one leg with five yellow cards and one red!*

● *This was Steaua Bucharest's fifth visit to Belgium in European competition. On their previous trips they had lost three games and drawn one. Their only qualification at the expense of a Belgian club was against Anderlecht in the semi-finals of the 1985/86 Champions' Cup, which they went on to win.*

● *The 0-0 draw meant that Antwerp were still awaiting their first home win in the competition.*

● *Antwerp captain Rudy Smidts had scored the winning goal for Belgium against Romania five months earlier in a World Cup qualifier in Brussels.*

Goalkeeping heroics deny Antwerp

Belgian Cup holders Antwerp produced one of their finest displays of the season in front of an embarrassingly small home crowd. But it was not enough to beat a Steaua Bucharest side who defended with everything they had and by every possible means - both fair and foul - to keep themselves in the tie.

Steaua's individual hero of the night was undoubtedly goalkeeper Dumitru Stingaciu. As Antwerp sharpshooter Alex Czerniatynski was at pains to point out after the game, "Without the exploits of their goalkeeper we would surely have had a 3-0 lead going into the return game." Time after time the Steaua number one kept Czerniatynski and his colleagues at bay to deprive them of what would have been a thoroughly deserved victory.

The pattern of the game was clear from the opening few minutes of play. Antwerp pressed forward in numbers, while Steaua, confirming the over-physical approach they had shown in earlier rounds, had four players booked - Gilca, Dobos, Bucur and Stan - in the opening half-hour. Stingaciu's first important save was from Czerniatynski after 15 minutes when he reacted brilliantly to the Antwerp number 11's glancing header from a corner. And after 30 minutes Jakovljevic should have made the breakthrough when he headed a clear chance over the bar from an unmarked position in the penalty area.

The second half saw more one-way traffic from the Belgians - and more heroics from the Steaua goalkeeper. Severeyns had a shot saved by the 'keeper's foot, then Jakovljevic saw his header palmed away as well. Bucur's sending off after an hour's play - for a foul on Segers - meant that Steaua withdrew even further into their defensive shell. Sburlea, a centre-back, was brought on for Vladoiu, a striker, and thanks to continued

good work from Stingaciu, who denied Czerniatynski and Lehnhoff (twice) in the closing stages, the Romanians eventually hung on for the goalless draw they had sought from the outset.

Antwerp coach Walter Meeuws was as frustrated as his players after the game and in an unsympathetic mood towards the opposition. "Only one team played to win, and that was us. We created eight to ten chances. They created none."

● *Bogdan Bucur - red-carded*

ILIE STAN
Steaua Bucharest

Most of the heroics for Steaua Bucharest in Antwerp were provided by their goalkeeper Dumitru Stingaciu. But another player who caught the eye was attacking midfield general Ilie Stan. Despite the one-way traffic in the direction of the Steaua goal for most of the game, the 25-year-old wasted precious seconds on a number of occasions with his ability to maintain possession and relieve the pressure on his overworked defence.
Until he made his belated Romanian national team debut as a substitute in a friendly against Mexico in August 1992, Stan was regarded as one of the best players in his country never to have gained full international recognition. And although manager Cornel Dinu did not call him up again during the course of the season, Stan appeared to be doing everything humanly possible to warrant further selection.
At the time of the Antwerp game he was riding high as the top scorer in the Romanian First Division, proving himself to be an indispensable asset in Steaua's quest for a first national title in four years.

CUP-WINNERS' CUP
Quarter-Final Second Leg

Wednesday 17th March 1993
Steaua Stadium, Bucharest

STEAUA BUCURESTI 1   ROYAL ANTWERP FC 1

Half-time 1-0 *Aggregate* 1-1 (Rotal Antwerp FC win on away goals) *Attendance* 30,000

		Goals				Goals
1	Dumitru STINGACIU			1	Stevan STOJANOVIC	
2	Ionel PIRVU			2	Wim KIEKENS	
3	Aurel PANAIT			3	Nico BROECKAERT	
4	Ion SBURLEA			4	Rudy TAEYMANS ❏ ■	
5	Constantin GILCA ❏			5	Rudy SMIDTS	
6	Daniel PRODAN			6	Didier SEGERS ❏	
7	Ion VLADOIU ‡			7	Ronny VAN RETHY †	
8	Ilie DUMITRESCU †	20		8	Patrick VAN VEIRDEGHEM ❏ ‡	
9	Iulian FILIPESCU			9	Francis SEVEREYNS	
10	Nica Basarab PANDURU			10	Hans-Peter LEHNHOFF	
11	Ionel FULGA ■			11	Alex CZERNIATYNSKI	82

Substitutes		*Substitutes*
Daniel IFTODE †74		Dragan JAKOVLJEVIC †65
Alexandru ANDRASI ‡82		Geert EMMERECHTS ‡85 ❏

Referee Leslie MOTTRAM (Scotland)

● *Antwerp were through to the Cup-winners' Cup semi-finals despite winning just a single one of their six games - the away leg of the second round tie against Admira Wacker.*

● *Alex Czerniatynski's sixth goal of the campaign enabled him to equal Karl Kodat as the club's highest ever goalscorer in Europe.*

● *Steaua began the match with three players suspended - Dobos, Bucur and Stan - and six more on a yellow card - Panduru, Panait, Dumitrescu, Sburlea, Gilca and Prodan.*

● *Antwerp had never previously won a European tie on the away goals rule. They were, however, eliminated by the rule back in 1974/75 when Ajax used it to knock them out of the UEFA Cup.*

● *Ilie Dumitrescu - opened the scoring*

FACTFILE

Late away goal puts Antwerp into semis

Belgian international Alex Czerniatynski proved to be Antwerp's hero for the second round in succession. He had scored five goals in the second round tie against Admira Wacker. Now his single goal, scored late in the game against Steaua in Bucharest, was sufficient to take Antwerp further than they had ever previously gone in European competition - into the Cup-winners' Cup semi-finals.

The 'Great Old', as Antwerp are fondly known in Belgium, were 1-0 down with just eight minutes to go when Czerniatynski rose to head in Hans-Peter Lehnhoff's inch-perfect cross. The locals could scarcely believe it. Their team had squeezed past Danish side AGF on the away goals rule in the last round after two late strikes in the same stadium, and now they were on the receiving end after having looked comfortable for so long.

The Romanians began the match with a great deal more spring in their step than they had shown in Antwerp. Their opening goal arrived after 20 minutes. Nica Basarab Panduru, their most enterprising player on the night, placed a free-kick into the penalty area. The ball fell invitingly to Ilie Dumitrescu and he beat Stojanovic from close range.

As play developed, the match became just as physical as the first contest in Belgium. The Scottish referee saw fit to reach for his notebook three times in the first half, and ten minutes after the interval Ionel Fulga became the second Steaua player to be sent off in the tie. Antwerp, though, could not make their numerical superiority pay, and 12 minutes later they were down to ten men themselves when defender Rudy Taeymans received his marching orders for his second bookable offence.

Steaua should have sewn the game up in the second half when Panduru, after a fine run upfield, set up Vladoiu for a glorious opportunity. But the Steaua striker's shot was well saved by Stojanovic. Moments later the significance of that miss became evident as Czerniatynski escaped from his marker Sburlea and joyously nodded Antwerp level with the all-important tie-clinching away goal.

● Ion Vladoiu - expensive miss

ALEX CZERNIATYNSKI
Royal Antwerp FC

The 1992/93 season was fast becoming an unforgettable one for Alex Czerniatynski. Almost single-handedly responsible for getting Antwerp through to the quarter-finals after his five-goal assault on Admira Wacker, he now created history for the club with his opportunely struck header in Bucharest. Moreover, this was a season in which he had been recalled to the Belgian national colours after a six-year absence and had promptly scored Belgium's winning goal in an important World Cup qualifier away to Czechoslovakia.
'Czernia', son of a Polish immigrant worker, enjoyed early stardom when he appeared for Belgium in the 1982 World Cup finals. He was an Antwerp player then, but moved to Anderlecht immediately after those finals and helped the Brussels club to win the UEFA Cup in his first season. After winning a Belgian championship medal with Anderlecht in 1985 Czerniatynski moved to Standard Liège where he spent four moderate seasons before his return to Antwerp, and another good UEFA Cup run, in 1989/90.

CUP-WINNERS' CUP
Quarter-Final First Leg

Tuesday 2nd March 1993
Feyenoord Stadium, Rotterdam

FEYENOORD 0 SPARTAK MOSKVA 1

Half-time 0-1 *Attendance* 33,187

		Goals			Goals
1	Ed DE GOEY		1	Stanislav CHERCHESOV	
2	Ulrich VAN GOBBEL		2	Dmitry KHLESTOV	
3	John DE WOLF		3	Andrey IVANOV ❑	
4	John METGOD †		4	Dmitry POPOV ‡	
5	Errol REFOS		5	Vladimir BESCHASTNYKH	
6	Peter BOSZ		6	Andrey CHERNYSHOV ❑ ■	
7	Arnold SCHOLTEN		7	Viktor ONOPKO	
8	Gaston TAUMENT		8	Valery KARPIN †	
9	József KIPRICH		9	Andrey PYATNITSKY	36
10	Rob WITSCHGE		10	Igor LEDYAKHOV	
11	Regi BLINKER ❑		11	Dmitry RADCHENKO ❑	

Substitute

Mike OBIKU †65

Substitutes

Nikolai PISAREV †70
Andrey GASHKIN ‡89

Referee Karl-Josef ASSENMACHER (Germany)

FACTFILE

● This match was the first of five in a busy and potentially crucial fortnight for Feyenoord. In addition to the European matches they had a Dutch Cup meeting with Ajax plus two important league matches against local rivals Sparta and leaders PSV.

● Spartak Moscow had won all three of their previous European ties against Dutch opposition - Den Haag in 1972/73, Haarlem in 1982/83 and Sparta in 1983/84. Curiously, John de Wolf, the Feyenoord defender, had been a goalscorer for Sparta in the first leg of that UEFA Cup third-round clash!

● Dmitry Radchenko, the Spartak Moscow striker, was being observed from the stands by Werder Bremen coach Otto Rehhagel and Barcelona assistant coach Bruins Slot.

Feyenoord furious over controversial goal

Spartak Moscow landed their third successive away win of the competition with a classy display in the Feyenoord Stadium. There was little doubt that they had done enough to deserve their victory. What was contentious, however, was the legitimacy of the goal that gave them their 1-0 win.

With nine minutes to go in the first half and the contest looking even at that stage, the Feyenoord defence pushed forward *en masse* almost to the halfway line. Spartak midfielder Igor Ledyakhov decided to chip the ball back into the Feyenoord half. His midfield colleague Valery Karpin ran on to it and with three Spartak players retreating from an offside position on the other side of the field, it seemed that the linesman would inevitably signal for offside. But his flag stayed down, Karpin ran on and Andrey Pyatnitsky, running unaccompanied through the middle, had the simplest of tasks to tap the ball in from Karpin's pass.

The Feyenoord defenders could not believe what was happening. Why had play not been stopped for offside? With captain John Metgod leading the protest, they rushed to the German linesman seeking explanation. They got none, but it seemed certain that he had ruled that the three 'offside' players were not interfering with play. Surely, however, that was the referee's decision, not the linesman's. But Feyenoord's pleas fell on deaf ears. The goal stood and that was that. They had to get on with the game and see if they could repair the damage themselves.

As so often happens in such circumstances where officials feel that in hindsight they may have made a mistake, decisions started to go in Feyenoord's favour after that, including a 'goal' from Beschastnykh just before half-time that was chalked off for no apparent reason. After the interval the Russians continued to create the better chances. Onopko, Pisarev and Beschastnykh all went close before Feyenoord responded with their best opportunity of the evening, Cherchesov being forced to save well from Witschge.

But 0-1 was how it remained, and although the Russians' celebrations were dampened somewhat by the sending off of their sweeper Andrey Chernyshov for a second bookable offence in the last minute, Spartak were beginning to look like serious contenders for the trophy. They had flattened Liverpool at Anfield. Now they had won in Rotterdam, where Feyenoord had not been beaten in Europe since 1986.

ANDREY PYATNITSKY
Spartak Moskva

Andrey Pyatnitsky's controversial winning strike in Rotterdam was his fourth European goal of the season, all of them having been scored away from home. The other three goals - two against Avenir Beggen and one against Liverpool - were all scored after the ties had virtually been decided, but this latest effort promised to be crucial. Pyatnitsky was widely recognised to be the most influential player on view against Feyenoord. He buzzed around in midfield to telling effect and laid on a number of chances for his team-mates with some astute passing. It was precisely those qualities which prompted Spartak Moscow to sign the 26-year-old from Pakhtakor Tashkent a year or so earlier. He had scored 10 goals for the Uzbekistan club in the last ever USSR Supreme League in 1991, and in 1992, after winning five caps in a row for the USSR/CIS national team, he played a prominent part in helping Spartak to their Russian League triumph.

CUP-WINNERS' CUP
Quarter-Final Second Leg

Thursday 18th March 1993
Torpedo Stadium, Moscow

SPARTAK MOSKVA 3 FEYENOORD 1

Half-time 1-1 *Aggregate* 4-1 *Attendance* 15,250

		Goals				Goals
1	Stanislav CHERCHESOV		1	Ed DE GOEY		
2	Dmitry KHLESTOV		2	Ulrich VAN GOBBEL ■		
3	Andrey IVANOV		3	John DE WOLF		
4	Dimitry POPOV		4	John METGOD		
5	Aleksandr BONDAR		5	Ruud HEUS ❑		
6	Igor LEDYAKHOV		6	Orlando TRUSTFULL		
7	Viktor ONOPKO ❑		7	Arnold SCHOLTEN		
8	Valery KARPIN	8, 81	8	Gaston TAUMENT		
9	Andrey PYATNITSKY ❑		9	József KIPRICH		14
10	Fyodor CHERENKOV ■		10	Rob WITSCHGE		
11	Dmitry RADCHENKO	89	11	Regi BLINKER ❑		
	Substitutes			*Substitutes*		

Referee Joël QUINIOU (France)

● *Vladimir Beschastnykh, the young Spartak Moscow striker, was suspended from appearing in this game by FIFA for his refusal to travel with the Russian team for the World Youth Cup in Australia.*

● *Feyenoord's defeat was their third in succession away from home.*

● *József Kiprich's goal maintained his record of scoring in every round. Moscow was a happy hunting ground for him. He had also scored twice there for Hungary in a European Championship qualifier against the Soviet Union 18 months earlier.*

● *Valery Karpin's two goals enabled him to draw up alongside Andrey Pyatnitsky as Spartak's top scorer in the competition with four goals.*

FACTFILE

● *Valery Karpin*

Late flurry takes Spartak into semis

With Russian President Boris Yeltsin amongst the 15,250 crowd, Spartak had more than just their usual supporters to impress as they sought to finish off what they had started in Rotterdam and qualify for their second European semi-final in three years.

It all started well for the reigning Russian champions when Valery Karpin caught the Feyenoord defence daydreaming in the eighth minute and ran through to fire a left-foot shot past Ed de Goey. This time there was no complaining about offside from Metgod and co.. They knew that on this occasion they, not the officials, were responsible for allowing their opponents to take the lead.

Wim van Hanegem's team were quick to strike back, though. Hungarian international József Kiprich, the only foreign player in the Feyenoord starting line-up, was allowed too much freedom on the right and he made Spartak pay with a brilliant finish, firing powerfully across Cherchesov into the net. Now, with an away goal in the bag, Feyenoord were very much back in the tie. One more goal and they would be in the driving seat. But the Russians, though less fluent than they had been before, continued to hold sway in midfield and there were precious few opportunities for the visitors to add to the scoreline.

Most of the second-half action took place in the Feyenoord half of the field, but the Dutch defended well and Ed de Goey, in particular, showed on a number of occasions just why he had been promoted to the Dutch national team as first-choice goalkeeper ahead of Ajax's Stanley Menzo with a succession of fine stops. Nine minutes from time, however, De Goey was to suffer a cruel blow which ultimately proved decisive in giving Spartak the ascendancy once again. Pyatnitsky blasted in a powerful low free-kick, De Goey dived at full stretch to make a save, but the ball hit the post and rolled across the line, where Karpin was waiting to scramble it into the net.

At 2-1 to Spartak, the tie was effectively over. But there was still plenty of time for further action and incident. With five minutes to go both teams were reduced to ten men when Feyenoord full-back Ulrich van Gobbel and Spartak's veteran midfielder Fyodor Cherenkov were sent off for fighting. Then, with the crowd whistling for full-time, Spartak got another goal. Dmitry Radchenko was the scorer, his coolly placed shot enabling him to keep up his record of scoring in every round as his team confirmed their place in the semi-finals.

JOHN DE WOLF
Feyenoord

Although he finished up on the losing side, John de Wolf impressed many observers with his tremendously gutsy performance in Moscow. It was no coincidence that he should gain a call-up for the Dutch national team a week later for the World Cup qualifier against San Marino. What was surprising, however, was that the big central defender should go on and score two goals!

De Wolf's one and only appearance for Holland before that had been back in 1987 when he appeared as a substitute in the team's last qualifier for the 1988 European Finals, which, of course, they went on to win. De Wolf was not a member of that victorious squad in Germany, but it is quite conceivable that at the age of 31 he will be back in the frame for the 1994 World Cup should the Dutch qualify. It is not just his physical appearance - tall, long-haired and bearded - that leaves accomplished strikers quaking in their boots. His ability to mark key opponents out of the game has been an important feature of Feyenoord's recent return to the big time both at domestic and European level.

CUP-WINNERS' CUP
Quarter-Finals Review

QUARTER-FINAL RESULTS

		1st leg	2nd leg	Agg.
Sparta Praha	Parma	0-0	0-2	0-2
Olympiakos	Atlético Madrid	1-1	1-3	2-4
Royal Antwerp FC	Steaua Bucuresti	0-0	1-1	1-1
(Royal Antwerp FC win on away goals)				
Feyenoord	Spartak Moskva	0-1	1-3	1-4

LEADING GOALSCORERS AFTER QUARTER-FINALS

6	Alex CZERNIATYNSKI (Royal Antwerp FC)
5	Ian RUSH (Liverpool)
4	Andrey PYATNITSKY (Spartak Moskva)
	József KIPRICH (Feyenoord)
	Valery KARPIN (Spartak Moskva)
	Torben CHRISTENSEN (AGF)
	Wynton RUFER (SV Werder Bremen)
	Yury NIKIFOROV (Chernomorets Odessa)
3	Dmitry RADCHENKO (Spartak Moskva)
	Ion VLADOIU (Steaua Bucuresti)
	Meny BASSON (Hapoel Petach-Tikva)

CUP-WINNERS' CUP

Tuesday 6th April 1993
Vicente Calderón Stadium, Madrid

ATLETICO MADRID 1 PARMA 2

Half-time 1-0 *Attendance* 50,000

		Goals			Goals
1	ABEL Resino		1	Marco BALLOTTA	
2	Juan Manuel LOPEZ ❏		2	Antonio BENARRIVO	
3	Antonio Muñoz "TONI"		3	Alberto DI CHIARA ❏	
4	Roberto SOLOZABAL 57 (og)		4	Lorenzo MINOTTI	
5	Juan VIZCAINO		5	Salvatore MATRECANO	
6	Juan Francisco Rodríguez "JUANITO" ❏ ‡		6	Georges GRÜN	
7	Manuel Sánchez "MANOLO" †		7	Alessandro MELLI †	
8	Bernd SCHUSTER ❏		8	Daniele ZORATTO ❏	
9	Manuel ALFARO		9	Tomas BROLIN	
10	ALFREDO Santaelena		10	Stefano CUOGHI	
11	LUIS GARCIA	44	11	Faustino ASPRILLA ❏	60

Substitutes

Juan SABAS †63

Francisco FERREIRA ‡75

Substitute

Fausto PIZZI †70

Referee Philip DON (England)

FACTFILE

● *Parma's victory was the first by an Italian club in the Vicente Calderón stadium for some 29 years.*

● *Philip Don was the second English referee to visit the Spanish capital in little over a month. His compatriot David Elleray had been in charge of the UEFA Cup quarter-final first leg between Real Madrid and Paris-Saint-Germain five weeks earlier.*

● *Victory extended Parma's unbeaten run in European football to nine games.*

● *Parma defender Luigi Apolloni was suspended from this tie after receiving yellow cards in both legs of the semi-final against Sparta Prague.*

Asprilla magic turns tie in Parma's favour

This was the third European tie involving Italian and Spanish clubs within the space of a year. The first meeting, between Barcelona and Sampdoria in the 1992 Champions' Cup final at Wembley, had gone Spain's way. Then, in the UEFA Cup, Napoli had gained some revenge for Italy by annihilating Valencia in the first round back in September. Now Parma and Atlético Madrid locked horns in the Cup-winners' Cup, with a place in another Wembley final awaiting the winners.

There was a tremendous atmosphere in the Vicente Calderón stadium. As Spain's last remaining representative in any of the three competitions, Atlético had become the sole focus of attention in their own country, and the home fans were determined to make the most of their top billing, providing a marvellous spectacle as the teams came on to the pitch, with firecrackers adding to the deafening noise and streamers raining down from every tier

The opening minutes of the game were littered with niggly fouls. Alessandro Melli might have made more of a poor back-pass midway through the half, but it was Atlético who finally opened the scoring just a minute before the interval. Mexican striker Luis García found a stylish finish to beat Ballotta in the Parma goal, but it was the fluency of the build-up play, involving Schuster and Manolo, that made the goal so special.

Luis García was denied a second goal early in the second half by a fine block-tackle from Benarrivo, and that was to prove the turning point in the match. Parma gradually began to assert themselves. Matrecano, in for regular number five Apolloni, had a penalty claim refused, then Melli shot over after working himself into a promising position in the penalty area. After 57 minutes the Italians got their deserved equaliser. It was officially credited as an own goal by Atlético's Spanish international defender Solozábal, but in reality it was Faustino Asprilla's goal. Found in space on the right by strike-partner Melli, his well-struck shot from just outside the area took a slight deflection off Solozábal's boot on its way into the net.

Just three minutes later, however, the Colombian striker contributed a second goal which he could justly claim to be all his own work. He met a hanging left-wing cross with a magnificent header on the run that gave Atlético 'keeper Abel no chance whatsoever. It proved to be the winning goal. Parma defended well for the last half-hour and, with Asprilla showing such devastating form up front, their counter-attacking continued to give Atlético big problems at the back right through to the final whistle.

FAUSTINO ASPRILLA
Parma

With Faustino Asprilla enjoying the hottest goal-scoring streak of his career, there was a great deal of interest shown in this match back in his homeland. Not only was the game being relayed live on Colombian television. There was also an unusually large Colombian contingent amongst the accredited press corps in the Vicente Calderón. Asprilla was clearly in no mood to let anyone down. His goalscoring touch proved to be the difference between the two sides, enabling Parma to have one foot in the final with half the tie still to play.

It had taken until the spring for Asprilla to come into bloom. Since joining the Italian Cup holders from Colombian side Nacional Medellín the previous summer the 23-year-old Olympic Games star had struggled to establish himself in the team and was more often than not asked to sit on the subs' bench as the season progressed. But then came his memorable strikes against Sparta Prague and Milan and suddenly there was no stopping him... as Atlético Madrid discovered to their cost.

CUP WINNERS' CUP
Semi-Final Second Leg

Thursday 22nd April 1993
Ennio Tardini Stadium, Parma

PARMA 0 ATLETICO MADRID 1

Half-time 0-0 *Aggregate* 2-2 (Parma win on away goals) *Attendance* 21,915

	Goals			Goals
1 Marco BALLOTTA		1 DIEGO Garrido		
2 Salvatore MATRECANO		2 Carlos AGUILERA †		
3 Antonio BENARRIVO		3 Antonio Muñoz "TONI" ❑		
4 Lorenzo MINOTTI		4 Roberto SOLOZABAL		
5 Luigi APOLLONI		5 TOMAS Reñones		
6 Georges GRÜN		6 DONATO Gama da Silva		
7 Alessandro MELLI ‡		7 Juan SABAS		78
8 Gabriele PIN		8 Bernd SCHUSTER		
9 Marco OSIO †		9 Juan VIZCAINO ■		
10 Stefano CUOGHI		10 ALFREDO Santaelena		
11 Tomas BROLIN		11 LUIS GARCIA ‡		
Substitutes		*Substitutes*		
Fausto PIZZI †76		Manuel ALFARO †58 ■		
Gianluca HERVATIN ‡88		Juan Francisco Rodríguez "JUANITO" ‡74 ■		

Referee Aron SCHMIDHUBER (Germany)

FACTFILE

● *Parma's triumph meant that, with Milan and Juventus also reaching the final in the other two competitions, Italian clubs had now reached 36 out of the 106 European finals, edging them closer to Spain's record figure of 37.*

● *Parma welcomed Luigi Apolloni back from suspension but were denied the services of both Alberto Di Chiara and Daniele Zoratto for the same reason.*

● *Although they reached their first European final, Parma's celebrations were spoiled somewhat by their first ever defeat in European competition.*

● *Juan Sabas's goal was the first conceded at home by Parma in the competition.*

● *Luigi Apolloni*

Parma hang on in dramatic finale

It was supposed to be a night of celebration for Parma. In the end it was, but not in the way that the team and their supporters had hoped. Having won the first leg in Madrid, the Italian Cup holders looked certainties to finish off the job with relative ease in front of their home crowd. But unsure whether to go for further goals and kill the tie off quickly or sit back and deny their opponents space, Nevio Scala's team very nearly threw it all away in an amazing final 15 minutes, during which Atlético Madrid scored a goal and, but for an incredible oversight by the German referee, would have had the opportunity to score a second from the penalty spot.

Parma's cause was not helped by the absence of first-leg hero Faustino Asprilla. He had been home to Colombia since the first leg and, to the horror of Parma officials, reported back for duty with a gashed leg, allegedly sustained in a 'domestic incident' although the precise cause of it was shrouded in doubt and was soon to become the subject of lengthy and lively debate in the Italian press. Without the Colombian, Parma lacked the necessary cutting edge up front to worry Atlético as they had done in Madrid. The first 45 minutes produced only one real chance, but Marco Osio snatched at it and Tomás was able to scramble off the line.

At the other end the Parma defence held firm for 75 minutes. But with qualification for the final so tantalisingly close, the players suddenly began to lose faith in themselves and handed Atlético the initiative. The first warning sign came when goalkeeper Marco Ballotta was called spectacularly into action from Aguilera's long-range shot. But the Italians failed to heed it and moments later they conceded a goal. Ballotta was the villain on this occasion, straying too far off his line and offering an unprotected target which Atlético striker Sabas found with an instinctive strike as the ball was played to him out of a *mêlée* on the edge of the area.

Now the Spaniards had the bit between their teeth. Swarming forward in numbers in search of a second goal that would put them into the final, they began to put the Parma defence in serious trouble for the first time in the tie. On one typical burst, Roberto Solozábal made his way into the penalty area only to be felled by a lunging tackle by Parma sweeper Lorenzo Minotti. It seemed a clear penalty, but to the disgust of the Spaniards, and the unexpected relief of the Italians, referee Schmidhuber refused to point to the spot. It was all too much for the Atlético players. Substitute Juanito got himself sent off for kicking out at Benarrivo after another, far less convincing, penalty appeal was waved away. And as the Atlético players continued to surround the German officials after the final whistle, two of them - Vizcaino and Alfaro - were shown the red card as well.

JUAN SABAS
Atlético Madrid

But for a dodgy refereeing decision, Juan Sabas might have gone down in the history books as the man who turned around the tie and put Atlético Madrid into their fourth European Cup-winners' Cup final. It was he who put the Spanish club back in the game with his neatly taken goal 12 minutes from time and there is every likelihood that he would have been asked to step forward for the decisive penalty if Herr Schmidhuber had correctly sanctioned Minotti's foul on Solozábal.

In such moments can careers be determined, and Sabas could certainly have done with the chance to earn some glory. After all, in his third season at Atlético the former taxi driver and Rayo Vallecano player was still some way off establishing himself as a first choice striker in the team. The match in Parma offered him only his second start of the competition and his first since the 6-1 thrashing of Maribor Branik in the opening round when he had also got his name on the scoresheet - from the penalty spot!

Wednesday 7th April 1993
Lenin Stadium, Moscow

SPARTAK MOSKVA 1 ROYAL ANTWERP FC 0

Half-time 1-0 *Attendance* 60,000

		Goals				Goals
1	Stanislav CHERCHESOV			1	Stevan STOJANOVIC	
2	Dmitry KHLESTOV			2	Nourédine MOUKRIM	
3	Andrey IVANOV			3	Nico BROECKAERT	
4	Dmitry POPOV			4	Wim KIEKENS ❑	
5	Vladimir BESCHASTNYKH ❑			5	Rudy SMIDTS ❑	
6	Andrey CHERNYSHOV			6	Dragan JAKOVLJEVIC ❑	
7	Valery KARPIN			7	Ronny VAN RETHY	
8	Ramiz MAMEDOV			8	Didier SEGERS	
9	Andrey PYATNITSKY	35		9	Francis SEVEREYNS	
10	Igor LEDYAKHOV			10	Hans-Peter LEHNHOFF †	
11	Dmitry RADCHENKO †			11	Alex CZERNIATYNSKI	
	Substitute				*Substitute*	
	Nikolai PISAREV †48				Gerry DE GRAEF †88	

Referee Leif SUNDELL (Sweden)

FACTFILE

● *Russian President Boris Yeltsin was again present in the stands to offer his support to Spartak.*

● *This was Antwerp's first away defeat of the competition and the first time that they had failed to score on their travels.*

● *Both teams went into the game with players missing through suspension. Spartak had to do without Onopko and Cherenkov, while Antwerp were denied the services of Emmerechts, Taeymans and Van Veirdeghem.*

● *Andrey Pyatnitsky's goal enabled the Spartak midfielder to prolong his sequence of scoring in every round.*

● *Antwerp had never previously played a European tie in Russia, nor, for that matter, in any part of the former Soviet Union.*

Narrow win for Spartak as chances go begging

After the way in which they had accounted for Liverpool and Feyenoord in the two previous rounds, Spartak Moscow were heavily fancied to reach their first European final by comfortably disposing of the competition's dark horses, Antwerp. 60,000 Russians braved a very cold night in Moscow to cheer their heroes on to what they trusted would be a convincing first leg win. But, as is so often the case in football, things did not exactly go to plan.

Walter Meeuws' side, clearly delighted to have reached this stage of a European competition for the first time in the club's history, adopted a nothing-to-lose attitude in the early part of the game and it very nearly produced a goal for them. Spartak were evidently not expecting the Belgians to come at them with such viguor and it was only the exploits of goalkeeper Cherchesov that prevented an early setback. Alex Czerniatynski, the tournament's leading goalscorer, was only just wide with a cross-shot early on. Then Lehnhoff, the German playmaker, brought a fine save out of Cherchesov with a 30-yard drive before Czerniatynski, again, tested the Spartak 'keeper with an instinctive hook-shot.

The first goal, however, was to be scored against the run of play. In what was their first attack of any substance, Spartak worked the ball out to Andrey Pyatnitsky on the right edge of the penalty area. His right-foot shot was instant and deadly, ripping into the net at the near post and giving the home team an undeserved lead.

Once ahead, Spartak began to exert their own spell of pressure on the Antwerp defence. Two clear chances were created. The first when, after a jinking run from Ledyakhov, Vladimir Beschastnykh smashed a shot against the post from 35 yards out, and the second when, after Antwerp 'keeper Stojanovic could only parry another long-range effort, Dmitry Popov slid his follow-up shot agonisingly across the face of the goal.

The half-time interval, however, saved Antwerp from a second goal and they emerged refreshed for the second period, reviving their early opening spell with another bout of pressure during which Czerniatynski had a penalty claim turned down and Lehnhoff's cross after a surge down the right was only inches away from the veteran Belgian international's outstretched boot. Spartak, as in the first half, finished the stronger, though. Pyatnitsky, their best outfield player, might have added to his five goals in the competition, but two late efforts from him failed to find the target and it was with a slim one-goal advantage that Spartak had to travel to Belgium for the return a fortnight later.

STANISLAV CHERCHESOV
Spartak Moskva

For all the attacking impetus they put into the game, Antwerp certainly deserved to score at least one goal in the Lenin stadium. But Stanislav Cherchesov, the Spartak goalkeeper, proved an insurmountable final barrier for Czerniatynski and co., and with Pyatnitsky scoring the only goal of the game at the other end, the Russians still looked to be in a commanding position to reach the final. Cherchesov began his career at Spartak, but was denied an opportunity to prove himself in the first team by the lasting briilliance of the great Rinat Dasaev. He moved to neighbours Lokomotiv for his first full season of action in 1988, but after Dasaev moved to Seville he was recalled and has been a regular in the Spartak line-up ever since, appearing in all eight of the club's matches during their 1990/91 Champions' Cup run and helping them to two national titles. Cherchesov will almost certainly be part of the Russian squad at the 1994 World Cup finals where he will continue to contest the number one jersey with Chelsea's Dmitry Kharin.

CUP WINNERS' CUP
Semi-Final Second Leg

Thursday 22nd April 1993
Bosuil Stadium, Antwerp

ROYAL ANTWERP FC 3 SPARTAK MOSKVA 1

Half-time 1-1 *Aggregate* 3-2 *Attendance* 17,000

		Goals				Goals
1	Stevan STOJANOVIC		1	Stanislav CHERCHESOV		
2	Patrick VAN VEIRDEGHEM ‡		2	Dmitry KHLESTOV		
3	Nico BROECKAERT		3	Andrey IVANOV		
4	Rudy TAEYMANS		4	Dmitry POPOV †		
5	Rudy SMIDTS		5	Nikolai PISAREV ❑		
6	Dragan JAKOVLJEVIC †	64	6	Andrey CHERNYSHOV		
7	Ronny VAN RETHY		7	Viktor ONOPKO ❑ ◼		
8	Didier SEGERS		8	Valery KARPIN ❑		
9	Francis SEVEREYNS		9	Andrey PYATNITSKY ❑		
10	Hans-Peter LEHNHOFF	76 (pen)	10	Igor LEDYAKHOV ❑		
11	Alex CZERNIATYNSKI	36	11	Dmitry RADCHENKO ‡		9
	Substitutes			*Substitutes*		
	Geert EMMERECHTS †81			Andrey GASHKIN †41		
	Nourédine MOUKRIM ‡85			Vladimir BAKSCHEV ‡43		

Referee Jorge MONTEIRO COROADO (Portugal)

FACTFILE

● *Dmitry Radchenko's goal, like that of his team-mate Pyatnitsky in the first leg, maintained a goal-a-round sequence for the Spartak forward.*

● *This was Antwerp's first home victory of the competition... against opponents who had won all three of their previous away games!*

● *Viktor Onopko became the third Spartak player to be sent off in the competition - a record that equalled that of their second-round opponents Liverpool.*

● *Alex Czerniatynski strengthened his position at the head of the Cup-winners' Cup goalscoring charts with his seventh goal of the competition.*

● *Viktor Onopko*

Mystery penalty puts underdogs in final

Despite conceding an early away goal to give their opponents an apparently decisive 2-0 aggregate lead, Antwerp recovered in dramatic fashion to score the three goals they needed and qualify for their first ever European final. Few were prepared to give the Belgians much hope of retrieving the one-goal deficit from the first leg. Before the match Antwerp coach Walter Meeuws was even ready to concede that "Spartak are the stronger team" before adding, optimistically, "but the stronger team does not always win!".

This tie was certainly a case in point. Spartak seemed to have everything in control right from the moment when Dmitry Radchenko headed home to put Spartak ahead after nine minutes. There were further opportunities for the Russians to score in the first period, but they seemed unconcerned at the chances they missed. After all, the tie looked to be sewn up already.

But the home side finally woke up and almost out of the blue they got an equaliser through - who else? - Alex Czerniatynski. That was an obvious blow to the visitors, but they had two more to suffer before the interval when their two most productive players up to that stage - midfielder Popov and goalscorer Radchenko - were forced to leave the field with injury.

Ominously for the Russians, the wheel of fortune was beginning to spin in Antwerp's favour. At the beginning of the second period they still looked to have matters in hand, but an excellent second goal for Antwerp in the 64th minute - a rising shot from ex-Yugoslav international Dragan Jakovljevic - had them looking worried for the first time in the contest.

As so often happens in major encounters of this ilk, luck was to prove the decisive factor. A penalty not given in the other semi-final had taken Parma through to Wembley. Now a far less obvious one was awarded to give Antwerp their all-important third goal. There appeared to be little of interest going on when the Portuguese referee suddenly noticed one of his linesman waving his flag. After consultation he approached Spartak defender Onopko and, to the amazement of everybody in the stadium, not only brandished a red card to the 1992 Russian Player of the Year but also pointed to the penalty spot! Unseen by everybody else, including the television cameras, the linesman had spotted an off-the-ball incident involving Onopko and Czerniatynski and that had been enough to persuade referee Monteiro Coroado to come to his decision. The onus now was on Hans-Peter Lehnhoff to convert the kick. He did so with considerable aplomb, sending Cherchesov the wrong way with a low shot into the corner that was met with understandable delirium in the stands. Antwerp were through to the final and a bewildered and bemused Spartak, their spirit gone, were left to wonder how they could possibly have let their chance slip away.

HANS-PETER LEHNHOFF
Royal Antwerp FC

Hans-Peter Lehnhoff showed nerves of steel to convert the contentious penalty which booked Antwerp's place in the Cup-winners' Cup final at Wembley. It was the Antwerp playmaker's first goal in Europe since the opening match of the campaign away to Glenavon, but while Czerniatynski had grabbed most of the headlines with his goalscoring exploits, Lehnhoff's contribution to the club's history making run had been equally important.
The 1992/93 season was Lehnhoff's sixth at Antwerp. Regarded as nothing more than a fair-to-middling talent when at Cologne in his native Germany, he has developed during his time in Belgium into one of the most respected all-round midfielders in the country. A regular scorer of goals - he had precisely 50 to his credit in the Belgian league at the time of this match - he creates even more thanks to his revered ability to find colleagues with killer through-balls.

CUP-WINNERS' CUP
Semi-Finals Review

SEMI-FINAL RESULTS

		1st leg	2nd leg	Agg.
Atlético Madrid	Parma	1-2	1-0	2-2
(Parma win on away goals)				
Spartak Moskva	Royal Antwerp FC	1-0	1-3	2-3

LEADING GOALSCORERS AFTER SEMI-FINALS

7	Alex CZERNIATYNSKI (Royal Antwerp FC)
5	Andrey PYATNITSKY (Spartak Moskva)
	Ian RUSH (Liverpool)
4	Dmitry RADCHENKO (Spartak Moskva)
	József KIPRICH (Feyenoord)
	Valery KARPIN (Spartak Moskva)
	Torben CHRISTENSEN (AGF)
	Wynton RUFER (SV Werder Bremen)
	Yury NIKIFOROV (Chernomorets Odessa)
3	Faustino ASPRILLA (Parma)
	LUIS GARCIA (Atlético Madrid)
	Ion VLADOIU (Steaua Bucuresti)
	Meny BASSON (Hapoel Petach-Tikva)

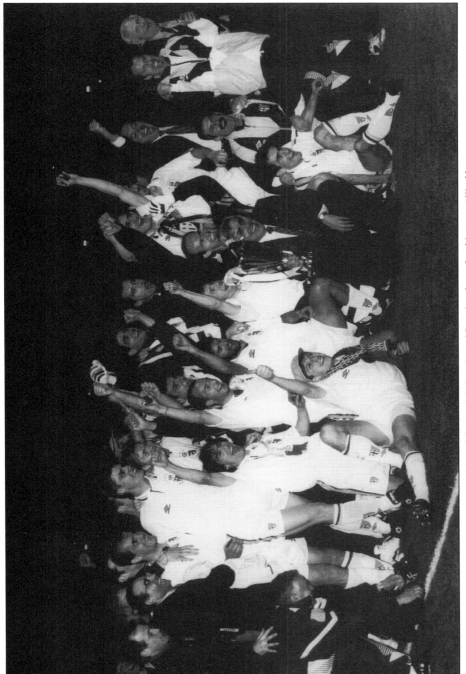

● *Parma celebrate following their Cup-winners' Cup triumph over Royal Antwerp at Wembley*

CUP WINNERS' CUP
Final

Wednesday 12th May 1993
Wembley Stadium, London

PARMA 3 ROYAL ANTWERP FC 1

Half-time 2-1 *Attendance* 37,393

		Goals				Goals
1	Marco BALLOTTA		1	Stevan STOJANOVIC		
2	Antonio BENARRIVO		2	Wim KIEKENS		
3	Alberto DI CHIARA ❑		3	Nico BROECKAERT ❑		
4	Lorenzo MINOTTI	9	4	Rudy TAEYMANS		
5	Luigi APOLLONI		5	Rudy SMIDTS		
6	Georges GRÜN		6	Dragan JAKOVLJEVIC †		
7	Alessandro MELLI	30	7	Ronny VAN RETHY		
8	Daniele ZORATTO †		8	Didier SEGERS ❑ ‡		
9	Marco OSIO ‡		9	Francis SEVEREYNS ❑	11	
10	Stefano CUOGHI	84	10	Hans-Peter LEHNHOFF		
11	Tomas BROLIN		11	Alex CZERNIATYNSKI		

	Substitutes		*Substitutes*
	Gabriele PIN †26		Patrick VAN VEIRDEGHEM †56
	Fausto PIZZI ‡75		Nourédine MOUKRIM ‡83

Referee Karl-Josef ASSENMACHER (Germany)

FACTFILE

● *This was the second successive season that Wembley Stadium had been allocated a European final. A year earlier it had also been the venue for the Champions' Cup final between Barcelona and Sampdoria.*

● *Like Werder Bremen and Monaco the year before, both Cup-winners' Cup finalists were appearing in a European final for the first time.*

● *The last time four goals had been scored in the Cup-winners' Cup final was in 1985 when Everton beat Rapid Vienna 3-1 in Rotterdam.*

● *Parma became the eighth different Italian club to win a European trophy.*

Parma spread wings to destroy Antwerp

Parma secured the first leg of an anticipated Italian treble with a comprehensive 3-1 victory over Antwerp at Wembley. It completed a quite extraordinary four-year cycle for Nevio Scala and his team. In 1990 Parma won promotion to Italy's Serie A for the very first time in their history. The following season they managed to qualify for Europe by finishing in sixth place. A year later they captured the Italian Cup and now, at the world-famous temple of football, they were tasting success at the highest possible level with victory in one of the European Cups. All in all, a quite astonishing achievement.

Antwerp, the 4/1 outsiders from Belgium, were never likely to stop Parma in their tracks. Their passage to the final had been scrappy and largely unimpressive. A penalty shoot-out, extra-time, the away goals rule and a controversial penalty had all combined to get them to Wembley, but against Parma they were to find themselves sadly out of their depth.

The match began very brightly. Czerniatynski was narrowly caught offside after just a couple of minutes when on the brink of racing clear, and at the other end a fine run on the right by Antonio Benarrivo resulted in a header by Melli which was well saved by Stevan Stojanovic. The Antwerp 'keeper had been a Champions' Cup final hero for Red Star Belgrade two years earlier against Marseille, but from the resulting corner he was to make an error which led to Parma's opening goal. As the kick came in, he could only flap at the ball. It fell to Parma skipper Lorenzo Minotti, who sent it spectacularly back into the far corner of the net with an elegant hook-shot.

Barely two minutes later, however, Antwerp were back in it. Czerniatynski broke through the middle, delivered a beautifully weighted pass through to his forward partner Francis Severeyns and the ex-Pisa striker clipped it past Ballotta in fine style to bring the scores level. There then followed a settling-down period in the game, but gradually Parma began to seize the initiative, with Benarrivo and Di Chiara, in particular, causing problems with their surging runs down the flanks. After half an hour they deservedly regained the lead, Melli heading in Osio's cross as Stojanovic again looked unconvincing in coming off his line. Just before the interval Melli should have been awarded a third goal when he finished off a brilliantly inventive free-kick move, but the German linesman mistakenly raised his flag and the goal was cancelled out.

In the second half Melli had countless other opportunities to sew up the match, but his erratic finishing let Antwerp off the hook. Not that his misses were crucial. Parma were running the show now and it seemed only a matter of time before they got another goal. It finally arrived six minutes from the end. A defence-splitting pass from Georges Grün sent Stefano Cuoghi free on the left. Again, Stojanovic hesitated in coming out to intercept it and that left him in no man's land face to face with the Parma midfielder. Cuoghi could have slipped it square to the unmarked Melli for a simple tap-in, but, influenced perhaps by the striker's earlier misses, he opted to go for glory himself and sent Stojanovic the wrong way with a curling shot inside the near post.

GEORGES GRÜN
Parma

With victory in the final coming against Belgian opposition, Parma's Cup-winners' Cup success tasted especially sweet for Georges Grün. The 30-year-old defender had an exceptional match at Wembley, cancelling out the threat of the competition's top goalscorer, his Belgian national team colleague Alex Czerniatynski, and even finding time to come forward and deliver the pass that led to Cuoghi's decisive third goal.

Grün has been one of the key figures in Parma's roller-coaster ride to success over the last three years. Signed up from Anderlecht the summer after Parma gained promotion to Serie A, he has missed only a handful of matches for the club and has helped form, together with Minotti and Apolloni, one of the best defences in Italy. With over 60 caps for his country, Grün has the responsibility of captaining Belgium to the World Cup finals in America precisely ten years after he made his first impressions on the international stage at the 1984 European Championships in France.

CUP-WINNERS' CUP
Review

TOP GOALSCORERS

7   Alex CZERNIATYNSKI (Royal Antwerp FC)
5   Andrey PYATNITSKY (Spartak Moskva)
     Ian RUSH (Liverpool)
4   Dmitry RADCHENKO (Spartak Moskva)
     József KIPRICH (Feyenoord)
     Valery KARPIN (Spartak Moskva)
     Torben CHRISTENSEN (AGF)
     Wynton RUFER (SV Werder Bremen)
     Yury NIKIFOROV (Chernomorets Odessa)
3   Alessandro MELLI (Parma)
     Faustino ASPRILLA (Parma)
     LUIS GARCIA (Atlético Madrid)
     Ion VLADOIU (Steaua Bucuresti)
     Meny BASSON (Hapoel Petach-Tikva)

RED CARDS

1   Ante SIMUNDZA (Maribor Branik)
     Michael CROWE (Glenavon)
     Balasz BÉRCZY (Újpesti TE)
     Paul STEWART (Liverpool)
     Marios CHARALAMBOUS (Apollon Limassol)
     Michael SCHÖNBERG (Hannover 96)
     John DE WOLF (Feyenoord)*
     René VAN ECK (FC Luzern)
     Brian BERTELSEN (FC Luzern)
     Bruce GROBBELAAR (Liverpool)
     Mike MARSH (Liverpool)
     Jozef CHOVANEC (Sparta Praha)
     Wynton RUFER (SV Werder Bremen)
     Michal HORNÁK (Sparta Praha)
     Bogdan BUCUR (Steaua Bucuresti)
     Rudy TAEYMANS (Royal Antwerp FC)
     Ionel FULGA (Steaua Bucuresti)
     Andrey CHERNYSHOV (Spartak Moskva)
     Fyodor CHERENKOV (Spartak Moskva)
     Ulrich VAN GOBBEL (Feyenoord)
     JUANITO (Atlético Madrid)
     Juan VIZCAINO (Atlético Madrid)
     Manuel ALFARO (Atlético Madrid)
     Viktor ONOPKO (Spartak Moskva)

later rescinded.

YELLOW CARDS

4   Viktor ONOPKO (Spartak Moskva)
     (inc. red card)

3   Anton DOBOS (Steaua Bucuresti)
     Geert EMMERECHTS (Royal Antwerp FC)
     Daniele ZORATTO (Parma)
     Alberto DI CHIARA (Parma)
     Juan Manuel LOPEZ (Atlético Madrid)
     Andrey CHERNYSHOV (Spartak Moskva)
     (inc. red card)
     Mike MARSH (Liverpool) (inc. red card)
     JUANITO (Atlético Madrid) (inc. red card)

2   BAKULA (Maribor Branik)
     MØRK (B 36)
     VILJANEN (TPS)
     BYRNE (Bohemians)
     PANDURU, STAN, GILCA (Steaua Bucuresti)
     KARATAIDIS, VLAHOS (Olympiakos)
     NELO, BOBÓ (Boavista FC)
     BÍLEK (Sparta Praha)
     VAN VEIRDEGHEM, LEHNHOFF,
     KIEKENS, SEGERS (Royal Antwerp FC)
     MESSLENDER (FC Admira Wacker)
     RAMSEY (Cardiff City)
     GRÜN, APOLLONI (Parma)
     PISAREV, BESCHASTNYKH, PYATNITSKY,
     LEDYAKHOV (Spartak Moskva)
     BURROWS (Liverpool)
     BURRI (FC Luzern)
     TOMAS, TONI (Atlético Madrid)
     SCHOLTEN, BLINKER (Feyenoord)
     HERZOG, WOLTER (SV Werder Bremen)

UEFA CUP

UEFA CUP
First Round First Leg

Tuesday 15th September 1992
Easter Road Park, Edinburgh

HIBERNIAN 2 RSC ANDERLECHT 2

Half-time 1-1 *Attendance* 14,213

		Goals
1	John BURRIDGE	
2	Willie MILLER ❏	
3	Graham MITCHELL	
4	Neil ORR	
5	Dave BEAUMONT	4
6	Murdo MacLEOD	
7	Michael WEIR ❏ ■	
8	Brian HAMILTON †	
9	Keith WRIGHT	
10	Darren JACKSON	
11	Pat McGINLAY	80

Substitute

Gareth EVANS †79

		Goals
1	Filip DE WILDE	
2	Bertrand CRASSON	
3	Wim KOOIMAN	
4	Philippe ALBERT	
5	Michel DE WOLF	
6	Bruno VERSAVEL	
7	Marc EMMERS †	
8	Peter VAN VOSSEN	67
9	Luc NILIS ‡	
10	Marc DEGRYSE ❏	37 (pen)
11	Danny BOFFIN	

Substitutes

Jean-François DE SART †8

Johan WALEM ‡87

Referee Hans-Jürgen WEBER (Germany)

SUMMARY

● Scotland's Skol Cup holders were under no illusions about the task that faced them if they wished to progress to the UEFA Cup second round. Whilst their illustrious Belgian opponents lined up a team containing 10 full internationals (Dutchman Wim Kooiman was the sole exception), Hibernian could boast only the experience of their veteran midfielder Murdo MacLeod and the one Scottish cap gained by striker Keith Wright. But no continental team relishes a trip to Scotland, and Anderlecht, for all the wealth of talent at their disposal, were obliged, like those before them, to roll their sleeves up and meet force with force in an abrasive encounter at Easter Road. Hibs, to the fervent joy of their supporters, took an early lead through Beaumont, but the Belgians got back on level terms when 40-year-old goalkeeper John Burridge brought down Versavel and Degryse converted the penalty. Van Vossen's lob and Weir's sending-off midway through the second period looked to have turned the tie irreversibly in Anderlecht's favour, but a late looping effort from McGinlay ensured that the Scottish team gained some reward for their committed display.

UEFA CUP
First Round Second Leg

Tuesday 29th September 1992
Constant Vanden Stock Stadium, Brussels

RSC ANDERLECHT 1 HIBERNIAN 1

Half-time 1-1 *Aggregate* 3-3 (Anderlecht win on away goals) *Attendance* 26,000

		Goals				Goals
1	Filip DE WILDE		1	John BURRIDGE		
2	Bertrand CRASSON		2	Willie MILLER		
3	Graeme RUTJES		3	Joe TORTOLANO ❏		
4	Philippe ALBERT ❏		4	Neil ORR		
5	Michel DE WOLF		5	Dave BEAUMONT		
6	Johan WALEM		6	Murdo MacLEOD		
7	Wim KOOIMAN †		7	Callum MILNE †		
8	Peter VAN VOSSEN		8	Brian HAMILTON		
9	Luc NILIS	5	9	Keith WRIGHT		
10	Marc DEGRYSE		10	Darren JACKSON		15
11	Danny BOFFIN		11	Pat McGINLAY		
	Substitute			*Substitute*		
	Bruno VERSAVEL †46			Gareth EVANS †80		

Referee Antonio MARTIN NAVARRETE (Spain)

● *Anderlecht went into this game confident of registering their 100th victory in European competition. Luc Nilis, with his 15th goal in Europe, appeared to set the Brussels club on their way as early as the fifth minute when he fired a first-time shot low into the corner of John Burridge's net. But Hibernian had not come as guests to a party. In fact, they achieved a milestone of their own when, just ten minutes later, new signing from Dundee United Darren Jackson latched on to a loose ball in the penalty area and shot past De Wilde for the equaliser. It was Hibs' 100th goal in the UEFA/Fairs' Cup. From then on both teams knew that they were in a game, and although the Belgians enjoyed the bulk of the possession, their opponents were at no time prepared to concede that they were second best. When Jackson missed a late chance, however, Hibs' gallant fight was over. Away goals decreed that Anderlecht were the winners, although the jeers of their supporters at the final whistle appeared to indicate that the moral victors were Scottish and wearing green.*

UEFA CUP
First Round First Leg

Wednesday 16th September 1992
Luis Casanova Stadium, Valencia

VALENCIA CF 1 NAPOLI 5

Half-time 0-1 *Attendance* 30,000

	Goals			Goals
1 José Manuel SEMPERE		1 Giovanni GALLI		
2 Enrique Sánchez "QUIQUE" ∎		2 Ciro FERRERA		
3 Francisco José CAMARASA ❏		3 Roberto POLICANO ❏		
4 Miodrag BELODEDICI		4 Fausto PARI		
5 Fernando GINER †		5 Massimo TARANTINO		
6 LEONARDO Nascimento ❏		6 Giancarlo CORRADINI ❏		
7 TOMAS González		7 Angelo CARBONE †		
8 ROBERTO Fernández	54	8 Jonas THERN		
9 Liuboslav PENEV		9 Antonio CARECA ‡		
10 FERNANDO Gómez		10 Gianfranco ZOLA		
11 ALVARO Cervera ‡		11 Daniel FONSECA	21,60,64,87,90

Substitutes

Carlos ARROYO †69

ELOY Olaya ‡72

Substitutes

Massimo CRIPPA ❏ †28

Giovanni FRANCINI ‡46

Referee Hubert FORSTINGER (Austria)

FACTFILE

● This was Napoli's biggest ever victory in European competition and the first time that they had ever managed five goals in one game. Equally, it was Valencia's heaviest home defeat in 20 seasons of competing in Europe.

● Both teams were previous winners of the competition. Napoli took the UEFA Cup in 1988/89 and Valencia twice won the old Inter-Cities Fairs' Cup in 1962 and 1963.

● Daniel Fonseca became the first player in the history of European Cup football to score all five of his team's goals in an away leg.

● Only one other player had ever previously scored five goals in a single European match for an Italian club - José Altafini for Milan in an 8-0 win against Union Luxembourg 30 years earlier!

● *Goalscorer Roberto*

Five-star Fonseca reigns in Spain

Napoli striker Daniel Fonseca scarcely endeared himself to the Valencia public before this match when he referred to the brief trial period he had spent at the club two years earlier as "the unhappiest days of my career." That comment alone was enough to guarantee the Uruguayan a barrage of boos and whistles every time he touched the ball. But the jeers did not last long. By the end of the match even the snubbed locals were forced to accept that the man they had let go had produced one of the most memorable individual performances in European Cup history.

Fonseca simply ripped Valencia apart. He opened the scoring for Napoli after 21 minutes, expertly converting a long diagonal pass from the right. Then, once the home side had equalised with a similarly fashioned goal from Roberto, he decided to subject the Valencia defence to a one-man demolition job in the last half hour. The result was four more goals, three from his favoured left foot and the last, and best, cheekily finished off with his right in the final minute after he had humiliated Sempere and co. for one last time.

5-1 to Napoli and all five goals to a player making his debut appearance in European competition! In one match Fonseca had scored as many European goals as Diego Maradona had managed in 25 European games for Napoli.

The tie, evidently, was over and for Valencia it was all too much to bear. For the first hour Guus Hiddink's side had matched their opponents and but for the superb goalkeeping of former Italian international Giovanni Galli would surely have added to the lone strike from Roberto. But Fonseca's late flurry was lethal, and the team which had not conceded a single goal

● Quique - sent off

in their first two Spanish League matches of the new campaign now had to ask serious questions about a much-vaunted five-man defence which contained two Spanish internationals (Quique and Giner) and new signing Miodrag Belodedici - the man who became the first player to win the Champions' Cup with two different clubs (Steaua Bucharest and Red Star Belgrade).

For Napoli, though, there was only celebration, and for Fonseca himself the added pleasure of revenge against the club that had rejected him.

DANIEL FONSECA
Napoli

Before this match Daniel Fonseca's biggest claim to fame was the late headed goal he scored in the 1990 World Cup first-round encounter against South Korea that enabled Uruguay to qualify for the knock-out phase. Following that tournament he made a permanent move to Italy, joining newly-promoted Cagliari from Uruguayan side Nacional of Montevideo.

After two seasons in Sardinia, where he scored 19 league goals in 50 Serie A appearances, Fonseca rejoined his former coach Claudio Ranieri on the Italian mainland at Napoli. Three days before the Valencia game the left-footed striker had celebrated his 23rd birthday by scoring twice in Napoli's 4-2 win at Foggia. But it was in the Luis Casanova Stadium, on his European debut, that Fonseca at last became a superstar in his own right. His exploits earned him the top mark of 10 in most Italian papers - almost as unprecedented an achievement as the five goals themselves!

UEFA CUP
First Round Second Leg

Wednesday 30th September 1992
San Paolo Stadium, Napoli

NAPOLI 1 VALENCIA CF 0

Half-time 1-0 *Aggregate* 6-1 *Attendance* 35,000

Goals   Goals

1	Giovanni GALLI	1	José Luis GONZALEZ
2	Carlo CORNACCHIA ❏	2	Miodrag BELODEDICI
3	Giovanni FRANCINI	3	Salvador González "BORO" ❏
4	Fausto PARI	4	Francisco José CAMARASA
5	Massimo TARANTINO	5	TOMAS González
6	Giancarlo CORRADINI	6	LEONARDO Nascimento
7	Massimo CRIPPA	7	Carlos ARROYO ❏
8	Jonas THERN	8	ALVARO Cervera
9	Antonio CARECA	9	Liuboslav PENEV †
10	Massimo MAURO ‡	10	FERNANDO Gómez
11	Daniel FONSECA † 9	11	ELOY Olaya

Substitutes   *Substitute*

Gianfranco ZOLA †46   Antonio José Gomes "TONI" †69

Angelo CARBONE ‡64

Referee Bo KARLSSON (Sweden)

<table>
<tr><td rowspan="1">

FACTFILE

</td><td>

● *This was the second time in three seasons that Valencia had fallen victim to Italian opposition in the UEFA Cup. Roma eliminated them in the second round of the 1990/91 competition on their way to the final. Valencia's only other encounters with Italian clubs had both ended in victory (against Inter and Roma) and had both taken place during the course of the club's back-to-back Fairs' Cup-winning campaigns in 1962 and 1963.*
● *6-1 was Napoli's best aggregate win and Valencia's worst aggregate defeat in Europe.*
● *For this game Napoli fielded only four survivors from their UEFA Cup-winning squad in 1988/89 - Francini, Corradini, Crippa and Careca. Goalkeeper Galli was also a European winner that year - in the Champions' Cup with Milan.*

</td><td>

● *Giovanni Galli*

</td></tr>
</table>

Formality for Napoli in the San Paolo

Since the triumphant first leg in Valencia a fortnight earlier things had not gone well for Napoli on the home front. A defeat at home to Inter and a draw away to newly-promoted Ancona had left Claudio Ranieri's team perilously close to the bottom of the Serie A table.

There was comfort of a sort, however, in the continuing goalscoring form of first-leg hero Daniel Fonseca. He had scored in each of those two league games and now, with less than ten minutes on the clock, he was to find a way through the Valencia defence once again to register his sixth goal of the tie and his tenth of the season in only six games!

The goal was a joint effort involving all three of Napoli's foreign stars. Swedish national team skipper Jonas Thern, a close-season signing from Benfica, threaded the ball through on the right for Careca, and when Valencia goalkeeper González, back in the team after being suspended for the first leg, failed to push the Brazilian's cross-shot to safety, Fonseca was there to apply the finishing touch and give Napoli the lead.

At that stage the Spaniards must have feared that another heavy defeat was on the cards. But Italian sides have never been ones to burn energy without good reason, and with qualification by now a foregone conclusion, Napoli spared their opponents any further anxiety by deciding simply to drop down a gear and see the match out to its conclusion without conceding a goal.

Evidence of this merciful approach came at half-time when Fonseca was substituted. It was clearly felt that the Uruguayan's legs would best be saved for another day when there was more at stake. The Napoli crowd, baying for more Spanish blood, appeared not to be in agreement with their coach's decision, but the fact that a player as accomplished as Gianfranco Zola was able to come on in Fonseca's stead helped to dull the sense of disappointment.

● *Napoli manager Claudio Ranieri*

So Napoli strolled home to take their place in round two, where they were joined by each of the other three Italian teams in the competition - Juventus, Roma and Torino. Valencia, meanwhile, joined Real Sociedad on the UEFA Cup scrapheap as the Spanish entry was, surprisingly, reduced by half after just one round.

ANTONIO CARECA
Napoli

The ace Brazilian goalgetter had to accept second billing to his fellow South American Daniel Fonseca in the Valencia tie, but it was his shot which brought about the only goal of the game in the San Paolo and he was a constant thorn in the side of the Valencia defence for the 90 minutes.

Careca is a name well-known throughout the footballing world and has been since the player scored five goals for Brazil in their 1986 World Cup campaign in Mexico. He quit São Paulo for San Paolo a year later and immediately established himself as one of the game's best all-round strikers, forming a formidable partnership with Diego Maradona and helping Napoli to both the UEFA Cup in 1989 and the Italian championship a year later. Careca was again prominent at Italia '90 and could conceivably still be a force, at 33, in next summer's World Cup in the United States.

UEFA CUP
First Round First Leg

Wednesday 16th September 1992
Monnikenhuize Stadium, Arnhem

VITESSE 3 DERRY CITY 0

Half-time 1-0 *Attendance* 5,692

		Goals				Goals
1	Raymond VAN DER GOUW		1	Dermot O'NEILL	
2	Roberto STRAAL		2	Paul MOONEY	
3	Erwin VAN DE LOOI		3	Peter HUTTON	
4	Theo BOS		4	Declan ROCHE ❑	
5	Arjan VERMEULEN		5	Paul CURRAN	
6	Martin LAAMERS		6	Stuart GAULD ❑	
7	John VAN DEN BROM	20,55	7	Paul CARLYLE	
8	René EIJER		8	Damien DUNLEAVY	
9	Bart LATUHERU		9	Paul HEGARTY †	
10	Hans VAN ARUM	90	10	Mark ENNIS ‡	
11	Philip COCU		11	Gregory KEARNEY	

Substitutes

Substitutes

Donal O'BRIEN †70

Paul JOHNSON ‡77

Referee João MARTINS PINTO CORREIA (Portugal)

● *These two clubs had met in the same competition only two years earlier, also in the first round. On that occasion Vitesse, making their European debut, had won 1-0 away and drawn 0-0 at home to take the tie before going on to reach the third round. This time the tie was reversed and there was every possibility that the goalless draw of the previous tie would be repeated, the reason being that Vitesse had scored only three goals in their last eight home matches in the Dutch league, a sequence stretching back almost eight months! Now, though, they matched that total in the course of just 90 minutes. Two goals from Dutch international midfielder John van den Brom, one in each half, plus a third in the final minute from Hans van Arum at last gave the goal-starved Vitesse fans something to smile about. Remarkably, there were as many as nine survivors from the previous encounter with Derry in the Vitesse starting line-up (Van de Looi and Cocu were the exceptions) compared with only four (Gauld, Curran, Carlyle and Hegarty) in the Irish team.*

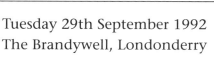

UEFA CUP
First Round Second Leg

Tuesday 29th September 1992
The Brandywell, Londonderry

DERRY CITY 1 VITESSE 2

Half-time 0-1 *Aggregate* 1-5 *Attendance* 3,500

		Goals				Goals
1	Dermot O'NEILL		1	Raymond VAN DER GOUW		
2	Paul MOONEY	60	2	Roberto STRAAL ❏		44
3	Peter HUTTON		3	Erwin VAN DE LOOI		
4	Declan ROCHE		4	Theo BOS		
5	Paul CURRAN		5	Arjan VERMEULEN		
6	Stuart GAULD		6	Martin LAAMERS	65	
7	Paul CARLYLE ‡		7	John VAN DEN BROM		
8	Damien DUNLEAVY		8	René EIJER		
9	Donal O'BRIEN		9	Bart LATUHERU †		
10	Mark ENNIS		10	Hans VAN ARUM		
11	Gregory KEARNEY ❏ †		11	Philip COCU		

Substitutes

Martin McCANN †75

Martin McGINLEY ‡89

Substitute

Richard ROELOFSEN †71

Referee Gylfi ORRASON (Iceland)

S U M M A R Y

● There was little or no chance of Derry City coming back from their 0-3 defeat in the first leg. Since returning to the European scene as League of Ireland representatives in 1988 (they had twice competed under the Northern Irish flag in the '60s) they had scored just once in seven matches. Furthermore, no team from the Irish Republic had won a European tie for over a decade! Derry did get another goal, scored by right-back Paul Mooney on the hour (he had scored before in Europe - a penalty for Irish league club Linfield against Dnepr in the 1989/90 Champions' Cup), but that came both before and after goals from the opposition. Vitesse's number two Roberto Straal put the Dutchmen ahead on the stroke of half-time and midfielder Martin Laamers restored the Arnhem club's lead on the night just five minutes after Mooney's equaliser. Vitesse's win was their fifth in six matches against teams from the British Isles and their third in succession on United Kingdom soil.

Tuesday 15th September 1992
Maladière Stadium, Neuchâtel

NEUCHATEL XAMAX FC 2   BK FREM 2

Half-time 0-2   *Attendance* 4,000

		Goals				Goals
1	Florent DELAY		1	Per WIND		
2	Guerino GOTTARDI		2	Tony CARLSEN		
3	Francis FROIDEVAUX ‡		3	Søren COLDING		
4	Hany RAMZY		4	Dan EGGEN ❏		
5	Stéphane HENCHOZ	22(og)	5	Peter FRANK ❏		
6	Philippe PERRET ❏		6	Søren FOLKMANN		
7	Beat SUTTER	51	7	Finn JENSEN ■		
8	José ZÉ MARIA		8	Michael NIELSEN		
9	Giuseppe MANFREDA	52	9	Marek CZAKON ‡		
10	Admir SMAJIC		10	Thomas THØGERSEN		
11	Charles WITTL †		11	Kim MIKKELSEN †		17
	Substitutes			*Substitutes*		
	Frédéric CHASSOT †25			Jimmi LÜTHJE †54		
	Philippe CRAVERO ‡78			Peter POULSEN ‡70		

Referee Marc BATTA (France)

SUMMARY

● *Seasoned campaigners Neuchâtel Xamax, competing in Europe for the eighth time in nine years, were clear favourites to win this tie against a semi-professional team which had not played European football since 1978 and in which virtually every player was making his European debut. The Swiss, coached by ex-West German international Uli Stielike, a former UEFA Cup winner with both Borussia Mönchengladbach (1975) and Real Madrid (1985), had reached the third round of the competition the previous season, but their hopes of a repeat performance looked to have been shattered with less than a quarter of the match gone. Only 22 minutes had passed and the lakesiders were already 0-2 down. Two goals as many minutes early in the second half, from international winger Beat Sutter and new striker Giuseppe Manfreda, eventually brought Xamax back into the game, but they could not find the winner and that left the Danes in jubilant mood at the finish, especially as they knew that by holding Xamax to a draw they had succeeded where the might of Celtic and Real Madrid had failed the season before.*

UEFA CUP
First Round Second Leg

Tuesday 29th September 1992
Idraetspark, Valby

BK FREM 4 NEUCHATEL XAMAX FC 1

Half-time 3-1 *Aggregate* 6-3 *Attendance* 3,476

		Goals				Goals
1	Per WIND		1	Florent DELAY		
2	Tony CARLSEN		2	Guerino GOTTARDI ■		
3	Lars BROUSTBO		3	Walter FERNANDEZ ❑		
4	Dan EGGEN		4	Hany RAMZY †		
5	Peter FRANK		5	Stéphane HENCHOZ ❑		
6	Søren FOLKMANN		6	Philippe PERRET ❑		
7	Henrik JENSEN	17	7	Beat SUTTER		
8	Søren COLDING †		8	José ZÉ MARIA		
9	Piotr HAREN	15, 33	9	Giuseppe MANFREDA	22	
10	Thomas THØGERSEN	54	10	Admir SMAJIC		
11	Kim MIKKELSEN ‡		11	Frédéric CHASSOT ‡		
	Substitutes			*Substitutes*		
	Michael NIELSEN †63			Philippe CRAVERO †36 ❑		
	Per LISDORF ‡70 ❑			Daniel FASEL ‡68 ❑		

Referee Marnix SANDRA (Belgium)

● Under Englishman Roy Hodgson in 1991/92 Neuchâtel Xamax were the most successful of the four Swiss clubs in European competition. Now, under Uli Stielike, they became the only one of the four Swiss participants to be knocked out in the first round. Worse still, they were eliminated in humiliating fashion after a disastrous defensive performance on the outskirts of Copenhagen. Two shocking errors of judgment from the normally ultra-reliable Egyptian World Cup sweeper Hany Ramzy, plus the sending-off of right-back Guerino Gottardi, cost the Swiss side any chance they had of reaching the second round. To their credit, Frem exploited Xamax's defensive lapses with ruthless application. Centre-forward Piotr Haren was the beneficiary of both of Ramzy's aberrations, in the 15th and 33rd minutes, and further goals from Henrik Jensen (a rebound after his penalty had hit the post) and Thomas Thøgersen (a precisely guided shot from the edge of the area) were enough to complete Frem's biggest ever victory in European competition.

Wednesday 16th September 1992
Lehen Stadium, Salzburg

SV CASINO SALZBURG 0   AJAX 3

Half-time 0-0   *Attendance* 10,000

		Goals				Goals
1	Herbert ILSANKER		1	Stanley MENZO		
2	Leopold LAINER ❑ †		2	Rob ALFLEN		
3	Heribert WEBER		3	Danny BLIND		
4	Kurt GARGER ❑		4	Wim JONK		
5	Ivo ERGOVIC ‡		5	Frank DE BOER		
6	Hannes REINMAYR		6	Marciano VINK		
7	Nikola JURCEVIC		7	Marc OVERMARS ❑		65
8	Gerald WILLFURTH		8	Michel KREEK		80
9	Herfried SABITZER		9	Stefan PETTERSSON		
10	Wolfgang FEIERSINGER		10	Dennis BERGKAMP		
11	Hermann STADLER ❑		11	Bryan ROY †		

Substitutes

Andreas LIPA †46
Andreas REISINGER ‡65

Substitute

Edgar DAVIDS †30 ❑   53

Referee Pierluigi PAIRETTIO (Italy)

● *UEFA Cup holders Ajax enjoyed a comfortable first defence of their trophy against a Salzburg side appearing in European competition for the first time in 12 years. The one and only time Ajax had played in Austria before was in the 1989/90 UEFA Cup. Then they had lost 0-1 to FK Austria before going out of the competition as a result of an infamous incident in the return leg when a Dutch fan threw an iron bar at the opposing goalkeeper and thereby deprived his team of a place in the Champions' Cup the following season. Now back at the forefront of the European game after their UEFA Cup win in May, Ajax were more than a match for Salzburg. The Austrians appeared to be overawed by their opponents' reputation and were lucky to be on level terms at half-time. But after the interval the Amsterdammers roared into overdrive and won the game with three goals from their youngsters Davids, Overmars and Kreek, the first two scoring on their European debuts (and getting their names taken) after replacing former wide players Bryan Roy and John van 't Schip in coach Louis van Gaal's exciting 3-4-3 formation.*

Wednesday 30th September 1992
Olympisch Stadium, Amsterdam

AJAX 3 SV CASINO SALZBURG 1

Half-time 1-0 *Aggregate* 6-1 *Attendance* 12,500

		Goals				Goals
1	Stanley MENZO		1	Otto KONRAD		
2	Sonny SILOOY		2	Leo LAINER ❑		
3	Danny BLIND		3	Heribert WEBER ❑		
4	Wim JONK		4	Kurt GARGER		
5	Frank DE BOER		5	Andreas REISINGER	57	
6	Marciano VINK		6	Peter HRSTIC ‡		
7	Marc OVERMARS		7	Nikola JURCEVIC		
8	Michel KREEK ‡		8	Gerald WILLFURTH		
9	Stefan PETTERSSON	27, 79	9	Herfried SABITZER †		
10	Dennis BERGKAMP	48	10	Wolfgang FEIERSINGER		
11	Edgar DAVIDS †		11	Hermann STADLER		

Substitutes

John VAN LOEN †60

Dan PETERSEN ‡69

Substitutes

Ivo ERGOVIC †63

Herbert ILSANKER ‡69

Referee Andrew WADDELL (Scotland)

● For all Ajax's recent successes in Europe (three finals and two trophies in the last six years), the club's record when playing in front of their own fans was far from impressive. Of their previous six European matches played in Amsterdam, Ajax could boast just a single victory - against Belgian side Gent. Salzburg may have been aware of that, but with a 0-3 deficit to make up from the first leg, they came to Amsterdam sound in the knowledge that their fate had already been sealed. They did manage to improve on their home-leg performance by actually scoring a goal (a superb first-time shot by Austrian international Andreas Reisinger) but that was negated by the fact that they again conceded three. Swedish striker Stefan Pettersson, whose last European appearance in the Olympic stadium had ended with a broken arm caused by an altercation with one of the corner flags in the 91/92 final, both opened the scoring and rounded it off. In the meantime Dennis Bergkamp continued his brilliant start to the season by grabbing Ajax's second with a marvellous right-foot volley from Frank De Boer's hanging left-wing cross.

UEFA CUP
First Round First Leg

Thursday 17th September 1992
Municipal Stadium, Guimarães

VITÓRIA GUIMARÃES 3 REAL SOCIEDAD 0

Half-time 2-0 *Attendance* 12,000

		Goals				Goals
1	MADUREIRA			1	Javier YUBERO	
2	BASÍLIO ❑			2	Miguel Angel FUENTES ❑	
3	MATIAS ❑			3	José María LUMBRERAS	
4	TANTA			4	Juan Antonio LARRAÑAGA	
5	DIMAS			5	Alberto GORRIZ	
6	PAULO BENTO ❑			6	Iñaki ALABA	
7	BASAULA Lemba			7	OCEANO	
8	PEDRO BARBOSA ‡	28		8	Andoni IMAZ	
9	ZIAD Tlemcani †			9	Meho KODRO ❑	
10	Dane KUPRESANIN	14, 76		10	CARLOS XAVIER ❑ †	
11	PAULO JORGE			11	Javier GURUCETA ‡	
	Substitutes				*Substitutes*	
	QUIM MACHADO †68				IMANOL Aguazil †32	
	QUIM BERTO ‡84				LUIS PEREZ ‡64	

Referee Sándor PUHL (Hungary)

SUMMARY

● *Vitória Guimarães and Real Sociedad went into this tie with very similar recent European pedigrees. This was the fourth time in six seasons that both clubs had qualified for Europe, and always in the same seasons (87/88, 88/89, 90/91 and, now, 92/93)! There was also a big Portuguese connection in the Real Sociedad team, with midfielders Oceano and Carlos Xavier both Portuguese internationals and coach John Toshack having previously been in charge of Sporting Lisbon. But this was to be an unhappy return for the trio. Guimarães, featuring not one Portuguese international themselves, put on a rousing performance, winning the match 3-0 and thereby bettering the 2-0 scoreline they achieved at home to another Spanish club, Atlético Madrid, on the way to reaching the UEFA Cup quarter-finals in 1986/87. Hero of the evening was two-goal Bosnian striker Dane Kupresanin, a close-season signing from Famalicão, who enjoyed a much more fruitful evening than his fellow countryman on the opposing side, former Yugoslav international and Velez Mostar striker, Meho Kodro.*

UEFA CUP
First Round Second Leg

Wednesday 30th September 1992
Atoxa Stadium, San Sebastián

REAL SOCIEDAD 2 VITÓRIA GUIMARÃES 0

Half-time 2-0 *Aggregate* 2-3 *Attendance* 19,200

		Goals				Goals
1	Javier YUBERO			1	MADUREIRA	
2	Miguel Angel FUENTES	23		2	BASÍLIO ❑	
3	José María LUMBRERAS ❑	6		3	MATIAS ❑	
4	Juan Antonio LARRAÑAGA			4	Herichi TAOUFIK ❑	
5	Iñaki ALABA			5	TANTA ❑	
6	IMANOL Aguazil †			6	PAULO BENTO	
7	OCEANO			7	QUIM MACHADO	
8	Andoni IMAZ ‡			8	PEDRO BARBOSA †	
9	Meho KODRO			9	ZIAD Tlemcani ‡	
10	CARLOS XAVIER			10	Dane KUPRESANIN	
11	Bittor ALKIZA			11	DIMAS	

Substitutes

José URIA †46

Mikel LOINAZ ‡65

Substitutes

PAULO JORGE †54 ❑

ARTUR JORGE ‡84

Referee Joël QUINIOU (France)

SUMMARY

● At the outset Real Sociedad knew that they had less than a one in ten chance of wiping away their first-leg 0-3 deficit and qualifying for the second round. But two goals in the first 23 minutes gave the passionate Atoxa crowd every reason to feel that their team would go on and win the tie. Long-serving midfielder José María Lumbreras was credited with the first goal after six minutes, although his speculative left-wing cross would certainly not have gone in without a deflection off the outstretched foot of a Guimarães defender. There was no doubt about the second goalscorer's identity as Miguel Angel Fuentes burst through the centre in acres of space before shooting accurately across the 'keeper. But that, surprisingly, was as far as the Spanish side got. Guimarães defended well for the remainder of the game and clung on for an aggregate 3-2 victory, giving them their first European success since a penalty shoot-out win over Belgian side Beveren in the second round of the 1987/88 UEFA Cup, and providing Portugal with its 12th victory in 28 European ties against Spanish opposition..

Wednesday 16th September 1992
Hillsborough, Sheffield

SHEFFIELD WEDNESDAY 8 SPORA LUXEMBOURG 1

Half-time 4-1 *Attendance* 19,792

		Goals				Goals
1	Chris WOODS		1	Fernand FELTEN		
2	John HARKES		2	Marco JANES		
3	Viv ANDERSON	23, 29	3	John KREMER		
4	Carlton PALMER		4	Patrick BEI		
5	Peter SHIRTLIFF		5	Ralph STANGE		
6	Paul WARHURST ‡	31, 73	6	Léon LAERA		
7	Graham HYDE †		7	Rico CARDONI ‡		
8	Chris WADDLE	9	8	Antonio SANTOPIETRO ❏		
9	Trevor FRANCIS		9	João CRUZ		11
10	Chris BART-WILLIAMS	60, 81	10	Jean-Marc RIGAUD †		
11	Nigel WORTHINGTON	65	11	Marc CHAUSSY		

Substitutes		*Substitutes*
Danny WILSON †69		Luc SEYLER †77
Nigel JEMSON ‡77		Luc MISCHO ‡85

Referee Freddy PHILIPPOZ (Switzerland)

SUMMARY

● *The draw could scarcely have been kinder to Sheffield Wednesday on their return to European football after a 29-year absence. But although they predictably tore the minnows of Spora Luxembourg apart with what amounted to little more than exhibition football, there was almost a tragic end to the evening for the Yorkshire club when, after colliding with Spora goalkeeper Fernand Felten in the process of scoring his second, and Wednesday's seventh, goal, makeshift striker Paul Warhurst had a fit whilst undergoing treatment for his injury and subsequently swallowed his tongue. Wednesday player/manager Trevor Francis, who had just completed his first 90 minutes of top-class football in almost 18 months, was succinct about the severity of Warhurst's predicament and made a point of paying tribute to the club's medical team - "Paul was pretty close to dying. In a situation like that, players are helpless. That is when you depend on the professionals. It is so important to have good staff "*

UEFA CUP
First Round Second Leg

Thursday 1st October 1992
Municipal Stadium, Luxembourg

SPORA LUXEMBOURG 1 SHEFFIELD WEDNESDAY 2

Half-time 1-2 *Aggregate* 2-10 *Attendance* 3,500

		Goals			Goals
1	Fernand FELTEN		1	Kevin PRESSMAN	
2	Marco JANES		2	John HARKES	
3	John KREMER		3	Roland NILSSON †	
4	Patrick BEI ‡		4	Julian WATTS	
5	Ralph STANGE		5	Nigel PEARSON	
6	Gilles THOMAS		6	Graham HYDE	
7	Léon LAERA		7	Danny WILSON	
8	Luc SEYLER		8	Mike WILLIAMS	
9	João CRUZ	20	9	Paul WARHURST ‡	36
10	Rico CARDONI †		10	Nigel JEMSON	
11	Marc CHAUSSY		11	Gordon WATSON	18

Substitutes

Antonio SANTOPIETRO †69

Pascal WAMPACH ‡81

Substitutes

Chris WADDLE †58

Carlton PALMER ‡60

Referee Gudmundur Stefán MARIASSON (Iceland)

SUMMARY

● *Just 15 days after his near-fatal injury in the first leg, Paul Warhurst was, remarkably, back on hand to score Sheffield Wednesday's winning goal in Luxembourg and complete the club's biggest ever victory margin in European competition. The 10-2 aggregate beat Wednesday's previous best of 8-2 against Dutch club DOS Utrecht in the 1963/64 Fairs' Cup. Despite taking the field with a severely weakened team, the Yorkshire club had little difficulty in seeing off the local part-timers. Reserve striker Gordon Watson scored 18 minutes into his European debut to give the English side the lead, and, as in the first leg, Spora striker João Cruz equalised just two minutes later, enabling him to have the distinction of being the only player in the club's history to score in both legs of a European tie. But that was all the locals had to celebrate as Warhurst again made his mark with his third goal of the tie to send Spora to their 21st defeat in 23 European matches.*

UEFA CUP
First Round First Leg

Wednesday 16th September 1992
Parc des Princes, Paris

PARIS SAINT-GERMAIN FC 2 PAOK 0

Half-time 2-0 *Attendance* 20,000

			Goals
1	Bernard LAMA		
2	Jean-Luc SASSUS		
3	Patrick COLLETER †		
4	RICARDO Gomes ❑		
5	Alain ROCHE		
6	Paul LE GUEN		
7	Laurent FOURNIER		
8	Vincent GUERIN		
9	François CALDERARO		
10	George WEAH	13, 24	
11	David GINOLA		

Substitute
Daniel BRAVO †83

			Goals
1	Tonci GABRIC		
2	Ioakim HAVOS		
3	Kostas MALIOUFAS		
4	Hristos HIONAS		
5	Alexandros ALEXIOU		
6	Kostas LAGONIDIS		
7	Kostas IKONOMIDIS		
8	Yorgos TOURSOUNIDIS		
9	Milan DJURDJEVIC		
10	Magdi TOLBA ❑ ‡		
11	Vagelis KALOGEROPOULOS ❑†		

Substitutes
Pavlos DERMITZAKIS †82
Nikos PLITSIS ‡88

Referee Brian McGINLAY (Scotland)

SUMMARY

● *This tie pitted together two coaches who had both recently taken teams to victory in the Champions' Cup. Paris Saint-Germain's Artur Jorge had led FC Porto to the title against Bayern Munich in 1987 and PAOK's Ljubomir Petrovic was in charge of Red Star Belgrade when they beat Marseille in 1991. Now Petrovic had to tackle French opposition once again, but PAOK were a far cry from the brilliant Red Star team of two years earlier. At the Parc des Princes the Greek side did little to suggest that they would trouble a team of Paris Saint-Germain's calibre. They failed to force Bernard Lama into a single save all evening and rarely suggested that they had come for anything other than an exercise in damage limitation. The French side should have punished them more severely than they did. Two almost identical headed goals from Liberian international George Weah in the first half were all they could muster from 90 minutes of complete domination. An over-cautious approach in the second half after the sending off of PAOK defender Alexandros Alexiou deprived them of a third goal which was there for the taking and which would surely have killed the tie.*

UEFA CUP
First Round Second Leg

Thursday 1st October 1992
Toumbas Stadium, Salonika

PAOK 0 PARIS SAINT-GERMAIN FC 2

(Match abandoned after 45 minutes; later awarded 0-3)
Half-time 0-2 *Aggregate* 0-4 *Attendance* 30,000

		Goals				Goals
1	Tonci GABRIC		1	Bernard LAMA		
2	Ioakim HAVOS		2	Jean-Luc SASSUS		32
3	Kostas MALIOUFAS		3	Patrick COLLETER		
4	Hristos HIONAS		4	RICARDO Gomes		
5	Nikos PLITSIS		5	Alain ROCHE		
6	Kostas LAGONIDIS †		6	Paul LE GUEN		
7	Kostas IKONOMIDIS		7	Laurent FOURNIER		
8	Yorgos TOURSOUNIDIS		8	Vincent GUERIN		
9	Milan DJURDJEVIC		9	George WEAH		15
10	Magdi TOLBA		10	VALDO Candido		
11	Mihalis LEONTIADIS		11	David GINOLA		

Substitute

Pavlos DERMITZAKIS †38

Substitutes

Referee John BLANKENSTEIN (Holland)

SUMMARY

● *Greek hooligans reared their ugly heads to bring their country's name into disrepute once again. PAOK were already destined for UEFA Cup elimination, 0-2 down on the night and 0-4 on aggregate, when a section of fans, which had earlier been chanting its disapproval of both the players and the club president, turned their vocal disaffection into violence. With the two teams in the dressing rooms at half-time, the Greek supporters began to hurl towards the police a variety of projectiles ranging from bottles to iron bars to slabs of concrete, before attempting to smash down a security fence and invade the pitch. Experienced Dutch referee John Blankenstein was in no doubt that the game had to be abandoned. He later explained: "I couldn't possibly restart the match. The situation was too dangerous. The supporters were continuing to throw things and with one fence already demolished, they could have come onto the pitch at any time." So while PAOK went out of the competition and awaited a harsh verdict from UEFA's disciplinary committee, Paris Saint-Germain deservedly moved into round two on the back of a convincing 45 minutes in one of the most hostile stadiums in Europe.*

UEFA CUP
First Round First Leg

Wednesday 16th September 1992
Achter de Kazerne Stadium, Mechelen

KV MECHELEN 2 ÖREBRO SK 1

Half-time 1-0 *Attendance* 5,000

		Goals				Goals
1	Michel PREUD'HOMME		1	Anders KARLSSON		
2	Davy GIJSBRECHTS		2	Ainars LINARDS		
3	Glen DE BOECK	63	3	Mikael ANDERSSON ‡		
4	Bart MAUROO		4	Thomas ANDERSSON		
5	Joël BARTHOLOMEEUSSEN		5	Magnus ERLINGMARK		
6	Stan VAN DEN BUYS		6	Hlynur STEFÁNSSON ❏		
7	Frank LEEN ‡		7	Mikael LINDQVIST †		
8	Klas INGESSON		8	Lars ZETTERLUND ■		
9	Patrick VERSAVEL		9	Sven DAHLQVIST		
10	Paul DE MESMAEKER		10	Hans HOLMQVIST		
11	René EYKELKAMP ❏ †	32	11	Miroslav KUBISZTAL		

Substitutes			*Substitutes*		
Kennet ANDERSSON †79			Pär MILLQVIST †56	83	
Peter JACOBS ‡90			Magnus SKÖLDMARK ‡85		

Referee Francesco BIANCHI (Switzerland)

● *Since taking eventual winners Milan to extra-time of a hard-fought Champions' Cup quarter-final in 1989/90, KV Mechelen had suffered a disastrous two seasons in Europe. Eliminated from the first round of the UEFA Cup in both 1990/91 and 1991/92, the former Cup-winners' Cup holders were determined to avoid an ignominious hat-trick of failures against Swedish side Örebro, competing in Europe for only the second time. Dutchman René Eykelkamp gave the home side an early boost when he volleyed home a left-wing cross after half an hour, and there was further good news for the locals when new sweeper Glen De Boeck exploited an error in the Swedish defence to head in a free-kick 18 minutes after the restart. But now, despite having a one-man advantage after Örebro's most experienced player, Lars Zetterlund, had been sent off in a rash challenge on his compatriot Kennet Andersson, Mechelen got nervous and the visitors took advantage. Polish striker Kubisztal set Icelandic international Stefánsson free on the left and his cross was converted from close range by former IFK Gothenburg midfielder Pär Millqvist.*

UEFA CUP
First Round Second Leg

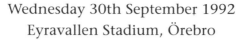

Wednesday 30th September 1992
Eyravallen Stadium, Örebro

ÖREBRO SK 0   KV MECHELEN 0

Half-time 0-0 *Aggregate* 1-2 *Attendance* 5,085

		Goals				Goals
1	Anders KARLSSON			1	Michel PREUD'HOMME	
2	Magnus SKÖLDMARK			2	Koen SANDERS	
3	Thomas ANDERSSON			3	Glen DE BOECK	
4	Tommy STÅHL †			4	Davy GIJSBRECHTS	
5	Magnus ERLINGMARK			5	Geert DEFERM ❑	
6	Hlynur STEFÁNSSON			6	Joël BARTHOLOMEEUSSEN	
7	Mikael LINDQVIST			7	Frank LEEN ❑	
8	Mikael ANDERSSON			8	Klas INGESSON	
9	Sven DAHLQVIST			9	Patrick VERSAVEL	
10	Ainars LINARDS			10	Kennet ANDERSSON	
11	Miroslaw KUBISZTAL			11	René EYKELKAMP	

Substitute

Richard LARSSON †67

Substitutes

Referee Svend Erik CHRISTENSEN (Denmark)

● *Thanks to their late away goal in the first leg, Örebro approached this tie with plenty of confidence. They had been beaten home and away by eventual winners Ajax on their European debut the season before, but now they had a real chance to beat another recent European trophy winner. A 1-0 win was all they needed, but it was certain to be tough against a side of Mechelen's calibre, especially as they themselves had been undergoing a difficult spell in the Swedish league, failing to qualify for the championship play-offs for the first time since they were promoted to the Allsvenskan in 1988. A crowd of over 5,000 - good by Örebro's standards - were there to offer their support, but hard though they tried, the home side, with only one member of Sweden's Euro '92 squad in their line-up (Erlingmark) as opposed to two on the other side (Ingesson and Andersson), could not find the goal they required. The Belgians, missing the injured Deferm, Peetermans and Vermant, were therefore mightily relieved to hang on to their first-leg lead and qualify for the UEFA Cup second round for the very first time.*

UEFA CUP
First Round First Leg

Tuesday 15th September 1992
Venoix Stadium, Caen

SM CAEN 3 REAL ZARAGOZA 2

Half-time 3-1 *Attendance* 5,134

		Goals				Goals
1	Philippe MONTANIER		1	Andoni CEDRUN		
2	Hippolyte DANGBETO ‡		2	Jesús Angel SOLANA ❏ †		
3	Hubert FOURNIER		3	Andreas BREHME		
4	Christophe POINT		4	Narciso JULIA		
5	Yvan LEBOURGEOIS †		5	Dario FRANCO		
6	Philippe AVENET		6	Javier AGUADO		
7	Benoît CAUET		7	Miguel PARDEZA	79	
8	Gabriel CALDERON		8	José GAY		
9	Stéphane PAILLE ❏	6, 37	9	Manuel PENA ‡		
10	Wilhelmus GORTER		10	GARCIA SANJUAN ❏	31	
11	Xavier GRAVELAINE	15	11	Dorin MATEUT		
	Substitutes			*Substitutes*		
	Joël GERMAIN †28			SERGI López †54 ❏		
	Faouzi ROUISSI ‡77			MOISES García ‡76		

Referee Kurt RÖTHLISBERGER (Switzerland)

SUMMARY

● *There were mixed emotions for the players, officials and supporters of Caen at the end of this dramatic and entertaining encounter. The French side had produced a stirring performance on their European debut to defeat Spain's Real Zaragoza. But a refereeing error 11 minutes from time had turned a comfortable and well-deserved 3-1 victory into a precariously narrow 3-2 final scoreline. Moises' double foul on Point and goalkeeper Montanier went unpunished by the officials and the Caen defenders simply stood in amazement as Pardeza walked the ball into the empty net. On the balance of play, Caen should have won the game comfortably. Zaragoza scored from their only two shots at goal, while the Normandy side created numerous opportunities without being able to add to their three first-half goals in the second period. Former French international Stéphane Paille got his name onto the scoresheet twice, but he owed both of his goals to the creativity of his attacking partner Xavier Gravelaine, scorer of the other Caen goal and indisputably the best player on the field.*

Thursday 1st October 1992
Romareda Stadium, Zaragoza

STADE MALHERBE
caen
CALVADOS BASSE-NORMANDIE

REAL ZARAGOZA 2 SM CAEN 0

Half-time 1-0 *Aggregate* 4-3 *Attendance* 15,000

		Goals				Goals
1	Andoni CEDRUN			1	Philippe MONTANIER	
2	Alberto BELSUE			2	Hippolyte DANGBETO	
3	Jesús Angel SOLANA			3	Faouzi ROUISSI	
4	SERGI López			4	Christophe POINT †	
5	Dario FRANCO			5	Yvan LEBOURGEOIS ❏	
6	Javier AGUADO			6	Hubert FOURNIER	
7	Miguel PARDEZA			7	Benoît CAUET	
8	José GAY ‡			8	Gabriel CALDERON ‡	
9	Francisco HIGUERA †			9	Stéphane PAILLE ❏	
10	Andreas BREHME ❏	24		10	Stéphane DEDEBANT	
11	Gustavo POYET	64		11	Xavier GRAVELAINE	

Substitutes			*Substitutes*	
MOISES García †52			Joël GERMAIN †66	
GARCIA SANJUAN ‡85 ❏			Wilhelmus GORTER ‡73	

Referee Howard KING (Wales)

SUMMARY

● *Real Zaragoza's two foreign stars, German Andreas Brehme and Uruguayan Gustavo Poyet, scored the goals which saw the Spanish team qualify for the second round at the expense of European debutants Caen. The French side's coach, former Swiss national boss Daniel Jeandupeux, made a curious team selection when he opted to play striker Stéphane Paille, scorer of two goals in the first leg, in the centre of defence. Moreover, he left Dutch midfielder Willy Gorter out of the team altogether. With first leg hero Gravelaine not enjoying the best of evenings, Caen offered little in attack. But even after Brehme had made up for an early missed penalty by giving the Spaniards the lead on 24 minutes, Jeandupeux, with his team now needing to score to qualify, would not free Paille to go and help out up front. Poyet's accurate, well-struck 25-yard shot after 64 minutes gave Zaragoza the two-goal cushion they were looking for and secured their place in the next round. Like compatriots Marseille against Sparta Prague in the Champions' Cup a year earlier, Caen had been unable to defend their first-leg 3-2 lead away from home and had gone out.*

UEFA CUP
First Round First Leg

Wednesday 16th September 1992
Városi Stadium, Vác

VÁC FC-SAMSUNG 1   FC GRONINGEN 0

Half-time 1-0   *Attendance* 3,500

		Goals				Goals
1	János KOSZTA			1	Patrick LODEWIJKS	
2	Tibor NAGY			2	Grafton HOLBAND	
3	Árpád HAHN			3	Claus BOEKWEG	
4	Imre ARANYOS			4	Ulrich WILSON	
5	János BÁNFI ❑			5	Erik VAN KESSEL	
6	Gábor KRISKA			6	Alex PIJPER	
7	János ROMANEK †			7	Lucian ILIE	
8	András ZOMBORI			8	Jos ROOSSIEN ❑	
9	László RÉPÁSI			9	Rick SLOR	
10	Antal SIMON			10	Milko DJUROVSKI ❑ ‡	
11	Antal FÜLE ‡	27		11	Mart VAN DUREN ❑ †	

Substitutes   *Substitutes*

László HORVÁTH †54   Ronald HAMMING †68

István SZEDLACSEK ‡70   Bert ZUURMAN ‡83

Referee George IONESCU (Romania)

SUMMARY

● *Vác FC-Samsung (formerly Váci Izzó MTE) were the revelation of the 1991/92 Hungarian season. Stalking Ferencváros all the way, they came within a whisker of lifting the Hungarian championship trophy for the first time. And as they prepared to take on Holland's FC Groningen in only their second European campaign, they were leading their domestic league once again after the first five matches of the new season. European perennials Groningen knew they had a game on their hands, especially as they were missing four regulars with injury - Meijer, Huizingh, Olde Riekerink and Veenhof - and goal-keeper Patrick Lodewijks was only just returning from a spell on the treatment table himself. The Dutch side, under new coach Pim Verbeek, went to Hungary for a draw and despite losing a goal mid-way through the first half they appeared to have the match under control. It was only in the last 15 minutes that Vác managed to establish a sustained bout of pressure. Fortunately Groningen survived that spell without conceding further goals, but at 0-1 down halfway through the tie, they clearly had their work cut out to retrieve the situation in the return.*

European Cups Review 1993

Wednesday 30th September 1992
Oosterpark Stadium, Groningen

FC GRONINGEN 1 VÁC FC-SAMSUNG 1

Half-time 0-1 Aggregate 1-2 Attendance 10,741

		Goals			Goals
1	Patrick LODEWIJKS		1	János KOSZTA	
2	Rick SLOR †		2	Tibor NAGY	
3	Claus BOEKWEG		3	Árpád HAHN †	
4	Ulrich WILSON		4	Imre ARANYOS	
5	Erik VAN KESSEL		5	János BÁNFI ❏	
6	Alex PIJPER		6	Gábor KRISKA	
7	Lucian ILIE		7	László HORVÁTH	
8	Jos ROOSSIEN		8	András ZOMBORI	
9	Hennie MEIJER		9	László RÉPÁSI	
10	Mart VAN DUREN		10	Antal SIMON ❏	
11	Harris HUIZINGH	57	11	Antal FÜLE ‡	44

Substitute

Ronald HAMMING †57

Substitutes

János ROMANEK †39

István SZEDLACSEK ‡79

Referee Esa PALSI (Finland)

● *For the first time since 1968/69 Hungary had only one team competing in the UEFA Cup, but Vác ensured that their country's interest in the competition would extend into the second round after this excellent performance in the Netherlands' northernmost footballing city. As in the first leg, Vác's goalscoring hero was 26-year-old former Honvéd striker Antal Füle. His well-executed goal just before half-time was an arrow in the heart of the home side. They now required no fewer than three goals in the second half to take the tie. They only managed one, scored in the 57th minute by first-leg injury victim Harris Huizingh. It was Groningen's second ignominious first-round exit from the UEFA Cup in successive seasons. Their 1991/92 campaign had been terminated early on by former East German side, Rot-Weiss Erfurt, and now their finances had been stung by yet another unlikely opponent from the East. Vác's triumph, meanwhile, meant extra kudos for the team and their enterprising coach, János Csank. With Ferencváros and Újpesti TE going out of the other two European competitions, Vác became the only Hungarian club to progress into the second round.*

UEFA CUP
First Round First Leg

Tuesday 15th September 1992
Laugardalsvöllur, Reykjavík

FRAM 0 1. FC KAISERSLAUTERN 3

Half-time 0-1 *Attendance* 1,500

		Goals			Goals
1	Birkir KRISTINSSON		1	Gerald EHRMANN	
2	Jón SVEINSSON		2	Axel ROOS	
3	Kristján JÓNSSON		3	Martin WAGNER ❏ ‡	63
4	Asgeir ASGEIRSSON		4	Thomas RITTER	
5	Valdimar KRISTÓFERSSON		5	Miroslav KADLEC	
6	Kristinn R. JÓNSSON		6	Wolfgang FUNKEL	
7	Pétur ARNTHÓRSSON †		7	Demir HOTIC	
8	Ingo INGÓLFSSON		8	Thomas DOOLEY	
9	Anton Björn MARKÚSSON ‡		9	Thomas VOGEL †	
10	Steinar GUDGEIRSSON		10	Michael ZEYER	
11	Jón RAGNARSSON		11	Marcel WITECZEK	30, 65
	Substitutes			*Substitutes*	
	Ómar SIGTRYGGSSON †78			Marcus MARIN †46	
	Gudmundur GÍSLASON ‡84			Thomas RICHTER ‡74	

Referee Thorbjørn AAS (Norway)

● *Unusually for an Icelandic club, Fram had put together an impressive sequence of results in Europe over the past couple of seasons. In 1990/91 they had comprehensively defeated Swedish side Djurgården in the first round of the Cup-winners' Cup before going out to eventual finalists Barcelona. A year later they had been denied a place in the second round of the Champions' Cup only by virtue of the away goals rule after holding Panathinaikos to two draws. It was a record to be proud of, but one for which German side Kaiserslautern showed little respect as they cruised to a comfortable victory in the Icelandic capital. Former World Youth Cup star Marcel Witeczek scored two of Kaiserslautern's three goals - his first in European competition - and new signing from Nuremberg, Martin Wagner, weighed in with the other to register the club's 100th goal in Europe. Fram, without their suspended player coach Pétur Ormslev organising the defence, simply had no answer to their opponent's incisive breaks and ended up, as in all six of their previous UEFA Cup matches, defeated and without a goal.*

UEFA CUP
First Round Second Leg

Tuesday 29th September 1992
Fritz Walter Stadium, Kaiserslautern

1. FC KAISERSLAUTERN 4 FRAM 0

Half-time 1-0 Aggregate 7-0 Attendance 23,197

		Goals				Goals
1	Gerald EHRMANN			1	Birkir KRISTINSSON	
2	Michael ZEYER			2	Jón SVEINSSON	
3	Martin WAGNER			3	Kristján JÓNSSON	
4	Thomas RITTER			4	Pétur ORMSLEV	
5	Miroslav KADLEC			5	Valdimar KRISTÓFERSSON	
6	Wolfgang FUNKEL			6	Ómar SIGTRYGGSSON †	
7	Demir HOTIC †			7	Pétur ARNTHÓRSSON	
8	Frank LELLE ∎			8	Ingo INGÓLFSSON	
9	Marcel WITECZEK	55, 76		9	Anton Björn MARKÚSSON ‡	
10	Oliver SCHÄFER			10	Steinar GUDGEIRSSON	
11	Stefan KUNTZ	29, 84		11	Jón RAGNARSSON	
	Substitutes				*Substitutes*	
	Marco HABER †36				Pétur ÓSKARSSON †65	
	Bjarne GOLDBAEK ‡46				Gudmundur GÍSLASON ‡70	

Referee ANSUATEGUI Roca (Spain)

● *Kaiserslautern's previous European match at the 'Betzenberg' held bitter memories for the club and its supporters. The team had been within a minute of eliminating Barcelona from the Champions' Cup when Bakero's header took the Spanish club through on away goals and on towards their first-ever Champions' Cup triumph. This fixture was evidently modest by comparison, but a sizeable crowd nevertheless turned up in force to demonstrate their loyalty and watch their team complete an easy qualification into round two. Marcel Witeczek repeated his two-goal tally of the first leg and his goals were sandwiched by another brace, from club captain Stefan Kuntz. Fram were never in the game and rarely looked like ending their barren goalscoring run in this competition, let alone avoiding yet another defeat. The 7-0 aggregate scoreline was Kaiserslautern's highest in Europe since an 8-1 triumph over Diósgyör of Hungary back in 1979.*

UEFA CUP
First Round First Leg

Wednesday 16th September 1992
Old Trafford, Manchester

MANCHESTER UNITED 0 TORPEDO MOSKVA 0

Half-time 0-0 *Attendance* 19,998

Goals

Goals

1 Gary WALSH	1 Aleksandr PODSHIVALOV
2 Dennis IRWIN	2 Gennady FILIMONOV
3 Lee MARTIN †	3 Maxim CHELTSOV
4 Steve BRUCE	4 Andrey AFANASYEV
5 Clayton BLACKMORE	5 Boris VOSTROSABLIN
6 Gary PALLISTER	6 Sergei SHUSTIKOV ‡
7 Andrey KANCHELSKIS	7 Gennady GRISHIN
8 Neil WEBB	8 Andrey MARTINOV
9 Brian McCLAIR	9 Andrey TALALAEV †
10 Mark HUGHES	10 Igor CHUGAYNOV
11 Danny WALLACE	11 Aleksei AREFIEV ❑

Substitute

Substitutes

Gary NEVILLE †87

Dmitry ULYANOV †74

Sergei SKACHENKO ‡79

Referee Aron SCHMIDHUBER (Germany)

SUMMARY

● This was Manchester United's 100th European match and their 50th at home. But with less than 20,000 fans turning up to support their team, the atmosphere was hardly conducive to celebration. The UEFA rule regarding the restricted use of non-nationals was particularly severe on the Old Trafford club with all their Irish, Welsh and Scottish players, but manager Alex Ferguson evidently forgot to read the smallprint when he omitted Welsh wonderkid Ryan Giggs from his line-up. Giggs, like his compatriot Clayton Blackmore, qualified as an 'affiliated foreigner' and could have been fielded alongside the fully-fledged 'foreigners' Hughes, McClair and Kanchelskis. Additionally, with Paul Ince suspended and Bryan Robson and Lee Sharpe injured, United were a long way from full strength. But they should still have had sufficient resources to break down a very young and inexperienced Torpedo side, competing for the first time in European competition under the Russian banner. As it was, the Muscovites held firm and only a Danny Wallace header in the second half, well saved by Podshivalov, seriously threatened to unlock their well-manned defence.

Tuesday 29th September 1992
Torpedo Stadium, Moscow

TORPEDO MOSKVA 0 MANCHESTER UNITED 0 (aet)

Half-time 0-0 *Aggregate* 0-0 (Torpedo win 4-3 on penalties) *Attendance* 11,357

		Goals				Goals
1	Aleksandr PODSHIVALOV		1	Peter SCHMEICHEL		
2	Gennady FILIMONOV ❑		2	Dennis IRWIN		
3	Maxim CHELTSOV ❑		3	Mike PHELAN ‡		
4	Andrey AFANASYEV		4	Steve BRUCE ❑		
5	Boris VOSTROSABLIN ‡		5	Neil WEBB		
6	Sergei SHUSTIKOV ❑		6	Gary PALLISTER		
7	Gennady GRISHIN		7	Danny WALLACE †		
8	Andrey TALALAEV		8	Paul INCE		
9	Aleksei AREFIEV		9	Brian McCLAIR ❑		
10	Igor CHUGAYNOV		10	Mark HUGHES ❑ ■		
11	Ivan PAZEMOV †		11	Ryan GIGGS		

Substitutes

Dmitry ULYANOV †84

Nikolai SAVICHEV ‡100

Substitutes

Bryan ROBSON †38

Paul PARKER ‡56

Referee Jan DAMGAARD (Denmark)

SUMMARY

● Torpedo Moscow had never been beaten in 25 previous European home games . That was some record, but Manchester United were well aware that they did not have to break it to take the tie. After the 0-0 draw at Old Trafford, any type of score draw would do. True to tradition, though, Alex Ferguson's team decided not to indulge in mathematics and went for the outright win. Torpedo showed touches of quality, but United were certainly the better side and it was only a lack of good fortune that prevented them from scoring that cherished away goal. With Mark Hughes sent off for a second bookable offence in the 88th minute, the visitors looked to have compromised their chances for extra-time. But still they created the best opportunities and yet still they couldn't score. In the end, all was settled by penalty kicks, and despite taking a 2-0 lead when the Russians missed their first two kicks, United could not capitalise. Bruce had his shot saved, McClair ballooned his over the bar and in sudden-death Pallister's miss consigned his club to the same fate they had endured on their previous UEFA Cup campaign - beaten on penalties by Videoton in the 1984/85 quarter-finals.

Tuesday 15th September 1992
Müngersdorfer Stadium, Cologne

1. FC KÖLN 2 CELTIC 0

Half-time 1-0 *Attendance* 26,000

		Goals				Goals
1	Bodo ILLGNER		1	Gordon MARSHALL		
2	Alfons HIGL		2	Tom BOYD		
3	Horst HELDT ‡		3	Dariusz WDOWCZYK		
4	Karsten BAUMANN		4	Mike GALLOWAY ❏		
5	Jan JENSEN	25	5	Tony MOWBRAY		
6	Andrzej RUDY		6	Gary GILLESPIE		
7	Hans-Dieter FLICK		7	Brian O'NEIL †		
8	Dirk LEHMANN †		8	Paul McSTAY		
9	Rico STEINMANN		9	Stuart SLATER ‡		
10	Pierre LITTBARSKI		10	Gerry CREANEY		
11	Frank ORDENEWITZ	82	11	John COLLINS		

Substitutes

Ralf STURM †88

Patrick WEISER ‡89

Substitutes

Peter GRANT †76

Charlie NICHOLAS ‡76

Referee Vadin ZHUK (Bielorussia)

● Reputations, if nothing else, deemed this one of the most attractive pairings of the UEFA Cup first round. Celtic, having achieved qualification 'by the back door' after the suspension of Yugoslav clubs, were embarking on their 29th European campaign. For Cologne, it was a 25th season of European football, and their 19th in the UEFA/Fairs' Cup, an appearance record bettered only by Italy's Internazionale with 21. But the Germans came into this first leg in shocking form. After six games in the Bundesliga they were bottom of the table with just a single point, and coach Jörg Berger's job was very much on the line. A convincing victory against Liam Brady's Celtic appeared to be his only salvation, and thanks to the benevolence of the Scottish team's defence, that is precisely what he obtained. Celtic, also going through a rough patch at home, committed two serious errors at the back to pre-empt both of the headed goals, one in either half, which secured Cologne's victory and put them firmly in control for the return in Glasgow.

UEFA CUP
First Round Second Leg

Wednesday 30th September 1992
Celtic Park, Glasgow

CELTIC 3 1. FC KÖLN 0

Half-time 2-0 *Aggregate* 3-2 *Attendance* 30,747

		Goals				Goals
1	Gordon MARSHALL		1	Bodo ILLGNER	
2	Mark McNALLY		2	Alfons HIGL	
3	Tom BOYD		3	Frank GREINER ❑	
4	Peter GRANT		4	Karsten BAUMANN	
5	Tony MOWBRAY		5	Jan JENSEN	
6	Mike GALLOWAY ❑		6	Andrzej RUDY	
7	Stuart SLATER †		7	Horst HELDT	
8	Paul McSTAY	36	8	Rico STEINMANN †	
9	Andy PAYTON ‡		9	Carsten KEULER ‡	
10	Gerry CREANEY	39	10	Patrick WEISER	
11	John COLLINS	80	11	Frank ORDENEWITZ	
	Substitutes			*Substitutes*	
	Joe MILLER †55			Henri FUCHS †54	
	Steve FULTON ‡88			Pierre LITTBARSKI ‡60	

Referee Guy GOETHALS (Belgium)

● Had Celtic's followers consulted the statistics beforehand, they would have been informed that, historically, their team stood only a one in four chance of overhauling their 0-2 deficit from the away leg. But not every team in Europe is able in such circumstances to draw on the support of 30,000 passionate and vociferous fans to will them to victory. At Parkhead, though, the atmosphere was electric and by half-time Cologne's first-leg advantage had been wiped out. Celtic skipper Paul McStay, with his first European goal for eight years, volleyed his side ahead after 36 minutes and young striker Gerry Creaney was on hand shortly afterwards to deflect John Collins' shot into the net and make it 2-0 on the night. Cologne brought on Fuchs and Littbarski, two attack-minded players, to try and get the crucial away goal after the interval, but it was to be Celtic's night. With extra-time looming, Collins twisted into the box on the left and fired past Bodo Illgner from a tight angle to take his team into round two. Manager Liam Brady had asked his side for a "special performance" and they had provided the perfect response.

UEFA CUP
First Round First Leg

Wednesday 16th September 1992
Sclessin Stadium, Liège

STANDARD LIEGE 5 PORTADOWN 0

Half-time 2-0 *Attendance* 12,000

		Goals				Goals
1	Gilbert BODART		1	Michael KEENAN		
2	Régis GENAUX ‡		2	Philip MAJOR		
3	Philippe LEONARD	55	3	Mario SCAPATICCI		
4	Stéphane DEMOL		4	Doug BELL ❏		
5	André CRUZ		5	Brian STRAIN		
6	Patrick VERVOORT		6	Alan STEWART		
7	Guy HELLERS		7	Anthony GORMAN		
8	Patrick ASSELMAN †	8, 45	8	Martin RUSSELL		
9	Alain BETTAGNO		9	Robert CASEY ‡		
10	Frans VAN ROOY ❏		10	David MILLS ❏ †		
11	Marc WILMOTS		11	Greg DAVIDSON		

Substitutes			*Substitutes*	
Michael GOOSSENS †48	52, 65		Peter MURRAY †58	
Mohamed LASHAF ‡77			Michael SURGEON ‡81	

Referee Haeem LIPKOVICH (Israel)

S U M M A R Y

● *Belgian clubs had been drawn against Irish League clubs 11 times before in European competition and had qualified every time - their best record against any country. But while Antwerp struggled against Glenavon in the Cup-winners' Cup, Standard Liège ensured themselves a gentle re-introduction to European football after a six-year absence by destroying Portadown in a completely one-sided match by five goals to nil. Despite their long absence from Europe, Standard had plenty of players with European experience in their side, and on the bench was coach Arie Haan, who had been a playing member in each of the three Ajax teams that won the Champions' Cup in the early '80s. But the goals were all scored by players making their European debut, with particular mention going to two-goal substitute striker Michael Goossens, just 18 years of age and with only a handful of first-team appearances behind him.*

UEFA CUP
First Round Second Leg

Tuesday 29th September 1992
Shamrock Park, Portadown

rfd

PORTADOWN 0 STANDARD LIEGE 0

Half-time 0-0 *Aggregate* 0-5 *Attendance* 2,500

		Goals				Goals
1	Michael KEENAN		1	Gilbert BODART		
2	Philip MAJOR		2	Régis GENAUX		
3	Peter MURRAY		3	Patrick VERVOORT		
4	Doug BELL ❏		4	Stéphane DEMOL		
5	Brian STRAIN		5	Philippe LEONARD		
6	Alan STEWART		6	Thierry PISTER		
7	David MILLS		7	Guy HELLERS		
8	Martin RUSSELL		8	Michael GOOSSENS †		
9	Robert CASEY		9	Henk VOS		
10	Stevie COWAN		10	Frans VAN ROOY		
11	Greg DAVIDSON		11	Marc WILMOTS		

Substitutes

Substitute

Mohamed LASHAF †72

Referee Georges RAMOS (France)

● *Portadown were never going to come back from a 0-5 first-leg defeat - no team ever had done in Europe - but they were able to salvage some pride by emulating mid-Ulster rivals Glenavon a fortnight earlier and holding Belgian opposition to a home draw. 0-0 was a dramatic improvement on Portadown's two home performances in the Champions' Cup in the past two seasons - 0-4 against Red Star Belgrade in 1991/92 and 1-8 versus FC Porto a year earlier - and it also maintained the club's unbeaten home record in the UEFA Cup. With qualification secure after the first leg, Standard simply went through the motions. At the forefront of their minds was the big local derby against FC Liège coming up the following Saturday, a match they needed to win to stay joint top of the Belgian league table alongside Anderlecht. Standard had faced four teams from Northern Ireland in the past - Linfield, Ards, Glenavon and Glentoran - and had always got the better of them. Now, after this comprehensive aggregate victory over Portadown, they had made it five out of five!*

UEFA CUP
First Round First Leg

Wednesday 16th September 1992
Parken, Copenhagen

FC KØBENHAVN 5 MP 0

Half-time 2-0 *Attendance* 8,430

		Goals				Goals
1	Palle PETERSEN		1	Stefan LINDSTRÖM	
2	Kenneth WEGNER		2	Jari HUDD	
3	Ivan NIELSEN ❑		3	Timo-Pekka VIITIKKO	
4	Michael GIOLBAS		4	Jokke KANGASKORPI ❑ †	
5	Lars Højer NIELSEN ‡	69(pen)	5	Jukka RUHANEN	
6	Pierre LARSEN	86	6	John ALLEN	
7	Jørgen Juul JENSEN †		7	Ilkka MÄKELÄ	
8	Iørn ULDBJERG	29	8	Juha KARVINEN	
9	Brian KAUS		9	Harri SAARELMA	
10	Martin JOHANSEN		10	Tibor GRUBOROVICS	
11	Michael JOHANSEN	12, 53	11	George LAWRENCE ‡	

Substitutes

Christian LØNSTRUP †76

Morten PETERSEN ‡88

Substitutes

Jari SARIOLA †61

Antti-Pekka NIKULA ‡88

Referee Marek KOWALCZYK (Poland)

● *Finnish part-timers MP of Mikkeli provided feeble opposition for the newly-formed FC København as the recently-refurbished Danish national stadium played host to its new permanent residents for the first time in European competition. FC København, a merger of the two Copenhagen clubs B 1903 and KB, was a new name on the European scene, but the actual team was not much different from the one which had reached the UEFA Cup quarter-finals the previous season as B 1903. Aiming to match that achievement under their new guise, the Danish club made light work of their opening assignment against MP. The Finns, languishing in the lower reaches of their domestic league, were outplayed for virtually the entire 90 minutes. Their 39-year-old goalkeeper Stefan Lindström had a busy evening and was forced to pick the ball out of his net on five occasions. Individual goalscoring honours went to Michael Johansen, one of two 20-year-old twins in the team, who scored his side's first and third goals.*

UEFA CUP
First Round Second Leg

Wednesday 30th September 1992
Urheilupuisto, Mikkeli

MP 1 FC KØBENHAVN 5

Half-time 0-4 *Aggregate* 1-10 *Attendance* 971

		Goals				Goals
1	Jozef ROBAKIEWICZ		1	Palle PETERSEN		
2	Jari HUDD		2	Christian LØNSTRUP		
3	Timo-Pekka VIITIKKO		3	Ivan NIELSEN		
4	Antti-Pekka NIKULA †		4	Michael GIOLBAS †		
5	Jukka RUHANEN		5	Lars Højer NIELSEN		8
6	John ALLEN	64	6	Pierre LARSEN		
7	Ilkka MÄKELÄ		7	Jørgen Juul JENSEN		
8	Juha KARVINEN		8	Iørn ULDBJERG		45
9	Harri SAARELMA		9	Brian KAUS ❑		
10	Jari SARIOLA ❑ ‡		10	Martin JOHANSEN		18, 32
11	George LAWRENCE		11	Anders BJERRE ‡		
	Substitutes			*Substitutes*		
	Niko TERÄSALMI †46			Søren LYNG †56		
	Pasi NUIJA ‡63			Brian RASMUSSEN ‡57		82

Referee Nikolai LEVNIKOV (Russia)

SUMMARY

● MP knew they were already out of the competition after their 0-5 trouncing in Copenhagen, but they still hoped to have the consolation of avoiding defeat in the UEFA Cup for the first time, if not registering their first victory. But once former PSV Eindhoven defender Ivan Nielsen had put the Danes in front after five minutes, Finnish dreams turned into another nightmare. Whereas Michael Johansen had scored twice for København in the first leg, his twin borther Martin bagged himself a brace this time as the visitors raced into a 4-0 lead after just 45 minutes. MP's lone bright spot of the evening came with a consolation goal from Englishman John Allen, whose only previous goal in Europe had been scored in the wrong net a season earlier against Spartak Moscow. With a 10-1 aggregate victory secured by substitute Brian Rasmussen's late effort, FC København joined Juventus, Panathinaikos, Eintracht Frankfurt and Sheffield Wednesday as the fifth team to reach double figures in the first round of the UEFA Cup.

UEFA CUP
First Round First Leg

Wednesday 16th September 1992
Widzew Stadium, Lódz

WIDZEW LÓDZ 2 EINTRACHT FRANKFURT 2

Half-time 2-0 *Attendance* 12,000

		Goals				Goals
1	Piotr WOJDYGA		1	Uli STEIN		
2	Marek GODLEWSKI ❑		2	Dietmar ROTH ❑		
3	Tomasz LAPINSKI		3	Ralf WEBER ‡		
4	Wieslaw CISEK		4	Uwe BINDEWALD		
5	Marek BAJOR		5	Manfred BINZ ❑		
6	Miroslaw MYSLINSKI ❑		6	Stefan STUDER ❑		
7	Bogdan JÓZWIAK ❑ ‡	19	7	Marek PENSKA		
8	Leszek IWANICKI		8	Ralf FALKENMAYER †		
9	Marek KONIAREK	26	9	Anthony YEBOAH	67	
10	Ryszard CZERWIEC †		10	Rudi BOMMER		
11	Andrzej MICHALCZUK		11	Axel KRUSE		

Substitutes

Pavel MIASZKIEWICZ †71

Zbigniew WYCISZKIEWICZ ‡76

Substitutes

Dirk WOLF †46 82

Frank MÖLLER ‡83

Referee SADIK Deda (Turkey)

● Widzew Lódz were back in Europe for the first time in six years and they made a tremendous start against one of the pre-tournament favourites Eintracht Frankfurt. Two goals up after 26 minutes, they threatened to hand out to Frankfurt the same type of punishment the German club had suffered from Brøndby in the first round of the UEFA Cup two years earlier when they were hammered 5-0. But the Polish side, coached by World Cup veteran Wladyslaw Zmuda, could not build on those early strikes from Bogdan Józwiak and Marek Koniarek, and in the second half they allowed the Germans back into the game. Ghanaian striker Anthony Yeboah reduced the deficit with a deflected shot after a penetrating move on the right, and substitute Dirk Wolf, who had come on at half-time, equalised late on when he was allowed too much space through the middle by the Widzew defence. With two precious away goals in the bag, Eintracht had completely altered the course of the tie and were now very firmly installed as favourites for the return in Frankfurt.

Wednesday 30th September 1992
Wald Stadium, Frankfurt-am-Main

EINTRACHT FRANKFURT 9 WIDZEW LÓDZ 0

Half-time 6-0 *Aggregate* 11-2 *Attendance* 11,200

		Goals			Goals
1	Uli STEIN		1	Piotr WOJDYGA	
2	Dietmar ROTH		2	Marek GODLEWSKI ❏	
3	Ralf WEBER		3	Tomasz LAPINSKI	
4	Uwe BINDEWALD		4	Wieslaw CISEK	
5	Manfred BINZ		5	Marek BAJOR	
6	Stefan STUDER ‡		6	Miroslaw MYSLINSKI	
7	Dirk WOLF		7	Andrzej SZULC	
8	Augustine OKOCHA		8	Leszek IWANICKI	
9	Anthony YEBOAH	20, 22, 36, 68	9	Marek KONIAREK	
10	Rudi BOMMER †		10	Ryszard CZERWIEC ‡	
11	Axel KRUSE	8, 14, 37	11	Andrzej MICHALCZUK †	
	Substitutes			*Substitutes*	
	Uwe BEIN †30	90		Bogdan JÓZWIAK †46	
	Uwe RAHN ‡44	83		Pawel MIASZKIEWICZ ‡56	

Referee Leslie MOTTRAM (Scotland)

● After the closeness of the first game, nobody could possibly have foreseen just how easily Eintracht Frankfurt would win this match. Not surprisingly, 9-0 was their biggest ever single-match victory in Europe. They had never previously exceeded six goals in a game. although they had managed 11 goals over two legs against Spora Luxembourg in the same competition just a year earlier! It was Widzew Lódz's heaviest defeat too. Their worst result previously in 40 European games was a 5-0 defeat by Ipswich Town in the 1980/81 season, the year the English club won the UEFA Cup. The men responsible for the demolition were Frankfurt's two strikers, Anthony Yeboah and Axel Kruse. Each player helped himself to a first-half hat-trick, with the Ghanaian adding another to his tally midway through the second half to bring his all-time total to eight goals in six European games. The scoring was completed with a goal each for Frankfurt's two substitutes, German internationals Uwe Rahn and Uwe Bein, both returning from injury to join in the fun.

UEFA CUP
First Round First Leg

Wednesday 16th September 1992
Idrottsparken, Norrköping

IFK NORRKÖPING 1 TORINO 0

Half-time 0-0 *Attendance* 10,000

		Goals				Goals
1	Lars ERIKSSON		1	Luca MARCHEGIANI		
2	Sulo VAATTOVAARA		2	Pasquale BRUNO		
3	Slobodan MAROVIC		3	Raffaele SERGIO ‡		
4	Peter LÖNN		4	Daniele FORTUNATO †		
5	Jonas LIND		5	Enrico ANNONI		
6	Jan KALÉN		6	Luca FUSI		
7	Patrik ANDERSSON †		7	Roberto MUSSI		
8	Per BLOHM	82	8	Walter CASAGRANDE		
9	Yevgeny KUZNETSOV		9	Carlos AGUILERA		
10	Jonny RÖDLUND		10	Enzo SCIFO		
11	Jan HELLSTRÖM		11	Giorgio VENTURIN		

Substitute

Mikael HANSSON †71

Substitutes

Sandro COIS †46

Gianluca SORDO ‡85

Referee Peter MIKKELSEN (Denmark)

● The previous season's UEFA Cup losing finalists Torino got their 92/93 campaign off to a shaky start with this narrow defeat in Sweden. Many important members of the team had left in the summer - notably Rafael Martín Vázquez to Marseille, Roberto Policano to Napoli, Roberto Cravero to Lazio and, for a world record fee of £13 million, Gianluigi Lentini to Milan - and this was evident in the team's disjointed display in Norrköping. On the balace of play, Torino did not deserve to lose, but with the Norrköping goalkeeper Lars Eriksson in superlative form and Torino's Brazilian striker Walter Casagrande not enjoying one of his better days in front of goal, the Italians failed to score the all-important away goal. And with only eight minutes remaining the home side scored out of the blue to win the game. Per Blohm, a long-haired midfielder capped once by Sweden, was the match-winner, his right-foot shot soaring past Marchegiani from the edge of the area to set his team up for a possible shock qualification.

UEFA CUP
First Round Second Leg

Thursday 1st October 1992
Delle Alpi Stadium, Turin

TORINO 3 IFK NORRKÖPING 0

Half-time 1-0 *Aggregate* 3-1 *Attendance* 17,783

		Goals				Goals
1	Luca MARCHEGIANI		1	Lars ERIKSSON		
2	Pasquale BRUNO		2	Sulo VAATTOVAARA	2 (og)	
3	Raffaele SERGIO		3	Slobodan MAROVIC		
4	Roberto MUSSI †		4	Peter LÖNN		
5	Enrico ANNONI		5	Jonas LIND		
6	Luca FUSI		6	Jan KALÉN		
7	Gianluca SORDO		7	Per BLOHM		
8	Walter CASAGRANDE ‡	77	8	Göran BERGORT †		
9	Carlos AGUILERA	80	9	Yevgeny KUZNETSOV ‡		
10	Enzo SCIFO		10	Jonny RÖDLUND		
11	Giorgio VENTURIN		11	Jan HELLSTRÖM		

Substitutes		*Substitutes*	
Andrea SILENZI †77		Mikael HANSSON †77	
Antonio ALOISI ‡79		Magnus SAMUELSSON ‡84	

Referee Aleksei SPIRIN (Russia)

● *Norrköping came to the Delle Alpi stadium with just one objective in mind. To hold on to what they had. Alas, after barely two minutes of the match, their plans lay in ruins. A deflected shot by Torino defender Pasquale Bruno put the Italians level on aggregate, and the Swedes knew that, barring success in a penalty shoot-out, they now had to score to survive. For the remaining 88 minutes, though, they appeared ill-inclined to veer away from their pre-programmed defensive tactics. The outcome was one-way traffic in the direction of the Norrköping goal where, once again, Swedish international goalkeeper Lars Eriksson performed heroically to keep his side in contention. The tie was finally settled in Torino's favour in the last quarter of an hour. Andrea Silenzi had just come on as an extra striker when, within seconds, he headed a cross down into the path of Walter Casagrande, who duly scored his seventh European goal in 12 games. Shortly afterwards, it was another South American striker, Carlos Aguilera, establishing an even better European strike-rate of nine goals in 11 games, who added the third, enabling Torino to join all five other Italian representatives in the next round.*

Wednesday 16th September 1992
Dr. Vacka Stadium, Prague

SLAVIA PRAHA 1 HEART OF MIDLOTHIAN 0

Half-time 0-0 *Attendance* 4,549

		Goals				Goals
1	Zdenek JÁNOS			1	Henry SMITH	
2	Michal PETROUS ❑			2	Graeme HOGG ❑	
3	Jan SUCHOPÁREK ❑			3	Tosh McKINLAY	
4	Jaroslav SILHAVY			4	Neil BERRY	
5	Patrik BERGER			5	Gary MACKAY	
6	Vladimir TATARCHUK	85		6	Peter VAN DE VEN	
7	Jirí LERCH			7	John ROBERTSON †	
8	Martin PENICKA			8	Derek FERGUSON ❑	
9	Pavel KUKA			9	IAN BAIRD ❑	
10	Radim NECAS			10	Ally MAUCHLEN	
11	Jirí NOVÁK †			11	Wayne FOSTER ‡	

Substitute

Stefan RUSNÁK †63

Substitutes

Scott CRABBE †60

Eamonn BANNON ‡72

Referee Sergei KHUSAINOV (Russia)

● *Slavia Prague's return to European football after a seven-year absence was anticipated with great interest by Czech football fans. Backed with financial aid from their wealthy American patron Boris Korbel, Slavia had been able to assemble an immensely promising side, and there was considerable expectation that they would go further this year iin Europe than they had ever gone before. That meant simply reaching the third round! With playmaker Radim Necas having joined the club in the summer from Baník Ostrava for a record internal Czechoslovakian fee and star striker Pavel Kuka agreeing to stay with the club despite several offers from abroad, Slavia certainly meant business. But Hearts, missing their Scottish international defender Craig Levein through suspension, were more than a match for them in the Czech capital. It was only a late lapse of concentration by goalkeeper Henry Smith which let in former Soviet Union international Vladimir Tatarchuk that denied them a worthy draw. But at 0-1 down Hearts knew that they had everything still to play for at Tynecastle.*

UEFA CUP
First Round Second Leg

Wednesday 30th September 1992
Tynecastle Park, Edinburgh

HEART OF MIDLOTHIAN 4 SLAVIA PRAHA 2

Half-time 3-1 *Aggregate* 4-3 *Attendance* 16,000

		Goals			Goals
1	Henry SMITH		1	Zdenek JÁNOS	
2	Graeme HOGG		2	Michal PETROUS	
3	Tosh McKINLAY ❑		3	Jan SUCHOPÁREK	
4	Craig LEVEIN	42	4	Jaroslav SILHAVY	14
5	Gary MACKAY	10	5	Bartolomej JURASKO	
6	Peter VAN DE VEN		6	Vladimir TATARCHUK	
7	John ROBERTSON		7	Dragisa BINIC †	
8	Alan McLAREN †		8	Martin PENICKA ❑ ■	
9	Ian BAIRD	21	9	Pavel KUKA	65
10	Glynn SNODIN ❑ ‡	79	10	Radim NECAS ‡	
11	Eamonn BANNON		11	Jirí LERCH ❑	

	Substitutes			*Substitutes*
	George WRIGHT †60			Patrik BERGER †74
	Tom WILSON ‡82			Jirí NOVÁK ‡79

Referee Rune LARSSON (Sweden)

● *This was without doubt one of the most exciting matches of the round. Sadly for Scottish football fans in general there were no television cameras to capture the action, but for the 16,000 Hearts supporters at Tynecastle it was a night to remember. Their team got off to the ideal start when they went 1-0 up on the night and level on aggregate after just 10 minutes. But Slavia soon equalised and from then on, in an enthralling topsy-turvy contest, qualification changed hands on no fewer than three occasions before Englishman Glynn Snodin fired home a 79th minute thunderbolt from the edge of the area to give Hearts a 4-2 victory and take them through to the next round. Amazingly, neither he nor the other Hearts marksmen - Gary Mackay, Ian Baird and Craig Levein - had ever previously scored in Europe! Manager Joe Jordan was a proud man: "It was a fabulous performance. Once or twice we could have lost it, but the players showed great character to win through. In terms of the quality of our goals and the excitement we generated, this was my best night in management."*

Wednesday 16th September 1992
Dinamo Stadium, Moscow

DINAMO MOSKVA 5 ROSENBORG BK 1

Half-time 1-0 *Attendance* 7,250

		Goals			Goals
1	Valery KLEYMENOV		1	Ola BY RISE	
2	Sergei TIMOFEEV ■	46	2	Øivind HUSBY	
3	Igor SKLYAROV	34, 62	3	Rune TANGEN	
4	Kakhaber TSKHADADZE		4	Bjørn Otto BRAGSTAD †	
5	Yury KALITVINTSEV ‡ ❑		5	Stig Inge BJØRNEBYE	
6	Sarkis OGANESYAN		6	Kåre INGEBRIGTSEN	
7	Yevgeny SMERTIN †		7	Øyvind LEONHARDSEN	
8	Viacheslav TSAREV ❑		8	Bent SKAMMELSRUD	
9	Omari TETRADZE	68	9	Karl-Petter LØKEN	75
10	Velli KASUMOV		10	Gøran SØRLOTH	
11	Igor SIMUTENKOV	57	11	Tore André DAHLUM ‡	
	Substitutes			*Substitutes*	
	Yury DROZDOV †79			Bjørn Tore KVARME †46	
	Badri SPANDERASHVILI ‡88			Roar STRAND ‡72	

Referee Karel BOHUNEK (Czechoslovakia)

SUMMARY

● *Rosenborg, containing several current Norwegian internationals, set out with considerable optimism that they could become the first Norwegian club to reach the second round of a European competition since they themselves had last managed it, against Linfield six years earlier in the Champions' Cup. But after 90 minutes in Moscow their dreams, realistic at the outset, were in tatters. They went into the match in confident mood, well on course for their third Norwegian Cup and League double in five years, and after half an hour everything looked fine until Dinamo defender Sklyarov put the Russians ahead with a free-kick from the edge of the area. That goal completely altered the course of the match, and in the same amount of time that Rosenborg had managed to keep the scoreline blank they suddenly conceded five goals. A late effort from the Norwegian league's top scorer in 1991, Karl-Petter Løken, was all Rosenborg could offer in reply, but that looked certain to be too little, too late to keep Norway's finest in the competition.*

UEFA CUP
First Round Second Leg

Wednesday 30th September 1992
Lerkendal Stadium, Trondheim

ROSENBORG BK 2 DINAMO MOSKVA 0

Half-time 1-0 *Aggregate* 3-5 *Attendance* 10,218

		Goals				Goals
1	Ola BY RISE			1	Valery KLEYMENOV	
2	Øivind HUSBY			2	Viacheslav TSAREV	
3	Rune TANGEN			3	Igor SKLYAROV	
4	Bjørn Otto BRAGSTAD			4	Kakhaber TSKHADADZE	
5	Stig Inge BJØRNEBYE			5	Yury KALITVINTSEV ❏	
6	Kåre INGEBRIGTSEN	8		6	Andrey KOBELEV	
7	Øyvind LEONHARDSEN			7	Yevgeny SMERTIN	
8	Bent SKAMMELSRUD			8	Sergei DERKACH	
9	Karl-Petter LØKEN	47		9	Sarkis OGANESYAN	
10	Gøran SØRLOTH			10	Velli KASUMOV ‡	
11	Tore André DAHLUM			11	Igor SIMUTENKOV †	
	Substitutes				*Substitutes*	
					Yury DROZDOV †69 ❏	
					Badri SPANDERASHVILI ‡89	

Referee Keith COOPER (Wales)

● *Only two clubs had ever successfully come back to win a European tie after losing the first leg 5-1 away from home. Rosenborg had a huge mountain to climb, and an excellent five-figure crowd turned up, more in hope than expectation, to see if they could do it. An early goal from international midfielder Kåre Ingebrigtsen, who had played his part in the Norwegian national team's shock World Cup victory over Holland a week earlier, was the early tonic Rosenborg needed, but there was no further scoring until Karl-Petter Løken's second goal of the tie just after the interval. The Russians began to feel the pressure in the second half, but with Rosenborg still requiring two goals to take the tie, there was no undue cause for alarm, and as the home side's resolve waned towards the end, Dinamo succeeded in hanging on to join city rivals CSKA, Spartak and Torpedo in the next round. As for Rosenborg, they could only reflect on what might have been and concentrate on qualifying for the 1993/94 Champions' Cup before the inevitable break-up of their talented side to the professional leagues of England and mainland Europe.*

SUMMARY

Wednesday 16th September 1992
Delle Alpi Stadium, Turin

JUVENTUS 6 ANORTHOSIS FAMAGUSTA 1

Half-time 3-0 *Attendance* 4,743

		Goals				Goals
1	Angelo PERUZZI		1	Nicos PANAYIOTOU	
2	Moreno TORRICELLI	75	2	Andreas PANAYIOTOU ❏	
3	Dino BAGGIO ❏		3	Andreas IOANNOU	
4	Roberto GALIA		4	Spyros KASTANAS	
5	Jürgen KOHLER		5	Kokos PANAYI	
6	Massimo CARRERA		6	Vassos TSAGARIS	
7	Paolo DI CANIO †		7	Temur KETSBAIA	84
8	David PLATT		8	Christakis KASSIANOS †	
9	Gianluca VIALLI	43, 62	9	Dimitris ASSIOTIS ‡	
10	Roberto BAGGIO	4	10	Nikolai KOSTOV	
11	Andreas MÖLLER ‡	11	11	Zacharias CHARALAMBOUS	

Substitutes | | | | *Substitutes* | |

	Antonio CONTE †41	46		Panayiotis POUNNAS †46	
	Fabrizio RAVANELLI ‡58			Christos KITTOS ‡67	

Referee László MOLNÁR (Hungary)

● *Juventus, who set out as the competition's joint top seeds along with city rivals Torino, had no diffi-culty getting back to grips with European football after their shock absence the previous season. Anorthosis of Cyprus provided limp opposition for a team containing the awesome-looking combined attacking talents of Vialli, Platt, Möller and Roberto Baggio. Baggio it was who opened the scoring after just four minutes with a neat left-footer from the edge of the area and thereafter it was plain sail-ing for the record Italian champions. Shooting practice was the order of the day, and the Juventus strike force appeared to have their sights well set. New signing Gianluca Vialli, whose previous European game, the Champions' Cup final between Sampdoria and Barcelona at Wembley, held few pleasant memories for him, pounced twice to score his 20th and 21st goals in European competition. A more surprising scorer was young full-back Moreno Torricelli who concluded a highly promising European debut with his team's sixth and last goal of the evening.*

UEFA CUP
First Round Second Leg

Tuesday 29th September 1992
Antonis Papadopoulos Stadium, Larnaca

ANORTHOSIS FAMAGUSTA 0 JUVENTUS 4

Half-time 0-2 *Aggregate* 1-10 *Attendance* 8,000

		Goals			Goals
1	Michalis KAVELIS		1	Angelo PERUZZI	
2	Andreas PANAYIOTOU		2	Massimo CARRERA ‡	
3	Andreas IOANNOU		3	Marco Antonio DE MARCHI	
4	Spyros KASTANAS		4	Antonio CONTE †	
5	Kokos PANAYI		5	Jürgen KOHLER	39
6	Vassos TSAGARIS		6	JÚLIO CÉSAR Silva	
7	Temur KETSBAIA		7	Paolo DI CANIO	
8	Panayiotis POUNNAS		8	Roberto GALIA	
9	Dimitris ASSIOTIS		9	Pierluigi CASIRAGHI	66, 89
10	Nikolai KOSTOV		10	David PLATT	
11	Zacharias CHARALAMBOUS †		11	Fabrizio RAVANELLI	14

Substitute		*Substitutes*	
Costas RIZOS †57		Dino BAGGIO †59	
		Luigi SARTOR ‡76	

Referee Brian HILL (England)

● *6-1 up from the first meeting in Turin, Juventus were able to rest some of their big names for this visit to the Cypriot town of Larnaca. Appearing in their change strip of yellow and blue, the Italians treated the fixture as little more than a training match. Of the five players who had scored goals in the first leg, only one, midfielder Antonio Conte, made the starting line-up this time and even he didn't last the 90 minutes. Anorthosis had never won a game in Europe and they were never likely to start against Juventus. Fabrizio Ravanelli, a silver-haired 23-year-old, opened the scoring early on, German defender Jürgen Kohler lashed home a spectacular second just before half-time and Italian international striker Pierluigi Casiraghi made the most of a rare outing in the Juventus first team with two soft goals in the second half. The final aggregate score of 10-1 was not a record for the Italians, but it was only the fifth time in their history that they had reached double figures for a single European tie.*

UEFA CUP
First Round First Leg

Wednesday 16th September 1992
Lokomotiv Stadium, Plovdiv

LOKOMOTIV PLOVDIV 2 AJ AUXERRE 2

Half-time 1-1 *Attendance* 5,000

		Goals				Goals
1	Vasil VASILIEV		1	Bruno MARTINI		
2	Radi RAIKOVSKI ❑		2	Stéphane MAZZOLINI ❑		
3	Petar PASHEV		3	William PRUNIER		
4	Rumen DIMITROV		4	Frank VERLAAT		
5	Ivan GOVEDAROV		5	Stéphane MAHE		
6	Valentin VALCHEV		6	Raphaël GUERREIRO		
7	Lazar VACHKOV		7	Christophe COCARD		73
8	Ayan SADAKOV ❑	33 (pen)	8	Daniel DUTUEL		
9	Simeon KRASTEV †		9	Gérald BATICLE		4
10	Dimitar CHOBANOV ‡		10	Corentin MARTINS		
11	Kostadin VIDOLOV	58	11	Pascal VAHIRUA †		

Substitutes

Dimitar KEKHAIOV †46

Stoian KARAPETROV ‡59

Substitute

Alain GOMA †82 ❑

Referee Fabio BALDAS (Italy)

S U M M A R Y

● *This was the second competitive match between Bulgarian and French teams within a week. Seven days earlier the Bulgarian national team had defeated their French counterparts 2-0 in a World Cup qualifier played in Sofia. Bruno Martini and Pascal Vahirua of Auxerre had played in that game, but there had been nobody on duty from Lokomotiv Plovdiv, a club returning to Europe after a nine-year absence. Lokomotiv's only international was their captain Ayan Sadakov, a veteran of the 1986 World Cup finals in Mexico and now back at his first club after a three-year stint in Portugal. Auxerre were the favourites to progress and they began positively, taking an early lead when centre-forward Gérald Baticle celebrated his European debut by heading in Vahirua's cross after four minutes. Goals from Sadakov and the impressive young forward Kostadin Vidolov swung the tie back in the home side's favour, but Cocard's 73rd-minute equaliser ensured that honours remained even in a match played in searing heat. The temperature at the 17.30 kick-off was an unforgiving 38 degrees!*

UEFA CUP
First Round Second Leg

Tuesday 29th September 1992
Abbé-Deschamps Stadium, Auxerre

AJ AUXERRE 7   LOKOMOTIV PLOVDIV 1

Half-time 4-1 *Aggregate* 9-3 *Attendance* 7,000

		Goals				Goals
1	Bruno MARTINI		1	Vasil VASILEV		
2	Thierry BONALAIR		2	Mikhail YUMERSKI		
3	William PRUNIER	12, 48	3	Petar PASHEV		
4	Frank VERLAAT		4	Rumen DIMITROV		
5	Stéphane MAZZOLINI		5	Ivan GOVEDAROV		
6	Raphaël GUERREIRO		6	Valentin VALCHEV †		
7	Christophe COCARD	11	7	Lazar VACHKOV		
8	Daniel DUTUEL		8	Ayan SADAKOV		22
9	Gérald BATICLE ‡	2, 66	9	Simeon KRASTEV ‡		
10	Corentin MARTINS		10	Stoian KARAPETROV		
11	Pascal VAHIRUA †	26	11	Kostadin VIDOLOV		
	Substitutes			*Substitutes*		
	Didier OTOKORE †55			Dimitar CHOBANOV †62		
	Lilian LASLANDES ‡67	80		Dimitar KEKHAIOV ‡75		

Referee Keith BURGE (Wales)

● *Auxerre had not been beaten at home in any competition since January 1991 (0-1 by Paris Saint-Germain), a sequence lasting 31 matches, so the chances of Lokomotiv Plovdiv progressing to the second round were minimal. And after 12 minutes of play, the Bulgarians' hopes had been extinguished completely. That was all the time it took for Auxerre to race into a 3-0 lead with goals from Baticle, Cocard and Prunier, all of them created by accurate crosses from the flanks. The Lokomotiv defence simply could not come to terms with Auxerre's adventurous 4-3-3 formation, with Cocard and Vahirua on the wings and Dutuel and Martins spraying passes to them from midfield. Four further goals followed Sadakov's unexpected strike midway through the first half. It gave Auxerre their best ever result in European competition. One more goal and they would have equalled the record scoreline for a French club in Europe, set a year earlier by Monaco's 8-0 thrashing of Swansea City in the Cup-winners' Cup.*

Wednesday 16th September 1992
Republican Stadium, Kiev

DINAMO KIEV 1 SK RAPID WIEN 0

Half-time 0-0 *Attendance* 17,000

		Goals				Goals
1	Valdemaras MARTINKENAS			1	Michael KONSEL	
2	Oleg LUZHNY ‡			2	Martin PUZA	
3	Akhrik TSVEIBA			3	Franz RESCH	
4	Anatoly DEMYANENKO			4	Andreas POIGER	
5	Sergei SHMATOVALENKO			5	Peter SCHÖTTEL ❑	
6	Pavel SHKAPENKO			6	Franz BLIZENEC	
7	Pavel YAKOVENKO	46		7	Franz WEBER	
8	Igor PANKRATYEV			8	Aleksandr METLITSKY	
9	Andrey ANNENKOV			9	Sergei MANDREKO ❑	
10	Viktor LEONENKO			10	Gerhard RODAX	
11	Vitaly MINTENKO †			11	Jan Åge FJØRTOFT	

Substitutes

Sergei KOVALETS †46

Nikolai ZUYENKO ‡81

Substitutes

Referee Antonio MARTIN NAVARRETE (Spain)

SUMMARY

● *Of all the teams representing newly-formed states in the 1992/93 Cups, Dinamo Kiev, of the Ukraine, were undoubtedly the most experienced, and the most respected, opponents. They had won the Cup-winners' Cup twice (in 1975 and 1986) and had reached the 1991/92 Champions' Cup semi-final group phase despite the gradual cessation of most of their best players to the West. Rapid Vienna, meanwhile, owed their UEFA Cup place to the ban on Yugoslav clubs. It was their 32nd European campaign, but the famous Austrian club had done nothing of note since reaching the Cup-winners' Cup final in 1985. In fact, their former stature in European football had never quite been regained since Kiev thrashed them 9-2 on aggregate on their way to winning the Cup-winners' Cup a year later. Pavel Yakovenko had been on the scoresheet for Kiev in the 4-1 away-leg victory of that tie, and he was to be the match-winner this time around, scoring the only goal of a closely-fought game a minute into the second half.*

UEFA CUP
First Round Second Leg

Wednesday 30th September 1992
Hanappi Stadium, Vienna

SK RAPID WIEN 3 DINAMO KIEV 2

Half-time 3-1 *Aggregate* 3-3 (Dinamo Kiev win on away goals) *Attendance* 16,000

		Goals				Goals
1	Michael KONSEL			1	Valdemaras MARTINKENAS	
2	Martin PUZA			2	Andrey ALEKSANENKO ‡	
3	Franz RESCH ❑			3	Akhrik TSVEIBA	
4	Andreas POIGER			4	Anatoly DEMYANENKO	
5	Peter SCHÖTTEL			5	Sergei SHMATOVALENKO	
6	Franz BLIZENEC ❑			6	Sergei KOVALETS	
7	Franz WEBER			7	Pavel YAKOVENKO †	
8	Sergei MANDREKO †	8		8	Sergei ZAETS ❑	
9	Stanislav GRIGA			9	Andrey ANNENKOV ■	
10	Gerhard RODAX			10	Viktor LEONENKO	45(pen), 87
11	Jan Åge FJØRTOFT	15, 38		11	Pavel SHKAPENKO	

Substitute

Prvoslav JOVANOVIC †73

Substitutes

Igor PANKRATYEV †46

Sergei REBROV ‡55

Referee Piero CECCARINI (Italy)

SUMMARY

● *This was undoubtedly one of the most exciting confrontations of the round. Rapid Vienna looked to have the match, and the tie, sewn up when they raced into a 3-0 lead after 38 minutes. But a needlessly conceded penalty just before half-time gave Dinamo Kiev heart just when they were on the verge of throwing in the towel, and despite losing their midfielder Annenkov in the second half for taking a swipe at an opponent, the Ukrainians were ultimately to snatch qualification just three minutes from time when Viktor Leonenko, who had scored the penalty earlier, soared above a static defence to head home the decisive away goal. Rapid players collapsed on the turf in desolation. It had all looked so rosy an hour or so earlier, with Norwegian international Jan Åge Fjørtoft, Rapid's top scorer for the past three seasons, scoring twice to add to the eighth-minute goal provided by ex-CIS international Sergei Mandreko. But Leonenko's two goals had knocked Rapid out and maintained Kiev's 100 % qualification record (five out of five) against Austrian teams in European competition.*

Wednesday 16th September 1992
Central Stadium, Craiova

ELECTROPUTERE CRAIOVA 0 PANATHINAIKOS 6

Half-time 0-2 Attendance 22,000

		Goals				Goals
1	Silviu LUNG		1	Jozef WANDZIK		
2	Ion DUDAN ❑		2	Stratos APOSTOLAKIS		
3	Stefan NANU		3	Hristos KALATZIS ❑		85
4	Sorin MOGOSANU		4	Marinos OUZOUNIDIS		
5	Gheorghe BITA		5	Nikos KARAYEORYIOU		
6	Vintila POPESCU		6	Kostas MAVRIDIS		
7	Ionel LUTA ❑		7	Dimitris SARAVAKOS †		
8	Ionel IRIZA †		8	Kostas ANTONIOU ❑		7
9	Marian CALAFETEANU		9	Krzysztof WARZYCHA ‡ 38, 53, 66		
10	Alin Mircea PAPA ‡		10	Kostas FRANTZESKOS		
11	Dumitru MITRITA		11	Spiros MARAGOS		70

Substitutes
Adrian ILIE †33
Cristian ALBEANU †46

Substitutes
Dimitris MARKOU †75
Yorgos DONIS ‡75

Referee Zbigniew PRZESMYCKI (Poland)

SUMMARY

● *Electroputere Craiova had stunned Romanian football followers by qualifying for Europe just a year after gaining promotion to the First Division. But they got a shock of their own on this, their European debut, with the visit of Greek giants Panathinaikos. 22,000 locals made their way to Craiova's Central stadium (the home ground of local rivals Universitatea) to see how Electroputere would fare at a higher level, but it did not take long for them to realise that their team were hopelessly out of their depth. A goal down after just four minutes, the Romanians were eventually ripped apart, conceding five further goals and failing to score once themselves. Polish international striker Krzysztof Warzycha was the chief architect of their demise with his three goals in 28 minutes either side of the interval. The 6-0 result was particularly astonishing because Panathinaikos's away record in Europe had been nothing short of atrocious - just four wins from 45 matches played, and none of those victories achieved by more than a one-goal margin!*

UEFA CUP
First Round Second Leg

Wednesday 30th September 1992
OAKA Stadium, Athens

PANATHINAIKOS 4 ELECTROPUTERE CRAIOVA 0

Half-time 1-0 *Aggregate* 10-0 *Attendance* 8,000

		Goals				Goals
1	Jozef WANDZIK			1	Silviu LUNG	
2	Stratos APOSTOLAKIS			2	Sorin MOGOSANU ‡	
3	Hristos KALATZIS	67		3	Samir Ionel ZAMFIR	
4	Marinos OUZOUNIDIS			4	Mihai MATEI	
5	Nikos KARAYEORYIOU			5	Gheorghe BITA	
6	Kostas MAVRIDIS †			6	Vintila POPESCU	
7	Dimitris SARAVAKOS	43		7	Ionel LUTA ❑	
8	Kostas ANTONIOU ‡			8	Alin Mircea PAPA	
9	Krzysztof WARZYCHA	58		9	Daniel PARASCHIV	
10	Kostas FRANTZESKOS	82		10	Gabriel POPESCU †	
11	Spiros MARAGOS			11	Marian CALAFETEANU	

Substitutes

Yorgos DONIS †46

Dimitris MARKOU ‡65

Substitutes

Dumitru MITRITA †32

Cristian ALBEANU ‡68

Referee Alphonse COSTANTIN (Belgium)

SUMMARY

● After the first leg rout in Craiova there was little at stake for either team in this return encounter in Athens, and it was no surprise that Panathinaikos cruised home comfortably to another convincing victory to boost their aggregate victory margin to double figures. 10-0 was by far Panathinaikos's best ever result in 28 years of competing in Europe, and the best for any Greek side. It was also the most comprehensive win of the round not just in the UEFA Cup, but in all three competitions. The Greeks had to wait until just before half-time for their first goal, and it was provided by their star player and captain, Dimitris Saravakos. A habitual scorer in European competition, Saravakos now took his total to 20 goals in Europe, all of them scored for Panathinaikos, including six in the 1987/88 UEFA Cup when he was the competition's joint top scorer. Krzysztof Warzycha scored his fourth goal of the tie to put Panathinaikos 2-0 up, and further strikes from Kalatzis and Frantzeskos merely ensured that the tie would go down in the record books.

UEFA CUP
First Round First Leg

Wednesday 16th September 1992
Luz Stadium, Lisbon

SL BENFICA 3 BELVEDUR IZOLA 0

Half-time 2-0 *Attendance* 12,000

		Goals				Goals
1	SILVINO			1	Dragan TALAJIC ❏	
2	VELOSO			2	Davor PERKAT	
3	HÉLDER			3	Amir RUZNIC	
4	WILLIAM	44 (pen)		4	Suarez KRAJA	
5	FERNANDO MENDES			5	Peter TOSIC	
6	Stefan SCHWARZ			6	Damir BAN	
7	VÍTOR PANEIRA	42, 73		7	Slaven CUCEK	
8	JOÃO PINTO			8	Danijel GREGORIC ‡	
9	RUI ÁGUAS			9	Igor ZOBEC	
10	Sergei YURAN †			10	Mladen RUDONJA	
11	Vasily KULKOV			11	Marjan CENDAK †	

Substitute

PACHECO †60

Substitutes

Virginio VELKOVSKI †46

Aljosa COTAR ‡83

Referee Periklis VASSILAKIS (Greece)

● With this match Belvedur Izola became the first Slovenian team to compete in the UEFA Cup, but not, it should be mentioned, the first from their country to play a competitive European game in the Stadium of Light. Olimpija Ljubljana had been thrashed 8-1 there by Benfica in the first round of the 1970/71 Cup-winners' Cup whilst representing Yugoslavia. Most experts predicted a similar fate for Belvedur. But Benfica had made a stuttering start to their season under new Croatian coach Tomislav Ivic and it showed as they struggled to find a way through the Slovenians' packed defence. With half-time approaching, right-winger Vítor Paneira at last broke the deadlock when he started and finished a smart three-man move, and shortly afterwards a penalty from Brazilian defender William made it 2-0. But only one further goal followed after the interval, another well-constructed effort from Vítor Paneira, and that was not enough to silence the jeering and whistling from the unimpressed Benfica fans sparsely dotted around the cavernous stadium.

UEFA CUP
First Round Second Leg

Wednesday 30th September 1992
Ivan Marion Stadium, Izola

BELVEDUR IZOLA 0 SL BENFICA 5

Half-time 0-1 *Aggregate* 0-8 *Attendance* 4,000

		Goals				Goals
1	Dragan TALAJIC		1	SILVINO		
2	Davor PERKAT		2	SAMUEL		
3	Amir RUZNIC		3	HÉLDER		
4	Suarez KRAJA		4	PAULO MADEIRA		
5	Peter TOSIC		5	VELOSO		
6	Damir BAN		6	JOSÉ CARLOS		
7	Slaven CUCEK		7	VÍITOR PANEIRA ‡		
8	Danijel GREGORIC †		8	PACHECO	20, 46, 65	
9	Igor ZOBEC		9	JOÃO PINTO	57	
10	Mladen RUDONJA		10	ISAÍAS		
11	Virginio VELKOVSKI ‡		11	Stefan SCHWARZ †		
	Substitutes			*Substitutes*		
	Samo ZUPANC †63			Vasily KULKOV †59		
	Marjan CENDAK ‡75			CÉSAR BRITO ‡61	87	

Referee Jaap UILENBERG (Holland)

SUMMARY

● *If the Lisbon Eagles had only hovered above their prey in the first leg, then they swooped and devoured the easy meat of Belvedur Izola in this match. The Slovenians defended like the European novices they were, committing mistake after mistake to allow their illustrious opponents to score almost at will. Two Portuguese internationals, yet non-regulars in the Benfica line-up, Pacheco and César Brito, were the players who benefitted most from this generosity, with the former scoring his first European hat-trick and the latter completing the demolition after coming on as a substitute to take his all-time European goals total to a highly impressive seven in 12 games, only six of which saw him on from the start. Once Pacheco had lobbed Talajic from the edge of the area after 20 minutes, the contest, if ever there was one, had come to an end. It was simply a question of how many more goals Benfica could score in a second half which turned into a living nightmare for the naive Belvedur defence.*

Wednesday 16th September 1992
Tivoli Stadium, Innsbruck

FC WACKER INNSBRUCK 1 ROMA 4

Half-time 1-3 *Attendance* 11,000

		Goals			Goals
1	Milan ORAZE		1	Giovanni CERVONE	
2	Helmut LORENZ		2	Luigi GARZYA ‡	
3	Michael STREITER ▢		3	Amedeo CARBONI ▢	
4	Robert WAZINGER		4	Walter BONACINA	
5	Andrzej LESIAK		5	Silvano BENEDETTI	
6	Harald SCHNEIDER		6	ALDAIR dos Santos	
7	Manfred LINZMAIER †		7	Claudio CANIGGIA	20
8	Michael BAUR ‡	34	8	Fausto SALSANO	
9	Václav DANEK		9	Ruggiero RIZZITELLI †	
10	Roland KIRCHLER		10	Giuseppe GIANNINI	15, 41
11	Christoph WESTERTHALER		11	Giovanni PIACENTINI	
	Substitutes			*Substitutes*	
	Alfred HÖRTNAGL †54			Roberto MUZZI †64	70
	Jürgen HARTMANN ‡74			Antonio COMI ‡75	

Referee Manuel DIAZ VEGA (Spain)

● *When Wacker Innsbruck changed their name to FC Swarovski Tirol in 1986, they immediately embarked on their most successful season ever in European competition, reaching the semi-finals of the UEFA Cup. So there was a certain optimism within the club that having reverted back to their former name in 1992 they might enjoy a similar run in the same competition. The first-round draw, however, was not kind to the Austrians, pairing them with Roma, UEFA Cup runners-up two years earlier. And in Innsbruck it was the Roma captain and former Italian international Giuseppe Giannini who was to do most to scupper the Austrian club's ambitions. His brilliant individual performance was crowned with two exceptional goals, the first after only a quarter of an hour when he nipped in ahead of his marker to steer home from six yards and the second with a majestic left-foot strike from distance. It was Giannini's first 'double' on the international stage, and with Caniggia and Muzzi adding further strikes, Roma had the tie all but sewn up with half of it still to play.*

UEFA CUP
First Round Second Leg

Wednesday 30th September 1992
Olimpico Stadium, Rome

ROMA 1 FC WACKER INNSBRUCK 0

Half-time 0-0 *Aggregate* 5-1 *Attendance* 23,093

		Goals				Goals
1	Giovanni CERVONE			1	Milan ORAZE	
2	Luigi GARZYA			2	Kurt RUSS	
3	Sebastiano NELA †			3	Michael STREITER ❏	
4	Giovanni PIACENTINI			4	Robert WAZINGER	
5	ALDAIR dos Santos			5	Andrzej LESIAK	
6	Antonio COMI			6	Harald SCHNEIDER	
7	Claudio CANIGGIA ‡			7	Roland KIRCHLER	
8	Thomas HÄSSLER	51		8	Michael BAUR	
9	Andrea CARNEVALE			9	Václav DANEK	
10	Giuseppe GIANNINI			10	Mario BEEN †	
11	Fausto SALSANO			11	Christoph WESTERTHALER ‡	
	Substitutes				*Substitutes*	
	Walter BONACINA †46				Alfred HÖRTNAGL †73	
	Ruggiero RIZZITELLI ‡50				Helmut LORENZ ‡80	

Referee Leif SUNDELL (Sweden)

SUMMARY

● With a 1-4 deficit to make up from the first leg, Innsbruck's chances of qualifying for the second round were virtually non-existent. They knew it, and so did Roma, who in typical Italian tradition simply went through the motions, ensuring first and foremost that their visitors were not allowed any encouragement from an early goal and only upping the tempo after the interval when it was clear that nothing could possibly go wrong. There was little to cheer for the 23,000 crowd, but one redeeming feature of Roma's generally uninspired display was the return to action of their German international Thomas Hässler. He had not played a competitive game since his world-class performances at the European Championship finals. But proof that his injured knee was back in full working order came in the 51st minute when he scored the only goal of the game with a wonderful swerving free-kick reminiscent of the ones he had scored for his country in Sweden.

UEFA CUP
First Round First Leg

Wednesday 16th September 1992
Sigma Stadium, Olomouc

SIGMA OLOMOUC 1 UNIVERSITATEA CRAIOVA 0

Half-time 0-0   Attendance 6,129

		Goals			Goals
1	Lubos PRIBYL		1	Eugen VARGA	
2	Michal KOVAR		2	Victor COJOCARU ❑	
3	Jan MAROSI		3	Emil SANDOI †	
4	Martin KOTULEK		4	Gheorghe BARBU	
5	Jirí VADURA ❑		5	Ovidiu STINGA ❑	
6	Milos SLABY †		6	Nicolae ZAMFIR	
7	Roman PIVARNÍK ‡		7	Silvian CRISTESCU ❑ ‡	
8	Radoslav LÁTAL		8	Daniel Emil MOGOSANU ❑	
9	Milan KERBR		9	Ionel Tersinio GANE	
10	Jirí BARBORÍK		10	Daniel Horatiu CIOLOBOC	
11	Martin GUZÍK		11	Danut MOISESCU	

Substitutes			Substitutes	
Tomás CAPKA †55	87		Catalin GIRLESTEANU †4	
Roman HANUS ‡72			Gheorghe CRAIOVEANU ‡88	

Referee Kaj John NATRI (Finland)

● *This all-Eastern European confrontation looked to be one of the most intriguing of the round. Universitatea Craiova had the more impressive track record in Europe - 17 previous campaigns and a UEFA Cup semi-final place in 1982/83 - but Sigma Olomouc could boast the better recent record. While Craiova had been knocked out sensationally by Apollon Limassol in the first round of the 1991/92 Champions' Cup, Olomouc had surprised eveybody by going through to the quarter-finals of the UEFA Cup in only their second year of European competition, beating former Champions' Cup winners Hamburg home and away in the process. Since then Olomouc had lost star player Pavel Hapal to another German side, Bayer Leverkusen, but the team had begun the domestic season well again under coach Karel Brückner. They also put up a good performance in this game, but were denied their solitary, winning goal until three minutes from time. It was scored by 21-year-old substitute Tomás Capka on his first appearance of the season in the first team.*

UEFA CUP
First Round Second Leg

Wednesday 30th September 1992
Central Stadium, Craiova

UNIVERSITATEA CRAIOVA 1 SIGMA OLOMOUC 2

Half-time 1-2 *Aggregate* 1-3 *Attendance* 15,000

		Goals				Goals
1	Eugen VODA		1	Lubos PRIBYL		
2	Victor COJOCARU		2	Michal KOVAR		
3	Emil SANDOI ❏		3	Jan MAROSI		
4	Ovidiu STINGA ❏		4	Martin KOTULEK		
5	Daniel Emil MOGOSANU		5	Jirí VADURA ❏		
6	Nicolae ZAMFIR ■		6	Roman PIVARNÍK		
7	Silvian CRISTESCU ‡		7	Roman HANUS †		
8	Daniel Horatiu CIOLOBOC		8	Radoslav LÁTAL		
9	Ionel Tersinio GANE	21	9	Milan KERBR	23, 42	
10	Danut MOISESCU		10	Jirí BARBORÍK ❏		
11	Gheorghe CRAIOVEANU ❏ †		11	Ivo LOSTÁK ‡		
	Substitutes			*Substitutes*		
	Dumitru PREDOI †60			Radoslav SINDELAR †80		
	Catalin GIRLESTEANU ‡61			Jirí HOMOLA ‡89		

Referee Egil NERVIK (Norway)

● *Three times in the past Universitatea Craiova had needed to come back from 0-1 defeats in the away leg of a European tie and each time they had managed it, the last occasion being on penalties against Spanish club Real Betis in the 1984/85 UEFA Cup. But the club had been thrown into turmoil since the first leg with the mass sacking of the first team coaching staff, led by Sorin Cîrtu, the man who had taken Craiova to the 'double' in 1990/91. The Romanians made a decent enough start, with new signing from city rivals Electroputere, 20-year-old Ionel Tersinio Gane, giving them the lead in the 21st minute. But the joy created by that goal was tempered just two minutes later when Olomouc striker Milan Kerbr, a scorer of three goals for the club during their previous season's UEFA Cup run, equalised. By half-time Kerbr had scored again, and the Czech side were firmly in control. Craiova required three goals in the second period to take the tie. They didn't manage one, and thus joined both Electroputere Craiova and Politehnica Timisoara, the other two Romanian UEFA Cup entrants, on the first round casualty list.*

Wednesday 16th September 1992
GKS Stadium, Katowice

GKS KATOWICE 0 GALATASARAY 0

Half-time 0-0 *Attendance* 5,000

		Goals				Goals
1	Janusz JOJKO			1	HAYRETTIN Demirbas	
2	Krzysztof MACIEJEWSKI			2	BÜLENT Korkmaz	
3	Grzegorz BORAWSKI			3	MERT Korkmaz	
4	Roman SZEWCZYK			4	Reinhard STUMPF	
5	Dariusz GRZESIK			5	Falko GÖTZ	
6	Zaza REVISHVILI			6	YUSUF Altintas ❏ ‡	
7	Piotr SWIERCZEWSKI ❏			7	MUHAMMET Altintas ❏	
8	Adam LEDWON			8	Elvir BOLIC	
9	Adam KUCZ			9	HAKAN Sükür	
10	Marek SWIERCZEWSKI			10	UGUR Tütüneker †	
11	Zdzislaw STROJEK †			11	HAMZA Hamzaoglu	

Substitute

Dariusz WOLNY †63

Substitutes

OKAN Buruk †69

ISMAIL Demiriz ‡85

Referee Lucian Mircea SALOMIR (Romania)

● This was GKS Katowice's seventh European campaign on the trot, but the Polish club had still never managed to progress beyond the second round. Conversely, Galatasaray had achieved some tremendous results in Europe in recent seasons. They established a Turkish record in 1988/89 by reaching the semi-finals of the Champions' Cup, and in 1991/92 they made it to the quarter-finals of the Cup-winners' Cup before putting up a brave fight against eventual winners Werder Bremen. In fact, it was primarily the performances of Galatasaray that had enabled the Turkish UEFA co-efficient to rise to such an extent that the country now had two UEFA Cup representatives for the first time since 1979/80. And having finished third in the 1991/92 Turkish championship, Galatasaray, suitably, were the first bene-ficiaries! Galatasaray's chances of making further waves in Europe increased after this dull goalless draw in Silesia. New German coach Karl-Heinz Feldkamp won the tactical battle with his Polish coun-terpart, Adolf Blutsch, and Galatasaray went away pretty much with what they had come for.

UEFA CUP
First Round Second Leg

Tuesday 29th September 1992
Ali Sami Yen Stadium, Istanbul

GALATASARAY 2 GKS KATOWICE 1

Half-time 1-0 *Aggregate* 2-1 *Attendance* 25,000

		Goals				Goals
1	HAYRETTIN Demirbas		1	Janusz JOJKO	
2	Reinhard STUMPF		2	Krzysztof MACIEJEWSKI	73
3	HAMZA Hamzaoglu ❑		3	Grzegorz BORAWSKI	
4	BÜLENT Korkmaz ❑		4	Roman SZEWCZYK ■	
5	Falko GÖTZ	55 (pen)	5	Dariusz GRZESIK	
6	OKAN Buruk		6	Zaza REVISHVILI	
7	UGUR Tütüneker †		7	Piotr SWIERCZEWSKI ■	
8	MUHAMMET Altintas		8	Adam LEDWON ■	
9	HAKAN Sükür ❑ ‡	30	9	Adam KUCZ	
10	TUGAY Kerimoglu		10	Marek SWIERCZEWSKI ❑	
11	ERDAL Keser ❑		11	Zdzislaw STROJEK †	

	Substitutes			*Substitute*	
	MERT Korkmaz †46			Dariusz WOLNY †46	
	Elvir BOLIC ‡88				

Referee Roger GIFFORD (Wales)

● *With this victory Galatasaray became the first of the four Turkish clubs in Europe to make it through to the second round - the other three were in action the following day. The Istanbul side knew they had to score to qualify, but just as importantly they could not afford to concede a goal. Away goals had been Katowice's route to success the previous season in the first round of the Cup-winners' Cup against Motherwell. But, fortunately for the Turks, by the time Maciejewski did score for the Poles, Galatasaray had already established a two-goal cushion. Hakan Sükür, Turkish football's promising new international centre-forward, scored the first, and he was followed onto the scoresheet in the second half by German sweeper Falko Götz, a man with particularly fond memories of this competition. He had gained a UEFA Cup winner's medal with Bayer Leverkusen in 1987/88 and was the competition's joint top scorer, along with fellow German Karl-Heinz Riedle, whilst playing for Cologne two years later. Now his penalty ultimately proved decisive in taking Galatasaray into round two.*

UEFA CUP
First Round First Leg

Tuesday 15th September 1992
National Stadium, Ta' Qali

FLORIANA 0 BORUSSIA DORTMUND 1

Half-time 0-1 *Attendance* 5,000

		Goals
1	David CLUETT	
2	James BRISCOE †	
3	David GALEA	
4	Jesmond DELIA	
5	Pierre BRINCAT	
6	John BUTTIGIEG	
7	Albert BUSUTTIL ‡	
8	Dennis CAUCHI	
9	Mark MILLER	
10	Brian CRAWLEY	
11	Kim WRIGHT	

Substitutes

Mario CARUANA †76
Mark MARLOW ‡86

		Goals
1	Stefan KLOS	
2	Knut REINHARDT	
3	Günter KUTOWSKI	
4	Bodo SCHMIDT	
5	Stefan REUTER	
6	Steffen KARL	
7	Thomas FRANCK ❏	
8	Michael ZORC	
9	Stéphane CHAPUISAT ‡	
10	Michael RUMMENIGGE	21
11	Flemming POVLSEN †	

Substitutes

Lothar SIPPEL †46
René TRETSCHOK ‡74

Referee Andreas GEORGIOU (Cyprus)

> ● *1991/92 German Bundesliga runners-up Borussia Dortmund could hardly have wished for a more appropriate first-round opponent as they embarked on their 11th European campaign with their sights very firmly set on winning the UEFA Cup. Not only did Floriana represent a comfortable passage into the second round. The Maltese side had also been their opening opponents the year they won their only previous European trophy. 13-1 was the aggregate score back in the 1965/66 season when Dortmund went on to capture the Cup-winners' Cup. In all the years since then Floriana had still never passed the first round in European competition, but they had shown an improvement in their last two European home games, holding Dundee United and Neuchâtel Xamax to goalless draws. Just one goal, scored for Dortmund by Michael Rummenigge after 21 minutes of a dull, uninspiring match, prevented the record champions of Malta from making it three in a row.*

UEFA CUP
First Round Second Leg

Tuesday 29th September 1992
Westfalen Stadium, Dortmund

BORUSSIA DORTMUND 7 FLORIANA 2

Half-time 2-2 Aggregate 8-2 Attendance 11,790

		Goals				Goals
1	Stefan KLOS		1	David CLUETT		
2	Knut REINHARDT ‡		2	James BRISCOE †		
3	Günter KUTOWSKI		3	David GALEA		
4	Ned ZELIC †		4	Jesmond DELIA	19 (og)	
5	Stefan REUTER		5	Pierre BRINCAT		
6	Thomas FRANCK	58	6	John BUTTIGIEG ❏		
7	Michael LUSCH		7	Albert BUSUTTIL ‡		
8	Michael ZORC	8	8	Dennis CAUCHI		
9	Frank MILL	72, 80, 90	9	Mark MILLER		
10	Michael RUMMENIGGE	66	10	Brian CRAWLEY	11, 18	
11	Flemming POVLSEN		11	Kim WRIGHT		

Substitutes

Gerhard POSCHNER †46

René TRETSCHOK ‡78

Substitutes

Mark MARLOW †69

Oscar MAGRI ‡72

Referee Denis McARDLE (Republic of Ireland)

SUMMARY

● 11,790 was a very small crowd by Borussia Dortmund's standards. But much of it had to do with the disappointment of events at the Westfalen Stadium four days earlier when Bundesliga leaders Bayern Munich had defeated the home side 2-1 before a full house in a dramatic top-of-the-table clash. Floriana were there to feel the backlash, but it was not until the second half that the home side's obvious superiority was reflected on the scoreboard. In fact, Floriana gave the Germans a horrible fright early on, going 2-1 up with two goals in seven minutes from their newly-signed Irish striker Brian Crawley before an own-goal quickly levelled the scores again. Ottmar Hitzfeld's half-time team-talk clearly had its effect on the Dortmund players and they destroyed their opponents with five goals in the second period. Veteran striker Frank Mill scored the last three to register his first hat-trick in Europe. The 7-2 final scoreline was Dortmund's second biggest European win, bettered only by their 8-0 success at home to the very same Floriana 27 years earlier!

UEFA CUP
First Round First Leg

Wednesday 16th September 1992
Politehnica Stadium, Timisoara

POLITEHNICA TIMISOARA 1 REAL MADRID 1

Half-time 0-1 *Attendance* 26,000

		Goals				Goals
1	Petrisor TOMA		1	Francisco BUYO		
2	Constantin VARGA ❑		2	RICARDO ROCHA		
3	Tiberiu CSIK		3	Mikel LASA ‡		
4	Adrian STOICOV		4	Miguel TENDILLO		
5	Ion ROSU ❑ ‡		5	Manuel SANCHIS		
6	Petru ANDREAS ❑		6	José TORIL		
7	Cristian CHINA		7	ALFONSO Pérez ❑		15
8	Adrian CRACIUN		8	Miguel González "MICHEL" †		
9	Ioan ULESAN		9	Iván ZAMORANO		
10	Octavian POPESCU		10	Luis MILLA		
11	Calin ROSENBLUM †		11	LUIS ENRIQUE Martínez		

Substitutes

Ovidiu CUC †46   61

Florin BATRINU ‡60

Substitutes

Francisco José Pérez VILLARROYA †46

Santiago ARAGON ‡75

Referee Ryszard WÓJCIK (Poland)

SUMMARY

● *Prior to this encounter no visiting team had ever managed to score an away goal against Politehnica Timisoara in European competition. Seven well respected teams had come and gone - MTK-VM, Honvéd, Celtic, West Ham, Lokomotive Leipzig, Atlético Madrid and Sporting Lisbon - and, remarkably, not one of them had found the net. But that record was to be broken after just 15 minutes when the Politehnica goalkeeper misjudged the flight of Míchel's high cross and 19-year-old Olympic Games star Alfonso Pérez headed into the empty net. That should have been the signal for Real, on their record-extending 37th European campaign, to go on and dominate the match. But the club from the 'revolution city' still had their unbeaten home record to defend, and after testing the Real defence on a number of occasions they finally made the breakthrough, to the delight of the big crowd, with a well-struck shot from another teenage striker, Ovidiu Cuc, after 61 minutes. The 1-1 final scoreline evidently suited both parties, Real in terms of qualification and Politehnica in terms of prestige.*

Tuesday 29th September 1992
Bernabéu Stadium, Madrid

REAL MADRID 4 POLITEHNICA TIMISOARA 0

Half-time 1-0 *Aggregate* 5-1 *Attendance* 40,000

		Goals			Goals
1	Pedro JARO		1	Petrisor TOMA	
2	RICARDO ROCHA		2	Constantin VARGA	
3	Francisco José Pérez VILLARROYA		3	Tiberiu CSIK	
4	Fernando Muñoz "NANDO"		4	Adrian STOICOV	
5	Manuel SANCHIS		5	Ion ROSU	
6	Fernando HIERRO ❏		6	Petru ANDREAS †	
7	Emilio BUTRAGUEÑO †		7	Emilian DIACONESCU ❏	
8	Miguel González "MICHEL"87		8	Adrian CRACIUN	
9	ALFONSO Pérez	28	9	Ovidiu CUC	
10	Luis MILLA ‡		10	Octavian POPESCU ‡	
11	José TORIL		11	Cristian CHINA	

Substitutes

Juan ESNAIDER †56	65	Florin MACAVEI †46	
LUIS ENRIQUE Martínez ‡56	57	Ioan ULESAN ‡63	

Referee Martin BODENHAM (England)

● *Politehnica Timisoara had performed admirably in the first leg, but they came to Madrid with little hope of causing a sensation and knocking Real Madrid out of the competition. Whilst the Romanians remained invincible at home in Europe, their record away from home was quite the opposite. They had played seven matches and lost the lot, the last occasion being a 7-0 thrashing by Sporting Lisbon two years earlier. Real welcomed their goalscoring midfielder Hierro back from suspension, but they were still without several first-choice stars, such as Zamorano, Prosinecki and Lasa. It was the man wearing Zamorano's number nine shirt, Alfonso, who repeated his feat of the first leg by opening the scoring for Real with an exquisitely placed diving header from Míchel's pass after 28 minutes. Three more goals followed after the break, with substitutes Luis Enrique and Esnaider both netting their first in European competition before Míchel, with a typically ferocious left-foot drive from the edge of the area, completed the scoring three minutes from time.*

UEFA CUP
First Round First Leg

Wednesday 16th September 1992
Fenerbahçe Stadium, Istanbul

FENERBAHÇE 3 BOTEV PLOVDIV 1

Half-time 2-0 Attendance 12,382

		Goals				Goals
1	ENGIN Ipekoglu			1	Georgi ANDONOV	
2	MÜJDAT Yetkiner			2	Trenko DUDOV	
3	SEMIH Yuvakuran			3	Georgi BORISOV	
4	Dzoni NOVAK			4	Ivan KOCHEV	
5	NURI Kamburoglu			5	Zaprian RAKOV	
6	OGUZ Çetin			6	Yasen PETROV ‡	
7	Candido GÉRSON			7	Krasimir DIMITROV	
8	RIDVAN Dilmen ‡			8	Todor ZAITSEV ❑	
9	Stanimir STOILOV †			9	Krasimir IVANOV	
10	TANJU Çolak	54 (pen)		10	Zvetozar DERMENDZHIEV	51
11	AYKUT Kocaman	14, 38		11	Stoian TOMOV †	

Substitutes

ILKER Yacioglu †75

ISMAIL Kartal ‡78

Substitutes

Bozhidar ISKRENOV †76

Anton SIVINOV ‡89

Referee Wieland ZILLER (Germany)

SUMMARY

● No fewer than eight European cities had two teams on view in the 1992/93 UEFA Cup, and Istanbul and Plovdiv were two of them, the others being Copenhagen, Turin, Lisbon, Moscow, Craiova and Edinburgh. The team lined up in Istanbul was virtually unrecognisable from that of the previous season, with only four players remaining. Fenerbahçe, runners-up in Turkey ahead of city rivals Galatasaray the previous season, also presented some new faces, notably their new foreign signings Novak and Stoilov, but their main strength lay as ever in their three-pronged international strike force of Ridvan, Tanju and Aykut. The latter two had scored 49 league goals between them in 1991/92 and they were to share Fenerbahçe's three goals this time as well, with Aykut scoring twice in the first half and Tanju hitting his first in Europe for four seasons in the second. Botev's only reply came from one of their newcomers, Zvetozar Dermendzhiev. It was his third UEFA Cup goal in successive seasons. He had previously scored for his former club Slavia Sofia against Omonia Nicosia in 1990/91 and Osasuna in 1991/92.

UEFA CUP
First Round Second Leg

Wednesday 30th September 1992
Botev Stadium, Plovdiv

BOTEV PLOVDIV 2 FENERBAHÇE 2

Half-time 2-1 *Aggregate* 3-5 *Attendance* 8,000

		Goals				Goals
1	Georgi ANDONOV		1	ENGIN Ipekoglu		
2	Trenko DUDOV		2	ISMAIL Kartal		
3	Georgi BORISOV ‡		3	SEMIH Yuvakuran		
4	Ivan KOCHEV †		4	Dzoni NOVAK †		
5	Zaprian RAKOV ❏		5	MÜJDAT Yetkiner		
6	Yasen PETROV ❏	41	6	NURI Kamburoglu ❏		
7	Georgi CHAKAROV		7	HAKAN Tecimer ■		
8	Todor ZAITSEV		8	RIDVAN Dilmen	36, 77	
9	Bozhidar ISKRENOV	5	9	Stanimir STOILOV		
10	Zvetozar DERMENDZHIEV		10	Candido GÉRSON		
11	Stoian TOMOV		11	AYKUT Kocaman		
	Substitutes			*Substitute*		
	Krasimir DIMITROV †75			ILKER Yacioglu †78		
	Rumen CHAKAROV ‡80					

Referee Michal LISTKIEWICZ (Poland)

SUMMARY

● There was excitement aplenty in Plovdiv as Botev sought to restore the city's pride after Lokomotiv's 7-1 thrashing at the hands of Auxerre the previous night. They got off to a magnificent start in their quest to haul back the first-leg 1-3 deficit when Bulgarian international winger Bozhidar Iskrenov, a member of his country's 1986 World Cup squad, put Botev in front after just five minutes. Another goal and the home side would be ahead on away goals. But they were ultimately to be foiled by two particular individuals on the opposing side. Goalkeeper Engin Ipekoglu was in brilliant form for the Turks, producing several spectacular saves, including one from the penalty spot, to keep his side in the game. And Ridvan Dilmen, Fenerbahçe's highly skilful but injury-prone forward, had one of his all too rare glory days, scoring two breakaway goals, his first in European competition, to steal the home side's thunder and put Fenerbahçe into the next round alongside Istanbul rivals Galatasaray. It was the first time that two Turkish clubs had reached the second round of the UEFA Cup in the same season.

Wednesday 16th September 1992
Hardturm Stadium, Zürich

GRASSHOPPER-CLUB ZÜRICH 1 SPORTING CP 2

Half-time 1-1 *Attendance* 15,000

		Goals				Goals
1	Pascal ZUBERBÜHLER		1	SÉRGIO		
2	Ramon VEGA		2	MARINHO ❏		
3	Ciriaco SFORZA		3	LEAL		
4	Heinz HERMANN ❏		4	BARNY		
5	Sigurdur GRÉTARSSON ❏		5	Stan VALCKX		
6	Harald GÄMPERLE		6	PEIXE		
7	Joël MAGNIN ❏ †		7	FIGO		
8	Adrian DE VICENTE ❏ ‡		8	FILIPE ❏		
9	ELBER de Souza Giovane		9	Andrzej JUSKOWIAK ‡	83	
10	Thomas BICKEL		10	Krasimir BALAKOV	44	
11	Alain SUTTER ❏	36 (pen)	11	CADETE †		

Substitutes

Mario CANTALUPPI †83

Murat YAKIN ‡85

Substitutes

AMARAL †74

CAPUCHO ‡89

Referee Philippe LEDUC (France)

SUMMARY

● *This confrontation looked intriguing enough when the draw was originally made in Geneva. Now, with Dutch coach Leo Beenhakker having moved to Grasshoppers from Real Madrid, it had added spice, for Beenhakker and his counterpart at Sporting, Englishman Bobby Robson, were old adversaries. The two had been in charge, respectively, of Holland and England at the 1990 World Cup finals and they had frequently been in opposing corners as the coaches of Ajax and PSV in the Dutch Premier Division. Both men were new to their clubs, but while Beenhakker was still unbeaten since his arrival, Robson had got off to a very poor start in the Portuguese League with only one victory in his first four matches. A penalty from Alain Sutter after 36 minutes looked to have aggravated the Englishman's predicament, but, backed by huge Portuguese support, Sporting replied soon after with a superb header by Bulgarian Krasimir Balakov from Leal's left-wing cross. And it was the Bulgarian again who produced an outstanding dribble to create Sporting's winner, scored by Olympic Games sensation Andrzej Juskowiak, with just seven minutes to go.*

UEFA CUP
First Round Second Leg

Wednesday 30th September 1992
José Alvalade Stadium, Lisbon

SPORTING CP 1 GRASSHOPPER-CLUB ZÜRICH 3 (aet)

Half-time 0-1 *Aggregate* 3-4 *Attendance* 40,000

		Goals				Goals
1	SÉRGIO ❑			1	Pascal ZUBERBÜHLER	
2	MARINHO			2	Ramon VEGA	
3	LEAL			3	Ciriaco SFORZA	
4	BARNY ❑			4	Murat YAKIN ‡	
5	Stan VALCKX			5	Harald GÄMPERLE	
6	PEIXE			6	Urs MEIER †	
7	FIGO ❑ ‡			7	Peter KÖZLE	
8	FILIPE			8	Adrian DE VICENTE	
9	Andrzej JUSKOWIAK †			9	ELBER de Souza Giovane	31, 110
10	Krasimir BALAKOV			10	Thomas BICKEL ❑	
11	CADETE	84		11	Alain SUTTER	
	Substitutes				*Substitutes*	
	AMARAL †68 ❑				Joël MAGNIN †81	84
	CAPUCHO ‡106				Mario CANTALUPPI ‡91 ❑	

Referee Helmut KRUG (Germany)

SUMMARY

● *In winning this match 3-1 after extra-time Grasshoppers became only the third club in European Cup history to come back successfully from a 1-2 home defeat in the first leg. Thanks to a magnificent performance in front of 40,000 hostile Portuguese fans, the Swiss record champions produced the shock of the round to move into the last 32. It was a bitter pill to swallow for Sporting and it raised questions about Bobby Robson's position as coach after barely a month in the job. It was the Englishman's third European failure in three years since his return to club management. Chief executioner for Grasshoppers was their Brazilian centre-forward Elber. He opened the scoring with a brilliant long-range header from Sutter's free-kick in the first half and after further goals for each side had taken the tie into extra-time, it was he again who settled the outcome with a brilliant strike ten minutes from the end. Controlling a through-ball with one touch of his left foot, he then blasted an unstoppable right-footer high into the net for one of the most spectacular, and significant, goals of the round.*

UEFA CUP
First Round Review

FIRST ROUND RESULTS

		1st leg	2nd leg	Agg.
Hibernian	RSC Anderlecht	2-2	1-1	3-3
(RSC Anderlecht win on away goals)				
Valencia CF	Napoli	1-5	0-1	1-6
Vitesse	Derry City	3-0	2-1	5-1
Neuchâtel Xamax FC	BK Frem	2-2	1-4	3-6
SV Casino Salzburg	Ajax	0-3	1-3	1-6
Vitória Guimarães	Real Sociedad	3-0	0-2	3-2
Sheffield Wednesday	Spora Luxembourg	8-1	2-1	10-2
Paris Saint-Germain FC	PAOK	2-0	3-0*	5-0
KV Mechelen	Örebro SK	2-1	0-0	2-1
SM Caen	Real Zaragoza	3-2	0-2	3-4
Vác FC Samsung	FC Groningen	1-0	1-1	2-1
Fram	1.FC Kaiserslautern	0-3	0-4	0-7
Manchester United	Torpedo Moskva	0-0	0-0aet	0-0
(Torpedo Moskva win 4-3 on penalties)				
1.FC Köln	Celtic	2-0	0-3	2-3
R Standard Liège	Portadown	5-0	0-0	5-0
FC København	MP	5-0	5-1	10-1
Widzew Lódz	Eintracht Frankfurt	2-2	0-9	2-11
IFK Norrköping	Torino	1-0	0-3	1-3
Slavia Praha	Heart of Midlothian	1-0	2-4	3-4
Dinamo Moskva	Rosenborg BK	5-1	0-2	5-3
Juventus	Anorthosis Famagusta	6-1	4-0	10-1
Lokomotiv Plovdiv	AJ Auxerre	2-2	1-7	3-9
Dinamo Kiev	SK Rapid Wien	1-0	2-3	3-3
(Dinamo Kiev win on away goals)				
Electroputere Craiova	Panathinaikos	0-6	0-4	0-10
SL Benfica	Belvedur Izola	3-0	5-0	8-0
FC Wacker Innsbruck	Roma	1-4	0-1	1-5
Sigma Olomouc	Universitatea Craiova	1-0	2-1	3-1
GKS Katowice	Galatasaray	0-0	1-2	1-2
Floriana	Borussia Dortmund	0-1	2-7	2-8
Politehnica Timisoara	Real Madrid	1-1	0-4	1-5
Fenerbahçe	Botev Plovdiv	3-1	2-2	5-3
Grasshopper-Club Zürich	Sporting CP	1-2	3-1aet	4-3

* UEFA decison. Match abandoned at half-time with Paris Saint-Germain FC leading 2-0.

UEFA CUP

UEFA CUP
Second Round First Leg

Wednesday 21st October 1992
Municipal Stadium, Guimarães

VITÓRIA GUIMARÃES 0 AJAX 3

Half-time 0-2 Attendance 8,000

Goals | | Goals

1	MADUREIRA		1	Edwin VAN DER SAR	
2	QUIM MACHADO		2	Rob ALFLEN	
3	Herichi TAOUFIK ❑		3	Danny BLIND	
4	TANTA		4	Wim JONK	
5	DIMAS †		5	Frank DE BOER	
6	PAULO BENTO		6	Marciano VINK	
7	PAULO JORGE ‡		7	Marc OVERMARS	
8	PEDRO BARBOSA		8	Michel KREEK	
9	ZIAD Tlemcani		9	Stefan PETTERSSON †	37
10	Dane KUPRESANIN		10	Dennis BERGKAMP ❑	48
11	LIMA		11	Edgar DAVIDS	1

Substitutes

JOÃO PINTO †46

PEDRO OLIVEIRA ‡68 ❑

Substitute

John VAN LOEN †46

Referee Václav KRONDL (Czechoslovakia)

SUMMARY

● 3-0 winners away from home against Salzburg in the first round, Ajax repeated the feat against Vitória Guimarães to extend their unbeaten run in the UEFA Cup to 15 matches. As in Austria, it was young left winger Edgar Davids who opened the scoring for the holders. Less than 60 seconds were on the clock when he raced onto Wim Jonk's clever through-ball and clipped the ball over the onrushing goalkeeper. It was a dream start for Ajax and from that moment on they looked the more assured of the two sides. Stand-in goalkeeper Edwin van der Sar had very little to do as the Portuguese found great difficulty in coming to terms with the Dutch team's tactical disposition. It was at the other end where most of the action took place. Swedish striker Stefan Pettersson had already had a goal dubiously disallowed before he increased Ajax's lead towards the end of the first half, finishing off a sweet three-man move with Bergkamp and Overmars. And it was Bergkamp himself who killed the tie stone dead with a marvellously executed third goal three minutes after the interval.

UEFA CUP
Second Round Second Leg

Wednesday 4th November 1992
Olympisch Stadium, Amsterdam

AJAX 2 VITÓRIA GUIMARÃES 1

Half-time 1-0 *Aggregate* 5-1 *Attendance* 25,000

		Goals				Goals
1	Edwin VAN DER SAR		1	JESUS		
2	Rob ALFLEN	60	2	BASÍLIO		
3	Danny BLIND		3	MATIAS		
4	Wim JONK		4	TANTA		
5	Frank DE BOER ‡		5	DIMAS ‡		
6	Marciano VINK †		6	GERMANO		
7	Marc OVERMARS		7	N'DINGA Mbote	57	
8	Michel KREEK		8	QUIM MACHADO		
9	Stefan PETTERSSON		9	ARTUR JORGE		
10	Dennis BERGKAMP	25	10	BASAULA Lemba †		
11	Edgar DAVIDS		11	PAULO JORGE		

Substitutes

Clarence SEEDORF †63

John VAN LOEN ‡78

Substitutes

JOÃO PINTO †53

LIMA ‡55

Referee Ilkka KOHO (Finland)

SUMMARY

● *On a night when Dutch rivals PSV and Feyenoord were both fighting for their European lives, Ajax, after their comfortable 3-0 victory in Portugal, were able to enjoy a relatively carefree 90 minutes in the Olympic stadium. Not that coach Louis van Gaal was taking any chances. Despite the fact that big league matches against MVV and Feyenoord were looming in the next few days, he decided to field the same first-choice eleven which had been victorious a fortnight earlier. Dennis Bergkamp's first-half free-kick goal was his tenth in European competition and it proved to be the highlight of a fairly low-key, passionless evening. Guimarães did have the satisfaction of piercing the Ajax defence on one occasion - a deflected shot from Zaire international N'Dinga - but the holders' 100% record so far in the competition was maintained when Rob Alflen headed in a Davids cross three minutes later. After the match Ajax discovered that with Barcelona, Werder Bremen, Monaco and Torino all going out of their respective competitions, they were the only European finalist from the previous season to survive the second round!*

Wednesday 21st October 1992
San Paolo Stadium, Naples

NAPOLI 0 PARIS SAINT-GERMAIN FC 2

Half-time 0-2 Attendance 35,378

Goals

Goals

1	Giovanni GALLI		1	Bernard LAMA ❑	
2	Ciro FERRARA		2	Jean-Luc SASSUS	
3	Massimo CRIPPA		3	Patrick COLLETER	
4	Fausto PARI ❑		4	RICARDO Gomes	
5	Giovanni FRANCINI		5	Alain ROCHE	
6	Giancarlo CORRADINI †		6	Paul LE GUEN	
7	Massimo MAURO		7	Laurent FOURNIER	
8	Jonas THERN		8	Vincent GUERIN ❑	
9	Antonio CARECA		9	George WEAH †	16, 35
10	Gianfranco ZOLA		10	VALDO Candido	
11	Daniel FONSECA		11	David GINOLA ‡	

Substitute

Roberto POLICANO †82 ❑

Substitutes

François CALDERARO †80

Daniel BRAVO ‡87

Referee Karl-Josef ASSENMACHER

SUMMARY

● Napoli's first-round demolition of Valencia looked increasingly to have been a flash in the pan as the Italian team's woeful start to the season plumbed new depths with this comprehensive home defeat. Napoli coach Claudio Ranieri, who was living on borrowed time in any case after his team had picked up just four points from six Serie A matches, found himself outwitted tactically by PSG's Portuguese coach Artur Jorge. The French team played with great discipline, stifling Napoli's much-lauded triumvirate of Careca, Zola and Fonseca and showing that, in Ginola, Valdo and Weah, they had exceptional attacking strengths of their own. Weah, the big Liberian centre-forward, was the undisputed man of the match. He took the field while still suffering from the after-effects of a flu bug, but nobody would have guessed it as he pounced twice in the first half, first with a volley from a Valdo free-kick, then with a header from a Ginola corner, to puncture Napoli's defence and, as PSG 's ambitious chief executive Michel Denisot put it, "write a new page in the history of the club".

Wednesday 4th November 1992
Parc des Princes, Paris

PARIS SAINT-GERMAIN FC 0 NAPOLI 0

Half-time 0-0 *Aggregate* 2-0 *Attendance* 43,605

		Goals			Goals
1	Bernard LAMA		1	Giovanni GALLI	
2	Jean-Luc SASSUS		2	Ciro FERRARA ❏	
3	Patrick COLLETER		3	Giovanni FRANCINI	
4	RICARDO Gomes		4	Giancarlo CORRADINI ❏	
5	Alain ROCHE ❏		5	Massimo TARANTINO ❏	
6	Paul LE GUEN		6	Fausto PARI	
7	Laurent FOURNIER		7	Angelo CARBONE ❏ †	
8	Vincent GUERIN		8	Jonas THERN	
9	George WEAH †		9	Massimo MAURO	
10	VALDO Candido		10	Gianfranco ZOLA ‡	
11	David GINOLA ‡		11	Daniel FONSECA	

Substitutes	*Substitutes*
François CALDERARO †88	Antonio CARECA †60
Daniel BRAVO ‡89	Massimo CRIPPA ‡77

Referee Joe WORRALL (England)

SUMMARY

● *Paris Saint-Germain's magnificent performance in the first leg ensured that the Parc des Princes was a virtual sell-out for the visit of the 1988/89 UEFA Cup winners. Unfortunately, though, the big crowd were to be denied the on-field excitement which befitted the occasion. The fact was that the tie had been won in Naples. True to his reputation, Artur Jorge instructed his players to secure qualification at all costs, not to take any risks or indulge in any unnecessary crowd-pleasing antics. As captain Paul le Guen said afterwards: "The objective was to qualify. Just to qualify." That meant an evening of few chances and precious little entertainment, but if PSG's approach was understandable, the same could not be said for that of the visitors. Coach Ranieri made the extraordinary decision to leave Careca on the bench and play with just Fonseca up front - this with his team needing at least two goals to qualify! Pragmatism was the order of the day. It put Paris-Saint-Germain into round three, but it meant the end for Napoli and, a week later, for their embattled coach.*

Tuesday 20th October 1992
Fritz Walter Stadium, Kaiserslautern

1.FC KAISERSLAUTERN 3 SHEFFIELD WEDNESDAY 1

Half-time 1-1 *Attendance* 20,802

		Goals				Goals
1	Gerald EHRMANN		1	Chris WOODS		
2	Bjarne GOLDBAEK		2	John HARKES		
3	Martin WAGNER		3	Nigel WORTHINGTON		
4	Thomas RITTER		4	Carlton PALMER		
5	Miroslav KADLEC		5	Nigel PEARSON ❏		
6	Wolfgang FUNKEL	6 (pen)	6	Viv ANDERSON		
7	Demir HOTIC		7	Danny WILSON		
8	Marco HABER		8	Chris WADDLE		
9	Marcel WITECZEK ❏	53	9	David HIRST ■		5
10	Oliver SCHÄFER		10	Paul WARHURST ‡		
11	Marcus MARIN †	51	11	Graham HYDE †		
	Substitute			*Substitutes*		
	Thomas VOGEL †61			Chris BART-WILLIAMS †60		
				Gordon WATSON ‡80		

Referee Joël QUINIOU (France)

SUMMARY

● *A disgraceful piece of play-acting by Kaiserslautern midfielder Marco Haber and a highly suspect performance by experienced French referee Joël Quiniou combined to give the home side the upper hand after the first leg of this attractive-looking second round tie. Sheffield Wednesday had a luckless night in all respects. It all started so brightly for them when David Hirst scored a beautiful diving header from after just five minutes. But just seconds later Kaiserslautern were harshly awarded a penalty after Anderson's poorly timed tackle on Witeczek. Funkel converted from the spot and the match was all-square again. The second controversial incident occurred at the end of the first half. Hirst certainly tapped Haber's ankle, but the German reacted almost as if his life was in danger from it. Alas, the referee was duped and Hirst was sent off. The second half, like the first, was evenly contested, but the Germans scored twice early on through strikers Marin and Witeczek and with Hirst off the field, Wednesday did not have the strength in numbers up front to convert any of their numerous chances and force their way back into the game.*

Wednesday 4th November 1992
Hillsborough, Sheffield

SHEFFIELD WEDNESDAY 2 1.FC KAISERSLAUTERN 2

Half-time 1-0 *Aggregate* 3-5 *Attendance* 27,597

		Goals			Goals
1	Chris WOODS		1	Michael SERR	
2	John HARKES †		2	Bjarne GOLDBAEK ❏	
3	Nigel WORTHINGTON		3	Thomas RICHTER	
4	Carlton PALMER		4	Thomas RITTER	
5	Nigel PEARSON ‡		5	Miroslav KADLEC	
6	Viv ANDERSON ❏		6	Thomas DOOLEY	
7	Danny WILSON	27	7	Demir HOTIC †	
8	Chris WADDLE		8	Marco HABER	
9	Gordon WATSON		9	Marcel WITECZEK ‡	62
10	Paul WARHURST		10	Oliver SCHÄFER	
11	John SHERIDAN	65	11	Marcus MARIN	
	Substitutes			*Substitutes*	
	Roland NILSSON †35			Michael ZEYER †63	76
	Chris BART-WILLIAMS ‡78			Thorsten LIEBERKNECHT ‡84	

Referee Sándor PUHL (Hungary)

SUMMARY

● *Revenge was in the air at Hillsborough as Sheffield Wednesday sought to punish the Germans for the injustices they felt they had suffered in the first game. Their objective was to win the game 2-0, but without the suspended Hirst it was sure to be a difficult task. As manager Trevor Francis stated beforehand, the Wednesday players needed no motivation and they were soon applying pressure on the Kaiserslautern rearguard in an effort to make the early breakthrough. That goal finally came in the 27th minute and it was scored by Northern Ireland international Danny Wilson. The siege on Serr's goal grew even more intense now, but in their search for a second goal the English side left themselves vulnerable at the back and on 62 minutes Marcel Witeczek crucially beat Viv Anderson for pace for the third time in the tie and netted his sixth goal of the competition after a brilliant run from the halfway line. Now the home side were back to square one again. John Sheridan's free-kick rapidly restored their hope, but all chances of qualification were finally extinguished when Kaiserslautern substitute Michael Zeyer struck the vistors' second away goal 14 minutes from the end.*

UEFA CUP
Second Round First Leg

Thursday 22nd October 1992
Valby Idraetspark, Copenhagen

BK FREM 0 REAL ZARAGOZA 1

Half-time 0-1 *Attendance* 2,852

		Goals				Goals
1	Per WIND		1	Andoni CEDRUN		
2	Søren COLDING †		2	Jesús Angel SOLANA ❑		
3	Tony CARLSEN ❑		3	ESTEBAN Gutiérrez		
4	Dan EGGEN		4	SERGI López		
5	Peter FRANK		5	Dario FRANCO		
6	Søren FOLKMANN ❑		6	Javier AGUADO		
7	Henrik JENSEN		7	Miguel PARDEZA		
8	Michael NIELSEN		8	Gustavo POYET	12	
9	Piotr HAREN ‡		9	Manuel PEÑA †		
10	Thomas THØGERSEN		10	Andreas BREHME		
11	Kim MIKKELSEN		11	José GAY ‡		

Substitutes		*Substitutes*	
Marek CZAKON †46		MOISES García †56	
Per LISDORF ‡63		Ignacio LIZARRALDE ‡64	

Referee Andrew WADDELL (Scotland)

SUMMARY

● *Spanish teams had long held the Indian sign over Danish sides in international competition. The great Danish national team of the mid-80s had both their 1984 European Championship and 1986 World Cup dreams shattered by Spain, and in 11 previous meetings between the two countries in European club competition the Spanish teams had qualified every time! So Frem, who had been surprisingly easy conquerors of Swiss side Neuchâtel Xamax in the first round, certainly had their hands full against a club which had progressed beyond the second round on no fewer than seven of their previous 11 European appearances. As expected, Frem did not enjoy the same sort of freedom up front which they had against Xamax. Zaragoza looked very secure at the back, with Dario Franco playing just in front of the defence in the traditional Argentinian 'number five' role. It was another South American, Uruguayan midfielder Gustavo Poyet, who scored the only goal of the game - a dipping right-footer which flew in from about 30 yards in the 12th minute.*

Second Round Second Leg

Tuesday 3rd November 1992
La Romareda Stadium, Zaragoza

REAL ZARAGOZA 5 BK FREM 1

Half-time 3-0 *Aggregate* 6-1 *Attendance* 12,000

		Goals				Goals
1	Andoni CEDRUN		1	Allan JENSEN		
2	Alberto BELSUE		2	Tony CARLSEN		
3	ESTEBAN Gutiérrez		3	Lars BROUSTBO		
4	SERGI López		4	Dan EGGEN		
5	Dario FRANCO †		5	Peter POULSEN		
6	Javier AGUADO		6	Søren FOLKMANN		
7	Miguel PARDEZA ‡		7	Finn JENSEN		
8	Gustavo POYET		8	Michael NIELSEN		
9	Jesús SEBA	40, 67	9	Marek CZAKON		
10	Dorin MATEUT	8, 39, 83	10	Jimmi LÜTHJE ‡		
11	José GAY		11	Kim MIKKELSEN †		

Substitutes			*Substitutes*		
GARCIA SANJUAN †46			Thomas THØGERSEN †14		
Francisco HIGUERA ‡73			Søren COLDING ‡57	74

Referee Arturo MARTINO (Switzerland)

SUMMARY

● *Real Zaragoza overwhelmed Frem to record their biggest aggregate victory in Europe for 28 years. Romanian Dorin Mateut, the winner of the European Golden Boot in 1988/89 when he scored a remarkable 43 goals for Dinamo Bucharest, was the individual star of the show. He had started just one Spanish League match in the 92/93 season before this game and had not been selected for the first leg in Denmark, but here he put Zaragoza into a 2-0 lead on the night with two opportunist goals in the first half before rounding off the evening's entertainment with a spectacular fifth - a rising shot from the left corner of the penalty area - eight minutes from time. The hat-trick was in fact to be a parting gift to Zaragoza. Just a week later Mateut was on his way to join the Romanian clan at Italian Serie A side Brescia. The other two goals, conversely, were scored by a newcomer, Jesús Seba, in what was only his third official game in the first team. He, like Mateut, demonstrated the knack of being in the right place at the right time to take Zaragoza comfortably into the third round of the UEFA Cup for the first time in 18 years.*

UEFA CUP
Second Round First Leg

Tuesday 20th October 1992
Westfalen Stadium, Dortmund

BORUSSIA DORTMUND 1 CELTIC 0

Half-time 0-0 Attendance 35,803

		Goals			Goals
1	Stefan KLOS		1	Pat BONNER	
2	Knut REINHARDT		2	Mark McNALLY ❑	
3	Bodo SCHMIDT		3	Tom BOYD	
4	Michael SCHULZ		4	Peter GRANT	
5	Stefan REUTER		5	Tony MOWBRAY ❑	
6	Michael LUSCH		6	Gary GILLESPIE	
7	Frank MILL ❑ †		7	Brian O'NEIL	
8	Michael ZORC		8	Paul McSTAY	
9	Stéphane CHAPUISAT	71	9	Stuart SLATER	
10	Michael RUMMENIGGE ‡		10	Gerry CREANEY †	
11	Flemming POVLSEN		11	John COLLINS	

Substitutes

Lothar SIPPEL †67

Gerhard POSCHNER ‡81

Substitute

Charlie NICHOLAS †89

Referee Ion CRACIUNESCU (Romania)

FACTFILE

● There were just two survivors on each side from the two clubs' last European meeting in the UEFA Cup five years earlier - Frank Mill and Michael Zorc of Dortmund and Peter Grant and Paul McStay of Celtic.
● Murdo MacLeod, a former player with both clubs, correctly predicted the 1-0 scoreline live on German television at the half-time interval.
● Paul McStay had become the most-capped Celtic player the previous week when he made his 62nd appearance for Scotland in a World Cup qualifier at home to Portugal.
● Stéphane Chapuisat's goal was his first in European competition for Borussia Dortmund.

● Paul McStay

Chapuisat strike just reward for Dortmund

A UEFA-restricted attendance of almost 36,000 filled the Westfalen Stadium for the first leg of this attractive second-round tie. Celtic came to Dortmund as well-known and respected opponents. Their first-round elimination of Cologne had impressed German observers and the local fans knew that their team would have to establish a healthy first-leg lead if they were not to suffer the same fate as the Rhinelanders a fortnight later in Glasgow.

Dortmund's plan to unhinge the Celtic defence was crystal clear from the opening moments of the match. With Lusch and Povlsen attacking down the right and Reinhardt and Chapuisat on the left, their intention was to draw the opposition out of their central positions and make space for the likes of Rummenigge and Zorc running in from midfield.

Throughout the first half Borussia controlled the play, but Liam Brady's side showed good discipline and managed to restrict the Germans to only a handful of chances. Defender Michael Schulz went nearest to breaking the deadlock, going close three times from set-pieces. But the best openings fell to Stéphane Chapuisat and Michael Rummenigge. The first effort was well saved by Bonner and the second merely found the side-netting. As for Celtic, they managed just one shot - a long-range attempt from their record signing Stuart Slater.

The pattern remained pretty much the same after the interval, with Celtic content to absorb all the pressure and deny the opposition space. But after Mill and Zorc wasted further chances to open the scoring, Dortmund finally found their way through with less than 20 minutes to go. Flemming Povlsen danced his way down the right, knocked in an excellent cross and there was Chapuisat, Dortmund's top scorer the previous season, to volley home past Bonner.

Can Can music burst out of the stadium speakers, the fans went wild, and Dortmund, at last, were in business.

But one goal was to be all they got. There were no further chances after that, except at the other end when Creaney sent a header wide from a Collins cross, and so the match finished with everything still in the balance for the second leg. Both sides viewed their chances of qualification with optimism. Dortmund had the lead, whereas Celtic knew that, in conceding just one goal, they had already done better than against Cologne in the previous round

● *Stuart Slater*

MICHAEL SCHULZ
Borussia Dortmund

An ever-present in Dortmund's 1991/92 Bundesliga campaign, when the club from the Ruhr were pipped for the title by Stuttgart on goal-difference, Michael Schulz was such a commanding figure in the Borussia defence that he was called up for the first time, at the age of 30, to the German national side in the spring of 1992. He made his debut in a friendly against Italy and was retained for the European Championship squad in Sweden, making just one appearance, as a substitute, against Scotland. The lanky centre-back gave further evidence of his growing reputation with a fine all-round performance against Celtic. He not only snuffed out the threat of the promising Gerry Creaney, but also found the time to come forward and fire three first-half headers at Pat Bonner's goal, one of which hit the top of the crossbar.

UEFA CUP
Second Round Second Leg

Tuesday 3rd November 1992
Celtic Park, Glasgow

CELTIC 1 BORUSSIA DORTMUND 2

Half-time 1-0 *Aggregate* 1-3 *Attendance* 31,578

	Goals			Goals
1 Pat BONNER		1 Stefan KLOS		
2 Mike GALLOWAY		2 Knut REINHARDT		
3 Tom BOYD		3 Bodo SCHMIDT ❏		
4 Peter GRANT		4 Michael SCHULZ ❏		
5 Tony MOWBRAY ❏		5 Stefan REUTER		
6 Gary GILLESPIE †		6 Günter KUTOWSKI †		
7 Stuart SLATER		7 Michael LUSCH		
8 Paul McSTAY		8 Michael ZORC ❏	57	
9 Charlie NICHOLAS		9 Stéphane CHAPUISAT	53	
10 Gerry CREANEY	13	10 Michael RUMMENIGGE ‡		
11 John COLLINS		11 Flemming POVLSEN		

Substitute

Joe MILLER †72

Substitutes

Uwe GRAUER †84
Steffen KARL ‡88

Referee Leif SUNDELL (Sweden)

FACT FILE

● *Celtic's elimination meant that for the 13th consecutive season the club would not be playing European football in the Spring.*

● *Dortmund's victory gave the Germans a UEFA Cup double over Celtic, having also eliminated the Scottish club in 1987/88.*

● *It was in Glasgow that Dortmund won their only European trophy. They defeated Liverpool 2-1 at Hampden Park in the 1966 Cup-winners' Cup Final.*

● *Gerry Creaney's goal was his second in successive European games at Celtic Park. He also scored against German opposition - Cologne - in the previous round.*

● *Gerry Creaney*

Celtic fail to take advantage of early goal

Hopes were high amongst the Celtic faithful that their team could come back from a first-leg deficit against German opposition for the second round in succession. They had come through spectacularly against Cologne in the previous round, and a crowd of over 30,000 expected a repeat performance from their heroes as Borussia Dortmund came to Celtic Park with only a fragile lead to protect.

But whereas Cologne had been propping up the Bundesliga when they arrived in Glasgow a month earlier, Dortmund were riding high in domestic competition and looking a fair bet again for the German League title.

The home side started well and pulled level on aggregate, courtesy of Gerry Creaney's excellent headed goal from a Collins cross after 13 minutes.

But Celtic's good fortune was to disappear in the second half. Eight minutes after the break Celtic lost possession on the halfway line. Michael Rummenigge, younger brother of the famous German international Karl-Heinz, broke forward and slid the ball into the path of Stéphane Chapuisat. With just one touch to control, the Dortmund number nine rifled the ball into the roof of Pat Bonner's net with his weaker right foot before running to celebrate in front of the jubilant travelling support.

That was the all-important away goal, and just four minutes later Dortmund had another. This time Chapuisat turned provider, setting up his captain Michael Zorc with a deft through-ball to give the Germans a 2-1 lead on the night, and a decisive 3-1 lead on aggregate.

For Celtic the tie was over. Three goals in the last half hour was just too much to ask from them against such a well-mar-

shalled Dortmund defence. They had failed to capitalise on their early breakthrough, hurrying their passes and snatching at chances when more composure was called for.

Disappointed Celtic manager Liam Brady was noble in defeat. "We have to hold our hands up and say the better side has gone through" he said, before adding "I wouldn't be surprised if Dortmund go all the way to the Final."

● Michael Zorc

STEPHANE CHAPUISAT
Borussia Dortmund

If Scottish fans had not paid too much attention to Stéphane Chapuisat during two impressive performances for Switzerland against Andy Roxburgh's national side in Berne, they could hardly fail to sit up and take notice of the 23-year-old striker now as his brilliant display at Parkhead put paid to Celtic's European ambitions for another year.

The son of a former Swiss international defender, Chapuisat developed rapidly in the early years of his career at Lausanne to become one of the hottest properties in Swiss football at the age of just 19, when he won his first national cap. After a brief spell at German club Bayer Uerdingen, Chapuisat moved to Dortmund and became an instant hit, scoring 20 Bundesliga goals in 1991/92 to take the 'Schwarzgelben' to the brink of the German championship.

UEFA CUP
Second Round First Leg

Wednesday 21st October 1992
Monnikenhuize Stadium, Arnhem

VITESSE 1 KV MECHELEN 0

Half-time 1-0 *Attendance* 9,499

		Goals				Goals
1	Raymond VAN DER GOUW		1	Michel PREUD'HOMME		
2	Roberto STRAAL		2	Koen SANDERS		
3	Erwin VAN DE LOOI		3	Glen DE BOECK		
4	Theo BOS		4	Davy GIJSBRECHTS		
5	Arjan VERMEULEN ❏		5	Geert DEFERM †		
6	Martin LAAMERS		6	Stan VAN DEN BUYS		
7	John VAN DEN BROM ❏	32	7	Frank LEEN		
8	René EIJER		8	Klas INGESSON		
9	Bart LATUHERU		9	Patrick VERSAVEL		
10	Hans VAN ARUM		10	Joël BARTHOLOMEEUSSEN ❏		
11	Philip COCU		11	René EYKELKAMP		

Substitutes

Substitute

Paul DE MESMAEKER †73

Referee Juan ANSATEGUI ROCA (Spain)

SUMMARY

● *A solitary goal from Vitesse captain John van den Brom was all that separated these two teams after a hard-fought duel in Arnhem. The Dutch international midfielder found a way past a tightly-packed Mechelen defence with a header after 32 minutes. It was the only time that Michel Preud'homme was beaten, but Vitesse coach Herbert Neumann, a man who had played professional football in four countries - Germany, Italy, Greece and Switzerland - was very satisfied with both the result and the performance of his team. With a reference to Mechelen's defence-at-all-costs approach, he said "In Belgium we will have more room to play in. By winning 1-0 we have put ourselves in a very good position." A few years earlier the Mechelen side had been full of Dutch players, and even had a Dutch coach in Aad de Mos when they won the Cup-winners' Cup in 1988. But for this match the only player returning to his country of origin was René Eykelkamp, and since he had been instructed to play up front all on his own, it was not a happy homecoming for the former Groningen striker.*

UEFA CUP
Second Round Second Leg

Tuesday 3rd November 1992
Achter de Kazerne Stadium, Mechelen

KV MECHELEN 0 VITESSE 1

Half-time 0-0 *Aggregate* 0-2 *Attendance* 10,000

		Goals			Goals
1	Michel PREUD'HOMME		1	Raymond VAN DER GOUW	
2	Koen SANDERS		2	Roberto STRAAL	
3	Glen DE BOECK		3	Erwin VAN DE LOOI †	
4	Davy GIJSBRECHTS		4	Theo BOS	
5	Geert DEFERM		5	Arjan VERMEULEN	
6	Stan VAN DEN BUYS		6	Martin LAAMERS	
7	Joël BARTHOLOMEEUSSEN		7	John VAN DEN BROM	
8	Klas INGESSON		8	René EIJER	
9	Paul DE MESMAEKER		9	Bart LATUHERU	
10	Kurt VAN GOMPEL †		10	Hans VAN ARUM ‡	
11	René EYKELKAMP		11	Philip COCU	74

Substitute

Patrick VERSAVEL †34

Substitutes

Huub LOEFFEN †56 ❑

Richard ROELOFSEN ‡89

Referee Arie FROST (Israel)

● *Vitesse set the ball rolling on an important week for Dutch football by repeating their 1-0 first-leg victory over Mechelen and reaching the third round of the UEFA Cup for the second time in as many appearances. After withstanding a barrage of early pressure from the Belgians, the Arnhem side, unchanged in personnel from the team which had both started and finished the first match, settled down to dictate the match for long periods. Theo Bos held the defence together superbly in his new sweeper role and it was left winger Philip Cocu who scored the tie-clinching away goal in the 74th minute with a vicious left-foot drive which caught Preud'homme out of position after a quickly taken throw-in. Defeat was difficult to swallow for Mechelen and their fans. They had gone out of the UEFA Cup after a 0-1 home defeat the previous season - to PAOK of Greece - and it was the same story now. Worse still for the club's disintegrating pride was the fact that they were the only one of the five Belgian clubs in European action during the week to be eliminated.*

UEFA CUP
Second Round First Leg

Wednesday 21st October 1992
Olimpico Stadium, Rome

ROMA 3 GRASSHOPPER-CLUB ZÜRICH 0

Half-time 3-0 *Attendance* 31,034

		Goals			Goals
1	Giovanni CERVONE ❑		1	Pascal ZUBERBÜHLER	
2	Luigi GARZYA		2	Ramon VEGA	
3	Amedeo CARBONI		3	Murat YAKIN	
4	Giovanni PIACENTINI		4	Heinz HERMANN	
5	Silvano BENEDETTI		5	Harald GÄMPERLE	
6	ALDAIR dos Santos		6	Urs MEIER ❑ ‡	
7	Sinisa MIHAJLOVIC		7	Peter KÖZLE	
8	Thomas HÄSSLER		8	Sigurdur GRÉTARSSON †	
9	Andrea CARNEVALE ❑ ■	18	9	ELBER de Souza Giovane	
10	Giuseppe GIANNINI †	42	10	Thomas BICKEL	
11	Ruggiero RIZZITELLI ‡	25	11	Alain SUTTER	
	Substitutes			*Substitutes*	
	Walter BONACINA †73			Joël MAGNIN †46	
	Fausto SALSANO ‡84			Massimo LOMBARDO ‡67	

Referee Heinz HOLZMANN (Austria)

● *Roma were full of confidence going into this match after their 4-1 victory over Inter the previous Sunday. And that confidence showed in a first half which they dominated from start to finish, scoring three goals without reply. Thomas Hässler did not get his name onto the scoresheet but he was certainly the key figure behind Roma's early attacking surge. His trickery on the right wing caused the Swiss defence no end of problems and it was from two of his crosses that Rizzitelli and Giannini scored Roma's second and third goals. The first had been scored by Andrea Carnevale, who owed his place in the team to Claudio Caniggia's participation for Argentina in the Intercontinental Cup in Saudi Arabia. But the ex-Italian international striker further soured an already shaky reputation by getting himself stupidly sent off shortly before Roma went 3-0 up. Grasshoppers gave a good account of themselves in the second half and as ten-man Roma inevitably went off the boil, they frequently came close - but not quite close enough - to snatching an all-important away goal.*

Tuesday 3rd November 1992
Hardturm Stadium, Zürich

GRASSHOPPER-CLUB ZÜRICH 4 ROMA 3

Half-time 1-2 *Aggregate* 4-6 *Attendance* 15,100

		Goals			Goals
1	Pascal ZUBERBÜHLER ■		1	Giovanni CERVONE	
2	Ramon VEGA		2	Luigi GARZYA	
3	Ciriaco SFORZA		3	Sebastiano NELA ❏ †	
4	Murat YAKIN		4	Giovanni PIACENTINI	
5	Harald GÄMPERLE	58	5	Silvano BENEDETTI	
6	Heinz HERMANN †		6	ALDAIR dos Santos	
7	Peter KÖZLE		7	Walter BONACINA ❏	
8	Adrian DE VICENTE ‡	36 (pen), 68	8	Thomas HÄSSLER	
9	ELBER de Souza Giovane		9	Claudio CANIGGIA	30
10	Thomas BICKEL		10	Giuseppe GIANNINI ‡	
11	Alain SUTTER	49	11	Ruggiero RIZZITELLI	7, 90
	Substitutes			*Substitutes*	
	Martin BRUNNER †60			Antonio TEMPESTILLI †74 ❏	
	Joël MAGNIN ‡76			Fausto SALSANO ‡80	

Referee Frans VAN DEN WIJNGAERT (Belgium)

● *Grasshoppers had come back from the dead in the first round against Sporting Lisbon and their powers of recovery were very much in evidence in this highly exciting second leg against Roma. As in the first match, the Italians were much too quick off the starting blocks for Leo Beenhakker's side. A marvellous header from Rizzitelli stretched Roma's aggregate lead to 4-0 after just seven minutes and with a third of the match gone the recalled Caniggia had further extended it to 5-0. The game was surely up for Grasshoppers now, but a generously awarded penalty just before the interval was miraculously to transform them in the second half. Three further goals in 23 minutes, beginning with Sutter's brilliant long-range shot and ending with De Vicente's finely judged glancing header, tore Roma apart. The Italians were down, but with the added cushion of an away goal to comfort them, they were not yet out and as the home side's fire burned out in the closing stages Rizzitelli settled everything with a wonderful last-minute solo goal to lower the curtain on a truly remarkable match.*

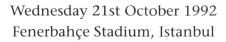

UEFA CUP
Second Round First Leg

Wednesday 21st October 1992
Fenerbahçe Stadium, Istanbul

FENERBAHÇE 1 SIGMA OLOMOUC 0

Half-time 1-0 *Attendance* 32,195

		Goals				Goals
1	ENGIN Ipekoglu			1	Lubos PRIBYL	
2	ISMAIL Kartal	36 (pen)		2	Michal KOVAR	
3	SEMIH Yuvakuran ❑			3	Ivo LOSTÁK	
4	Dzoni NOVAK			4	Martin KOTULEK	
5	MÜJDAT Yetkiner			5	Robert FIALA	
6	OGUZ Çetin ❑			6	Jirí HOMOLA ❑	
7	SENOL Ustaömer			7	Roman HANUS	
8	RIDVAN Dilmen			8	Radoslav LÁTAL	
9	ILKER Yacioglu †			9	Milan KERBR ❑	
10	Candido GÉRSON			10	Jirí BARBORÍK	
11	AYKUT Kocaman			11	Roman PIVARNÍK	
	Substitute				*Substitute*	
	TANJU Çolak †61				Petr KIRSCHBAUM †83	

Referee Lube SPASOV (Bulgaria)

SUMMARY

● *The feeling in Turkey was that the draw had offered Fenerbahçe the perfect opportunity to progress beyond the second round in Europe for only the second time in 23 attempts and for the first time in 29 years. Sigma Olomouc had been UEFA Cup quarter-finalists the previous season, but they held no great fears for the Istanbul club, especially as Fenerbahçe's Czechoslovakian coach, Jozef Venglos, was sure to know all about them. A large and predictably noisy crowd turned up to see if their team could put the Moravians to the sword and kill the tie after the first leg, but by the end of the 90 minutes it was anybody's guess which of the two teams would progress into the next round. Olomouc, despite missing a number of key players through injury, had restricted Fenerbahçe to just one goal, and a harshly-awarded penalty at that, to give themselves at least an even chance of retrieving the deficit back in Czechoslovakia.*

UEFA CUP
Second Round Second Leg

Wednesday 4th November 1992
Sigma Stadium, Olomouc

SIGMA OLOMOUC 7 FENERBAHÇE 1

Half-time 3-1 *Aggregate* 7-2 *Attendance* 10,152

		Goals
1	Lubos PRIBYL	
2	Michal KOVAR	
3	Jan MAROSI †	51
4	Martin KOTULEK	
5	Jiří VADURA	80
6	Milos SLABY ❑	
7	Roman HANUS ❑	9 (pen), 90
8	Radoslav LÁTAL ❑	
9	Milan KERBR	12
10	Jiří BARBORÍK	34
11	Roman PIVARNÍK	
	Substitutes	
	Robert FIALA †61	76
	Jiří KABYL ‡76	

		Goals
1	ENGIN Ipekoglu	
2	ISMAIL Kartal ■	
3	SEMIH Yuvakuran	
4	Dzoni NOVAK	
5	MÜJDAT Yetkiner	
6	OGUZ Çetin ❑	
7	SENOL Ustaömer ❑	
8	RIDVAN Dilmen ‡ ❑	
9	Stanimir STOILOV †	
10	Candido GÉRSON ■	
11	AYKUT Kocaman ❑	38
	Substitutes	
	HAKAN Tecimer †29 ■	
	NURI Kamburoglu ‡83	

Referee Emanuel MONTEIRO COROADO (Portugal)

SUMMARY

● *Three Fenerbahçe players were sent off as Sigma Olomouc raced to their most comprehensive victory ever in European competition. Despite having conceded two goals in the first 12 minutes and another later on, the Turks were still just a goal away from qualification at half-time after Aykut's superb first-time left-foot volley had reduced the deficit to 3-1, and 3-2 on aggregate. But Jozef Venglos's team completely lost their discipline after the interval and Olomouc punished them for it with four further goals, the pick of which was the first, from skipper Jan Marosi, a marvellously timed low, skidding shot direct from a corner. There were six goals and six different goalscorers on the Olomouc scoresheet until Roman Hanus, who had opened the scoring from the penalty spot, grabbed a second in the last minute. Almost inevitably, Fenerbahçe accused the Portuguese referee of bias, but in truth they only had themselves to blame, as was recognised by club president Metin Asik, who resigned in shame after the match...only to re-appoint himself a few days later when Fenerbahçe defeated city rivals Galatasaray in a table-topping Turkish league clash!*

UEFA CUP
Second Round First Leg

Wednesday 21st October 1992
Wald Stadium, Frankfurt am Main

EINTRACHT FRANKFURT 0 GALATASARAY 0

Half-time 0-0 *Attendance* 40,802

		Goals				Goals
1	Uli STEIN		1	HAYRETTIN Demirbas		
2	Dietmar ROTH		2	Reinhard STUMPF		
3	Ralf WEBER		3	BÜLENT Korkmaz		
4	Uwe BINDEWALD		4	YUSUF Altintas †		
5	Manfred BINZ		5	Falko GÖTZ		
6	Stefan STUDER		6	TUGAY Kerimoglu		
7	Dirk WOLF		7	UGUR Tütüneker		
8	Augustine OKOCHA		8	MUHAMMET Altintas		
9	Anthony YEBOAH		9	HAKAN Sükür		
10	Uwe RAHN †		10	OKAN Buruk		
11	Axel KRUSE		11	MUSTAFA Kocabey ‡		

Substitutes

Rudi BOMMER †81

Substitutes

MERT Korkmaz †80

Elvir BOLIC ‡89

Referee Brian McGINLAY (Scotland)

SUMMARY

● *Galatasaray had been to Germany twice before in the past four seasons for important European matches and now, as then, they were able to call upon huge support from the local Turkish community. The red and yellow favours of the Istanbul club were as prominent all over the Wald Stadium as they had been in Cologne's Müngersdorfer Stadium back in 1989 and in Bremen's Weser stadium a few months earlier. And once again the Turkish fans left the stadium at the end of the match with reason to be satisfied by their team's performance. Galatasaray's German coach, Karl-Heinz Feldkamp, waged a tactical battle with his Frankfurt counterpart Dragoslav Stepanovic and came out the winner thanks in no small part to the defensive contributions of his two German players, Falko Götz and Reinhard Stumpf. The hosts badly missed playmaker Uwe Bein and at times, with strikers Yeboah and Kruse struggling to impose themselves up front, it looked as if Frankfurt were being forced to pay some sort of perverse price for having exhausted their goal supply in that first-round hammering of Widzew Lódz.*

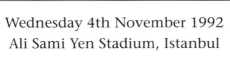

GALATASARAY 1 EINTRACHT FRANKFURT 0

Half-time 1-0 *Aggregate* 1-0 *Attendance* 29,546

		Goals			Goals
1	HAYRETTIN Demirbas		1	Uli STEIN	
2	Reinhard STUMPF		2	Dietmar ROTH	
3	BÜLENT Korkmaz		3	Stefan STUDER ‡	
4	YUSUF Altintas		4	Uwe BINDEWALD	
5	Falko GÖTZ		5	Manfred BINZ	
6	TUGAY Kerimoglu		6	Michael KLEIN	
7	UGUR Tütüneker	6	7	Augustine OKOCHA	
8	MUHAMMET Altintas ❏		8	Rudi BOMMER ❏	
9	HAKAN Sükür		9	Anthony YEBOAH	
10	OKAN Buruk ‡		10	Uwe BEIN †	
11	Elvir BOLIC †		11	Axel KRUSE ❏	

Substitutes

MERT Korkmaz †80

ISMAIL Demiriz ‡88

Substitutes

Jørn ANDERSEN †70

Edgar SCHMITT ‡78

Referee Pierluigi PAIRETTO (Italy)

SUMMARY

● *Galatasaray went into the history books with this narrow, but amply deserved 1-0 victory. No Turkish team had ever eliminated a side from the German Bundesliga in nine previous attempts. But a goal in the sixth minute from Turkish international midfielder Ugur Tütüneker changed that record forever. The goal was Ugur's first in Europe since he hit a brace against Neuchâtel Xamax on the way to helping Galatasaray into the 1989 Champions' Cup semi-finals, and it came about as a result of Frankfurt striker Axel Kruse's miscued clearance from a corner. The ball fell unexpectedly to Ugur and he whacked it gleefully home past Uli Stein. Kruse might have atoned for his error in the second half with an equaliser, but his effort hit the post and that was Frankfurt's last chance of staying in the competition. Victory celebrations for Galatasaray lasted long into the night, not just in Istanbul but all over Germany where thousands of 'Gastarbeiter' were able to go to work the following morning with broad smiles beaming from their faces!*

Thursday 22nd October 1992
Delle Alpi Stadium, Turin

TORINO 1 DINAMO MOSKVA 2

Half-time 0-1 *Attendance* 26,943

Goals   Goals

1	Luca MARCHEGIANI		1	Valery KLEYMENOV ❏	
2	Pasquale BRUNO ❏		2	Sergei TIMOFEEV	56 (o.g.)
3	Raffaele SERGIO †		3	Igor SKLYAROV †	
4	Daniele FORTUNATO		4	Kakhaber TSKHADADZE	
5	Enrico ANNONI ❏		5	Viacheslav TSAREV	
6	Luca FUSI		6	Andrey KOBELEV	
7	Gianluca SORDO ‡		7	Yevgeny SMERTIN	
8	Walter CASAGRANDE		8	Sergei DERKACH	
9	Carlos AGUILERA		9	Omari TETRADZE	
10	Enzo SCIFO		10	Velli KASUMOV ‡	45
11	Giorgio VENTURIN		11	Igor SIMUTENKOV	69

Substitutes   *Substitutes*

Andrea SILENZI †74   Igor VARLAMOV †88 ❏

Roberto MUSSI ‡8   Sarkis OGANESYAN ‡90

Referee Helmut KRUG (Germany)

SUMMARY

● *The remarkable success of the four Moscow clubs was rapidly becoming the story of the season in Europe, and Dinamo Moscow wrote a fresh chapter with this superb victory in the Delle Alpi Stadium against Torino. Emiliano Mondonico's team were rocked on their heels by a tremendously committed and powerful performance from the young Russian team. Italian national coach Arrigo Sacchi was one of many onlookers in the stadium who could not fail to be impressed with the manner in which Dinamo took the game to Torino and never allowed them to settle into any kind of rhythm. It did not help Torino's cause that their South American front pairing of Aguilera and Casagrande were both in patchy form up front. Their other foreigner, Belgian Enzo Scifo, was indirectly responsible for Torino's only goal of the game - an own goal by Timofeev - but against that Dinamo scored twice at the right end, with Simutenkov securing a 2-1 win in the 69th minute after Russian League top goalscorer Velli Kasumov had opened the scoring on the stroke of half-time.*

UEFA CUP
Second Round Second Leg

Thursday 5th November 1992
Dinamo Stadium, Moscow

DINAMO MOSKVA 0 TORINO 0

Half-time 0-0 *Aggregate* 2-1 *Attendance* 13,000

Goals   Goals

1	Valery KLEYMENOV		1	Luca MARCHEGIANI
2	Sergei TIMOFEEV ❑		2	Pasquale BRUNO
3	Igor SKLYAROV ❑		3	Raffaele SERGIO
4	Kakhaber TSKHADADZE		4	Roberto MUSSI
5	Yury KALITVINTSEV †		5	Enrico ANNONI ■
6	Andrey KOBELEV		6	Luca FUSI †
7	Igor VARLAMOV		7	Gianluca SORDO ‡
8	Sergei DERKACH		8	Walter CASAGRANDE ❑
9	Omari TETRADZE		9	Carlos AGUILERA
10	Velli KASUMOV ‡		10	Enzo SCIFO ❑
11	Igor SIMUTENKOV ■		11	Giorgio VENTURIN ❑

Substitutes

Viacheslav TSAREV †64 ❑   Andrea SILENZI †47
Sarkis OGANESYAN ‡87   Paolo POGGI ‡69

Referee Jozef MARKO (Czechoslovakia)

● Torino were well known in Italian football circles for their so-called 'grinta' (determination) and also their ability to strike on the counter-attack. These qualities were certainly required once again in Moscow if they were to stay in the competition after their home-leg defeat. The boggy pitch, alas, was hardly conducive to their style of play. Favouring defences, it enabled Dinamo to adopt a much less ambitious stance than they had shown in the first leg and frustrate the Torino forwards by simply massing bodies in defence and leaving no way through. Dinamo goalkeeper Valery Kleymenov also did his fair share to keep the Italians at bay when they did manage to lift the ball out of the mud and shoot at goal, and he was the player to receive most acclaim when the final whistle sounded to signal Dinamo's passage into round three for the second year in a row. But while Dinamo ensured that Russian interest remained in all three competitions, Torino had gone the way of three other 91/92 European finalists - Barcelona, Monaco and Werder Bremen - all eliminated after losing their home leg.

UEFA CUP
Second Round First Leg

Wednesday 21st October 1992
Luz Stadium, Lisbon

SL BENFICA 5 VÁC FC-SAMSUNG 1

Half-time 1-0 *Attendance* 25,000

		Goals				Goals
1	SILVINO		1	János KOSZTA		
2	JOSÉ CARLOS		2	Tibor NAGY		
3	HÉLDER		3	Árpád HAHN		
4	WILLIAM	79 (pen)	4	Imre ARANYOS		
5	VELOSO		5	Péter BERECZKI		
6	Stefan SCHWARZ		6	Gábor KRISKA ‡		
7	VÍTOR PANEIRA ‡		7	János ROMANEK †		
8	PACHECO	58 (pen)	8	László HORVÁTH ❑		
9	PAULO SOUSA		9	László RÉPÁSI		
10	Sergei YURAN ❑ †	42	10	Antal SIMON		
11	ISAÍAS	55, 85	11	István SZEDLACSEK		82
	Substitutes			*Substitutes*		
	Aleksandr MOSTOVOY †72			Elek NYILAS †60		
	RUI COSTA ‡79			Zoltán SWARCZ ‡81		

Referee Ryszard WÓJCIK (Poland)

SUMMARY

● *The last time Benfica had taken on a Hungarian side in European competition they had eclipsed Honvéd 9-0 on aggregate in the 1989/90 Champions' Cup. Vác were in fine domestic form coming into this match, but like Honvéd before them, they were to find themselves hopelessly out of their depth in the Stadium of Light. It took Benfica a while to get going, but once Yuran had given them the lead just before half-time, the floodgates opened and all their territorial dominance was finally translated onto the scoresheet. Benfica had scored four second-half goals in their previous European fixture, away to Belvedur Izola, and now they repeated the dose against Vác. Two penalties, both legitimately awarded for fouls on the elusive Pacheco, and two excellent strikes from Isaías put the Portuguese side out of reach for the second leg in Hungary. Vác grabbed a goal of their own from one of their rare attacks when Szedlacsek lobbed Silvino after appearing to be yards offside. But it was a consolation, and nothing more, for the outclassed Hungarians.*

Wednesday 4th November 1992
Városi Stadium, Vác

VÁC FC-SAMSUNG 0   SL BENFICA 1

Half-time 0-1   *Aggregate* 1-6   *Attendance* 3,000

		Goals				Goals
1	János KOSZTA		1	SILVINO		
2	Tibor NAGY		2	JOSÉ CARLOS		
3	Péter BERECZKI ∎		3	PAULO MADEIRA		
4	Imre ARANYOS		4	WILLIAM		
5	János BÁNFI		5	VELOSO †		
6	Gábor PUGLITS ∎		6	HÉLDER		
7	János ROMANEK		7	VÍTOR PANEIRA		
8	Elek NYILAS		8	PAULO SOUSA		
9	László RÉPÁSI ‡		9	Stefan SCHWARZ	14	
10	Antal SIMON		10	Aleksandr MOSTOVOY ❏ ‡		
11	Antal FÜLE †		11	ISAÍAS		

Substitutes		*Substitutes*	
István SZEDLACSEK †38		FERNANDO MENDES †30	
László HORVÁTH ‡73		RUI COSTA ‡68	

Referee OGUZ Sarvan (Turkey)

SUMMARY

● *In the two weeks since the first leg in Lisbon there had been a succession of internal rumblings at Benfica, and they had concluded with the sacking of Croatian coach Tomislav Ivic, guilty, it was alleged, of failing to form an amicable dialogue with the three Russian players at the club - Yuran, Kulkov and Mostovoy. It was another member of the club's foreign contingent, Swedish international Stefan Schwarz, who found his name in the headlines, for all the right reasons, after this match. He it was who scored the only goal of the game after 14 minutes to seal Benfica's passage into the third round. The goal was also a personal landmark for the midfielder, who, in 20 previous European Cup outings for both Malmö and Benfica, had never once found the net. With only 3,000 spectators present to witness their demise, hard-up Vác came out losers in all respects. Their plight was symptomatic of the sorry state of Hungarian football in general. Their elimination meant that for the fifth year in a row not one Hungarian club had managed to progress beyond the second round of any of the three European competitions.*

U E F A   C U P
Second Round First Leg

Wednesday 21st October 1992
Constant Vanden Stock Stadium, Brussels

RSC ANDERLECHT 4 DINAMO KIEV 2

Half-time 2-1 Attendance 15,000

		Goals				Goals
1	Filip DE WILDE		1	Valdemaras MARTINKENAS		
2	Bertrand CRASSON		2	Oleg LUZHNY ❑		
3	Graeme RUTJES		3	Akhrik TSVEIBA		
4	Philippe ALBERT		4	Anatoly DEMYANENKO		
5	Michel DE WOLF		5	Sergei SHMATOVALENKO †		
6	Johan WALEM		6	Sergei KOVALETS		
7	Wim KOOIMAN †		7	Stepan BETSA ‡		
8	Peter VAN VOSSEN	60	8	Sergei ZAETS		
9	Luc NILIS	24	9	Igor PANKRATYEV ❑		
10	Marc DEGRYSE	37	10	Viktor LEONENKO	54	
11	Danny BOFFIN		11	Pavel SHKAPENKO	20	
	Substitute			*Substitutes*		
	Bruno VERSAVEL †29	51		Nikolai ZUYENKO †46		
				Vladimir SHARAN ‡70		

Referee Frederick McKNIGHT (Northern Ireland)

SUMMARY

● *Both of these teams had competed in the last-eight of the Champions' Cup the previous season, but while Anderlecht had strengthened their squad considerably since then with the addition of Albert, Emmers and Van Vossen, Dinamo Kiev had been obliged to sell off some of their big names, notably Salenko and Yakovenko. So it was something of a surprise when the Ukrainians took the lead after 20 minutes, Shkapenko plotting a successful route through the Anderlecht offside trap. The Belgians responded admirably, though, and goals from Nilis and Degryse put them firmly in control at half-time. Three goals were to follow in the 15-minute spell after the interval, two for Anderlecht, including a rare header for Dutchman Peter van Vossen, and one for Kiev, a third away goal of the tournament for Viktor Leonenko, and that left the tie nicely poised at 4-2 to the Belgians. The victory was Anderlecht's 100th in European competition, but they would have to wait another two weeks to see if it had any lasting value.*

UEFA CUP
Second Round Second Leg

Wednesday 4th November 1992
Republican Stadium, Kiev

DINAMO KIEV 0 RSC ANDERLECHT 3

Half-time 0-1 Aggregate 2-7 Attendance 24,000

		Goals			Goals
1	Valdemaras MARTINKENAS		1	Filip DE WILDE	
2	Oleg LUZHNY		2	Bertrand CRASSON	
3	Akhrik TSVEIBA ‡		3	Graeme RUTJES	
4	Anatoly DEMYANENKO		4	Philippe ALBERT	
5	Sergei SHMATOVALENKO		5	Michel DE WOLF	
6	Sergei KOAVLETS		6	Johan WALEM	
7	Sergei VOLOTIOK †		7	Bruno VERSAVEL	
8	Sergei ZAETS		8	Peter VAN VOSSEN	
9	Igor PANKRATYEV		9	Luc NILIS †	61, 67
10	Viktor LEONENKO		10	Marc DEGRYSE	
11	Pavel SHKAPENKO		11	Peter VAN VOSSEN ❏	20

Substitutes	*Substitutes*
Sergei REBROV †46	Wim KOOIMAN †73
Yury GRITSYNA ‡61	

Referee Rune PEDERSEN (Norway)

SUMMARY

● *Anderlecht travelled to rainy Kiev with an impressive away record to defend. They had won all five of their away games so far in the Belgian league and had reached this stage of the competition as a result of their two away goals in the first round against Hibernian. For the first 20 minutes, however, that unbeaten sequence looked likely to be broken as the Ukrainians surged forward in numbers towards Filip de Wilde's goal. But once Van Vossen, with another header, had put the Belgians in front, the home side's assault subsided and Anderlecht began to dominate. They should have increased their lead when Marc Degryse missed a penalty after Nilis had been fouled by Luzhny, but it mattered not. The second half belonged almost exclusively to the Belgian league leaders, and in particular to Luc Nilis. The highly-gifted striker, who, remarkably, had never scored once for the Belgian national team in 18 appearances, took his goal tally in European Cup football to 19 in 40 games with two brilliant long-range strikes that amply demonstrated his extraordinary talent.*

UEFA CUP
Second Round First Leg

Tuesday 20th October 1992
OAKA Spiros Louis Stadium, Athens

PANATHINAIKOS 0 JUVENTUS 1

Half-time 0-0 *Attendance* 70,000

		Goals				Goals
1	Jozef WANDZIK			1	Angelo PERUZZI	
2	Stratos APOSTOLAKIS			2	Moreno TORRICELLI	
3	Marinos OUZOUNIDIS			3	Dino BAGGIO ❑	
4	Leonidas HRISTODOULOU			4	Roberto GALIA	
5	Yannis KALITZAKIS			5	Jürgen KOHLER ❑	
6	Kostas MAVRIDIS			6	Massimo CARRERA	
7	Yorgos DONIS			7	Antonio CONTE	
8	Kostas ANTONIOU			8	David PLATT	79
9	Krzysztof WARZYCHA			9	Fabrizio RAVANELLI †	
10	Kostas FRANTZESKOS			10	Roberto BAGGIO	
11	Spiros MARAGOS			11	Andreas MÖLLER	

Substitutes

Substitute

Pierluigi CASIRAGHI †53

Referee Bo KARLSSON (Sweden)

SUMMARY

● *Both Panathinaikos and Juventus had struck ten goals apiece in disposing of their modest first-round opponents. But this encounter, watched by a huge crowd, was never likely to produce a similar goal feast. Juventus had never been happy visitors to Athens. In three previous European meetings with Panathinaikos they had lost two of the away legs and drawn the other one. And in 1983 the Greek capital was also the venue for their shock 1-0 defeat by Hamburg in the Champions' Cup final. But now, at last, the Turin club were to taste victory, and for that they had to thank Englishman David Platt, who fired in the only goal of the game with a precise right-foot shot 11 minutes from time. Roberto Baggio, fresh from signing a new extension to his contract, also had an influential evening, as did Juventus goalkeeper Angelo Peruzzi, who made a number of fine saves, including one magnificent point-blank stop from Panathinaikos's most dangerous player, Frantzeskos. But it was Platt who had most to be pleased about after a performance which was generally recognised to be his most complete so far since his summer transfer from Bari.*

UEFA CUP
Second Round Second Leg

Wednesday 4th November 1992
Delle Alpi Stadium, Turin

JUVENTUS 0 PANATHINAIKOS 0

Half-time 0-0 *Aggregate* 1-0 *Attendance* 21,592

		Goals				Goals
1	Angelo PERUZZI		1	Jozef WANDZIK		
2	Moreno TORRICELLI		2	Stratos APOSTOLAKIS ❏		
3	Marco Antonio DE MARCHI		3	Marinos OUZOUNIDIS ❏		
4	Roberto GALIA		4	Leonidas HRISTODOULOU		
5	Jürgen KOHLER		5	Yannis KALITZAKIS		
6	Massimo CARRERA ❏		6	Kostas MAVRIDIS		
7	Antonio CONTE		7	Yorgos DONIS †		
8	David PLATT		8	Nikos KARAYEORYIOU		
9	Gianluca VIALLI ❏		9	Krzysztof WARZYCHA		
10	Roberto BAGGIO		10	Kostas FRANTZESKOS ‡		
11	Andreas MÖLLER ❏		11	Spiros MARAGOS ❏		
	Substitutes			*Substitutes*		
				Kostas ANTONIOU †53		
				Yorgos KAFES ‡77		

Referee Mario VAN DER ENDE (Holland)

SUMMARY

● Whistles and boos rang around the cavernous Delle Alpi stadium after this uneventful goalless draw. Granted Juventus were into the next round. But fans of the Turin club expect more than just results and qualification from their highly-paid idols. They want to see performances worthy of the club's great European tradition. But on this occasion they were to be sorely disappointed. Juventus had scored five goals against Ancona in the Italian league the previous weekend, but against Panathinaikos they could not find the target once. Gianluca Vialli, who had missed the first leg, had yet another poor match up front for his new club, and first-leg hero David Platt was as anonymous as he had been adventurous in Athens. Only Roberto Baggio, of the front players, delivered the goods and he was very unfortunate to have a perfectly valid goal ruled offside by the Dutch officials. But it was goalkeeper Peruzzi once again who spared Juve's blushes, imposing himself on the match with a string of important interventions to ensure his team's presence in the third round.

UEFA CUP
Second Round First Leg

Wednesday 21st October 1992
Tynecastle Park, Edinburgh

HEART OF MIDLOTHIAN 0   R STANDARD LIEGE 1

Half-time 0-1   Attendance 16,897

		Goals				Goals
1	Henry SMITH		1	Gilbert BODART		
2	Graeme HOGG		2	Régis GENAUX		
3	Tosh McKINLAY		3	Patrick VERVOORT ❑		
4	Craig LEVEIN †		4	Stéphane DEMOL		
5	Gary MACKAY		5	André CRUZ †		
6	Peter VAN DE VEN		6	Alain BETTAGNO		7
7	John ROBERTSON		7	Guy HELLERS		
8	Derek FERGUSON ‡		8	Michael GOOSSENS		
9	Ian BAIRD ❑		9	Philippe LEONARD ❑		
10	Glynn SNODIN		10	Frans VAN ROOY		
11	Eamonn BANNON		11	Marc WILMOTS ❑		

Substitutes		*Substitute*
Alan McLAREN †46		Thierry PISTER †46
Iain FERGUSON ‡73		

Referee Gerhard KAPL (Austria)

SUMMARY

● *Hibernian had been somewhat unlucky to lose on away goals to Anderlecht in the first round, and now the other Edinburgh club, Hearts, also had reason to complain at their lack of good fortune against Belgian opposition. Standard Liège were under siege for much of the game, but somehow they managed to hang on to the 1-0 lead which in-form midfielder Alain Bettagno had given them as early as the 7th minute when he rose unchallenged to head in Patrick Vervoort's left-wing corner. The Hearts fans, who had been encouraged to turn up in numbers after their team's exciting victory over Slavia Prague in the first round, got firmly behind their team. But with Baird being awarded a free-kick instead of a penalty when bundled down by Leonard just inside the area and Snodin having a free-kick deflected onto a post, the Scottish side did not get the break they needed. And as their attacks became more and more infrequent late in the game, goalkeeper Henry Smith found himself having to make three important saves from Vervoort, Van Rooy and Hellers to keep Hearts in the tie.*

Wednesday 4th November 1992
Sclessin Stadium, Liège

R STANDARD LIEGE 1 HEART OF MIDLOTHIAN 0

Half-time 0-0 Aggregate 2-0 Attendance 25,000

		Goals				Goals
1	Gilbert BODART †		1	Henry SMITH		
2	Régis GENAUX		2	Alan McLAREN		
3	Patrick VERVOORT		3	Tosh McKINLAY		
4	Stéphane DEMOL		4	Craig LEVEIN		
5	André CRUZ		5	Gary MACKAY ‡		
6	Philippe LEONARD		6	Peter VAN DE VEN		
7	Guy HELLERS		7	John ROBERTSON		
8	Alain BETTAGNO		8	Derek FERGUSON		
9	Michael GOOSSENS		9	Ian FERGUSON		
10	Frans VAN ROOY		10	John MILLAR ❏ †		
11	Marc WILMOTS	62	11	Ally MAUCHLEN		

Substitute

Jacky MUNARON †46

Substitutes

Glynn SNODIN †67 ❏

Wayne FOSTER ‡73

Referee Philippe LEDUC (France)

SUMMARY

● *Since the first leg Hearts and Standard had become involved in an increasingly hostile war of words. It had begun when Standard coach Arie Haan, unimpressed with the Scottish side's physical approach, had labelled them "a rugby team" and escalated to a depressing peak when the Hearts team bus was stoned by Standard fans as it arrived at the ground. Joe Jordan's men were understandably in no mood to change their style of play for this return leg and the first half an hour was almost a replica of the first game. Hearts poured forward in search of a goal but could not score and Standard survived to the interval with their 1-0 lead still intact. The Belgians had a new goalkeeper for the second half but Munaron was called into action far less frequently than Bodart as the Scottish attacks began to peter out. The only goal arrived at the other end and was scored by Belgian international Marc Wilmots. Goossens and Cruz came close to extending Standard's advantage late on, but the scoreline was already quite sufficient to take Standard further than they had been in Europe for over a decade.*

UEFA CUP
Second Round First Leg

Wednesday 21st October 1992
Abbé-Deschamps Stadium, Auxerre

AJ AUXERRE 5 FC KØBENHAVN 0

Half-time 2-0 *Attendance* 20,000

		Goals			Goals
1	Bruno MARTINI		1	Palle PETERSEN	
2	Thierry BONALAIR		2	Christian LØNSTRUP	
3	William PRUNIER		3	Ivan NIELSEN	
4	Frank VERLAAT †		4	Michael GIOLBAS	
5	Stéphane MAHE		5	Lars Højer NIELSEN †	
6	Raphaël GUERREIRO		6	Pierre LARSEN	
7	Christophe COCARD ‡		7	Jørgen Juul JENSEN	
8	Daniel DUTUEL		8	Nicolai WAEL ❏	
9	Gérald BATICLE	15, 40, 80	9	Brian KAUS	
10	Corentin MARTINS	53	10	Martin JOHANSEN	
11	Pascal VAHIRUA		11	Anders BJERRE	
	Substitutes			*Substitute*	
	Alain GOMA †46			Brian RASMUSSEN †65	
	Didier OTOKORE ‡81	90			

Referee László VAGNER (Hungary)

● FC København went into this match with a quite extraordinary record. The club, formed less than four months earlier, had yet to lose a match in official competition! They were still unbeaten after 12 matches of the Danish league, they had destroyed MP of Finland on their European debut and had just knocked Brøndby out of the Danish Cup. But Auxerre had shown in the previous round against Lokomotiv Plovdiv just how ruthless they could be on their home ground when the mood took them, and this was to be another of those nights. Right from the opening whistle Auxerre tore into their opponents, and by the end of the match the Danish side's proud record had not merely been broken. It had been smashed into smithereens, with goalkeeper Palle Petersen having endured the most miserable of evenings between the posts. The star of the show for Auxerre was Gérald Baticle. He doubled his goal tally of the first round with a brilliant hat-trick to make himself joint top goalscorer in the competition alongside Napoli's Daniel Fonseca.

Wednesday 4th November 1992
Parken, Copenhagen

FC KØBENHAVN 0   AJ AUXERRE 2

Half-time 0-0   Aggregate 0-7   Attendance 3,000

		Goals				Goals
1	Palle PETERSEN			1	Bruno MARTINI	
2	Kenneth WEGNER			2	Thierry BONALAIR	88
3	Ivan NIELSEN			3	William PRUNIER	
4	Michael GIOLBAS			4	Frank VERLAAT	
5	Lars Højer NIELSEN †			5	Stéphane MAHE	
6	Pierre LARSEN			6	Raphaël GUERREIRO	
7	Christian LØNSTRUP			7	Christophe COCARD	
8	Iørn ULDBJERG			8	Daniel DUTUEL	
9	Michael MANNICHE ‡			9	Gérald BATICLE †	64
10	Brian KAUS			10	Corentin MARTINS	
11	Michael JOHANSEN			11	Pascal VAHIRUA ‡	

Substitutes	*Substitutes*
Anders BJERRE †50	Lilian LASLANDES †64
Jørgen Juul JENSEN ‡72	Alain GOMA ‡80

Referee Philip DON (England)

● 5-0 down from the first leg, FC København had only pride to play for in front of a small crowd in the Danish national stadium. They gave as good as they got for an hour, but a spectacular individual goal from Christophe Cocard put the visitors in the lead after 64 minutes and a second Auxerre victory was sealed with full-back Thierry Bonalair's fulminating left-foot shot just two minutes from the end. In both games Auxerre had demonstrated the art of finishing to an almost merciless degree and they now went into the hat for the third-round draw having amassed a grand total of 16 goals from their four matches - more than any other team in the competition. Guy Roux was evidently delighted with his team's progress: "With qualification to the next round, four UEFA points out of four and not a single booking in either leg, there is not much more anybody could have asked of us." He would also be able to boast later that Auxerre's 7-0 aggregate was the biggest victory margin of the round, not just in the UEFA Cup but in all three competitions put together!

Wednesday 21st October 1992
Bernabéu Stadium, Madrid

REAL MADRID 5 TORPEDO MOSKVA 2

Half-time 3-2 Attendance 43,000

		Goals				Goals
1	Francisco BUYO		1	Aleksandr PODSHIVALOV		
2	RICARDO ROCHA		2	Gennady FILIMONOV		
3	Mikel LASA		3	Maxim CHELTSOV		
4	Fernando Muñoz "NANDO"		4	Andrey AFANASYEV		
5	Manuel SANCHIS		5	Dmitry ULYANOV		
6	Fernando HIERRO	8, 28, 32	6	Sergei SHUSTIKOV		36
7	Emilio BUTRAGUEÑO †		7	Gennady GRISHIN		39
8	Miguel González "MICHEL"	85 (pen)	8	Yury TISHKOV		
9	Iván ZAMORANO	52	9	Boris VOSTROSABLIN †		
10	Robert PROSINECKI ‡		10	Igor CHUGAYNOV		
11	LUIS ENRIQUE Martínez		11	Aleksei AREFIEV		

Substitutes		*Substitute*
ALFONSO Pérez †63		Nikolai SAVICHEV †46 ❑
Luis MILLA ‡65		

Referee Frans VAN DEN WIJNGAERT (Belgium)

SUMMARY

● *Real Madrid had lost at home to Spartak Moscow in the Champions' Cup quarter-final two seasons earlier, and another team from the Russian capital were to give them a nasty fright before they eventually finished as comfortable 5-2 winners. It all looked plain sailing for Real after 32 minutes. They were 3-0 up, and deservedly so, thanks to a hat-trick of exceptional quality by their goalscoring midfielder Hierro, all of his goals having been created from dead-ball situations by Míchel. But Torpedo had not abandoned hope, and before the half was out they had stunned the Bernabéu crowd into silence by scoring twice in three minutes, both goals coming out of nothing, speculative shots from outside the penalty area. Chilean striker Iván Zamorano went halfway towards restoring Real's three-goal advantage when he prodded in his first European goal seven minutes after the restart - again as a result of a Míchel corner - but it was not until five minutes from the end that the Spaniards completed their recovery when Míchel himself deservedly got his name on the scoresheet from the penalty spot.*

UEFA CUP
Second Round Second Leg

Wednesday 4th November 1992
Torpedo Stadium, Moscow

TORPEDO MOSKVA 3 REAL MADRID 2

Half-time 1-1 *Aggregate* 5-7 *Attendance* 6,500

		Goals				Goals
1	Aleksandr PODSHIVALOV		1	Pedro JARO		
2	Gennady FILIMONOV		2	Miguel CHENDO ∎		
3	Maxim CHELTSOV		3	Francisco José Pérez VILLARROYA		
4	Andrey AFANASYEV		4	Fernando Muñoz "NANDO"		
5	Mikhail MURASHOV	77	5	Manuel SANCHIS ∎		
6	Sergei SHUSTIKOV ❏		6	Fernando HIERRO		56
7	Gennady GRISHIN ❏		7	Emilio BUTRAGUEÑO		
8	Yury TISHKOV	61	8	Miguel González "MICHEL" ‡		
9	Andrey TALALAEV ‡	11	9	Iván ZAMORANO †		9
10	Igor CHUGAYNOV		10	Robert PROSINECKI		
11	Aleksei AREFIEV †		11	LUIS ENRIQUE Martínez		
	Substitutes			*Substitutes*		
	Dmitry ULYANOV †72			ALFONSO Pérez †58		
	Ivan PAZEMOV ‡79			Luis MILLA ‡62		

Referee Jaap UILENBERG (Holland)

● *Whilst the three other Moscow teams - CSKA, Spartak and Dinamo - all completed magnificent second-round triumphs against, respectively, Barcelona, Liverpool and Torino, Torpedo could not quite make up the deficit from their first encounter in Madrid. Nevertheless, they departed with their heads held high. After all, they had eliminated a big European name of their own - Manchester United - in the first round and against Real Madrid they had not only managed to come twice from behind to preserve their long-standing unbeaten home record in Europe, but had also recorded a famous victory over European football's most successful club. 3-2 was the final score on the night, although frankly there was never any real hope that Torpedo could actually win the tie once Zamorano had given Real the lead early in the first half and Hierro had restored it 11 minutes after the interval. But goals by Yury Tishkov and Mikhail Murashov, both, like Talalaev's earlier effort, scored with the head, ensured that the Russian fans went home happy despite their team's exit from the competition.*

UEFA CUP
Second Round Review

SECOND ROUND RESULTS

		1st leg	2nd leg	Agg.
Vitória Guimarães	Ajax	0-3	1-2	1-5
Napoli	Paris Saint-Germain FC	0-2	0-0	0-2
1.FC Kaiserslautern	Sheffield Wednesday	3-1	2-2	5-3
BK Frem	Real Zaragoza	0-1	1-5	1-6
Borussia Dortmund	Celtic	1-0	2-1	3-1
Vitesse	KV Mechelen	1-0	1-0	2-0
Roma	Grasshopper-Club Zürich	3-0	3-4	6-4
Fenerbahçe	Sigma Olomouc	1-0	1-7	2-7
Eintracht Frankfurt	Galatasaray	0-0	0-1	0-1
Torino	Dinamo Moskva	1-2	0-0	1-2
SL Benfica	Vác FC Samsung	5-1	1-0	6-1
RSC Anderlecht	Dinamo Kiev	4-2	3-0	7-2
Panathinaikos	Juventus	0-1	0-0	0-1
Heart of Midlothian	R Standard Liège	0-1	0-1	0-2
AJ Auxerre	FC København	5-0	2-0	7-0
Real Madrid	Torpedo Moskva	5-2	2-3	7-5

LEADING GOALSCORERS AFTER SECOND ROUND

6 Marcel WITECZEK (1.FC Kaiserslautern)
   Gérald BATICLE (AJ Auxerre)
   Daniel FONSECA (Napoli)
5 George WEAH (Paris Saint-Germain FC)
   Anthony YEBOAH (Eintracht Frankfurt)
4 PACHECO (SL Benfica)
   Luc NILIS (RSC Anderlecht)
   Fernando HIERRO (Real Madrid)
   Krzysztof WARZYCHA (Panathinaikos)
3 Stefan PETTERSSON (Ajax)
   Dennis BERGKAMP (Ajax)
   Dorin MATEUT (Real Zaragoza)
   John VAN DEN BROM (Vitesse)
   Giuseppe GIANNINI (Roma)
   Ruggiero RIZZITELLI (Roma)
   AYKUT Kocaman (Fenerbahçe)
   Milan KERBR (Sigma Olomouc)
   Viktor LEONENKO (Dinamo Kiev)
   Peter VAN VOSSEN (RSC Anderlecht)
   Christophe COCARD (AJ Auxerre)
   Paul WARHURST (Sheffield Wednesday)
   Axel KRUSE (Eintracht Frankfurt)
   Frank MILL (Borussia Dortmund)

UEFA CUP

THIRD ROUND DRAW

Tuesday 24th November 1992
Olympisch Stadium, Amsterdam

AJAX 2 1.FC KAISERSLAUTERN 0

Half-time 1-0 *Attendance* 46,000

		Goals			Goals
1	Stanley MENZO		1	Michael SERR	
2	Sonny SILOOY		2	Bjarne GOLDBAEK	
3	Danny BLIND		3	Martin WAGNER ❑	
4	Wim JONK	83	4	Thomas RITTER	
5	Frank DE BOER		5	Miroslav KADLEC	
6	Marciano VINK		6	Thomas DOOLEY	
7	Marc OVERMARS		7	Demir HOTIC ‡	
8	Michel KREEK		8	Michael ZEYER	
9	Rob ALFLEN †		9	Marcel WITECZEK	
10	Dennis BERGKAMP		10	Oliver SCHÄFER †	
11	Edgar DAVIDS ‡	1	11	Marcus MARIN	

Substitutes   *Substitutes*

Ron WILLEMS †76   Marco HABER †53

Clarence SEEDORF ‡82   Bernhard WINKLER ‡84

Referee Howard KING (Wales)

SUMMARY

● *Holders Ajax kept their long unbeaten UEFA Cup run going with this emphatic 2-0 victory against Kaiserslautern. The Germans had been thrashed 5-0 by Feyenoord on their only previous visit to Holland - in the 1976/77 UEFA Cup - and a similar punishment looked to be a possibility when Edgar Davids slipped in front of a ball-watching Kaiserslautern defence to put Ajax in the lead in the very first minute. It was the third round in succession that the young left-winger had scored Ajax's opening goal of the tie. But the Amsterdam side failed to capitalise on that early breakthrough and it was not until seven minutes from the end that midfield schemer Wim Jonk gave his team some breathing space for the return fixture with a second goal. It was Jonk's first European goal since his magnificent strike against Torino in the final the previous season, and once again it came from a well-struck shot from outside the area. That goal completed a miserable night for the German club. Before the match 50 of their skinhead followers had been arrested for causing trouble and refused entry into the stadium.*

UEFA CUP
Third Round Second Leg

Tuesday 8th December 1992
Fritz Walter Stadium, Kaiserslautern

1.FC KAISERSLAUTERN 0 AJAX 1

Half-time 0-1 *Aggregate* 0-3 *Attendance* 27,111

		Goals				Goals
1	Michael SERR		1	Stanley MENZO		
2	Bjarne GOLDBAEK †		2	Sonny SILOOY		
3	Axel ROOS ❑		3	Danny BLIND		
4	Thomas RITTER ❑		4	Wim JONK		
5	Miroslav KADLEC		5	Frank DE BOER		
6	Oliver SCHÄFER		6	Marciano VINK ❑		
7	Demir HOTIC ❑		7	Marc OVERMARS		
8	Jan ERIKSSON ‡		8	Rob ALFLEN	42	
9	Marcel WITECZEK		9	Stefan PETTERSSON		
10	Thomas VOGEL		10	Dennis BERGKAMP		
11	Marcus MARIN		11	Edgar DAVIDS		
	Substitutes			*Substitutes*		
	Frank LELLE †46					
	Michael ZEYER ‡76					

Referee Emanuel MONTEIRO COROADO (Portugal)

SUMMARY

● *2-0 up from the first leg and unbeaten away from home in Dutch league and European fixtures for over a year, Ajax had every reason to feel confident of making further progress in the competition. On the other hand, Kaiserslautern had won each of their last ten home games in Europe and had not been beaten there since October 1980. Something had to give, and Kaiserslautern coach Rainer Zobel unwittingly gave Ajax confidence by moving six-goal Marcel Witeczek from centre-forward to the left-back position normally occupied by the suspended Martin Wagner. The move was a concession to the threat posed by Marc Overmars on the right wing, but the youngster was to be the star of the show and it was from one of his runs that the only goal of the game ensued. His neat pass inside was knocked back by Marciano Vink into the path of Rob Alflen, who just managed to stab the ball past Serr before the defenders closed in. The tie was all over from this moment and Ajax proceeded to put on a show in the second half. It was six wins out of six for Ajax now, an exact repeat of their performance in the first three rounds a year earlier.*

UEFA CUP
Third Round First Leg

Tuesday 24th November 1992
Westfalen Stadium, Dortmund

BORUSSIA DORTMUND 3 REAL ZARAGOZA 1

Half-time 3-0 *Attendance* 35,917

		Goals				Goals
1	Stefan KLOS		1	Andoni CEDRUN		
2	Knut REINHARDT		2	Jesús Angel SOLANA ❏ ■		
3	Bodo SCHMIDT		3	ESTEBAN Gutiérrez		
4	Michael SCHULZ		4	SERGI López		
5	Stefan REUTER		5	Dario FRANCO		51
6	Thomas FRANCK ❏ ‡		6	Javier AGUADO		
7	Michael LUSCH		7	Miguel PARDEZA		
8	Michael ZORC	23 (pen)	8	Gustavo POYET ❏		
9	Stéphane CHAPUISAT	12	9	Francisco HIGUERA ‡		
10	Michael RUMMENIGGE †		10	Andreas BREHME		
11	Flemming POVLSEN	42	11	José GAY † ❏		

Substitutes

Lothar SIPPEL †78

Ned ZELIC ‡82

Substitutes

GARCIA SANJUAN †58

Manuel PEÑA ‡69

Referee David ELLERAY (England)

SUMMARY

● *With Kaiserslautern having a difficult task against holders Ajax, most German hopes of European glory rested with their only other survivors, Borussia Dortmund. Ottmar Hitzfeld's side had looked trophy-winning material against Celtic in the previous round and were in even better form in the first half of this encounter. Zaragoza were possibly still reeling from their 6-1 thrashing by Barcelona the previous weekend, but the home side showed them little mercy. Dortmund's first goal was a gem, scored, almost inevitably, by Stéphane Chapuisat, after 13 minutes. The Swiss striker showed both skill and pace to twist past his markers before finding the net with a delightful chip. Ten minutes later Dortmund were 2-0 up thanks to captain and spot-kick expert Michael Zorc. And three minutes before the interval Flemming Povlsen was on hand to convert Knut Reinhardt's cross and put Dortmund three up. The Spaniards regained some composure in the second half and were rewarded with a goal from Argentinian Dario Franco, who headed in a Brehme free-kick to keep his team's chances alive for the second leg.*

Tuesday 8th December 1992
La Romareda Stadium, Zaragoza

REAL ZARAGOZA 2 BORUSSIA DORTMUND 1

Half-time 1-0 *Aggregate* 3-4 *Attendance* 39,000

		Goals			Goals
1	Andoni CEDRUN		1	Stefan KLOS	
2	Andreas BREHME	90 (pen)	2	Knut REINHARDT	
3	ESTEBAN Gutiérrez		3	Bodo SCHMIDT	
4	Narciso JULIA		4	Michael SCHULZ	
5	Dario FRANCO		5	Ned ZELIC ❑	
6	Javier AGUADO		6	Günter KUTOWSKI ❑	
7	Miguel PARDEZA		7	Michael LUSCH	
8	Gustavo POYET ❑	26	8	Michael ZORC	
9	Francisco HIGUERA ❑		9	Stéphane CHAPUISAT	62
10	Jesús SEBA †		10	Gerhard POSCHNER	
11	José GAY		11	Flemming POVLSEN	

Substitute

GARCIA SANJUAN †59

Substitutes

Referee Hubert FORSTINGER (Austria)

SUMMARY

● *Statistically, Zaragoza had a one in three chance of rescuing qualification after their 1-3 defeat in Dortmund, but Spanish teams had a long-standing reputation for their second-leg turnarounds. There was certainly no shirking from the home team in the first ten minutes during which two of their players received yellow cards for taking their enthusiasm too far. One of them, Gustavo Poyet, who thus incurred his second booking of the tie, made amends soon afterwards by swivelling in the box to plant a cross-shot beyond Klos and give Zaragoza the lead. The Spaniards continued to impose themselves, but with a little under half an hour to go they were rocked on their heels when, out of the blue, Dortmund got an equaliser. It was that man Chapuisat again who scored it, his fourth goal in as many games, and it left Zaragoza with a mountain to climb if they were to stay in the competition. The best they could muster in reply was a last-minute penalty by Andreas Brehme after Schulz had harshly been adjudged to have held down Pardeza in the box. But that was too late to save them.*

Tuesday 24th November 1992
Parc des Princes, Paris

PARIS SAINT-GERMAIN FC 0 RSC ANDERLECHT 0

Half-time 0-0 Attendance 32,402

		Goals				Goals
1	Bernard LAMA		1	Filip DE WILDE		
2	Antoine KOMBOUARE		2	Bertrand CRASSON		
3	Patrick COLLETER		3	Graeme RUTJES		
4	RICARDO Gomes		4	Philippe ALBERT ■		
5	Alain ROCHE		5	Michel DE WOLF		
6	Paul LE GUEN		6	Wim KOOIMAN		
7	Laurent FOURNIER		7	Bruno VERSAVEL		
8	Vincent GUERIN		8	Peter VAN VOSSEN †		
9	George WEAH		9	Luc NILIS		
10	VALDO Candido		10	Mark DEGRYSE ❏		
11	David GINOLA ❏ ■		11	Danny BOFFIN		

Substitutes   *Substitute*

Johan WALEM †89

Referee Angelo AMENDOLIA (Italy)

FACTFILE

● Going into this game Anderlecht were on top of the Belgian League, two points ahead of Standard Liège, while Paris-Saint-Germain were joint top in France alongside Nantes.

● Paris Saint-Germain's only previous European tie against Belgian opposition took place a decade earlier in the Cup-winners' Cup. On that occasion they were eliminated in the quarter-finals by Waterschei, 2-3 on aggregate after extra-time, after winning the home leg 2-0.

● No fewer than seven of the Anderlecht players who took the field against Paris Saint-Germain were appearing at the Parc des Princes for the second time in 1992. Crasson, Albert, Versavel, Nilis, Degryse, Boffin and Walem had all played there for Belgium against France in a friendly international the previous March.

De Wilde keeps unlucky PSG at bay

Anderlecht's Croatian coach Luka Peruzovic dogmatically stated his team's ambition before the game. "We have come to Paris to score a goal." It was no empty claim. For Anderlecht had managed five goals on foreign soil in the two previous rounds, and back home in Belgium they had taken maximum points from their first six away games of the season, hitting an incredible 21 goals in the process.

However, the sequence was to end in the Parc des Princes despite the fact that Anderlecht enjoyed a one-man advantage for 35 minutes of play. That was the time which elapsed between the sending-off of Paris Saint-Germain's David Ginola for a second bookable offence midway through the first half and the red card shown by the Italian referee to Anderlecht's Philippe Albert for his wild challenge on man of the match Valdo.

The good news for the Belgians, though, was that Paris SG did not find the target either. They certainly threatened to, no more so than in the last few minutes when first Fournier screwed the ball just wide after shaking off Boffin's challenge and then Guérin saw his shot saved at point-blank range by De Wilde after finding himself free on the edge of the six-yard box.

De Wilde gave a true captain's performance all evening and it was purely down to his exploits that Anderlecht managed to avoid defeat. The French side were the better team throughout, at 11-a-side, 10-a-side or even when the visitors had their one-man advantage. But with Ginola off the field early on, five-goal Weah having a bad night up front and luck not going their way,

● Filip De Wilde

they had to content themselves at the end of an exciting, yet goalless, game with having thwarted Anderlecht's ambition to score an away goal.

In truth, the Belgians had rarely looked like scoring that goal. Perhaps the sight of Paris 'keeper Bernard Lama had something to do with that. Having broken his nose during a French League match against Auxerre the previous weekend, he took the field sporting a sinister-looking face mask of the type worn by 'Hannibal the Cannibal' in the hit film, "Silence of the Lambs"!

VALDO
Paris Saint-Germain FC

Nobody tried harder to unlock the Anderlecht defence than Paris SG's Brazilian midfielder Valdo. He was a constant scourge to the Belgians, bringing out a fine one-handed save from Filip De Wilde in the first half, going close with a free-kick in the second and leading his markers a merry dance from first minute to last with a wonderful exhibition of dribbling skills.

Valdo came to Paris from Benfica in the summer of 1991 in a joint deal involving his fellow Brazilian Ricardo. The two players were key members of the Benfica side which reached the Champions' Cup final in 1990, losing eventually to Milan in Vienna. On the international stage Valdo enhanced his reputation with some fine displays at the 1990 World Cup, where he appeared from the start in all four of Brazil's matches. If his 1992/93 form is anything to go by, he should be making a World Cup re-appearance in the States next summer assuming, of course, that Brazil maintain their record of never having failed to qualify.

UEFA CUP
Third Round Second Leg

Tuesday 8th December 1992
Constant Vanden Stock Stadium, Brussels

RSC ANDERLECHT 1 PARIS SAINT-GERMAIN FC 1

Half-time 0-0 *Aggregate* 1-1 *Attendance* 25,000

		Goals				Goals
1	Filip DE WILDE			1	Bernard LAMA	
2	Bertrand CRASSON			2	Jean-Luc SASSUS †	
3	Graeme RUTJES			3	Patrick COLLETER	
4	Alain VAN BAEKEL			4	RICARDO Gomes	
5	Michel DE WOLF			5	Alain ROCHE	
6	Johan WALEM			6	Paul LE GUEN	
7	Bruno VERSAVEL			7	Laurent FOURNIER ❏	
8	Peter VAN VOSSEN			8	Vincent GUERIN	
9	Luc NILIS			9	François CALDERARO	
10	John BOSMAN	53		10	VALDO Candido	
11	Danny BOFFIN			11	Daniel BRAVO ‡	

Substitutes				*Substitutes*		
				Antoine KOMBOUARE †66 ❏	76	
				Francis LLACER ‡90		

Referee Kurt RÖTHLISBERGER (Switzerland)

● *Paris Saint-Germain's qualification enabled France to have three teams left in Europe in the spring for only the third time ever. The previous two occasions were in 1979/80 and 1989/90.*

● *Three players were suspended from this game as a result of misdemeanours in the first leg. Philippe Albert and Marc Degryse of Anderlecht and David Ginola of Paris Saint-Germain.*

● *John Bosman's goal was the first conceded by Paris SG in their European campaign.*

● *This was the first time Anderlecht had been eliminated by a French club from European competition. In previous meetings they had knocked Lens out of the UEFA Cup in 1983/84 and Metz out of the Cup-winners' Cup in 1988/89.*

FACTFILE

Kombouaré's header takes Paris SG through

Despite being held to a goalless draw at home in the first meeting, Paris Saint-Germain had good reason to believe that they could still make it through to the UEFA Cup quarter-finals for the first time. 2-0 victories away from home against both PAOK and Napoli in the last two rounds were evidence enough that the French side were not afraid of travelling, nor of appearing in front of hostile crowds.

In a week when Auxerre and Marseille also had decisive matches against Belgian opposition, Paris SG appeared to have the most difficult task of the three, especially with their counter-attacking specialist, Ginola, out through suspension and top scorer Weah missing with a leg injury. François Calderaro and Daniel Bravo were the replacement strike force and the latter should have made a dramatic entrance with a goal in the fifth minute. But he miscued his header completely and Anderlecht were let off the hook.

After an evenly-balanced first half, still without goals, the home side began to pick up the pace in the early moments of the second period. Lama was tested twice by Versavel and Nilis before Bosman, in for the suspended Degryse, beat him with a flying header from Van Vossen's left-wing cross. The first goal of the tie had been scored at last - after nearly two and a half hours of football!

Anderlecht were ahead, but they could not afford to relax. The away goals rule left them still vulnerable. They had benefitted from it in the first round against Hibernian, but now it was to cause their downfall.

Van Vossen had just missed a glorious opportunity to settle the tie when, with the clock showing less than a quarter of an hour to go, Paris SG won a corner on the left. Valdo swung it in and Antoine Kombouaré, the former Nantes defender, who had come on as a substitute just a few minutes earlier, rose in between two Anderlecht defenders to meet the ball at the near post and glance it astutely into the far corner.

It was no more than the French side deserved. They had shown tremendous character, had never given up hope and, on the balance of the two legs, had unquestionably been the better side.

Now, having eliminated one of the pre-tournament favourites, Artur Jorge's men could stride forward into the quarter-finals full of confidence and ready to take on any of the big guns still left in the competition.

BERNARD LAMA
Paris Saint-Germain FC

The 'Man in the Mask' from the first leg became 'Man of the Match' in the second. Bernard Lama did his prospects of ousting Bruno Martini from the French national team jersey no harm whatsoever with a brave and confident performance in Brussels. His feline frame was alive to all danger from the Anderlecht forwards and his save from Van Vossen, in particular, was just as crucial to his team's success as Kombouaré's goal moments later.

Paris Saint-Germain became Lama's fifth club in as many seasons when he joined them from Lens in the summer of 1992. After a number of years with Lille, his first club, he spent just a single season each with Metz, Brest and Lens before his big-money move to the capital. Now, though, he would seem to be settled at last in Paris, where, amongst other things, he benefits from the coaching experience of former French national 'keeper Joël Bats.

Tuesday 24th November 1992
Sclessin Stadium, Liège

R STANDARD LIEGE 2 AJ AUXERRE 2

Half-time 1-0 *Attendance* 16,600

		Goals			Goals
1	Gilbert BODART		1	Bruno MARTINI	
2	Régis GENAUX ❑		2	Alain GOMA	
3	Patrick VERVOORT		3	William PRUNIER ❑	
4	Stéphane DEMOL		4	Frank VERLAAT ■	55
5	André CRUZ		5	Stéphane MAHE	
6	Thierry PISTER ❑ ‡		6	Raphaël GUERREIRO	
7	Guy HELLERS		7	Christophe COCARD	
8	Alain BETTAGNO †		8	Daniel DUTUEL	
9	Michael GOOSSENS	9, 48	9	Gérald BATICLE	71
10	Frans VAN ROOY		10	Corentin MARTINS	
11	Marc WILMOTS		11	Pascal VAHIRUA †	

Substitutes	*Substitute*
Mohamed LASHAF †61	Stéphane MAZZOLINI †78
Philippe LEONARD ‡78	

Referee James McCLUSKEY (Scotland)

SUMMARY

● *Standard Liège had only themselves to blame for failing to establish a big first-leg lead. For 50 minutes they steamrollered Auxerre into submission, scoring two goals when double that amount would not have been an unjust reflection of the play. But, astonishingly, the Frenchmen came back to score twice themselves and put themselves in a promising position for the return. Young striker Michael Goossens was the man who set Standard up for what appeared to be a comfortable win by scoring both of their goals. His first was steered in from an acute angle and the second came early in the second half when he reacted first in the box to a knock-on from a throw-in. Dutchman Frank Verlaat was Auxerre's chief protagonist. The sweeper nodded in his team's first goal after 55 minutes and found himself up front once again to lay on Gérald Baticle's seventh goal of the competition before getting himself sent off shortly afterwards. Auxerre boss Guy Roux gave an ironic summing-up of his team's display: "We had one half-chance all match and scored two goals!"*

Tuesday 8th December 1992
Abbé-Deschamps Stadium, Auxerre

AJ AUXERRE 2 R STANDARD LIEGE 1

Half-time 0-0   *Aggregate* 4-3   *Attendance* 18,300

		Goals				Goals
1	Bruno MARTINI			1	Gilbert BODART	
2	Stéphane MAZZOLINI			2	Régis GENAUX ■	
3	William PRUNIER			3	Patrick VERVOORT	
4	Stéphane MAHE ❑			4	Stéphane DEMOL	
5	Franck RABIRAVONY †			5	André CRUZ †	
6	Raphaël GUERREIRO			6	Thierry PISTER	
7	Christophe COCARD			7	Guy HELLERS	
8	Daniel DUTUEL	71		8	Alain BETTAGNO	
9	Gérald BATICLE	81		9	Michael GOOSENS	
10	Corentin MARTINS			10	Frans VAN ROOY	
11	Pascal VAHIRUA ‡			11	Marc WILMOTS	88

Substitutes		*Substitute*
Christophe REMY †83		Philippe LEONARD †80
Didier OTOKORE ‡85		

Referee Patrick KELLY (Republic of Ireland)

SUMMARY

● *Inspired by their team's home performances in earlier rounds and by the unexpected comeback in Liège, the good people of Auxerre turned out in force once again to will their team into the UEFA Cup quarter-finals for the second time in four seasons. With two away goals to comfort them, Auxerre knew they had to keep their goal intact to win the tie, but with three key defenders - Bonalair, Goma and the suspended Verlaat - all missing, that was no easy task. Yet for much of the game, despite the intensity of the contest and the excitement generated in the stands by the sell-out crowd, 0-0 looked to be the likeliest result. But the expulsion of Standard's young right-back Régis Genaux after an hour's play gave Auxerre the extra boost they needed and they took full advantage by scoring two goals in ten minutes, the first a volleyed chip from Baticle, who had earlier been denied by an acrobatic save from Bodart, and the second from man of the match Daniel Dutuel. Wilmots' late strike for Standard ensured a nervous finish for the home fans but it came too late to save the Belgians from elimination.*

Wednesday 25th November 1992
Dinamo Stadium, Moscow

DINAMO MOSKVA 2 SL BENFICA 2

Half-time 0-1 Attendance 6,000

		Goals				Goals
1	Valery KLEYMENOV		1	SILVINO		
2	Sarkis OGANESYAN †		2	JOSÉ CARLOS		
3	Igor SKLYAROV		3	HÉLDER ▢		
4	Kakhaber TSKHADADZE ▢		4	WILLIAM ▢		
5	Yury KALITVINTSEV	75	5	VELOSO		
6	Andrey KOBELEV		6	Stefan SCHWARZ		
7	Yevgeny SMERTIN ‡		7	VÍTOR PANEIRA		
8	Sergei DERKACH	88	8	PAULO SOUSA		
9	Omari TETRADZE		9	Aleksandr MOSTOVOY		
10	Velli KASUMOV		10	Sergei YURAN †		
11	Igor VARLAMOV		11	ISAÍAS	36, 54	

Substitutes	*Substitute*
Nikolai KAVARDAEV †58 ▢	PAULO MADEIRA †81 ▢
Aleksei SAVCHENKO ‡79	

Referee John BLANKENSTEIN (Holland)

● Benfica's trip to Moscow got off to a dramatic start when their flight out of Lisbon had to be recalled after a phone call had been received stating that there was a bomb aboard the aircraft. Fortunately that turned out to be a hoax, but there was nothing untoward about the weather that greeted the Benfica party when they eventually touched down in Moscow. The Russian winter had already begun in earnest, and it was on a snow-covered pitch and in sub-zero temperatures that they had to take on a Dinamo side which had just completed its league season, finishing third behind the two Spartaks of Moscow and Vladikavkaz. In the circumstances, Benfica put on a quite splendid performance. Two goals from Brazilian striker Isaías had them two up with just a quarter of an hour to go. But the home side refused to surrender and late goals from Kalitvintsev and Derkach ensured that the tie was not yet over. After all, Dinamo had won away at Torino in the previous round, and all three of the other Russian teams - CSKA, Spartak and Torpedo - had also won ties after being held at home.

UEFA CUP
Third Round Second Leg

Tuesday 8th December 1992
Luz Stadium, Lisbon

SL BENFICA 2 DINAMO MOSKVA 0

Half-time 0-0 *Aggregate* 4-2 *Attendance* 50,000

		Goals				Goals
1	SILVINO		1	Valery KLEYMANOV		
2	JOSÉ CARLOS		2	Sergei TIMOFEEV		
3	HÉLDER		3	Igor SKLYAROV ❏		
4	WILLIAM		4	Kakhaber TSKHADADZE ❏		
5	VELOSO		5	Yury KALITVINTSEV		
6	Stefan SCHWARZ		6	Andrey KOBELEV ❏ †		
7	VÍTOR PANEIRA †		7	Yevgeny SMERTIN ‡		
8	PAULO SOUSA		8	Sergei DERKACH		
9	RUI COSTA		9	Omari TETRADZE		
10	Sergei YURAN ‡	57	10	Velli KASUMOV		
11	ISAÍAS	52	11	Viacheslav TSAREV		
	Substitutes			*Substitutes*		
	RUI ÁGUAS †67			Igor VARLAMOV †69		
	PACHECO ‡83			Aleksei SAVCHENKO ‡76		

Referee Gheorghe CONSTANTIN (Romania)

● *Russia's interest in the UEFA Cup ended in front of 50,000 spectators in the Stadium of Light. Dinamo became, after Torpedo a round earlier, the second of the four Moscow clubs to fall by the wayside, leaving just CSKA in the Champions' Cup and Spartak in the Cup-winners' Cup to pursue their European dreams. As in Moscow, it was Isaías who became the central figure in the game when he headed home Vítor Paneira's cross to give Benfica the lead on the night. The Brazilian had now scored ten goals in two seasons of European football. Only Luc Nilis of Anderlecht could match that achievement. No other player as yet had taken his two-season tally into double figures. Sergei Yuran became the next closest challenger when he scored Benfica's second goal five minutes later to register his ninth over the past two seasons. More significantly, the former Dinamo Kiev striker's goal ensured Benfica's place in the quarter-finals, the 18th time in their history that the club had reached the last eight of a European competition.*

UEFA CUP
Third Round First Leg

Wednesday 25th November 1992
Olimpico Stadium, Rome

ROMA 3 GALATASARAY 1

Half-time 0-0 *Attendance* 23,980

	Goals			Goals
1 Giuseppe ZINETTI		1 HAYRETTIN Demirbas	
2 Giovanni PIACENTINI †		2 Reinhard STUMPF	
3 Amedeo CARBONI ❑ ■		3 BÜLENT Korkmaz ❑	
4 Walter BONACINA		4 YUSUF Altintas	
5 ALDAIR dos Santos	59, 90	5 Falko GÖTZ	
6 Antonio COMI		6 TUGAY Kerimoglu	
7 Sinisa MIHAJLOVIC ❑ ‡		7 UGUR Tütüneker ■	
8 Thomas HÄSSLER ❑		8 Elvir BOLIC ❑ †	
9 Andrea CARNEVALE		9 HAKAN Sükür	85
10 Giuseppe GIANNINI ❑		10 OKAN Buruk	
11 Ruggiero RIZZITELLI		11 ERDAL Keser ❑	
Substitutes		*Substitute*	
Roberto MUZZI †55	80	SUAT Kaya †79	
Fausto SALSANO ‡73			

Referee Bernd HEYNEMANN (Germany)

SUMMARY

● *This was the first of two important games in four days for Roma. Coming up the following Sunday was the Rome derby, and for the first 45 minutes of this encounter it appeared as if Vujadin Boskov's side were simply warming up for that big Serie A clash with Lazio. But the apathy of their first-half display disappeared once Ugur had been sent off for an ugly off-the-ball incident. Seizing their one-man advantage, Roma were a team transformed after the interval, and after 59 minutes they finally got the breakthrough. It came not from one of their recognised goalscorers, but from Brazilian centre-back Aldair, chosen in preference to Claudio Caniggia. Roma looked to have gained a secure foothold on the tie when substitutes Salsano and Muzzi combined to produce a second goal after 80 minutes. But a disastrous goalkeeping error by Zinetti let in Hakan five minutes later and, as things stood, the Turks seemed likely to go away the happier. Aldair, however, was to have the final word. His stunning 35-yard strike flashed in off the post beyond a stupefied Hayrettin and the Italians were back in control.*

UEFA CUP
Third Round Second Leg

Wednesday 9th December 1992
Ali Sami Yen Stadium, Istanbul

GALATASARAY 3 ROMA 2

Half-time 1-1 Aggregate 4-5 Attendance 22,868

		Goals			Goals
1	HAYRETTIN Demirbas		1	Giuseppe ZINETTI	
2	Reinhard STUMPF ‡		2	Luigi GARZYA	
3	TAYFUN Hut †		3	Walter BONACINA	
4	YUSUF Altintas		4	Giovanni PIACENTINI	
5	Falko GÖTZ ❑		5	Silvano BENEDETTI	
6	MERT Korkmaz		6	Antonio COMI	
7	ISMAIL Demiriz		7	Claudio CANIGGIA ‡	7
8	MUHAMMET Altintas		8	Thomas HÄSSLER	47
9	HAKAN Sükür		9	Sinisa MIHAJLOVIC	
10	TUGAY Kerimoglu		10	Giuseppe GIANNINI	
11	MUSTAFA Kocabey	27, 58	11	Ruggiero RIZZITELLI †	

Substitutes			*Substitutes*	
ARIF Erdem †51	75		Andrea CARNEVALE †67	
HAMZA Hamzaoglu ‡67			Fausto SALSANO ‡80	

Referee Peter MIKKELSEN (Denmark)

● *Roma continued to demonstrate just how erratic their performances could be away from home. Twice, at the beginning of each half, they seemed to have the tie wrapped up, but, as in Zürich five weeks earlier, the Italians were to find themselves battling desperately to save their qualification in the latter stages when they should have been cruising gracefully into the next round. Having put out Frankfurt in the previous round, the Turks were reasonably optimistic of making further progress at Roma's expense. Still, they were taking no chances. The scheduled 13.00 kick-off time was brought back five minutes because they felt it might bring them bad luck! But as the clock struck 13.02 Galatasaray were already picking the ball out of the net. Mustafa's equaliser 20 minutes later gave the home crowd something to cheer, but a fantastic strike from Hässler just after half-time restored Roma's advantage. From then on, though, it was all Galatasaray and by the final whistle, despite being eliminated, they could at least celebrate only the second ever victory by a Turkish club against a side from Serie A.*

UEFA CUP
Third Round First Leg

Thursday 26th November 1992
Monnikenhuize Stadium, Arnhem

VITESSE 0   REAL MADRID 1

Half-time 0-0   *Attendance* 13,000

		Goals				Goals
1	Raymond VAN DER GOUW		1	Pedro JARO		
2	Roberto STRAAL		2	Luis RAMIS		
3	Erwin VAN DE LOOI		3	Mikel LASA		
4	Theo BOS		4	Fernando Muñoz "NANDO"		
5	Arjan VERMEULEN		5	Luis MILLA		
6	Martin LAAMERS		6	Fernando HIERRO	73	
7	John VAN DEN BROM		7	ALFONSO Pérez		
8	René EIJER ❏		8	Miguel González "MICHEL"		
9	Bart LATUHERU		9	Iván ZAMORANO ‡		
10	Hans VAN ARUM ❏ †		10	Robert PROSINECKI †		
11	Philip COCU		11	LUIS ENRIQUE Martínez		

Substitute

Huub LOEFFEN †75

Substitutes

Miguel CHENDO †68

Juan ESNAIDER ‡81

Referee Kaj John NATRI (Finland)

● *The Monnikenhuize Stadium in Arnhem was the setting for Real Madrid's 250th European match. Needless to say, this was an all-time appearance record in European competition, although Real had only just pipped their arch-rivals Barcelona to the landmark. The Catalans had played 248 times on the European stage when CSKA Moscow surprisingly knocked them out of the Champions' Cup. And fittingly Real celebrated their achievement with a victory - their 142nd - thanks to a single goal - their 542nd - scored by Hierro - his fifth in three games - after 73 minutes. Vitesse had plenty of opportunities to spoil the Spaniards' party, but they were too obliging in front of goal and Hierro's free-kick condemned them to an ill-deserved defeat. Irrespective of the two clubs' differing European pedigrees, the result was something of a surprise. Real had won just twice on their travels in the first three months of the season and had not won an away leg in Europe for six matches, their last victory, ironically enough, having been achieved just 50 km away, in Utrecht, 13 months earlier.*

Thursday 10th December 1992
Bernabéu Stadium, Madrid

REAL MADRID 1 VITESSE 0

Half-time 1-0 *Aggregate* 2-0 *Attendance* 20,000

		Goals				Goals
1	Francisco BUYO ❏			1	Raymond VAN DER GOUW	
2	Luis RAMIS			2	Roberto STRAAL	
3	Mikel LASA			3	Erwin VAN DE LOOI	
4	Fernando Muñoz "NANDO"			4	Theo BOS	
5	Manuel SANCHIS			5	Arjan VERMEULEN	
6	Luis MILLA			6	Martin LAAMERS	
7	Emilio BUTRAGUEÑO			7	John VAN DEN BROM	
8	Miguel González "MICHEL"			8	Huub LOEFFEN	
9	Iván ZAMORANO †	31		9	Bart LATUHERU	
10	Robert PROSINECKI			10	Hans VAN ARUM ❏	
11	LUIS ENRIQUE Martínez ‡			11	Philip COCU	

Substitutes

ALFONSO Pérez †46
Francisco LLORENTE ‡72

Substitutes

Referee Leslie MOTTRAM (Scotland)

● *Real Madrid, 1-0 winners in the first leg, duly secured a record 27th European quarter-final appearance with a repeat scoreline in the Bernabéu. But the club's ever-demanding supporters were far from impressed by the manner of the team's qualification. And rightly so. The fact was that Real had been preposterously lucky to win the game. They had taken the lead through a close-range Zamorano header in the first half but never looked likely to increase that advantage. Indeed, the second half was pretty much one-way traffic in the direction of Buyo's goal. As in the first leg, Vitesse had their chances to score, but from the best of them, both created by the ubiquitous Martin Laamers, Van den Brom aimed a free header straight at the Real 'keeper and Van Arum saw another aerial strike cannon back off the crossbar. Vitesse thus exited without a goal but with their pride very much intact, while Real, who had also suffered the indignity of losing 2-0 to poor relations Rayo Vallecano the previous weekend, appeared to be entering a crisis period, with new coach Benito Floro's job very much on the line.*

UEFA CUP
Third Round First Leg

Wednesday 25th November 1992
Sigma Stadium, Olomouc

SIGMA OLOMOUC 1 JUVENTUS 2

Half-time 0-1 *Attendance* 18,000

		Goals				Goals
1	Lubos PRIBYL		1	Angelo PERUZZI		
2	Michal KOVAR		2	Moreno TORRICELLI		
3	Jan MAROSI	89	3	Marco Antonio DE MARCHI		
4	Martin KOTULEK		4	Dino BAGGIO ❏		76
5	Jirí VADURA ❏		5	Jürgen KOHLER		
6	Milos SLABY ‡		6	Massimo CARRERA		
7	Roman HANUS		7	Antonio CONTE ❏		
8	Radoslav LÁTAL ❏		8	Roberto GALIA ❏		
9	Milan KERBR		9	Gianluca VIALLI †		
10	Jirí BARBORÍK †		10	Andreas MÖLLER ‡		23
11	Roman PIVARNÍK		11	Pierluigi CASIRAGHI		

Substitutes

Martin GUZÍK †78
Jirí KABYL ‡84

Substitutes

Fabrizio RAVANELLI †61
Paolo DI CANIO ‡82

Referee Joaquín URIO VELAZQUEZ (Spain)

S U M M A R Y

● *Sigma Olomouc had not been beaten at home in any of their previous seven European ties, including two against ex-Champions' Cup winners Hamburg and Real Madrid, but they met their match at last against Juventus. The Italians were good value for their third straight away win of the competition. In the absence of injury victims Roberto Baggio and David Platt, German international Andreas Möller came into his own and bossed the game with tremendous authority from the centre of the field. He was also responsible for opening the scoring. But if his classic 30-yard curler was textbook stuff, the same could hardly be said about Juventus's second goal. A long punt from Peruzzi dissected the Czechoslovakians' offside trap and Olomouc 'keeper Pribyl saw fit to come out of his area and head the ball away. Alas for him, it fell straight to Dino Baggio, who then proceeded to chip the ball back over his head from all of 40 yards! The only blot on the Italians' efficient, well-organised display came in the final minute when Marosi scored a consolation goal for Olomouc direct from a corner.*

UEFA CUP
Third Round Second Leg

Thursday 10th December 1992
Delle Alpi Stadium, Turin

JUVENTUS 5 SIGMA OLOMOUC 0

Half-time 2-0 Aggregate 7-1 Attendance 5,047

		Goals			Goals
1	Angelo PERUZZI		1	Lubos PRIBYL	
2	Moreno TORRICELLI		2	Michal KOVAR	
3	Marco Antonio DE MARCHI		3	Jan MAROSI	
4	Antonio CONTE ‡		4	Martin KOTULEK	
5	Jürgen KOHLER		5	Michal GOTTWALD †	
6	Massimo CARRERA		6	Milos SLABY	
7	Paolo DI CANIO		7	Roman HANUS ‡	
8	Roberto GALIA		8	Robert FIALA	
9	Gianluca VIALLI †	6, 50	9	Milan KERBR	
10	Andreas MÖLLER	46	10	Jirí BARBORÍK	
11	Pierluigi CASIRAGHI	29	11	Roman PIVARNÍK	
	Substitutes			*Substitutes*	
	Fabrizio RAVANELLI †60	70		Ivo LOSTÁK †33	
	Nicola RAGAGNIN ‡77			Jirí KABYL ‡64	

Referee Joël QUINIOU (France)

● *Gianluca Vialli took time out from a troublesome barren spell in the Italian league to score two spectacular goals and lead Juventus's charge into the UEFA Cup quarter-finals. The former Sampdoria striker was on target as early as the sixth minute with a wonderful first-time shot from just outside the area. The ball started out well wide of the target before bending back beautifully to find the top corner. Vialli's second goal was just as majestic, a bullet header from a Möller free-kick that flew into the net before the Olomouc 'keeper had time to move. That goal put Juventus 4-0 up on the night, with Casiraghi and Möller having also found the target earlier on. But even with Vialli off the field, the home side had not finished. His replacement, Fabrizio Ravanelli, crashed in a fifth goal after a comedy of errors in the Olomouc defence had presented him with the ball in yards of space on the edge of the area. With a 5-0 triumph on the night and a 7-1 victory on aggregate, Juventus had completed the third-round programme with the most convincing performance of any of the UEFA Cup contenders.*

UEFA CUP
Third Round Review

THIRD ROUND RESULTS

		1st leg	2nd leg	Agg.
Ajax	1.FC Kaiserslautern	2-0	1-0	3-0
Borussia Dortmund	Real Zaragoza	3-1	1-2	4-3
Paris Saint-Germain FC	RSC Anderlecht	0-0	1-1	1-1
(Paris Saint-Germain win on away goals)				
R Standard Liège	AJ Auxerre	2-2	1-2	3-4
Dinamo Moskva	SL Benfica	2-2	0-2	2-4
Roma	Galatasaray	3-1	2-3	5-4
Vitesse	Real Madrid	0-1	0-1	0-2
Sigma Olomouc	Juventus	1-2	0-5	1-7

LEADING GOALSCORERS AFTER THIRD ROUND

8   Gérald BATICLE (AJ Auxerre)

6   Marcel WITECZEK (1.FC Kaiserslautern)
    Daniel FONSECA (Napoli)

5   ISAÍAS (SL Benfica)
    Fernando HIERRO (Real Madrid)
    George WEAH (Paris Saint-Germain FC)
    Anthony YEBOAH (Eintracht Frankfurt)

4   Stéphane CHAPUISAT (Borussia Dortmund)
    Michael GOOSSENS (R Standard Liège)
    Gianluca VIALLI (Juventus)
    PACHECO (SL Benfica)
    Luc NILIS (RSC Anderlecht)
    Krzysztof WARZYCHA (Panathinaikos)

UEFA CUP

UEFA CUP
Quarter-finals First Leg

Tuesday 2nd March 1993
Bernabéu Stadium, Madrid

REAL MADRID 3 PARIS SAINT-GERMAIN FC 1

Half-time 2-0 *Attendance* 70,000

		Goals				Goals
1	Francisco BUYO		1	Bernard LAMA		
2	Luis RAMIS		2	Jean-Luc SASSUS ❑ †		
3	Mikel LASA ❑		3	Patrick COLLETER ❑		
4	Fernando Muñoz "NANDO"		4	RICARDO Gomes		
5	Manuel SANCHIS ❑		5	Alain ROCHE ■		
6	Fernando HIERRO		6	Paul LE GUEN		
7	Emilio BUTRAGUEÑO ‡	31	7	Laurent FOURNIER ❑		
8	Miguel González "MICHEL"	90	8	Vincent GUERIN		
9	Iván ZAMORANO	34	9	George WEAH ‡		
10	Luis MILLA ❑ †		10	VALDO Candido		
11	LUIS ENRIQUE Martínez		11	David GINOLA		49

Substitutes

Francisco LLORENTE †58

Juan ESNAIDER ‡62

Substitutes

Francis LLACER †64

Daniel BRAVO ‡84

Referee David ELLERAY (England)

FACTFILE

● *Real Madrid had won all four of their previous European confrontations with French teams, including two Champions' Cup final victories over Stade Reims (1956 and 1959).*

● *Prior to this match Real Madrid had dropped just one point at home in their 14 Spanish League matches. They had also won all three of their European matches in the Bernabéu.*

● *Three days earlier Real had gone top of the Spanish League for the first time in the season after a 2-1 victory at home to Deportivo La Coruña.*

● *David Ginola's goal was the sixth (out of eight) that Paris Saint-Germain had scored from a corner in their UEFA Cup campaign.*

● *Míchel*

Late penalty floors luckless French

Before the game Real Madrid president Ramón Mendoza was presented with a plaque by UEFA chief Lennart Johansson to commemorate the club's achievement at having played 250 matches in European competition. But those spectators in the Bernabéu who had witnessed many of Real's great European games in the past would have been hard pressed, at the final whistle of this one, to have recalled another encounter in which their team was so fortunate to come away with a victory.

On the balance of play Paris Saint-Germain certainly deserved far better than a 3-1 defeat. They dominated the match for large periods, with young French international David Ginola giving a virtuoso performance on the left wing and George Weah causing all sorts of problems for the Real defence.

Real's collective teamwork did not impress, but veteran Spanish internationals Míchel and Butragueño were both on song, and it was their quick-thinking which brought about the first Real goal against the run of play. While the Paris SG defenders were still quibbling over whether Real had earned themselves a throw-in or a corner, Míchel swung the ball over to the far post where Butragueño, unchallenged, headed in. Once in front, Real grew in confidence and another piece of Míchel/Butragueño magic opened the door for Iván Zamorano to hook the second.

Incredibly, at half-time, Real were 2-0 up. But Paris SG were not finished, and after 49 minutes they got the goal they deserved. The faintest of touches from Ginola at the near post deflected in Valdo's corner for what was almost a replica of Kombouaré's goal in Brussels a round earlier.

But if the French sensed the tide was turning in their favour they were wrong. Luck was to desert them for the remainder of the game. First Ginola was blatantly brought down in the area by Sanchis, but the English referee simply waved play on. Then, with just a minute remaining, left-back Colleter burst into the Real area only to see his shot come back off Buyo's legs. Real immediately regained possession. Zamorano served Llorente, who clearly looked offside, but the ball fell to Míchel and his shot was saved on the line by Roche. Unfortunately for the Frenchman, he was adjudged to have deflected the ball away with his hand, which meant a red card for him and a penalty for Real. That was not the end of it, though. Míchel blasted the spot-kick towards goal, Lama pushed the ball upwards, it hit the crossbar and fell back into play where Míchel, following up, bundled it into the net as Valdo failed to connect with his attempted clearance.

EMILIO BUTRAGUEÑO
Real Madrid

Emilio Butragueño earned worldwide fame when he scored four goals in Spain's 5-1 defeat of Denmark at the 1986 World Cup in Mexico. But it is in European club competition that he has consistently proved his worth over the years. Although Real Madrid still chase that elusive seventh Champions' Cup, El Buitre, as he is commonly known in Spain, has done as much as anybody to retain Real Madrid at the forefront of European club football over the past decade.
Butragueño's goal against Paris-Saint-Germain was his 25th in European competition. More particularly, it meant that he had scored at least one European goal in each of the past nine seasons, that is, every one of his seasons at Real Madrid. That constitutes a unique record for any current player and one which Butragueño will surely be keen to prolong into a 10th season in 1993/94, especially if, as seems likely under the regime of current Spanish national team coach Javier Clemente, his days of international football are now at an end.

Thursday 18th March 1993
Parc des Princes, Paris

PARIS SAINT-GERMAIN FC 4 REAL MADRID 1

Half-time 1-0 *Aggregate* 5-4 *Attendance* 46,000

		Goals				Goals
1	Bernard LAMA		1	Francisco BUYO		
2	Jean-Luc SASSUS ❑ ‡		2	RICARDO Rocha		
3	Patrick COLLETER		3	Mikel LASA		
4	RICARDO Gomes		4	Fernando Muñoz "NANDO"		
5	Antoine KOMBOUARE	90	5	Luis RAMIS		
6	Paul LE GUEN		6	Fernando HIERRO		
7	Amara SIMBA †		7	Emilio BUTRAGUEÑO †		
8	Vincent GUERIN		8	Miguel González "MICHEL"		
9	George WEAH	33	9	Iván ZAMORANO		90
10	VALDO Candido	87	10	Robert PROSINECKI		
11	David GINOLA	81	11	LUIS ENRIQUE Martínez ‡		

Substitutes

Daniel BRAVO †73

Bruno GERMAIN ‡77

Substitutes

Francisco José Pérez VILLARROYA †65 ❑

ALFONSO Pérez ‡81

Referee Sándor PUHL (Hungary)

FACTFILE

● *Paris Saint-Germain's victory completed a European treble for France, with Auxerre eliminating Ajax in the same competition and Marseille thrashing CSKA Moscow 6-0 in the Champions' League.*

● *By a strange irony, injury-time match-winner Antoine Kombouaré would not have been playing had regular libero Alain Roche not been suspended following his sending-off in injury-time of the first leg!*

● *Real Madrid's official team sheet contained only 15 players, the reason being that they had originally selected young Argentinian striker Juan Esnaider as one of the substitutes, only to discover, just in time, that he was the fourth foreigner in the 16. Brazilian Ricardo Rocha, Croatian Prosinecki and Chilean Zamorano were already in the starting eleven.*

● *Qualification was worth £20,000 a man for each of the Paris SG players.*

Sensational climax in Parc des Princes

The Parc des Princes had witnessed many great sporting occasions in the past, but this incredible game topped just about everything that had gone before. In one of the most remarkable climaxes to a match in European Cup history, Paris Saint-Germain eventually beat Real Madrid 5-4 on aggregate to go through to their first-ever European semi-final.

The poor state of the Parc des Princes pitch was something of a concern for players and spectators alike before kick-off, but once the match got underway the sense of occasion overcame all that. Paris Saint-Germain pressed forward with great purpose. Their football was bright, intelligent and varied, and after 33 minutes they scored the first of the two goals they needed to win the tie. Once again, it came from a corner. This time it was Weah who rose unmarked to head in Valdo's inswinger from the left.

Early in the second half Weah wasted a glorious opportunity to make it 2-0 when Buyo saved his left-foot shot, and for a period after that the home side began to flag. But just when it appeared that Real, unambitious throughout, had got what they came for, Paris Saint-Germain scored. Fittingly it was David Ginola, the undisputed man of the tie, who got the goal with an immaculate half-volley from the edge of the area. But with the result now going against them, the Spaniards came out of their shell and twice came close to scoring. Substitute Alfonso might have had a penalty when he went down in the area, but he should certainly have scored moments later with a free header just a couple of yards out. Instead, Paris SG went upfield and scored a third goal, Valdo slotting the ball home after cheekily dummying his Brazilian compatriot Ricardo Rocha.

The match was some four minutes into stoppage time, with the crowd screaming for the final whistle, when, amazingly, Real scored. A free-kick on the left was knocked down in the danger area where arch-poacher Zamorano pushed it through Lama's legs to shrieks of disbelief and horror all around the stadium. It looked as if Real had managed another of their famous great escape acts and that extra-time was inevitable. But still the Hungarian referee refused to blow the final whistle. The clock had reached 96 minutes when Paris SG got a free-kick 35 yards out on the right. Valdo curled it in and, timing his run to perfection, centre-back Antoine Kombouaré rose to meet the ball with a wonderful glancing header. The ball was in the net, Paris Saint-Germain had won, and, for the 46,000 spectators, the Parc des Princes had suddenly been transformed into a theatre of fulfilled dreams

DAVID GINOLA
Paris-Saint-Germain FC

Some players remain synonymous with great games. David Ginola will long be revered in Paris as the man who did most to knock Real Madrid out of the UEFA Cup. His man-of-the-match performance in Madrid, where he scored once and should have had a penalty, was one thing. To repeat the feat in Paris was another. Ginola scored what looked to be the decisive goal and also had a hand in the one that really was when he earned the free-kick from which Kombouaré sent the Parc des Princes crowd into ecstasy.

Ginola earned early fame as a 20-year-old with Toulon, but a move to the ill-fated Matra Racing Paris in 1988 failed to pay off. After two years there he moved to Brittany, to Brest, but there again the club got into financial trouble and back he came to the capital, to PSG. That was midway through the 1991/92 season, and since then he has blossomed again, establishing himself at last in the French national team after being controversially left out of Michel Platini's Euro '92 squad.

Tuesday 2nd March 1993
Olimpico Stadium, Rome

ROMA 1 BORUSSIA DORTMUND 0

Half-time 0-0 *Attendance* 41,351

		Goals				Goals
1	Giovanni CERVONE		1	Stefan KLOS		
2	Luigi GARZYA		2	Günter KUTOWSKI		
3	Giovanni PIACENTINI ❏		3	Bodo SCHMIDT		
4	Walter BONACINA ❏ ■		4	Michael SCHULZ		
5	Silvano BENEDETTI		5	Ned ZELIC		
6	ALDAIR dos Santos ‡		6	Gerhard POSCHNER		
7	Sinisa MIHAJLOVIC	67	7	Stefan REUTER ❏		
8	Thomas HÄSSLER		8	Michael ZORC		
9	Andrea CARNEVALE †		9	Stéphane CHAPUISAT		
10	Giuseppe GIANNINI		10	Michael RUMMENIGGE		
11	Ruggiero RIZZITELLI ❏		11	Flemming POVLSEN †		

Substitutes			*Substitute*	
Roberto MUZZI †77			Lothar SIPPEL †81	
Antonio TEMPESTILLI ‡88				

Referee Mario VAN DER ENDE (Holland)

FACTFILE

● *According to Italian television coverage, Dutch referee Van der Ende blew for the end of both halves 15 seconds before time!*

● *An estimated 8,000 Borussia Dortmund fans made the trip to Rome.*

● *Dortmund were unable to include their new signing, Matthias Sammer, who had scored for his former club Internazionale against Roma in the Italian League earlier in the season. His transfer to Dortmund had not been completed until after the January 15 deadline, which meant that he was ineligible to play.*

● *In each of their three previous European games against Italian sides Dortmund had been eliminated after losing the away leg and drawing at home.*

● *Matthias Sammer*

Narrow win for home side in rainy Rome

A single goal scored midway through the second half by Roma's Yugoslav midfielder Sinisa Mihajlovic gave the Italian side a narrow, but potentially decisive, first-leg advantage in this first meeting between Bundesliga and Serie A representatives for two and a half years.

Rain fell throughout the evening as Roma, fresh from a morale-boosting Italian League victory over Juventus just two days earlier, set about establishing the kind of first-leg advantage that had accounted for both Grasshoppers and Galatasaray in the previous two rounds. They did not begin well, though, and it was Dortmund who looked more likely to draw first blood in a rather muted first half. 37 minutes had gone when Borussia defender Michael Schulz tested Cervone with a crisp left-footer that the Roma 'keeper pushed for a corner at full stretch. That aroused Roma and it was not long before Giuseppe Giannini found himself with a glorious chance to open the scoring at the other end. Stefan Klos was equal to the Roma captain, however, and at half-time the score remained 0-0.

If Dortmund had looked marginally the better team in the first period, they disappeared completely from the game after the interval. Suddenly their passing became inacurate and, denied room for manoeuvre through the centre, they were also unable to find any joy out wide on the flanks, where they were normally so dangerous. Meanwhile, Roma's pressure increased. Giannini was again foiled by Klos, Carnevale sent another chance just over the bar, then, after a spell of frantic activity in the Dortmund goalmouth, Mihajlovic struck to give Roma the lead. Dortmund could not clear their lines properly and as the ball fell invitingly for him on the left corner of the penalty area, the former Red Star Belgrade star lashed in a formidable shot with his weaker right foot. It skimmed off the turf and came to rest in the corner of Klos's net.

Walter Bonacina's sending off in the 78th minute (for his second bookable offence) inspired a late rally by Dortmund, and it was Schulz again who rapped Cervone's knuckles with another well-struck shot in the closing seconds. But Roma held on to their advantage and Dortmund coach Ottmar Hitzfeld was left to reflect on the situtation his team now found themselves in:

"It looked like it would be a 0-0 draw. It is typical of such a game that it should be decided by a speculative shot. It will be very difficult for us to pull back a 0-1 deficit against a team which has scored at least two goals away from home in every round."

SINISA MIHAJLOVIC
Roma

Sinisa Mihajlovic's goal against Dortmund, his first in Europe for Roma, came at just the right time for the former Red Star Belgrade man. After a promising start to his first season in Italian football, where he had particularly endeared himself to the Roma fans with his ferocious left-footed free-kicks, Mihajlovic looked to have gone into a slump and was no longer an automatic choice as one of the three foreigners in the side. Mihajlovic was a prominent member of the Red Star team which won the Champions' Cup in 1991. He arrived at the club from Vojvodina midway through that 1990/91 season and went on to score the free-kick in the semi-final against Bayern Munich that helped the club through to the final against Marseille in Bari. Mihajlovic had an even better season for Red Star the following season, scoring four more goals in Europe and leading the side to a third successive championship triumph. But for the belated ban on Yugoslavia, he would probably also have starred at Euro '92 in Sweden.

UEFA CUP
Quarter-final Second Leg

Thursday 18th March 1993
Westfalen Stadium, Dortmund

BORUSSIA DORTMUND 2 ROMA 0

Half-time 1-0 *Aggregate* 2-1 *Attendance* 35,800

Goals

Goals

1	Stefan KLOS	
2	Knut REINHARDT	
3	Günter KUTOWSKI	
4	Michael SCHULZ ❏	41
5	Ned ZELIC	
6	Gerhard POSCHNER ‡	
7	Stefan REUTER	
8	Michael ZORC	
9	Lothar SIPPEL	46
10	Michael RUMMENIGGE †	
11	Flemming POVLSEN	

Substitutes

Steffen KARL †78

Uwe GRAUER ‡88

1	Giovanni CERVONE	
2	Luigi GARZYA	
3	ALDAIR dos Santos	
4	Giovanni PIACENTINI ❏	
5	Silvano BENEDETTI	
6	Antonio COMI	
7	Sinisa MIHAJLOVIC ❏	
8	Thomas HÄSSLER	
9	Roberto MUZZI †46	
10	Giuseppe GIANNINI ❏	
11	Ruggiero RIZZITELLI	

Substitute

Andrea CARNEVALE †46

Referee Václav KRONDL (Czechoslovakia)

FACTFILE

● *This was Roma's first defeat for 13 games. A week earlier they had made headlines by beating Milan 2-0 in the first leg of the Italian Cup semi-finals - the Italian champions' first defeat in a year.*

● *In Europe, however, this was Roma's third successive away defeat after losses in the previous two rounds in Zürich and Istanbul.*

● *Claudio Caniggia was left out of the Roma side in favour of first-leg match-winner Sinisa Mihajlovic despite scoring goals in each of his last two games.*

● *Dortmund's victory was their seventh in succession at the Westfalen Stadium in European competition.*

● *Claudio Caniggia*

Reserve striker nods Dortmund into semis

Given Roma's previous away record in the competition - nine goals in three games - few would have backed them to surrender their 1-0 advantage from the first leg. But Vujadin Boskov, fearing that the Germans would prove tougher nuts to crack in defence than any of their earlier opponents, opted for caution. Counter-attack specialist Claudio Caniggia, a goalscorer in each of the previous three away legs, was surprisingly left in the stands, with another top striker, Andrea Carnevale, demoted to the substitutes' bench.

Dortmund coach Ottmar Hitzfeld had also taken a gamble with his selection up front. Stéphane Chapuisat, a goalscorer in all four of the team's matches in the second and third rounds, was not deemed fit enough to start. His place up front went to Lothar Sippel, a close-season signing from Frankfurt.

Sippel, though, like the rest of the team, could make little headway in the first half against a well-marshalled Roma defence. The principal feature of the opening period was Knut Reinhardt's fleeting raids down the left, and it was a free-kick from the Dortmund left-back which led to the home side's opening goal just four minutes before the interval. Roma sweeper Antonio Comi failed to get any distance with his clearance and Michael Schulz, the defender who had come closest to scoring for his team in the first leg, drilled the ball back into the corner of the net via a slight deflection.

Loud cheers heralded the half-time whistle, but the noise was even greater after just 18 seconds of the restart. That was all the time it took for Dortmund to go 2-0 up. Again Reinhardt was involved. He took a quick throw-in, the ball was promptly returned to him and he lofted in a superb cross which Sippel, catching the Roma defence unawares so early in the half, headed with power and precision into the Roma net. Now the Italians had to come out and play. Carnevale was on the pitch now and he and Schulz were to have several heated exchanges as the match became increasingly physical. Schulz had just seen his name go into the referee's book when, from the resulting Hässler free-kick, Silvano Benedetti sent tremors round the ground with a brilliant header that struck the inside of the left-hand post before Kutowski cleared it to safety.

That was the closest Roma were to come, though, and after enduring three minutes of stoppage time Dortmund players and fans were relieved to hear the final whistle that signalled their first qualification for a European semi-final in 27 years.

KNUT REINHARDT
Borussia Dortmund

The UEFA Cup was familiar territory for Knut Reinhardt. Five years earlier he had been a member of the last German team to capture the trophy, Bayer Leverkusen. As a teenager, he had played in eight of Leverkusen's matches on their way to that unexpected triumph, including the second leg of the final which they won 3-0 at home to Español before taking the trophy after a penalty shoot-out.

As a reward for his part in Leverkusen's success, Reinhardt was given his national team debut for West Germany in a friendly against the Soviet Union the following September. But the speedy left-back had to wait another two years for his second cap and it was not until October 1992 that he made his first appearance in the starting line-up, against Mexico, by which stage his performances for Dortmund in both domestic and European competition had marked him out as a potential long-term successor to World Cup hero Andreas Brehme.

Thursday 4th March 1993
Luz Stadium, Lisbon

SL BENFICA 2 JUVENTUS 1

Half-time 1-0 *Attendance* 50,000

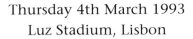

		Goals			Goals
1	SILVINO		1	Angelo PERUZZI	
2	JOSÉ CARLOS †		2	Massimo CARRERA	
3	HÉLDER		3	Moreno TORRICELLI ❑	
4	Carlos MOZER ❑		4	Dino BAGGIO	
5	VELOSO		5	Jürgen KOHLER	
6	PAULO SOUSA		6	JÚLIO CÉSAR Silva	
7	VÍTOR PANEIRA ❑	11, 80	7	Antonio CONTE	
8	Stefan SCHWARZ		8	Roberto GALIA †	
9	JOÃO PINTO		9	Gianluca VIALLI ‡	59 (pen)
10	Sergei YURAN ‡		10	Roberto BAGGIO	
11	ISAÍAS		11	Andreas MÖLLER	

Substitutes		*Substitutes*
RUI ÁGUAS †63		Paolo DI CANIO †52
PACHECO ‡66		Marco Antonio DE MARCHI ‡85

Referee Guy GOETHALS (Belgium)

● *This was the third top-level encounter in eight days betwen Portuguese and Italian teams after the Portugal-Italy World Cup qualifier and Porto-Milan in the Champions' Cup. It was also the first to be won by the Portuguese side.*

● *The defeat was Juventus's first of the season in Europe.*

● *Benfica had signed national team star Paulo Futre since the previous round. But he was ineligible to play on two counts. Not only was he signed after the permitted deadline, he also played European football earlier in the season for Atlético Madrid.*

● *In the World Cup qualifier between Portugal and Italy the previous week all three Italian goals in the 3-1 win had been scored by Juventus players - Roberto Baggio, Pierluigi Casiraghi and Dino Baggio.*

Vítor Paneira double gives Benfica victory

The list of quarter-finalists in the UEFA Cup looked to be one of the strongest for years, stronger even perhaps than the line-up in the Champions' League. But in terms of historical prestige, there is no doubt that the pairing of Benfica and Juventus stood out as the tie of the round.

As the first leg approached, however, neither of the two great clubs was enjoying a particularly fruitful season in domestic competition. Benfica trailed Portuguese leaders FC Porto by four points, while in Italy, Juventus were in a lowly sixth place some 14 points behind all-conquering Milan.

That said, Benfica had won their last five Portuguese League matches without conceding a goal in any of them, so they did go into the game with a certain amount of confidence, and that was borne out by the enterprising way in which they took the play to Juventus from the start. After 11 minutes the 50,000 crowd even had a goal to shout about. Portuguese international right-winger Vítor Paneira was the scorer. After a beautifully worked one-two with Sergei Yuran, he showed great composure and confidence to sweep the ball home first time into the far corner. So delighted was the Benfica number seven with his exploit that he promptly earned himself a yellow card for over-celebrating the goal out on the left touchline!

Benfica looked the more controlled side during the remainder of the first half, especially with young Paulo Sousa scheming like a veteran in his deep-lying central midfield role. He looked precisely the type of player that Juventus had been aching to have in their team for years. He certainly outshone all of the current Juventus midfielders on this occasion, which begged the question why coach Trapattoni had left out Englishman David Platt in favour of Brazilian sweeper Júlio César, who had only just returned from injury.

The one Juventus player who did seem to rise to the occasion was striker Gianluca Vialli. He struck the Benfica crossbar with a formidable overhead effort in the first half before grabbing his team's equaliser from the penalty spot just before the hour mark. There was no disputing the decision. Silvino was just beaten to Dino Baggio's through-ball by Andy Möller and he pulled the German's legs from under him. The penalty looked to have got Juventus off the hook, but with just ten minutes left Benfica deservedly took the lead again with a second goal from Vítor Paneira. It came about as a result of a superb run and cross on the left by Isaías. Peruzzi hesitated in going to collect the ball as it whistled across his six-yard box and Vítor Paneira slid in to lift the ball into the roof of the net and give his side victory.

VÍTOR PANEIRA
SL Benfica

Before his two-goal match-winning performance against Juventus, Vítor Paneira had not been on the scoresheet for Benfica since just before Christmas. It was a timely return to form for the 27-year-old midfielder who, after a positive start to the season, was beginning to waver in his contributions and had been left out of the Portuguese national side against Italy a week earlier as a result. Vítor Paneira first came to the attention of Portuguese football followers at the beginning of the 1988/89 season. He had just arrived at Benfica from Second Division Vizela and made an immediate impact with his crafty forays on the right side of midfield. Less than two months after his First Division debut he was called up to the national team and he proceeded to play in all of the team's seven internationals that season, scoring three goals to boot. Now, after five seasons with Benfica, he is generally considered to be one of the finest players in the country.

UEFA CUP
Quarter-final Second Leg

Wednesday 17th March 1993
Delle Alpi Stadium, Turin

JUVENTUS 3   SL BENFICA 0

Half-time 2-0 *Aggregate* 4-2 *Attendance* 51,697

		Goals			Goals
1	Angelo PERUZZI		1	SILVINO †	
2	Massimo CARRERA ❑		2	VELOSO	
3	Moreno TORRICELLI		3	HÉLDER ❑	
4	Dino BAGGIO	43	4	Carlos MOZER	
5	Jürgen KOHLER	2	5	PAULO MADEIRA ‡	
6	JÚLIO CÉSAR Silva		6	PAULO SOUSA	
7	Andreas MÖLLER ❑ †		7	VÍTOR PANEIRA	
8	Antonio CONTE		8	Stefan SCHWARZ	
9	Gianluca VIALLI		9	JOÃO PINTO ❑	
10	Roberto BAGGIO ‡		10	Sergei YURAN	
11	Giancarlo MAROCCHI		11	RUI COSTA	

Substitutes			*Substitutes*	
Roberto GALIA †55 ❑			NENO †2	
Fabrizio RAVANELLI ‡65 ❑	67		RUI ÁGUAS ‡46	

Referee Peter MIKKELSEN (Denmark)

● *Victory for Juventus meant revenge for the 0-3 aggregate defeat they suffered at the hands of Benfica in the 1967/68 Champions' Cup semi-final - the only previous meeting of the two clubs in European competition.*

● *Juventus's victory was particularly sweet for coach Giovanni Trapattoni as it came on his 54th birthday.*

● *Victory enabled Juventus to reach a European semi-final for the 14th time in their history.*

● *Nine players started the game with one yellow card to their name from previous matches. Two of them, Carrera of Juventus and Hélder of Benfica, were booked again, meaning automatic suspension from their next match.*

● *Giovanni Trapattoni*

Controversial strike paves way for Juventus

This was heralded as Juventus's 'Match of Truth'. They had slipped almost to halfway in the Serie A table after a shock weekend reverse in Brescia and there were even calls from some quarters for the sacking of Giovanni Trapattoni, the man who had led the club to all three European trophies in the past.

What Juventus desperately needed to calm the nerves of both players and supporters was an early goal, and that is precisely what they got thanks to a controversial oversight by the Danish referee. Less than two minutes had elapsed when, from a corner on the left, Dino Baggio rose to challenge Benfica goalkeeper Silvino. The Italian international clearly elbowed Silvino in the face, but Mikkelsen allowed play to carry on and as a Benfica defender inadvertently knocked the ball back to his prostrate goalkeeper, the ball kindly rebounded from his body into the path of Jürgen Kohler, who tapped it into the empty net without difficulty. The match could hardly have begun more depressingly for Benfica. They now stood a goal behind and their goalkeeper was forced to leave the field on the stretcher with a suspected broken nose.

Not long afterwards Benfica's cruel luck continued when Mozer, their Brazilian centre-back, had a goal disallowed for pushing his opponent. But his defensive partner Hélder could certainly count himself fortunate to stay on the field when, after an earlier booking for deliberate hand-ball, he hacked Gianluca Vialli down on the edge of the area. But if Mikkelsen showed leniency on that occasion, further punishment for the Portuguese side was not long in coming. It came in the shape of a second goal, and Dino Baggio, the man who had earlier put Silvino out of the game, was the scorer, shooting in from close range after Vialli had flicked on a corner.

Juventus were now firmly in the driving seat, but they too had their injury woes in the second half when their two most creative players, Baggio and Möller, had to be withdrawn from the action. But the man who replaced Möller, Fabrizio Ravanelli, was to be the chief protagonist in the last quarter of the match. With his first touch he headed just over after a brilliant cross on the run by Vialli. Then, with a much more difficult chance moments later, he fired Juventus into a 3-0 lead with a low left-foot cross-shot. The same player even had time to miss another opening created by the ever-industrious Vialli and get himself booked before the referee blew for the end of the match, signalling the *Bianconeri's* third semi-final qualification in successive European campaigns.

GIANLUCA VIALLI
Juventus

Although he did not get his name onto the scoresheet, Gianluca Vialli was the man most responsible for seeing off Benfica in the Delle Alpi Stadium. He had a hand in all three goals and was a constant menace to the Portuguese defence with his pace and aggression up front. Vialli's fine display was not, however, symptomatic of his first year at Juventus. The club had paid a small fortune to prize the player away from his beloved Sampdoria, but by the time that Benfica came to Turin he had scored a measly four goals for Juventus in the Italian League and had also missed a penalty in a vital championship game against Milan in the autumn.

At Sampdoria, however, Vialli remains a legend. He scored 86 goals in 223 Serie A matches for the club, including a top-scoring 19 in their historic championship-winning season of 1990/91. He also scored the two extra-time goals that beat Anderlecht in the 1990 Cup-winners' Cup final and was on target six times in Sampdoria's run to the Champions' Cup final at Wembley in 1991/92.

UEFA CUP
Quarter-final First Leg

Wednesday 3rd March 1993
Abbé-Deschamps Stadium, Auxerre

AJ AUXERRE 4 AJAX 2

Half-time 2-2 *Attendance* 17,000

		Goals				Goals
1	Bruno MARTINI		1	Stanley MENZO		
2	Alain GOMA		2	Sonny SILOOY		
3	William PRUNIER †		3	Danny BLIND ❏		
4	Frank VERLAAT	16	4	Wim JONK †		
5	Stéphane MAZZOLINI		5	Frank DE BOER ❏		
6	Raphaël GUERREIRO		6	Marciano VINK		45
7	Christophe COCARD		7	Rob ALFLEN		
8	Daniel DUTUEL	90	8	Edgar DAVIDS		
9	Gérald BATICLE ‡		9	Stefan PETTERSSON		3
10	Corentin MARTINS	43	10	Dennis BERGKAMP		
11	Pascal VAHIRUA	81	11	Marc OVERMARS ‡		
	Substitutes			*Substitutes*		
	Thierry BONALAIR †61			Michel KREEK †55		
	Lilian LASLANDES ‡80			Jari LITMANEN ‡85		

Referee Arcangelo PEZZELLA (Italy)

FACTFILE

● This was Ajax's first defeat in 19 European matches. They had not lost a match since going down 0-1 to FK Austria in a UEFA Cup first round match on 14 September 1989.

● Five Ajax players - Bergkamp, Jonk, Overmars, Silooy and De Boer - appeared in Holland's World Cup qualifying match against Turkey a week earlier.

● Daniel Dutuel's last-minute strike was Auxerre's 18th goal in four UEFA Cup games at the Abbé-Deschamps Stadium - an average of four and a half goals per game!

● The 18.15 kick-off was delayed by a few minutes as a result of fireworks thrown onto the pitch by the Ajax fans.

● *Marciano Vink*

Late goals send holders to shock defeat

Ajax's long unbeaten European run had to come to an end at some time. But they did not expect it to happen in the humble surroundings of Auxerre. The French provincial club had been in dire form since their victory over Standard Liège in the third round back in December. Since the turn of the year they had lost all hope of a first-ever French championship success. A run of seven matches without a win, including five straight defeats without a single goal, had only just ended the previous weekend. Ajax, on the other hand, had been in vibrant form during the same period, scoring goals aplenty - 24 in five games - before an unfortunate defeat at PSV scuppered their title ambitions too.

Ajax began the tie as clear favourites to reach the semi-finals and, as in the previous two rounds, they got off to the perfect start with a goal in the early seconds of the game. Stefan Pettersson was the man on target, bundling the ball in from close range after Vink had knocked on Jonk's free-kick. The holders had not conceded a goal in any of their previous first-leg games, but records like that don't last for ever and it was their old boy, Frank Verlaat, the Auxerre sweeper, who broke it when he equalised with a splendid left-foot volley after 16 minutes.

By half-time there had been two further goals, one for each side. Corentin Martins gave Auxerre the lead with a superbly executed free-kick, which bypassed a seven-man wall before nestling in the top corner of the motionless Stanley Menzo's net. Then, just before the half-time whistle, Ajax levelled the scores again through Marciano Vink after some splendid close-control in the penalty area from Dennis Bergkamp.

The 2-2 scoreline clearly suited the side from Amsterdam, and for the bulk of the second half they seemed happy to control the pace of the game in their inimitable way, retaining possession at will and almost beckoning their opponents to come and take the ball off them, as if in a practice match. But the confidence, some would say arrogance, was to drain from Ajax in the last ten minutes of the match. Not for the first time, the side were let down by their goalkeeper Stanley Menzo. He completely misjudged an inswinging right-wing corner from Pascal Vahirua and the ball flew into the net via his palms to put Auxerre in front again.

In the fourth minute of injury-time Ajax's first European defeat for three and a half years was complete. Daniel Dutuel, feeding off a delicate through-ball from Laslandes, broke clear through the middle and beat Menzo with a shot that went in off the far post. Predictably, the crowd went wild. Now, for the first time, they really believed that the holders could be toppled.

FRANK VERLAAT
AJ Auxerre

"Mine was a very important goal, Not, I stress, because it was against my old club, but because it was in the quarter-final of the UEFA Cup."
Who did Frank Verlaat think he was kidding? Judging by the celebrations after he had smashed home Auxerre's first goal to bring the scores level at 1-1, the Dutchman had just achieved a lifelong ambition! Certainly it is reasonable to say that Verlaat did not get a fair crack of the whip during his early years at Ajax. Although he played as a teenager for the club in the final of the Cup-winners' Cup against Lokomotive Leipzig in 1987, he never established himself in the team over the next couple of seasons and eventually found himself offloaded to Switzerland in one of the least publicised of Ajax's many recent foreign sales. Verlaat subsequently spent three impressive years with Lausanne before his move to Auxerre in the 1992 close season, although he still awaits his first international call-up for Holland.

UEFA CUP
Quarter-final Second Leg

Tuesday March 16th 1993
Olympisch Stadium, Amsterdam

AJAX 1   AJ AUXERRE 0

Half-time 0-0 Aggregate 3-4 Attendance 43,000

		Goals			Goals
1	Edwin VAN DER SAR		1	Bruno MARTINI	
2	Sonny SILOOY ❑		2	Alain GOMA	
3	Danny BLIND †		3	William PRUNIER	
4	Rob ALFLEN		4	Frank VERLAAT	
5	Frank DE BOER	60	5	Franck RABARIVONY	
6	Marciano VINK ‡		6	Raphaël GUERREIRO ❑	
7	Marc OVERMARS		7	Christophe COCARD	
8	Michel KREEK		8	Daniel DUTUEL	
9	Stefan PETTERSSON		9	Gérald BATICLE †	
10	Dennis BERGKAMP		10	Corentin MARTINS	
11	Edgar DAVIDS		11	Pascal VAHIRUA	

Substitutes

Clarence SEEDORF †16

Johnny HANSEN ‡56

Substitute

Laurent CHIECHELSKI †88

Referee Kurt RÖTHLISBERGER (Switzerland)

FACTFILE

● *This was the first game of Auxerre's UEFA Cup campaign in which they failed to score a goal. They had managed at least two in all seven of their previous matches.*

● *Ajax's elimination meant that, after second-round exits for Barcelona and Werder Bremen in the other two competitions, all three trophy holders had been eliminated before the semi-finals.*

● *Auxerre's aggregate victory took France level with Holland in European confrontations between the two countries. Both nations now had eight qualifications each.*

● *Ajax had never previously been knocked out of Europe by a French club. They had won all three of their previous ties against Marseille (twice) and Strasbourg.*

Defence holds firm as Auxerre stun holders

BRUNO MARTINI
AJ Auxerre

There was a touch of *déjà vu* about Auxerre's trip to Amsterdam. The previous season they had also held a two-goal lead before travelling to face another of European football's biggest names, Liverpool. On that occasion, however, their nerve had failed them and they were eliminated after going down 3-0 at Anfield. Now they needed to draw on that experience and prove that they could indeed compete for the highest stakes in Europe.

It looked as if any safety-first policy Auxerre might have been considering had been thrown out of the window as they attacked Ajax right from the kick-off. Ajax coach Louis van Gaal had responded to the critics by leaving out goalkeeper Stanley Menzo in favour of his deputy, Edwin van der Sar. But the youngster began in calamitous fashion. Kicking the ball around his area like a schoolboy in a playground, he lost possession and an almighty scramble ensued, with each of Auxerre's three-pronged strike-force, Cocard, Baticle and Vahirua, having a chance to score but failing to do so. That was a real let off for the home side, but the danger had by no means passed. An exquisite run on the left by Vahirua ended with another opportunity for Cocard, but he could only graze the top of the bar with his shot.

Eventually Ajax weathered the storm and began to dictate the play. By half-time Dennis Bergkamp had escaped from his watch-dog, Raphaël Guerreiro, three times, but he too could not find the net. His first effort curved just wide of the post, then he placed a header on top of the crossbar and finally he was denied a penalty after a surge through the centre of the Auxerre defence.

The second half was played almost exclusively in the Auxerre half. And on the hour a moment's hesitation in the French side's defence cost them a goal, with defender Frank de Boer heading in unmarked from Alflen's free-kick. It was backs to the wall from now on for Auxerre. Cocard and Vahirua came back to help out as the team fought desperately to cling onto their narrow lead.

Goalkeeper Bruno Martini was in inspired form in the Auxerre goal, and it was his double intervention in the last minute that denied both Pettersson and Bergkamp. Referee Röthlisberger spared the French side any further torment when he blew the final whistle after just ten seconds of injury time, this despite two major stoppages earlier in the half. Ajax coach Van Gaal was not impressed. This had been his first major defeat since taking over the reins of the club 18 months earlier. But for Auxerre coach Guy Roux, who had committed himself to the club for five more years earlier in the week, this was undoubtedly his finest hour.

If Bruno Martini had a point to prove to French national coach Gérard Houllier, who had dropped him for the World Cup qualifier against Israel a month earlier, he certainly made it in Amsterdam. Auxerre needed all the experience and know-how of their 30-year-old 'keeper to withstand the constant pressure imposed on them by the Ajax forwards in the second half, and he obliged with a faultless performance to steer Auxerre into the previously uncharted waters of a European semi-final. Martini has spent over a decade at Auxerre and has been first choice there since his predecessor, Joël Bats, moved to Paris Saint-Germain in 1985. He also followed Bats into the French national jersey, assuming the role on a permanent basis when Bats retired from international football following France's failure to qualify for the 1990 World Cup. Subsequently, it was not until Martini's 21st cap that France lost a game in which he had been selected from the start.

QUARTER-FINAL RESULTS

		1st leg	2nd leg	Agg.
Real Madrid	Paris Saint-Germain FC	3-1	1-4	4-5
Roma	Borussia Dortmund	1-0	0-2	1-2
SL Benfica	Juventus	2-1	0-3	2-4
AJ Auxerre	Ajax	4-2	0-1	4-3

LEADING GOALSCORERS AFTER QUARTER-FINALS

8 Gérald BATICLE (AJ Auxerre)
6 George WEAH (Paris Saint-Germain FC)
   Marcel WITECZEK (1.FC Kaiserslautern)
   Daniel FONSECA (Napoli)
5 Iván ZAMORANO (Real Madrid)
   Gianluca VIALLI (Juventus)
   ISAÍAS (SL Benfica)
   Fernando HIERRO (Real Madrid)
   Anthony YEBOAH (Eintracht Frankfurt)
4 VÍTOR PANEIRA (SL Benfica)
   Stefan PETTERSSON (Ajax)
   Stéphane CHAPUISAT (Borussia Dortmund)
   Michael GOOSSENS (R Standard Liège)
   PACHECO (SL Benfica)
   Luc NILIS (RSC Anderlecht)
   Krzysztof WARZYCHA (Panathinaikos)
3 MICHEL (Real Madrid)
   Fabrizio RAVANELLI (Juventus)
   Edgar DAVIDS (Ajax)
   Gustavo POYET (Real Zaragoza)
   Michael ZORC (Borussia Dortmund)
   Claudio CANIGGIA (Roma)
   Pierluigi CASIRAGHI (Juventus)
   Andreas MÖLLER (Juventus)
   Dennis BERGKAMP (Ajax)
   Dorin MATEUT (Real Zaragoza)
   John VAN DEN BROM (Vitesse)
   Giuseppe GIANNINI (Roma)
   Ruggiero RIZZITELLI (Roma)
   AYKUT Kocaman (Fenerbahçe)
   Milan KERBR (Sigma Olomouc)
   Viktor LEONENKO (Dinamo Kiev)
   Peter VAN VOSSEN (RSC Anderlecht)
   Christophe COCARD (AJ Auxerre)
   Paul WARHURST (Sheffield Wednesday)
   Axel KRUSE (Eintracht Frankfurt)
   Frank MILL (Borussia Dortmund)

UEFA CUP

Tuesday 6th April 1993
Delle Alpi Stadium, Turin

JUVENTUS 2 PARIS SAINT-GERMAIN FC 1

Half-time 0-1 *Attendance* 42,792

		Goals				Goals
1	Michelangelo RAMPULLA		1	Bernard LAMA		
2	Moreno TORRICELLI		2	Bruno GERMAIN		
3	Giancarlo MAROCCHI †		3	Patrick COLLETER		
4	Dino BAGGIO ❑		4	RICARDO Gomes		
5	Jürgen KOHLER ❑		5	Antoine KOMBOUARE		
6	JÚLIO CÉSAR Silva ❑		6	Paul LE GUEN		
7	Antonio CONTE ❑		7	Laurent FOURNIER		
8	David PLATT		8	Vincent GUERIN		
9	Gianluca VIALLI		9	George WEAH	23	
10	Roberto BAGGIO	54, 90	10	VALDO Candido		
11	Fabrizio RAVANELLI		11	David GINOLA		

Substitute

Paolo DI CANIO †31 ❑

Substitutes

Referee Antonio MARTIN NAVARRETE (Spain)

FACTFILE

● *This was the third European meeting of the two clubs in ten years. On both previous occasions Juventus had won the tie and gone on to win the trophy - the Cup-winners' Cup in 1983/84 and the UEFA Cup in 1989/90.*

● *Of the 23 players on view, only one of them - Juventus's Giancarlo Marocchi - had appeared in the last encounter between the two sides three and a half years earlier.*

● *This was the first time that Juventus had come from a goal behind to win a European game since a UEFA Cup third round first-leg match against Karl-Marx-Stadt of East Germany in November 1989.*

● *Roberto Baggio's goals were his 11th and 12th goals in Europe for Juventus and his first since the opening match of the campaign against Anorthosis Famagusta.*

Baggio brings late relief to Juventus

For the third European fixture in a row Paris Saint-Germain conceded a last-minute goal. Míchel and Zamorano of Real Madrid had done it in the last round and now it was the turn of Roberto Baggio, with a magnificent curling free-kick, to puncture the Paris defence seconds before the final whistle and give his team the psychological advantage of a first-leg lead.

It was a very important goal for Juventus. A week earlier they had been knocked out of the Italian Cup on the away goals rule, and now the UEFA Cup offered them their only hope of salvaging a trophy from another hit-and-miss season. Prospects of a convincing victory over the French side were not helped by a long list of absentees, notably the suspended Carrera, Galia and Möller and the injured Casiraghi and Peruzzi. And dissatisfaction with the team was evident from the large banks of empty seats in the Delle Alpi stadium.

Juventus did not begin well. They created a handful of half chances in the opening 45 minutes, but not much more. Fabrizio Ravanelli, a replacement for the absent Möller and Casiraghi, wasted the best of those opportunities, and the significance of that miss was put into perspective when the visitors struck out of the blue in the 23rd minute to open the scoring. It was a fabulous goal, created by David Ginola and finished in confident style by George Weah. The African had now scored seven goals in the competition, five of them away from home and, after his second-round double in Naples, three of them in Italy.

Artur Jorge's men were good value for their half-time lead. They were stroking the ball around purposefully in much the same way as they had done away to Real Madrid in the quarter-final. The elusive Ginola was on song again and he nearly scored a spectacular second goal after the interval following a solo run of fully 60 yards from his own half. But as the French began to withdraw more men into defence to protect their lead, Juventus started to assert themselves in the second period and they were rewarded with an equaliser after 54 minutes, Roberto Baggio firing home powerfully from the right edge of the 'D'.

It remained at one goal each until the final seconds. Paris SG were clinging on desperately when Kombouaré brought down Vialli just outside the penalty area. It was a suicidal mistake to make against a team with Roberto Baggio in their ranks. The kick was perfectly positioned for the Juventus number ten to curl it expertly over the wall and beyond the despairing dive of Lama. Juventus were off the hook. Paris Saint-Germain were cursing themselves for failing once again to keep their defence tight right through to the final whistle.

ROBERTO BAGGIO
Juventus

UEFA Cup victory meant so much to Roberto Baggio. Because for all his undoubted genius, the star of the Italian national team had never previously won a major trophy of any description. His team had often finished runner-up, as his former club, Fiorentina, had done in this very competition. But Baggio had never been a winner, and his two marvellously struck goals against Paris Saint-Germain were testimony to his determination to rectify that as soon as possible.
Since the demise of Diego Maradona, many consider Roberto Baggio to be the finest footballer in the world. His gifts are immense. Ball skills, vision, fancy footwork, passing accuracy, goalscoring. He has the lot. A true footballing entertainer, he is one of those rare individuals who justify the entrance fee by their mere presence on the field. With Baggio you never quite know what to expect next. He has so many tricks up his sleeve. World Cup '94 is just waiting to be graced by his extraordinary talent.

UEFA CUP
Semi-final Second Leg

Thursday 22nd April 1993
Parc des Princes, Paris

PARIS SAINT-GERMAIN FC 0 JUVENTUS 1

Half-time 0-0 *Aggregate* 1-3 *Attendance* 46,152

		Goals			Goals
1	Bernard LAMA		1	Michelangelo RAMPULLA	
2	Laurent FOURNIER †		2	Moreno TORRICELLI ❏	
3	Patrick COLLETER ❏ ‡		3	Marco Antonio DE MARCHI	
4	RICARDO Gomes		4	Roberto GALIA	
5	Alain ROCHE ❏		5	Massimo CARRERA	
6	Paul LE GUEN		6	JÚLIO CÉSAR Silva	
7	Antoine KOMBOUARE		7	Giancarlo MAROCCHI	
8	Vincent GUERIN		8	David PLATT	
9	George WEAH		9	Gianluca VIALLI	
10	VALDO Candido		10	Roberto BAGGIO ❏ ‡	76
11	David GINOLA		11	Andreas MÖLLER †	

Substitutes

Amara SIMBA †60

Bruno GERMAIN ‡79

Substitutes

Pierluigi CASIRAGHI †65

Paolo DI CANIO ‡85

Referee Jaap UILENBERG (Holland)

FACTFILE

● *Juventus's three suspended players - Kohler, Conte and Dino Baggio - were all directly replaced by the three players under suspension for the first leg in Turin - Carrera, Galia and Möller.*

● *This was the 12th game of the season in which Michelangelo Rampulla had been in goal for Juventus and they had not lost a single one of them.*

● *No fewer than eight of the Paris Saint-Germain players who started the game were under threat of suspension. Only Weah, Valdo and Le Guen could afford a yellow card if they wanted to play in the next game.*

● *This was the first time that Paris Saint-Germain had ever lost a European tie playing the second leg in the Parc des Princes.*

● *David Platt*

Disciplined Juventus reach ninth Euro final

Paris in the springtime had never experienced such a severe case of football fever. All tickets for the game had been sold out within three hours of going on sale and there was great optimism in the French capital that 'PSG' would make it third time lucky in their meetings with Juventus and progress to their first ever European final.

Juventus, however, and in particular their coach Giovanni Trapattoni, had been through this experience many times in the past, and they knew exactly what to do in order to hang on to their precious first-leg advantage. In essence, it meant forming a wall of defenders 30 yards in front of Rampulla's goal and plugging every conceivable gap with extra reinforcements when danger threatened.

The French side had enormous difficulty making any sort of breakthrough in the first half, although, in fairness, they were not helped by some strange offside decisions by the Dutch linesman. Other than that, there was one good chance from Weah which Rampulla did well to save, but overall Paris SG seemed to lack the necessary creativity to carve out any real clear-cut openings.

For the first 25 minutes of the second half there was little change to the storyline, but then came the game's most controversial incident. George Weah, attempting to latch onto the ball in the penalty area, was wrestled to the ground by Carrera and then tripped by the Juventus defender's outstretched foot. It had to be a penalty, but referee Uilenberg was having none of it and just waved play on. It was a shameful decision, but it served to bring the crowd to life at last and shortly afterwards Weah went close with a header from a Ginola cross.

Within minutes, though, the Parisians had fallen silent again. The referee again appeared to be on the Italian team's side when he not only wrongly awarded a free-kick to Juventus after a supposed foul by Colleter on Baggio - the Italian clearly tripped over his own feet - but then booked Colleter for booting the ball away. Worse then followed when, from the ensuing Marocchi free-kick, Platt headed the ball back for Vialli and his shot was deflected past Lama by Baggio for his third goal of the tie. The home side redoubled their efforts in the closing minutes, but Rampulla denied Weah, Le Guen and Ginola and then Júlio César cleared a ball off the line in the last minute.

Juventus were through to their ninth European final. It had been a disciplined, pragmatic performance from Trappatoni's men, but one which, as the boos from the stands indicated, had needed more than its fair share of good fortune.

JÚLIO CÉSAR
Juventus

With Jürgen Kohler suspended, Júlio César had to assume extra responsibility in helping to make Juventus's rearguard action effective. The Parc des Princes was a ground on which he had played on numerous occasions before during his four-year spell in the French League, and indeed there were three players on the opposing side - Colleter, Guérin and Le Guen - with whom he had played together at Brest. On familiar territory and in familiar company, the big Brazilian produced a towering performance and was one of the genuine heroes of his team. When Juventus signed Júlio César from Montpellier in 1990 for £1 million, there were several raised eyebrows in Italy. After all, was this not a man who had been unable to claim a place in Brazil's Italia '90 squad and who had barely rated a mention in international football circles since his displays in Mexico four years earlier? Juventus obviously did not think so, and it is fair to say that in his three years at the club he has successfully made a nonsense of that cut-price transfer fee.

UEFA CUP
Semi-final First Leg

Tuesday 6th April 1993
Westfalen Stadium, Dortmund

BORUSSIA DORTMUND 2 AJ AUXERRE 0

Half-time 0-0 *Attendance* 35,800

Goals

		Goals
1	Stefan KLOS	
2	Gerhard POSCHNER	
3	Günter KUTOWSKI	
4	Bodo SCHMIDT	
5	Ned ZELIC	
6	Michael LUSCH ‡	
7	Stefan REUTER	
8	Michael ZORC	87
9	Stéphane CHAPUISAT	
10	Michael RUMMENIGGE	
11	René TRETSCHOK †	

Substitutes

Steffen KARL †46   58
Ulf RASCHKE ‡81

		Goals
1	Bruno MARTINI	
2	Alain GOMA	
3	William PRUNIER	
4	Frank VERLAAT	
5	Stéphane MAZZOLINI	
6	Raphaël GUERREIRO	
7	Christophe COCARD ❑	
8	Daniel DUTUEL	
9	Gérald BATICLE	
10	Corentin MARTINS ❑	
11	Pascal VAHIRUA	

Substitutes

Referee Frans VAN DEN WIJNGAERT (Belgium)

FACTFILE

● *The 35,800 attendance in the Westfalen stadium was equivalent to approximately the entire population of Auxerre! All tickets had been snapped up within two hours of going on sale a fortnight earlier.*

● *Dortmund striker Stéphane Chapuisat and Auxerre defender Frank Verlaat were former colleagues together at Swiss club Lausanne-Sports.*

● *In 11 seasons of European competition spanning over 60 matches Dortmund had never before faced French opposition in Europe. Likewise, this was Auxerre's first ever contest against a team from Germany.*

● *Having scored 24 goals in their first seven matches of the campaign, Auxerre had now gone two successive games without scoring once.*

● *Michael Lusch*

First blood to determined Dortmund

Borussia Dortmund went into their first European semi-final for 27 years with four key players unable to take the field and another, striker Stéphane Chapuisat, well short of full fitness. In addition to the suspension of defender Michael Schulz and the continued ineligibility of Matthias Sammer, Dortmund had to make do without the bedridden Knut Reinhardt and, most depressingly of all, long-term injury victim Flemming Povlsen. The Dane had torn ligaments in his right knee the previous weekend and could say goodbye to football for the next six months at least. Auxerre, on the other hand, were virtually at full strength and it must have been at the forefront of the French players' minds that the club would never have a better opportunity of reaching a European final.

Sadly, though, Guy Roux's men were to offer only fleeting glimpses of the fine attacking football that had characterised their progress through earlier rounds. The Germans, with so many enforced changes to their usual line-up, inevitably looked disorganised early on, but Auxerre were not courageous enough to go out and punish them and although they were happy to reach the half-time interval with the score still goalless, they had been given a number of warnings that Dortmund were beginning to find their rhythm, notably just before the interval when a succession of headers caused panic in the Auxerre defence. Zorc was the first on target, forcing Martini to tip over, then Reuter nodded across goal before Tretschok had his effort saved on the goal-line.

With Michael Rummenigge evidently not enjoying the unfamiliar experience of playing up front alongside a half-fit Stéphane Chapuisat, Dortmund coach Ottmar Hitzfeld opted to change things at half-time, bringing on Steffen Karl for Tretschok. And it worked. Just moments after Verlaat had survived a penalty appeal when the ball hit his hand, the Dutchman's luck disappeared when substitute Karl's shot deflected up off his thigh to beat Martini and put Dortmund ahead.

Now the Dortmund pressure intensified and Auxerre could hardly get the ball out of their own half. Martini made two good saves from Lusch and Karl and then, after 81 minutes, surpassed himself by saving a penalty kick from the normally ultra-reliable Michael Zorc. In truth, it should not have been a penalty in the first place. Chapuisat, demonstrating an irritating tendency towards playacting throughout the match, had clearly dived over Prunier's outstretched leg. But six minutes later the Dortmund captain was able to make amends with a bullet header from Poschner's corner that beat Martini all ends up and gave Dortmund what appeared to be a decisive 2-0 first-leg lead.

MICHAEL ZORC
Borussia Dortmund

It is a mark of the respect which Borussia Dortmund fans feel for their captain that they were still chanting Michael Zorc's name after he had missed the late penalty which could have sealed Dortmund's first-leg victory. Obviously encouraged by this show of affection, Zorc responded in the best possible fashion, redeeming himself with a superb header that nearly ripped the net off its hinges.

Zorc is one of a dying breed of loyal one-club men. He has been with Dortmund all his career and has made over 300 Bundesliga appearances for the team. A hard-working midfielder, just as effective in possession as he is in trying to win it back, Zorc has received international recognition late in his career. He was well into his 31st year when Berti Vogts called him up for the brief tour to South America at the end of 1992. Making his debut as a substitute against Brazil, he has held his place in the team ever since and could yet be a joker in the German pack at next year's World Cup in the USA.

UEFA CUP
Semi-final Second Leg

Tuesday 20th April 1993
Abbé-Deschamps Stadium, Auxerre

AJ AUXERRE 2 BORUSSIA DORTMUND 0 (aet)

Half-time 1-0 *Aggregate* 2-2 (Dortmund win 6-5 on penalties) *Attendance* 18,500

		Goals			Goals
1	Lionel CHARBONNIER		1	Stefan KLOS	
2	Alain GOMA †		2	Knut REINHARDT	
3	William PRUNIER ❏		3	Bodo SCHMIDT	
4	Frank VERLAAT	72	4	Michael SCHULZ ❏	
5	Stéphane MAHE		5	Ned ZELIC ‡	
6	Raphaël GUERREIRO ❏ ■		6	Günter KUTOWSKI ❏ ■	
7	Christophe COCARD ❏		7	Michael LUSCH †	
8	Daniel DUTUEL		8	Michael ZORC	
9	Gérald BATICLE ‡		9	Stéphane CHAPUISAT	
10	Corentin MARTINS ❏	8	10	Michael RUMMENIGGE	
11	Pascal VAHIRUA		11	Steffen KARL	

Substitutes   *Substitutes*

Moussa SAIB †100   Frank MILL †74

Lilian LASLANDES ‡106   Uwe GRAUER ‡105

Referee Serge MUHMENTHALER (Switzerland)

FACTFILE

● *This was only the third penalty shoot-out of the season in Europe. The other two had both been in the first round back in September, with Torpedo Moscow beating Manchester United in the UEFA Cup and Antwerp eliminating Glenavon in the Cup-winners' Cup.*

● *Only 1500 tickets were available to Dortmund fans for the game. An estimated crowd of 20,000 had gathered back in Dortmund city centre to watch the game being relayed live on a giant screen.*

● *An important absentee for Auxerre was injured goalkeeper Bruno Martini. The French international would surely have been an asset in the penalty shoot-out having saved Zorc's spot-kick in the first leg.*

● *The leading scorer in the UEFA Cup, Auxerre's eight-goal Gérald Baticle, failed to score for the fourth game in a row.*

Heartbreak for Auxerre in shoot-out drama

France had three clubs seeking a European final place, and Auxerre were the first into action. Guy Roux's men had not done themselves justice in the first leg, but as previous had shown, they were a different proposition at home. A full house had assembled to offer all the vocal and visual support they could muster. The rest was down to the players.

There was a dream start for the Frenchmen when Corentin Martins opened the scoring after just eight minutes. Daniel Dutuel chipped the ball forward, Martins chested it down and as Schmidt let the ball go past him, the Auxerre number ten gleefully despatched it across Stefan Klos into the far corner. Dortmund's policy was to try and hit back straight away with a crucial away goal. Karl and Chapuisat both had chances before Rummenigge brought a fine save out of Auxerre's stand-in goalkeeper Lionel Charbonnier. But there was to be no equaliser from that spell of pressure and Dutuel came within inches of bringing the aggregate scores level when he hit the bar in the 37th minute after a superb pass from Vahirua.

The second half produced two early chances, one for each team's number nine, but Chapuisat, after beating Mahé and Goma, clipped his shot fractionally wide and Baticle then saw his first-time shot saved by Klos. Then came the Auxerre equaliser, with Verlaat outjumping everybody else to nod in a Vahirua free-kick. With the tie all square at two apiece, the French side decided to go for the jugular and in the last 20 minutes they launched an onslaught on the Dortmund goal. Vahirua went close four times, Cocard had an effort saved on the line and finally Martins fired in a firm low drive. The goal of deliverance would not come, though, and the match went into extra-time.

By now tiredness had crept in and the extra 30 minutes produced little action of note. Just a lot of niggly fouls and stray passes, plus the sendings-off of Dortmund's Kutowski and Auxerre's Guerreiro. And so to penalties, and to some remarkably accurate shooting from both teams. Karl, Chapuisat, Reinhardt, Schulz and Zorc all found the net for Dortmund, and with Vahirua, Prunier, Laslandes, Verlaat and Dutuel doing likewise with their five kicks for Auxerre, it was down to sudden death. Rummenigge scored Dortmund's sixth, but Stéphane Mahé, only in the side because of an injury to regular left-back Stéphane Mazzolini, suffered the agony of seeing his timid shot saved by Stefan Klos. That was that. Dortmund were through to the final. The tearful Auxerre players, having given everything they had, were out of the competition.

CORENTIN MARTINS
AJ Auxerre

Auxerre midfielder Corentin Martins was one of several who played out of their skins in the French side's attempt to qualify for a first-ever European final. Martins scored the opening goal and played a key role in keeping the team's heart pumping with his indefatigable work in midfield. This was the 23-year-old's first season in European football, but he looked as if he had been competing at this level for years.

Martins was born of Spanish parentage in Brest, the western seaport on the Brittany peninsular. He joined the local team Brest-Armorique as a youngster and remained there until the club was forced out of business under a mountain of debt halfway through the 1991/92 season. Guy Roux, always a man with an eye for potential, brought him to Auxerre and the story since has been one of continued success, with Martins receiving his first French international cap as a substitute against Austria in March 1993 and then making his first full appearance a week after his impressive display against Dortmund in the World Cup game against Sweden in Paris.

UEFA CUP
Semi-final Review

SEMI-FINAL RESULTS

		1st leg	2nd leg	Agg.
Juventus	Paris Saint-Germain FC	2-1	1-0	3-1
Borussia Dortmund	AJ Auxerre	2-0	0-2 aet	2-2

(Borussia Dortmund win 6-5 on penalties)

LEADING GOALSCORERS AFTER SEMI-FINALS

8 Gérald BATICLE (AJ Auxerre)
7 George WEAH (Paris Saint-Germain FC)
6 Marcel WITECZEK (1.FC Kaiserslautern)
   Daniel FONSECA (Napoli)
5 Iván ZAMORANO (Real Madrid)
   Gianluca VIALLI (Juventus)
   ISAÍAS (SL Benfica)
   Fernando HIERRO (Real Madrid)
   Anthony YEBOAH (Eintracht Frankfurt)
4 Roberto BAGGIO (Juventus)
   Michael ZORC (Borussia Dortmund)
   VÍTOR PANEIRA (SL Benfica)
   Stefan PETTERSSON (Ajax)
   Stéphane CHAPUISAT (Borussia Dortmund)
   Michael GOOSSENS (R Standard Liège)
   PACHECO (SL Benfica)
   Luc NILIS (RSC Anderlecht)
   Krzysztof WARZYCHA (Panathinaikos)
3 Corentin MARTINS (AJ Auxerre)
   Frank VERLAAT (AJ Auxerre)
   MICHEL (Real Madrid)
   Fabrizio RAVANELLI (Juventus)
   Edgar DAVIDS (Ajax)
   Gustavo POYET (Real Zaragoza)
   Claudio CANIGGIA (Roma)
   Pierluigi CASIRAGHI (Juventus)
   Andreas MÖLLER (Juventus)
   Dennis BERGKAMP (Ajax)
   Dorin MATEUT (Real Zaragoza)
   John VAN DEN BROM (Vitesse)
   Giuseppe GIANNINI (Roma)
   Ruggiero RIZZITELLI (Roma)
   AYKUT Kocaman (Fenerbahçe)
   Milan KERBR (Sigma Olomouc)
   Viktor LEONENKO (Dinamo Kiev)
   Peter VAN VOSSEN (RSC Anderlecht)
   Christophe COCARD (AJ Auxerre)
   Paul WARHURST (Sheffield Wednesday)
   Axel KRUSE (Eintracht Frankfurt)
   Frank MILL (Borussia Dortmund)

● Juventus, UEFA Cup winners 1993

UEFA CUP
Final First Leg

Wednesday 5th May 1993
Westfalen Stadium, Dortmund

BORUSSIA DORTMUND 1 JUVENTUS 3

Half-time 1-2 Attendance 37,000

		Goals				Goals
1	Stefan KLOS		1	Angelo PERUZZI		
2	Knut REINHARDT		2	Massimo CARRERA		
3	Thomas FRANCK †		3	Marco Antonio DE MARCHI		
4	Bodo SCHMIDT		4	Dino BAGGIO		26
5	Uwe GRAUER		5	Jürgen KOHLER		
6	Michael LUSCH		6	JÚLIO CÉSAR Silva		
7	Stefan REUTER		7	Antonio CONTE ❏		
8	Michael ZORC ‡		8	Giancarlo MAROCCHI ❏		
9	Stéphane CHAPUISAT		9	Gianluca VIALLI		
10	Michael RUMMENIGGE ❏	2	10	Roberto BAGGIO †		31, 74
11	Gerhard POSCHNER		11	Andreas MÖLLER ‡		

Substitutes

Frank MILL †46

Steffen KARL ‡71

Substitutes

Paolo DI CANIO †76

Roberto GALIA ‡88

Referee Sándor PUHL (Hungary)

FACTFILE

- Dortmund had not lost a European match in their home stadium since a 1-6 defeat by Manchester United in the 1964/65 Fairs' Cup.
- May 5th was also the date of Borussia Dortmund's previous European final appearance - the 1966 Cup-winners' Cup final, which they won against Liverpool at Hampden Park, Glasgow.
- Each of the two teams contained one player who was appearing against his old club. Andy Möller of Juventus and Stefan Reuter of Dortmund.
- Dortmund striker Stéphane Chapuisat was playing his second match against Italian opposition in five days. The previous Saturday he had been in the Switzerland side that beat Italy 1-0 in a World Cup qualifier.

● *Michael Rummenigge*

'Baggiomania' breaks out in Dortmund

The Westfalen Stadium was sold out once again as Borussia Dortmund strove to maintain their 100% home record in the competition and establish a useful first-leg advantage to take to Turin. But this was to be a night on which the German side, and their supporters, would have to accept second best. Outsmarted both technically and tactically by experienced, in-form opponents, their dreams of European glory were destroyed above all by one man - Juventus superstar Roberto Baggio.

In the post-match analysis there was a body of opinion which felt that Dortmund might have scored too early for their own good, but that thought was certainly not on the spectators' minds when Michael Rummenigge smashed in Reinhardt's cross after just 62 seconds. It was a goal worthy of his famous brother and one which sent the home fans into wild celebration.

Further Dortmund goals might have followed in a lively opening spell, with Lusch shooting just wide after a poor defensive clearance and Poschner having an even better effort pushed for a corner by Peruzzi. But Juventus soon began to weather the storm. Andy Möller, booed at every touch by his former supporters, had already struck the bar with an early chip before he made a complete hash of a far easier chance just eight yards out. Soon after that, however, Juventus got the equaliser they had been threatening. A well-worked free-kick ended with Dino Baggio creating space for himself and beating Klos with a precise left-foot shot into the far corner. There was even worse to come for the home fans five minutes later when the other Baggio, Roberto, shot Juventus in front. Dortmund coach Hitzfeld had assigned Thomas Franck to man-mark the Juventus number ten throughout the match, but he was nowhere in sight as the ball was swung over into the area by Vialli, and Baggio, standing almost on the penalty spot, had all the time in the world to shoot past Klos and give Juventus the lead.

As the teams changed ends, the Italians had firmly taken control of the game. Their second-half policy was to absorb Dortmund's pressure and hit their opponents on the counter. With players of the calibre of Baggio, Möller and Vialli in attack, they threatened to score each time they broke away. Baggio had one effort cleared off the line by Schmidt after an hour but he made no mistake in the 74th minute after good work from Vialli and Möller had wrongfooted the Dortmund defence. Swivelling majestically onto the ball, he expertly found the one corner of the goal that was open to him. Stefan Klos could only stand motionless and watch as the ball rolled beyond him and over the goalline via the left-hand upright.

In many ways Juventus had produced the perfect game plan for an important away fixture in Europe. The defence, symbolised by Kohler's faultless performance against the dangerous Chapuisat, had held firm, whilst the brilliance of Roberto Baggio had tormented the depleted Dortmund back-line at the other end. Theoretically, the tie was only half over, but for all except the most optimistic German supporters, the UEFA Cup final of 1993 had already been won and lost in Dortmund.

JÜRGEN KOHLER
Juventus

Whilst most of the post-match headlines focussed on Roberto Baggio, there were many who pointed to the outstanding defensive display of Jürgen Kohler as an equally decisive factor in giving Juventus such a strong first-leg advantage. The 27-year-old, playing on his native soil, succeeded in completely marking Dortmund's lone recognised striker, Stéphane Chapuisat, out of the game. Not many other defenders could claim to have done that over the past two seasons.

Kohler is now universally recognised as one of the best central defenders in the business and there are few strikers who ever get the better of him. He began his career with Waldhof Mannheim and had spells with both Cologne and Bayern Munich before moving to Juventus in 1991. A World Cup winner in 1990, he has established himself as an immovable element in the Juventus defence. While fellow 'stranieri' Platt, Möller and Júlio César played musical chairs with their team selections during the season, Kohler was never dropped once.

JUVENTUS 3 BORUSSIA DORTMUND 0

Half-time 2-0 *Aggregate* 6-1 *Attendance* 62,781

Goals

1	Angelo PERUZZI	
2	Massimo CARRERA	
3	Moreno TORRICELLI †	
4	Marco Antonio DE MARCHI ❑	
5	Jürgen KOHLER	
6	JÚLIO CÉSAR Silva	
7	Roberto GALIA ❑	
8	Dino BAGGIO	5, 43
9	Gianluca VIALLI ‡	
10	Roberto BAGGIO	
11	Andreas MÖLLER	65

Substitutes

Paolo DI CANIO †66
Fabrizio RAVANELLI ‡80

Goals

1	Stefan KLOS	
2	Knut REINHARDT	
3	Bodo SCHMIDT	
4	Michael SCHULZ	
5	Ned ZELIC ❑	
6	Gerhard POSCHNER	
7	Stefan REUTER ‡	
8	Steffen KARL	
9	Lothar SIPPEL	
10	Michael RUMMENIGGE †	
11	Frank MILL	

Substitutes

Thomas FRANCK †43
Michael LUSCH ‡66

Referee John BLANKENSTEIN (Holland)

FACTFILE

● *Victory gave Juventus their fifth European trophy success. They had previously won the Champions' Cup in 1985, the Cup-winners' Cup in 1984 and the UEFA Cup in both 1977 and 1990.*

● *Roberto Galia was the only survivor from the Juventus team the last time they held aloft the UEFA Cup after beating Fiorentina three years earlier.*

● *Although Italian clubs had won the UEFA Cup on four previous occasions, this was the first time that the winning team had been able to collect the trophy in front of their home fans.*

● *Dortmund were without three key players through injury - Chapuisat, Povlsen and Zorc. On the other hand, Schulz, Zelic and Sippel were all back in the team after missing the first leg.*

Juventus stroll to record third triumph

DINO BAGGIO
Juventus

There had been little doubt about the outcome of the final after the first leg in Dortmund. But despite an evening of torrential rain in Turin, over 60,000 Juventus fans came to the Delle Alpi stadium to witness the completion of the club's fifth European trophy success, establishing club record gate receipts of approximately £2 million in the process.

Juventus coach Giovanni Trapattoni had publicly warned his team against complacency before the game. Still fresh in his memory was the dramatic UEFA Cup third round tie in 1988/89 when his team Inter were knocked out on away goals by Bayern Munich, having won the first leg 2-0 in Munich. But if this German-Italian confrontation was to go the same way, then Dortmund had to score early. Instead, it was Juventus who got the quick breakthrough, with Dino Baggio, scorer of Juventus's opening goal in the first leg, again finding the target with a crashing left-foot shot after he had been served by Vialli's astute back-heel.

At 4-1 down Dortmund were dead and buried. Two long-range efforts from Schulz and Reinhardt came very close to getting the match back to all-square on the night, but the better chances in the first half all fell to the Italians, with Kohler having a header cleared off the line and Roberto Baggio, sent clear by Möller, bringing the best out of Klos in the Dortmund goal. Just a minute after that, Juventus duly got their second goal. Once again the scorer was Dino Baggio, with his second goal of the evening, third of the tie and fifth of the competition. Möller floated over a free-kick and Baggio rose superbly to head in off the inside of the post.

With the contest long since over, Juventus spared themselves any unnecessary exertions in the second period. The crowd had already begun to celebrate, sending Mexican waves around the stadium and letting out shouts of "Olé" every time a Juventus player touched the ball. They even had a third goal to celebrate, although, frankly, the scorer, Andy Möller, knew very little about it as the ball ricocheted into the net off his leg as a Dortmund defender attempted to boot the ball clear after a dangerous move on the left. Roberto Baggio also treated the crowd to some of his party tricks. He might have brought the house down after one sensational slalom run, but he tried to take on just one man too many and the chance of a shot at goal disappeared.

Not that it mattered. Juventus had already won the trophy by the biggest final victory margin in UEFA Cup history, captain Baggio had his first major honour in football and coach Trapattoni had steered the club to their 15th major title under his command.

No player had scored three goals in a European final since Borussia Mönchengladbach's Jupp Heynckes against FC Twente in the UEFA Cup final of 1975. So Juventus defender-cum-midfielder Dino Baggio had plenty to be proud of as he added two first-half strikes in Turin to the one which had opened Juventus's account in Dortmund. After all, this was a player who had only scored four goals in three full seasons of Serie A football with Torino, Inter and Juventus!

A player of exceptional versatility, Dino Baggio began his career at Torino as a central defender. Juventus bought him from their city rivals in 1991 but were obliged to loan him out for a season to Inter as part of the complicated arrangement which allowed coach Trapattoni to move to Juventus in the opposite direction. Since returning to Juventus at the start of the 92/93 season, Baggio has established himself as a fixture in the Italian national team, even scoring twice in their World Cup campaign, including one magnificent blockbuster against Portugal.

UEFA CUP
Review

TOP GOALSCORERS

8 Gérald BATICLE (AJ Auxerre)
7 George WEAH (Paris Saint-Germain FC)
6 Roberto BAGGIO (Juventus)
   Marcel WITECZEK (1.FC Kaiserslautern)
   Daniel FONSECA (Napoli)
5 Dino BAGGIO (Juventus)
   Iván ZAMORANO (Real Madrid)
   Gianluca VIALLI (Juventus)
   ISAÍAS (SL Benfica)
   Fernando HIERRO (Real Madrid)
   Anthony YEBOAH (Eintracht Frankfurt)
4 Andreas MÖLLER (Juventus)
   Michael ZORC (Borussia Dortmund)
   VÍTOR PANEIRA (SL Benfica)
   Stefan PETTERSSON (Ajax)
   Stéphane CHAPUISAT (Borussia Dortmund)
   Michael GOOSSENS (R Standard Liège)
   PACHECO (SL Benfica)
   Luc NILIS (RSC Anderlecht)
   Krzysztof WARZYCHA (Panathinaikos)

RED CARDS

2 HAKAN Tecimer (Fenerbahçe)
1 Michael WEIR (Hibernian)
   QUIQUE (Valencia CF)
   Finn JENSEN (BK Frem)
   Guerino GOTTARDI (Neuchâtel Xamax FC)
   Alexandros ANDREOU (PAOK)
   Lars ZETTERLUND (Örebro SK)
   Mark HUGHES (Manchester United)
   Martin PENICKA (Slavia Praha)
   Sergei TIMOFEEV (Dinamo Moskva)
   Andrey ANNENKOV (Dinamo Kiev)
   Nicolae ZAMFIR (Universitatea Craiova)
   Piotr SWIERCZEWSKI (GKS Katowice)
   Roman SZEWCZYK (GKS Katowice)
   Adam LEDWON (GKS Katowice)
   David HIRST (Sheffield Wednesday)
   Andrea CARNEVALE (Roma)

Pascal ZUBERBÜHLER (Grasshopper-Club Zürich)
ISMAIL Kartal (Fenerbahçe)
Candido GÉRSON (Fenerbahçe)
Enrico ANNONI (Torino)
Igor SIMUTENKOV (Dinamo Moskva)
Péter BERECZKI (Vác FC-Samsung)
Igor PUGLITS (Vác FC-Samsung)
Jesús Angel SOLANA (Real Zaragoza)
David GINOLA (Paris Saint-Germain FC)
Philippe ALBERT (RSC Anderlecht)
Frank VERLAAT (AJ Auxerre)
Régis GENAUX (R Standard Liège)
UGUR Tütüneker (Galatasaray)
Amedeo CARBONI (Roma)
Alain ROCHE (Paris Saint-Germain FC)
Walter BONACINA (Roma)
Raphaël GUERREIRO (AJ Auxerre)

YELLOW CARDS

4 Dino BAGGIO (Juventus)
   Alain ROCHE (Paris Saint-Germain FC)
   (inc. red card)
   Jesús Angel SOLANA (Real Zaragoza)
   (inc. red card)
3 Jirí VADURA (Sigma Olomouc)
   Antonio CONTE (Juventus)
   Roberto GALIA (Juventus)
   Sergei TIMOFEEV (Dinamo Moskva)
   (inc. red card)
   Piotr SWIERCZEWSKI (GKS
   Katowice) (inc. red card)
   Enrico ANNONI (Torino) (inc. red card)
   Philippe ALBERT (RSC Anderlecht)
   (inc. red card)
   Régis GENAUX (R Standard Liège)
   (inc. red card)
   Amedeo CARBONI (Roma) (inc. red card)
   Walter BONACINA (Roma) (inc. red card)
   Raphaël GUERREIRO (AJ Auxerre)
   (inc. red card)

EUROPEAN ROLL OF HONOUR

CHAMPIONS' CUP

1956	Real Madrid (Esp)
1957	Real Madrid (Esp)
1958	Real Madrid (Esp)
1959	Real Madrid (Esp)
1960	Real Madrid (Esp)
1961	SL Benfica (Por)
1962	SL Benfica (Por)
1963	Milan (Ita)
1964	Internazionale (Ita)
1965	Internazionale (Ita)
1966	Real Madrid (Esp)
1967	Celtic (Sco)
1968	Manchester United (Eng)
1969	Milan (Ita)
1970	Feyenoord (Hol)
1971	Ajax (Hol)
1972	Ajax (Hol)
1973	Ajax (Hol)
1974	FC Bayern München (Frg)
1975	FC Bayern München (Frg)
1976	FC Bayern München (Frg)
1977	Liverpool (Eng)
1978	Liverpool (Eng)
1979	Nottingham Forest (Eng)
1980	Nottingham Forest (Eng)
1981	Liverpool (Eng)
1982	Aston Villa (Eng)
1983	Hamburger SV (Ger)
1984	Liverpool (Eng)
1985	Juventus (Ita)
1986	Steaua Bucuresti (Rom)
1987	FC Porto (Por)
1988	PSV (Hol)
1989	Milan (Ita)
1990	Milan (Ita)
1991	Crvena zvezda Beograd (Yug)
1992	FC Barcelona (Esp)
1993	Olympique Marseille (Fra)

CUP-WINNERS' CUP

1961	Fiorentina (Ita)
1962	Atlético Madrid (Esp)
1963	Tottenham Hotspur (Eng)
1964	Sporting CP (Por)
1965	West Ham United (Eng)
1966	Borussia Dortmund (Frg)
1967	FC Bayern München (Frg)
1968	Milan (Ita)
1969	Slovan Bratislava (Tch)
1970	Manchester City (Eng)
1971	Chelsea (Eng)
1972	Rangers (Sco)
1973	Milan (Ita)
1974	1.FC Magdeburg (Gdr)
1975	Dinamo Kiev (Urs)
1976	RSC Anderlecht (Bel)
1977	Hamburger SV (Frg)
1978	RSC Anderlecht (Bel)
1979	FC Barcelona (Esp)
1980	Valencia CF (Esp)
1981	Dinamo Tbilisi (Urs)
1982	FC Barcelona (Esp)
1983	Aberdeen (Sco)
1984	Juventus (Ita)
1985	Everton (Eng)
1986	Dinamo Kiev (Urs)
1987	Ajax (Hol)
1988	KV Mechelen (Bel)
1989	FC Barcelona (Esp)
1990	Sampdoria (Ita)
1991	Manchester United (Eng)
1992	SV Werder Bremen (Ger)
1993	Parma (Ita)

FAIRS/UEFA CUP

1958	FC Barcelona (Esp)
1960	FC Barcelona (Esp)
1961	Roma (Ita)
1962	Valencia CF (Esp)
1963	Valencia CF (Esp)
1964	Real Zaragoza (Esp)
1965	Ferencváros (Hun)
1966	FC Barcelona (Esp)
1967	Dinamo Zagreb (Yug)
1968	Leeds United (Eng)
1969	Newcastle United (Eng)
1970	Arsenal (Eng)
1971	Leeds United (Eng)
1972	Tottenham Hotspur (Eng)
1973	Liverpool (Eng)
1974	Feyenoord (Hol)
1975	Borussia M'gladbach (Frg)
1976	Liverpool (Eng)
1977	Juventus (Ita)
1978	PSV (Hol)
1979	Borussia M'gladbach (Frg)
1980	Eintracht Frankfurt (Frg)
1981	Ipswich Town (Eng)
1982	IFK Göteborg (Swe)
1983	RSC Anderlecht (Bel)
1984	Tottenham Hotspur (Eng)
1985	Real Madrid (Esp)
1986	Real Madrid (Esp)
1987	IFK Göteborg (Swe)
1988	Bayer 04 Leverkusen (Frg)
1989	Napoli (Ita)
1990	Juventus (Ita)
1991	Internazionale (Ita)
1992	Ajax (Hol)
1993	Juventus (Ita)

OTHER BOOKS PUBLISHED BY SPORTS PROJECTS

THE EUROPEAN FOOTBALL YEARBOOK 93/94

The bible of European football... over 1,100 pages

Available October 1993 • ISBN 0-946866-14-7

PLAYING IN EUROPE 93/94

A who's who guide to the teams and players in Europe's three major club competitions... 304 pages

Available September 1993 • ISBN 0-946866-13-9

PREMIER REVIEW 1993

A complete match-by-match record of the first ever season of the FA Premier League... 256 pages

Available now • ISBN 0-946866-11-2

ASTON VILLA REVIEW 1993

A complete match-by-match record of the Premier League title challengers' season... 160 pages (hardback)

Available now • ISBN 0-946866-09-0

NEWCASTLE UNITED REVIEW 1993

A complete match-by-match record of the Football League champions' season... 160 pages (hardback)

Available now • ISBN 0-946866-10-4

Sports Projects Ltd.,
188 Lightwoods Hill,
Smethwick, Warley,
West Midlands, B67 5EH.
Telephone 021 643 2729